D1238292

Empowerment versus Oppression

Empowerment versus Oppression
Twenty First Century Views of Popular Romance Novels

Edited by

Sally Goade

CAMBRIDGE SCHOLARS PUBLISHING

Empowerment versus Oppression: Twenty First Century Views of Popular Romance Novels, edited by
Sally Goade

This book first published 2007 by

Cambridge Scholars Publishing

15 Angerton Gardens, Newcastle, NE5 2JA, UK

British Library Cataloguing in Publication Data
A catalogue record for this book is available from the British Library

For my mother, Dr. Barbara Gunn,
my favorite romance coconspirator

TABLE OF CONTENTS

ACKNOWLEDGEMENTS

This book would not exist without the Southwest Texas Popular Culture Association and American Popular Culture Association, whose joint conference I have had the privilege to participate in over the last six years. In 2005 I had the honor of co-chairing the Romance Fiction panel with Paul Fleming, who had chaired it alone (and quite efficiently) for several years. These acknowledgments must begin with Paul, who graciously handed the opportunity for editing a collection of papers from the 2004 and 2005 conferences to me when Cambridge Scholars Publishing (CSP) editors expressed interest. With five contributors committed to the project, we had an excellent nucleus on which to build, and I asked Amanda Millar and Andy Nercessian of CSP if I could send out an all-inclusive call for papers. I would like to thank all of the respondents to that call, as it was an impressive array indeed of twenty-first century views on romance. To the contributors who were accepted and have persisted through all the editing stages, you have my utmost respect and thanks for your thorough research, innovative ideas, and commitment to see the project through, not to mention your frequent words of encouragement to me.

To Amanda Millar, thank you for your interest in the original idea of the book and your early support, and to Andy Nercessian, an extra helping of thanks for your patience, guidance, and confidence. I owe heartfelt thanks to my graduate assistant, Elizabeth Romero, who helped me to decipher the technicalities of indexing, compared edited and revised versions of chapters with a finely honed sense of detail, and most of all, put up with my John Denver music collection and brought me snacks and encouraging words during our evening work sessions.

Finally, thank you to my husband Dan for believing in every project I have undertaken since we first met as teenagers—you are simply amazing.

INTRODUCTION

SALLY GOADE

This book's title comes from the central question evident in popular romance criticism for at least the past thirty years: Are women readers (and writers) oppressed by their commitment to a narrative with an essentially patriarchal, heterosexual relationship at its center, or are they somehow empowered by their ability to create, escape to, and transform the romance narrative into a vehicle for reimagining women's freedom within relationships? In writing that question, I realize that I immediately slanted my wording toward the latter view, and that is probably because I began to analyze romance novels during my doctoral work in English in 1997, with the benefit of having the work of critics such as Janice Radway, Tania Modleski, and Kay Mussell on which to build. These critics and many others gave us theories with which to agree, tinker, and argue; even more importantly, they laid the premise that popular romance deserves a close examination, that it is a dynamic, changing genre despite (even perhaps because of) its formulaic elements, and that it is a genre to which readers are particularly important. This last focus is true in great part because notables as early as Miguel de Cervantes and Jane Austen have "diagnosed" readers, worrying about the effects of romance on the populace, but it is also true because readers sometimes cross over into being authors and critics themselves (as certainly both Cerventes and Austen did).

The nucleus of this collection is comprised of five papers presented on the Romance Fiction panels at the Southwest Texas Popular Culture and American Popular Culture Associations' annual conferences in 2004 and 2005, chaired first by Paul Fleming in 2004 and then co-chaired by Paul and me in 2005. With this exciting and varied collection of conference papers in hand, Cambridge Scholars Publishing editor Andy Nercessian then encouraged me to solicit additional submissions, which I did through an inclusive call for papers in the summer of 2005. In sifting through proposals for this collection, I kept an eye out for submissions with something new to add to the conversation about romance novels, whether it be a new perspective from a unique group of readers (we hear from readers in Hong Kong and India), an examination of a particular romance subtype (included are Christian, African-American, and Gothic novels, as well as those set in Las Vegas and the Middle East), or a new way of presenting a critical response (here we have a romance novelist's controversial reflection, a critique of the industry as a creative enterprise, an examination of how students negotiate with romance in the classroom, and well known critics "rewriting" their favorite romances).

No matter the perspective, each contributor must at some point address the question of empowerment versus oppression, as have nearly all earlier romance novel critics and authors who have written about the genre. In part, the complexity of the question's answer depends on the definition of "romance novel" with which we are working. The term "romance" is fraught with complications and potential misunderstanding. The earliest prose works (not poetry or drama) were romances—the term "novel" that we now know so well was not coined until the eighteenth century. At that time the romance was finally defined simply because authors felt a need to distinguish it from the new form—novels. Romances were then defined as containing an element of the fantastic and novels as being more realistic and about everyday life (Reeve 111). Novels have, of course, changed considerably since they were first defined, so that now novels may contain many elements of the original romance genre, including the supernatural, fantasy, magic, and even time travel. In his definition of romance for *The Encyclopedia of Fantasy*, Brian Attebery states that when romance "is used to identify particular kinds of literature it is usually part of a compound." "Women's romance," "western romance," and "scientific romance" are all usable compounds, and each can then be referred to as a genre on its own terms even while all share the general generic label of romance. Attebery notes that "some critics use this trend as an excuse to bump 'romance' up a level from genre to mode" (820). Attebery's discomfort with calling romance a mode and labeling its variations as genres may well be a reaction to the practice of drawing strict lines between forms of romance.

Many categories ("genres" or "sub-genres") of popular fiction, including mystery, science fiction, and fantasy, are offshoots of the big romance genre. What most people call "romance novels" represent one more genre within a genre. These are novels written primarily for women by women, and they focus on the developing relationship of one man and one woman (homosexual romances are a newer innovation and still focus on one monogamous couple). Romance novels are also marked by a convention that harks back to Greek and Shakespearean comedies—the "happy ending" in marriage or betrothal. In her 2003 book, *A Natural History of the Romance Novel*, Pamela Regis gives a comprehensive description of key elements, such as the happy ending, and her work builds on earlier descriptions of romance "formula," notably those of Janice Radway and John Cawelti (an early mentor of Kay Mussell). Regis makes an intriguing observation that marriage, often thought to be *the* happy ending for romance, may actually come at any point in the narrative. According to Regis, betrothal—the admission of committed love—and freedom for the heroine through her relationship to the hero are the culmination of the romance plot, no matter when legal marriage occurs in the narrative (30). For novelists such as Diana Gabaldon (the *Outlander* series), who write multiple books in a series focused on the same couple, unavoidable separation and ecstatic rejoining can serve the "betrothal" element. Northrup Frye calls this separation of the committed couple the "Penelope motif," coined for Ulysses and Penelope's long-awaited reunion in *The Odyssey* (Frye 80). Variations such as the use of long-term marriage and even interesting, complex storylines for other characters can blur the lines between the romance novel and other literature. However, Cawelti's 1976 description of a focus on the developing relationship and a "moral fantasy" in which the love between hero and heroine overcomes all obstacles still rests at the core of other definitions (Cawelti 40-42).

Add to the potential confusion over the romance genre that the literary time periods in England from approximately 1785 to 1830 and in North America from approximately 1830 to 1865 are called Romantic Periods, that the philosophy springing from these periods is called "Romanticism," and that popular media has its own Valentine's Day version of "romance," and it is easy to see why the term nearly always requires explanation. At a recent talk on romance given to a group of professors from several disciplines, I began by asking them who among them had ever read a romance novel. Only about three of the twenty-five raised their hands. When I asked if any had read Charlotte Brontë's *Jane Eyre* or Jane Austen's *Pride and Prejudice,* the hands came up, but so did the surprised expressions, for surely these great classics could not be considered "romance novels." Indeed Frye, in his analysis of romance (*The Secular Scripture*), notes that while Austen critiques the romance narrative (and thus helps to transform it), she is also very careful that the right heroine ends up with the right hero in the end, satisfying the romance reader even as the reader feels herself a little above the typical narrative (39-40). Similarly, to romance readers who like to feel a little above the average consumer, a contemporary author such as Gabaldon, who has scoffed a bit at romance novels on her website and playfully alludes to the genre's stereotypes in her novels, still keeps the story focused on the central hero and heroine, making sure that they are either reunited or that the stage is set for reunion at the end of each novel.

Literary critics have long studied the big romance genre and all of its offshoots. However, for centuries and particularly with an early twentieth century preference for realistic literature, precursors of the modern romance novel have been seen as somehow less than other literature. Robert Scholes has identified this distinction as one between "literature" and "non-literature," and he calls it an "invidious distinction," a construction of difference that stems from an artificial hierarchy in the discipline of English that reinforces the schism readers sometimes feel between what they learn in the classroom and what they enjoy in their personal lives (5). Interestingly, in online and group discussions among romance readers, the readers will often distinguish "their" genre from "literary fiction," reinforcing the difference (even though most continue to read in both categories) with the kind of distinction that Radway describes in an early article on Book-of-the-Month Club editors' choices between "serious fiction" and more "popular" choices (527-28). The connections between canonical romance (those works accepted as "classics") and popular romance novels have been repeatedly noted, however, in overviews given by romance critics such as Modleski (*Loving with a Vengeance* 15) and Mussell (*Fantasy and Reconciliation* 8), and extended in more depth by Regis's 2003 study.

Within the essays collected here, critics give varying degrees of credence to the idea that what they are analyzing may not be seen as literature; however, one of the gifts given to us by earlier critics is that the value of examining romance, its variations, and its effects no longer has to be rationalized for several pages in every critique before the critic feels justified in continuing. Within this collection, Glen Thomas describes the flourishing Harlequin-Mills and Boon romance industry in Australia throughout Chapter Two; Eva Chen (Chapter Three) cites 2003 statistics showing romance novels accounting for 50% of all popular fiction sales (30); Guy Mark Foster (Chapter Eight) cites industry analysis showing annual sales of romance novels at "$1.41 billion worldwide at the end of the last millennium" (106). Chapters written on specific types of romance (Christian, Gothic, African-American) demonstrate the vigor of the industry in that many specialized types and category lines remain ever more viable. The very popularity of romance novels serves to merit study, even if only to find out the answer to the facetious question Mussell first asked in the title of a 1982 article, "But Why Do They Read Those Things?" One of Radway's key purposes in her 1984 book (cited by every romance critic on the planet), *Women, Patriarchy, and Popular Culture*, was to discover—through ethnographic study—how readers use romance novels. Modleski's work in the same time period stressed the importance of studying romance because of the light it could shed on how women fantasize, negotiate, and function within a patriarchal society (*Loving with a Vengeance* 112-14).

These critics, along with many others, established the question that still resonates in this book's title. Radway and Modleski, while often perceived as having markedly divergent interpretations of romance reading, actually both note oppression and empowerment for women in reading the romance. The oppression comes through a view of women's "false consciousness" in accepting as natural a cultural narrative that keeps them static in power relations, even perpetuating the narrative themselves as writers and eager readers (Radway 210; Modleski 113). The empowerment is described by Radway through accounts of women defiantly stealing time from their domestic chores for the novels and triumphantly identifying with strong heroines who extricate themselves from ticklish situations even while maintaining their heroes' undying admiration (93-101). While Mussell also argued for women taking a good, long look at the narrative of love conquers all that they were accepting in her early work, by 1997, she was writing the introduction to a *Paradoxa* issue on romance in which she notes remarkable innovations in the genre that also illustrate its potentially empowering effects. Mussell's observations center on two elements in the evolving romance novel: the many types that now exist (making one interpretation of romance's effects highly problematic) and the increasingly blurred lines between readers, authors, and critics, showing the influence that each group has on the others and even the ways in which individuals may affect the genre by serving in more than one position ("Where's Love Gone?" 6).

Both of the elements noted by Mussell are represented in this collection, which is framed with a first chapter by a romance author critiquing her genre and a final chapter in which notable critics try rewriting their favorite romances. Candice Proctor first came to my attention in the early summer of 2005 when a proposal she had submitted to the Romance Writers of America (RWA) publication, *Romance Writers Report* (*RWR*), caused controversy on the Romance Readers Anonymous Listserv (RRA-L) to which I subscribe. Proctor describes how the controversy came to be and her response to it in her "Postscript" to the original essay, both of which are published here as Chapter One. The essay was not published by *RWA*, but it did appear on Proctor's website. Proctor's approach in "Why We Don't Get No Respect" is to put some of the responsibility for the genre's reputation with the general public on to the authors. Intrigued by Proctor's entertaining and direct essay when she submitted it, I decided that it was my "editorial duty" to read one or two of Proctor's romance novels as well. Six novels later, I have to admit that Proctor's novels have a new fan, and I have even included one of the romances (along with Proctor's essay) in the 2006 rendition of the Women's Romance Fiction course I teach. Proctor's website gives details on the seven romance novels she has published, as well as the new "mystery/thriller" novels that she has now begun to publish under the name C. S. Harris.

In response to what he sees as a "dead end" in textual studies of romance, Glen Thomas has focused his attention on the business of romance and within that business, the creativity possible. In Chapter Two, "Romance: The Perfect Creative Industry? A Case Study of Harlequin-Mills and Boon Australia," Thomas examines the production and consumption of romance novels, with particular attention to how the industry has flourished in Australia, where he is a professor at the Queensland University of Technology. While Thomas sheds light on the often-neglected marketing and production elements of popular romance, his study also highlights the interactive nature of production and consumption, the effect that readers and their interests actually have on the genre.

Thomas's study of the Australian romance industry is only the first of four chapters that lend an international perspective to this collection. Chapter Three is Eva Y. I. Chen's analysis of pleasure in the romance. Working from her position as an English professor at the National Cheng-Chi University in Taipei, Taiwan, Chen traces the complex progression of pleasure as a concept in romance criticism. Her comprehensive overview and detailed analysis identify pleasure as originally a concept linked to oppression (the "opiate" of the people) and then a concept that has swung perhaps excessively toward empowerment, as "a concept standing for reader's agency that is divorced from power politics and textual control" (31). As with the concepts of oppression and empowerment themselves, one of the implications of Chen's study is that pleasure can never be identified as only one idea.

For the reader moving through this collection in order, Chapters One through Three will give a representative sample of varying perspectives, and Chapter Four will offer the first study of a specific type. While Emily A. Haddad is examining the trope of captivity specifically in Harlequin"sheikh novels," she brings to bear many earlier analyses of captivity in romance. Reading her work enhanced my own understanding of the inverted captivity narratives in romances with Native American heroes, a motif I had first seen described by Kate McCafferty in a 1994 *Journal of Popular Culture* article. However, in addition to shedding light on the function of captivity in romance narratives, Haddad's chapter is also a striking example of what Chen calls the impossibility of "divorc[ing]" romance from "the cultural and political" (Chen 39). Haddad asks this key question:

> If Harlequins can make heterosexual women feel better about their relations with men, could they not also make white, western women (Harlequin's primary readership) feel better about inter-cultural or inter-ethnic relations? (53-54)

To answer this question, Haddad analyzes changes in the way the captivity trope is enacted in novels published since the beginning of the United States-Iraq war in March 2003. The result is a fascinating glimpse at how fantasy can collide with and be irrevocably changed by reality; it is also an unflinching look at the racial stereotypes that can so often underlie fantasies of exotic danger.

Chapters Five and Six address a different kind of danger in romance, the realization of the Gothic in film and literature. In "Derailed by Detail: DuMaurier, Hitchcock, and *Rebecca*" (Chapter Five), Andrea Austin examines the famous film based on the 1938 novel that spawned the twentieth-century reincarnation of the Gothic novel, a form that had first reached great popularity in the eighteenth century. Austin's discussion of the conflict Hitchcock felt in making the film goes to the heart of what often characterizes the romance genre as "feminine," showing that "the film presents a counter-aesthetics, working feverishly to contain and neutralize the feminine agency of the detail" (71). In her 1995 *Art of Darkness: A Poetics of Gothic*, Anne Williams contends that there are overlapping and yet separate masculine and feminine forms of the Gothic (1), and Austin's chapter gives us a comprehensive analysis of how these two may converge.

The "Gothic revival" (as Modleski called it) that began with *Rebecca* and was critiqued mercilessly by critics such as Joanna Russ ("Somebody's Trying to Kill Me and I Think It's My Husband") seemed to die out with the advent of the popular historical romance in the 1970s and 1980s, novels that provided several alternatives to category romance. Deborah Lutz's "The Haunted Space of the Mind: The Revival of the Gothic Romance in the 21st Century" details a later emergence of the Gothic romance in the genre's most recent novels. Lutz has a 2006 book in which she focuses attention on the lover-villain-Byronic hero figure in romance (*The Dangerous Lover: Gothic Villains, Byronism, and the Nineteenth-Century Seduction Narrative*), and her thorough knowledge of the most modern Gothic's roots in earlier literature gives her study a depth that readers will find most valuable.

From the Gothic, we move to an entirely different romance novel type with Chapter Seven, Rebecca Barrett-Fox's "Hope, Faith, and Toughness: An Analysis of the Christian Hero." Christian novels would seem to be the perfect alternative for Christian readers who want narratives that combine their religious beliefs with romance and that they can trust to be sexually conservative. Indeed, demand for the novels is great enough that Barrett-Fox describes them as part of "an entire industry" that has built up around them, although interestingly, it is one "devoted to defining, clarifying, protecting, nurturing, defending, promoting, and teaching biblical masculinity" (93). A fascinating element of this chapter is the argument *against* the books from several Christian sources, and the argument echoes non-religious protests against romance readers lost in fantasy, not appreciating reality nor working as hard as possible to make reality the best it can be. Barrett-Fox gives these arguments a thorough airing, but her conclusion is a fascinating one, involving the possibility for transformation through the novels, not only for women, but for definitions of masculinity as well.

In Chapter Eight, Guy Mark Foster examines the fast-growing African-American romance novel, looking particularly at black women authors who portray inter-racial relationships in which the heroine is black and the hero white. Noting that industry "figures suggest that black women have been readers of popular romances since the genre first emerged with the appearance of Harlequin in the late 1940s," Foster explores ways in which those readers have had to negotiate with the texts in order to take pleasure in a narrative with a white couple, particularly a white hero, at its center (106). While romance novels in which heroes and heroines are both black now flourish, one of the negotiations black readers have made is to envision romance with inter-racial overtones, a psychological move that brings longstanding conflict into play, especially for politically aware black women who struggle with white men's role in the historical past. Noting that "the subject of contemporary black women's sexual relationship to white men largely comprises an unmapped terrain within the mainstream African American literary canon" (125), Foster describes the ways in which several African American romance authors are boldly creating their own maps.

Chapters Nine and Ten both address a connection between India and the popular romance, but they do so in very different ways. In "'I find some Hindu practices, like burning widows, utterly bizarre': Representations of Sati and Questions of Choice in *Veils of Silk*," Maura Seale uses textual analysis of a Mary Jo Putney novel as a starting place to reveal "the racial and imperial politics of the romance genre" that "have not received much scholarly attention" (132). As Haddad examines the political and cultural underpinnings of exotic danger fantasies in Middle Eastern captivity narratives, so Seale examines the stereotypes and seductive views of otherness that underlie fantasies of Indian life. Seale's description of sati and of a Putney novel heroine's "choice" to run from the pyre at her husband's death invokes an impression of false independence, one the heroine definitely exercises in the novel but one that is dependent on a stereotypical view of cultural practice. In contrast, Jayashree Kamble approaches romance novels from the perspective of how they may help Indian women to break through gender stereotypes and cultural constraints. In Chapter Ten ("Female Enfranchisement and the Popular Romance: Employing an Indian Perspective"), Kamble uses results from a survey she conducted of romance readers in India, as well as textual analysis and her own experience as an Indian woman, to show how romance reading may indeed open a broader world of individual choice.

Amy Lee takes still another approach in drawing the parallel between a culture of readers and the texts themselves in Chapter Eleven, "Forming a Local Identity: Romance Novels in Hong Kong." She views romance as a reflection of Hong Kong's history, particularly in the late twentieth to early twenty-first centuries, showing that "the evolution of the romance novel in Hong Kong reflects quite accurately the change of attitude towards gender identity" (174). Lee's analysis is thorough in its presentation of history and of popular literature's progression within that history. Writing as a part of the bilingual and hybrid culture of Hong Kong, Lee's familiarity with Hong Kong culture gives her an important vantage point, and her examination of how romanticized fantasy of urban life and changing mores reflect the culture highlights the ways in which popular culture and texts may parallel each other in many venues.

One unexpected venue is the American iconic city of Las Vegas, Nevada, and in Chapter Twelve ("City of Fantasy: Romance Novels in Las Vegas") Eva Stowers gives us a lighthearted and perceptive glimpse into how the public's perception of Las Vegas is reflected in the many romance novels set in that glittering city. A Nevada native myself, I am especially intrigued by the increasing attention that Stowers notes the authors now give to the desert landscape of their setting, moving perhaps a little beyond the glitz and fantasy of the casino world.

Chapters Thirteen and Fourteen conclude the collection by exploring the responses of two unique and important groups of romance readers. "Understanding the Pleasure: An Undergraduate Romance Reading Community" (Chapter Thirteen) is my description of the ways in which students in my "Women's Romance Fiction" course negotiate with the romance narrative. Some of the students taking the course, which originated at a women's college, have entered without believing that they will ever truly be romance readers. They have entered out of curiosity, for a needed requirement, or because they want to understand the romance's appeal. Others are romance readers already or discover quickly that they enjoy the texts immensely, and so they appreciate the class as a way to understand their own attraction and somehow make it feel legitimate academically. All of these students negotiate with a variety of texts as they balance their attraction or aversion to romance with what they learn about the popular genre's connection to the literary canon. A sample syllabus for the course is attached as a chapter appendix.

Chapter Fourteen is the exciting culmination of a doctoral project that promises to go much further in book form. Mary Beth Tegan began with an idea to have well known romance critics revisit their favorite works from the genre, "revising" their storylines. "Becoming Both Poet and Poem: Feminists Repossess the Romance" is the result. The participating critics include Modleski, Mussell, Jan Cohn, Nancy K. Miller, Theresa Gregor, Slyia Kelso, Pat Koski, and several others, including Tegan herself. Some chose to revise canonical classics (*Jane Eyre* and Margaret Mitchell's *Gone with the Wind* are among them), while others chose contemporary romances. We are given a sample of each critic's approach to revising romance, as well as thoughtful commentary from Tegan, who honestly analyzes the effects of the parameters and process she set up for the project as well as the project's ultimate results. In the end, Tegan invites other romance analysts to help her extend the chapter as she completes her upcoming book, to join her and the participating critics in "collapsing further the distinction between critic and reader, subject and object" (273).

Tegan's chapter and much of the collection speak to the blurred lines between author, critic, and reader that Mussell described in 1997, one of the elements that would point to the power of readers to help transform the genre from within. In the end, though this book's title accurately describes the question that haunts each study of romance's relationship with its readers, inevitably we have created a false dichotomy. For as even a healthy romantic relationship will both empower and constrain a woman (and her partner), in striking a bargain with the romance narrative, women romance readers are simultaneously bound to a patriarchal system and emboldened by their own choice and creativity within that system. As individual readers very often grow, change their tastes, and demand innovation in the books they enjoy, so individual critics and criticism itself also grow and stretch, moving beyond first observations to note innovations in the genre and their effects. It is important that those of us published here not suddenly proclaim ourselves as the "new" voices of romance criticism and as such, somehow discreetly separate from earlier "feminist" critics. By definition, those of us interested in and analyzing women's texts are practicing feminist criticism, and we are building on and benefiting from earlier writers who brought popular romance into the critical light. Lawrence Grossberg has said that empowerment and exploitation of the consumer can be simultaneous (7). For romance readers, critics, and even authors, the key may well be continued awareness of both possibilities.

Works Cited

Attebery, Brian. "Romance." *The Encyclopedia of Fantasy*. Ed. John Clute and John Grant. New York: St. Martin's P, 1997.
Cawelti, John. *Adventure, Mystery and Romance*. Chicago: U of Chicago P, 1976.
Frye, Northrup. *The Secular Scripture: A Study of the Structure of Romance*. Cambridge, MA: Harvard UP, 1976.
Gabaldon, Diana. "Frequently Asked Questions." Home page. 26 Jan. 2003. 31 Jan. 2003. <http://www.cco.caltech.edu/~gatti/gabaldon/gabaldon.html>
———.*Outlander*. New York: Dell, 1991.
Goade, Sally. "'And with the land, our spirits so blended'" Interrelated Frontier Quests of Self in Contemporary Historical Romance—A Study of Rosanne Bittner's *Savage Destiny* Series." DA Paper. Idaho State U, 1999.
Grossberg, Lawrence. *Bringing It All Back Home: Essays on Cultural Studies*. Durham: Duke U P, 1997.

Krentz, Jayne Ann, ed. *Dangerous Men and Adventurous Women: Romance Writers on the Appeal of the Romance.* Philadelphia: U of Pennsylvania P, 1992.

Leavis, F. R. *The Great Tradition: A Study of the English Novel.* Garden City, NY: Doubleday, 1954.

McCafferty, Kate. "Palimpsest of Desire: The Re-Emergence of the American Captivity Narrative as Pulp Romance." *Journal of Popular Culture* 27:4 (1994): 43-56.

Modleski, Tania. *Loving with a Vengeance: Mass-Produced Fantasies for Women.* Hamden, CT: Archon, 1982.

Mussell, Kay. "'But Why Do They Read Those Things?'": The Female Audience and the Gothic Novel." *Female Gothic.* Ed. Juliann E. Fleenor. Montreal: Eden P, 1983.

———.*Fantasy and Reconciliation: Contemporary Formulas of Romance Fiction.* Westport, CT: Greenwood P, 1984.

———. "Where's Love Gone? Transformations in Romance Fiction and Scholarship." *Paradoxa* 3:1-2 (1997): 3-14.

Proctor, Candice. *Candice Proctor writing as . . . .* 24 Aug. 2006. 24 Aug. 2006 <http://candiceproctor.com/index.html>.

Rabine, Leslie W. *Reading the Romantic Heroine.* Ann Arbor: U of Michigan P, 1985.

Radway, Janice. "The Book-of-the-Month Club and the General Reader: On Uses of 'Serious' Fiction." *Critical Inquiry* 14:3 (1988): 516-38.

———.*Reading the Romance: Women, Patriarchy, and Popular Literature.* Chapel Hill: U of North Carolina P, 1984.

Reeve, Clara. *The Progress of Romance.* 1785, rpt. New York: The Facsimile Text Society, 1930. 111.

Regis, Pamela. *A Natural History of the Romance Novel.* Philadelphia: U of Pennsylvania P, 2003.

Richardson, Samuel. *Pamela or Virtue Rewarded.* 1740. New York: W. W. Norton, 1993.

Romance Readers Anonymous Listserv. Adm. Preeti Singh. 2005. Kent State University (listserv@listserv.kent.edu). 24 Aug. 2006 <http://ww.toad.net/~dolma/>.

Russ, Joanna. "Somebody's Trying to Kill Me and I think It's My Husband: The Modern Gothic." *Female Gothic.* Ed. Juliann E. Fleenor. Montreal: Eden P, 1983.

Scholes, Robert. *Textual Power: Literary Theory and the Teaching of English.* New Haven, CT: Yale UP, 1985.

Williams, Anne. *Art of Darkness: A Poetics of Gothic.* Chicago: U of Chicago P, 1995.

CHAPTER ONE

THE ROMANCE GENRE BLUES
OR WHY WE DON'T GET NO RESPECT

CANDICE PROCTOR

Being a romance writer who reinvents yourself as a mystery and thriller writer is a bit like being a man in drag: people perceive you differently, treat you differently, and genuinely believe you are different.

When I began my new Regency-era mystery series and people would ask me what kinds of books I wrote, I would still answer, "historical romances." But once I actually sold *What Angels Fear*, I would occasionally say, "mysteries." Well, instead of sly smirks and condescending *oh's,* suddenly I was getting widened eyes and admiring gushes. I will admit, initially it was gratifying. Ah, respect at last. Then I started getting pissed.

As a former history professor who has spent a sizable chunk of her life moving around the world, I have always brought a carefully researched sense of time and place to my novels. My romances are just as meticulously plotted and contain the same well-developed characters as my mysteries and thrillers. Yet my romances—despite their hefty advances and starred *Publishers Weekly* reviews—are seen as being less worthy of respect than my hardcover mystery. Why?

In the process of preparing for my new career as a mystery/thriller writer, I slogged my way through literally hundreds of poorly written *New York Times (NYT)* bestselling mysteries and thrillers. I encountered cardboard characters, leaky contrived plots, and whopping historical and factual errors. Yes, there are some embarrassingly awful romance writers hitting the *NYT*. But they are no worse than the hack thriller writers, derivative fantasy gurus, and franchised suspense Names who for some reason are accorded more respect. In pondering this phenomenon, I have identified eight possible explanations, some easily dismissed, others more telling.

Romances are formulaic

This explanation—although often advanced—is just plain silly. All genre fiction is formulaic by definition. In fact, nothing is more formulaic than a mystery, and thrillers aren't that far behind. Yet for some reason, romances are criticized for being formulaic when other genres are not.

True, the mating dance ritual tends to follow the same steps, and the Kama Sutra delineated the various ways to make love hundreds of years ago. But then, there are also only so many ways to kill (everything else is just embellishment), and when it comes to motives, they can all be reduced to the standard four: money, revenge, love/lust, and fear.   As for another international conspiracy/terrorist attack/plot to end the world? Please.

Readers like to think they're learning something from their fiction

For many readers, fiction is Education Lite.   Novels with pathologist protagonists contain all sorts of juicy tidbits about forensic science; legal thrillers teach the curious about the law, while political thrillers give them a peek at the nasty inside maneuverings of our government. What do romances teach?

Well, some women read historical romances to learn about history. Unfortunately, while some historical romance writers, such as Laura Kinsale and LaVyrle Spencer, are meticulous in their research, far too many treat their books like adult versions of playing dress ups. As a result, readers seriously interested in history are more likely to go to historical mysteries or straight historicals.

What romances really have to teach are emotional lessons about love: how to tell a good man from a bad one, the importance of honesty in a relationship, the value of trust. These are worthy lessons. Unfortunately, the inescapable reality is that emotions are not valued very highly in our society, probably because they are of more interest to women than men (see #4 below). Then there is the fact that while not too many readers have committed murder or plotted to end the world, most have fallen in love and had sex. It's one of the reasons romances traditionally had their greatest appeal among the young (I'm not going to touch the reasons why today's teenagers seem to prefer fantasy over romance).

There are also those who would argue that some of these "love lessons" are not particularly well taught. True, we have moved on from the days when romance heroes routinely raped their heroines and—instead of being castrated, jailed, or at the very least jilted—were forgiven simply because they acted on the mistaken assumption that the women involved were no longer "pure." But all too many romance heroes are still sulky, bad-tempered, borderline abusive men who are miraculously redeemed by the love of a good woman. I don't know about you, but that's one lesson I don't want my daughters to learn. There are enough codependent women in this world as it is.

The most popular romance writers aren't necessarily—or even usually—the best "writers," but simply the ones who most successfully hit their readers' fantasies

This is true. But it is only slightly less true of thriller/suspense/fantasy writers.

Some of today's successful thriller/suspense/fantasy writers create wonderful characters, write riveting dialogue, and have a memorable way with words. They are rare. Most of the genre writers hitting the *NYT* today are there because their pacing is nicely modeled to appeal to an audience weaned on television, or because they came up with a really, really clever high concept (even if it was badly executed).

Who hasn't read the hyper successful thriller writer who resorts to the laughable tactic of having both his protagonist and his antagonist gaze at their reflections in order to describe them, who regularly stops his story's action for a series of information dumps clumsily framed as flashbacks, and makes so many historical and factual errors that he has spawned a small industry devoted to detailing his best howlers? At the moment, I am listening to the audiotape of a book by a hugely successful male writer of non-happily-ever-after love stories. His point of view bounces around like the proverbial ping pong ball, there isn't a hint of conflict anywhere (let alone on every page), and he spent the entire first half of his book presenting his main characters' backstories in a narrative that would have put me to sleep if I hadn't been counting reps. The fantasy he's writing to? That it's never too late to find true love (even if the characters must ultimately lose out in order to maintain the author's claim to pseudo-literary status).

While many people do not like to admit it, the fact remains that all genre writing is about satisfying readers' fantasies. Some of these fantasies are easy to spot: No matter how bad things look, a hero will save the world from destruction. A clever detective can and will catch each and every killer. Good always triumphs over Evil.

Other fantasies are admittedly subtler. My husband recently read three mysteries in a row, each by a different (male) writer, in which the protagonists were all laughably the same: a middle-aged male, happily free from the demands of any and all dependent females and living a Huck Finn-type life in a cabin in the Everglades/on a boat in the Caribbean/in a Florida marina. Everyone see the secondary fantasy at work here?

It has been suggested that one of the reasons sales of traditional romances (as opposed to, for instance, chick lit or romantic suspense) have flattened lately may be because the fantasy that romance writers are selling—the idea that love is the most important thing in the world, and that a woman can find lasting happiness in the arms of one man—simply isn't as widely held as it once was. Of course that still does not explain why female fantasies are ridiculed when male fantasies are not. Except, is this common assumption really true?

The first time I visited my friendly neighborhood used bookstore, I was stunned to wander into a room labeled Men's Fiction. Here was a genre I didn't even know existed: books about gritty, macho men fighting wars, riding the range, breaking all the rules as soldiers of fortune. I have recently come to know one of those writers, and he is very good (he even ghost wrote five books for a bestselling romance writer who shall remain nameless). I have never heard the authors of these books complain about their lack of recognition and respect. They know that what they're writing appeals only to their target audience, they know why, and they accept it.

It's the patriarchy's fault

This rationale goes something like this: romances are despised because these are books written by women and for women, and things related to women are always despised in patriarchal societies such as ours. This argument is the darling of academics and women's studies-types (as a card-carrying feminist who authored a scholarly book on attitudes toward gender discrimination in Revolutionary France, I can say that).

Yes, it is true that women are still what Simone de Beauvoir called "le deuxieme sex." We are still scantily represented in the US Congress. Professions dominated by women (whether secretaries in the US or doctors in the old USSR) are still underpaid and lacking in prestige. But while all that doubtless plays a part, it is also a convenient excuse that can all too easily keep us from engaging in the kind of soul-searching we need to be doing.

Think about this: Anne Rice, J. K. Rowling, Sue Grafton, and Sue Monk Kidd are all women writers. While Rice and Rowling appeal equally to both genders, I suspect that a hefty majority of those reading Grafton and Kidd are women. Yet their books are not despised as being written by women and for women.

The romance genre rewards quantity over quality

Many romance writers churn out three, six, even ten books a year. I use the expression *churn out* deliberately. While there are some rare, gifted authors who can write wonderful stories in clear, insightful prose at an astonishing pace, most such books are frankly abysmal (although some could have been wonderful if their authors had spent another six to nine months writing them).

This is a genre where advertising budgets are small and name recognition is therefore very important. The more books an author produces, the better known she becomes, and the more books she sells. Hey, presto, she's on the bestseller lists. If all a reader wants is to mainline her fantasy fix, I guess that's all right. But is it really so surprising when other people look at these books and label them "trash"?

By focusing on the tastes of "hardcore" romance readers, the genre narrowed itself down to the extent that a potentially broader readership has been lost

This is an interesting hypothesis.

Look at the way mysteries have expanded in the last thirty years. Where once we had mainly British manor house whodunits and hardboiled American private detectives, we now have police procedurals, historical mysteries, cozies, serial killer suspenses, etc, etc, etc.

What happened with the romance genre during the same period? The opposite. From the diversity of the early years, romances narrowed down to the point that not long ago a major house announced that their historical romance authors would only be allowed to set books in Regency or Victorian England, or Scotland. If you didn't want to write contemporary romantic comedies, romantic suspense, or pseudo-historical, sexy romps with Regency dukes or men in kilts, you were pretty much out of luck. True, things do seem to be getting better. As romance imprints watch their share of the market dip, they are scrambling to try to attract new readers. But it's going to take the industry a long time to live down the bride/secret baby/cowboy/Navy SEAL stereotype. Like the old bodice ripper tradition that still plagues us, this is something we did to ourselves.

It's because of the sex

This is a touchy one. Not all romances even have sex. Besides, why should romances be the only books despised for their steamy sex? Other genres have sex too, right?

I have this theory that a big part of the appeal of serial killer novels is the illicit thrill some people get from reading about kinky, deviant sex. I know, I know: everyone who reads them says they like finding out how serial killers think (see Education Lite). Except that Charles Gramlich, a friend of mine who not only writes horror and fantasy but also happens to be a professor of psychology at Xavier University, says that the portrayals of serial killers in most suspense books are way, way off base. And is it really a coincidence that as serial killer books have waned in general popularity, the genre has found a new home amongst romance writers now writing romantic suspense?

A few years ago, when some of the better selling romance writers started toning down the sex in their books in an attempt to go mainstream (and acquire more "respect"), readers became downright angry. Some savvy new writers, all too eager to fill their books with explicit, repetitive sex scenes, saw their sales shoot up high enough to land them on the *NYT*.

Romance writers tend to get really, really irate when people accuse them of writing pornography for women. We think of pornography as something exploitative and dehumanizing, we think of *Hustler*, we think of *men's* pornography. That isn't what turns women on. Women are turned on by Rhett sweeping Scarlett up into his arms and snarling, "Frankly, my dear, I don't give a damn." Women are turned on by…romance. And we know it.

Look at the way we promote our genre and ourselves

Intrigued by the skyrocketing popularity of a newish fantasy writer, I recently pulled one of her books off the shelf in my local bookstore, opened it at random, and found myself reading a graphic description of three people engaged in a sex sandwich. Nothing I had read about this author even hinted at the blatant erotica in her books. (And here I thought she was making the *NYT* because she was a good writer!)

Now we all know that kinky sex is a big, big part of why that author's books are selling so well. But she has somehow managed to escape the snide winking and smirking directed at romance writers. How?

Because she doesn't use sex and pink hearts to market her books.

You know what I'm talking about. I'm talking about the cheesy covers that still appear all too often: the traditional torrid clench, or the newer ones featuring a bare-chested male model (usually headless, for some bizarre reason) posed with his hand dangling strategically, suggestively, near his crotch (I am indebted to Monica Jackson for her hilarious blog, "Got coochy for that hint o' dick?"). I'm talking about the male model contests and the authors who promote themselves by handing out red garters and chocolate body sauce. And then there are the authors' websites that scream, "Sizzling Sensuality! Hot Heroes!"

Why do we do this to ourselves? Because this embarrassing kind of nonsense helps sell the books. We might hate to admit it, but the fact remains that many women read our books as much for the sexual titillation as for the romance, and we know it.

Don't get me wrong: I enjoy sex every bit as much as the next person. I have no moral or religious objections to healthy erotic representations of human sexuality in art, print, or film. But since I'm no longer thirteen, I admit I find it beyond boring to read about the sex act in repetitive, excruciating, gratuitous detail, while lurid purple prose makes me want to cringe.

Like it or not, things like pink feather boas, life-sized, cardboard cutouts of the Topaz man, and ridiculously clichéd titles taint the image of the entire genre. All those red garters and hint o' dick covers may help boost individual print runs, but at what price? As long as the industry indulges in this kind of nonsense and encourages quantity over quality, respect will remain illusive. We can either change that, or embrace it and just quit whining.

Postscript

When the above essay appeared on my website in July of 2005, I heard from numerous romance writers and readers, some from as far away as Australia and Europe. Most welcomed the essay's analysis and responded positively to its conclusions. But a significant minority reacted with near hysteria to one of their "own" breaking ranks and failing to recite the officially sanctioned line as recently articulated in a series of articles in the *Romance Writers Report*—i.e., romances are fabulous stories with wonderful characters and positive messages of empowerment and commitment created by some of the best writers writing. I was accused of everything from arrogance and condescension to having no love for the genre, despising happy endings, scorning sex scenes, and even disliking pink. Curiously enough, it was the suggestion that a romance's success depends mainly on how well it does or does not satisfy its readers' fantasies that aroused some of the most emotional reactions.

Whether we like it or not, modern genre fiction typically fails or succeeds commercially not so much because of the "quality" of its writing (by which I mean vivid characterizations, graceful use of prose, avoidance of clichés, etc) but because of the extent to which it plugs into reader fantasies. Those of us who are in this business as a business rather than as a hobby like to see ourselves as professionals, and part of being a professional is learning to take long, realistic looks at our business.

Yes, the romance industry gets some undeservedly bad press; there are some incredibly bright, talented women in the genre who write graceful, emotionally rewarding stories. But we do ourselves a severe disservice if we continue to tell ourselves and each other that what we have here is simply an image problem based on blind prejudice. There appears to be a common but oddly naïve belief among romance writers that if we could just reeducate the public and get them to actually read our books, then everyone would see that they were wrong about the genre. In fact, many of the complaints I examine in my essay come from women who read our books—or who used to.

As an historian, I have been trained to analyze. The general public's perception of the romance genre comes from something, and those with the genre's best interests at heart would do well to listen to what our critics are saying rather than simply dismissing their comments out of hand. Much of the public's perception of our industry comes from the titles, the covers, the prose, the way we promote ourselves, the things we write about and the way we write about them. The dilemma is that these are the same things that help sell our product to our most dedicated readers and may not even be things we want to change.

Titles and covers are mostly—although not entirely—out of writers' control; the other issues are not. Our genre has been enormously successful in the past. It recently went through a severe crisis and is now, it seems, emerging as something quite different. Can't we have a frank, adult conversation about where we go from here and how we get there?

Candice Proctor

Candice Proctor graduated Phi Beta Kappa, summa cum laude with a degree in Classics before going on to earn an MA and PhD. in history. A former academic, she has taught at the University of Idaho and Midwestern State University in Texas. She also worked as an archaeologist on a variety of sites, including a Hudson's Bay Company Fort in San Juan Island; a Cherokee village in Tennessee; a prehistoric kill site in Victoria, Australia; and a Roman cemetery and medieval manor house in Winchester, England. Most recently, she spent many years as a partner in an international business consulting firm. Her publications include seven historical romances, the Sebastian St. Cyr Regency mystery series, and a nonfiction historical study of the French Revolution. Her novels are available worldwide and have been translated into some sixteen different languages. Proctor is also a Hurricane Katrina survivor and is currently rebuilding her home in New Orleans, Louisiana.

CHAPTER TWO

ROMANCE:
THE PERFECT CREATIVE INDUSTRY?
A CASE STUDY OF HARLEQUIN-MILLS
AND BOON AUSTRALIA

GLEN THOMAS

This paper forms part of an ongoing project that examines romance writing, publishing, and reading in Australia as a Creative Industry. The aims of the overall project are three fold:

1. To examine the conditions of production of romance novels
2. To analyze the way in which romance fiction is consumed
3. To outline and map the romance milieu within Australia as a Creative Industry.

I have taken this approach because it is apparent that textual studies of romance fiction have, in my opinion, reached a dead end. Textual analysis of romance fiction has, over decades, shown that romance fiction is highly conservative, based upon normative views of heterosexual romance, and, in the opinion of most critics on the topic, disempowering for women. Certainly, romances have traditionally been regarded by feminist critics as a means of reinforcing sex-role stereotypes of both men and women. For example, Modleski argues that romances "inevitably increase the reader's own psychic conflicts, thus creating an even greater dependency on the literature" (57). In the same vein, Snitow argues that romance novels "reveal and pander to [women's] impossible fantasy life," in that these texts depict a world of romance between men and women that is unattainable (320). Further, Snitow suggests that in romance, "the price for needing emotional intimacy is that [the heroine] must passively wait, must anxiously calculate" (320); these conclusions are echoed by Dubino in her analysis. In this framework, readers are perceived to be passive victims of a patriarchal society that perpetuates itself through myths of female subservience in romantic relationships. Readers are perceived to absorb this patriarchal ideology without any negotiation or engagement with its ideological underpinnings. The justification for this approach is found in the characterization of women in romance novels as young, inexperienced virgins who seek an ideal (usually wealthy) husband; indeed, such characterizations do persist in recent Mills & Boon Sweet Romance novels published in 2000-2003 (see, for example, *Life with Riley*, *Professor and the Nanny*, *City Girl in Training*), but these are now becoming the exception rather than the rule.

Above all these critical studies of romance stands the imposing figure of Janice Radway, whose *Reading the Romance* (first published in 1984) broke new ground (at the time) for the study of romance fiction and romance readers. Radway's study, however, is twenty-two years old this year; since she completed her work, romance fiction and the romance market have both changed quite considerably. Lines of romance novels have proliferated, to the effect that readers now have more choice of romantic fiction than ever before. In Australia, for instance, Harlequin-Mills & Boon publishes twelve different lines (loosely, novels with generic similarities) of romance novels in this country alone. These lines include, among others,

Sweet Romances
Sexy Romances
Medical Romances
Desire
Intrigue
Temptation
Intimate Moments

Within these lines, some 61 different titles are published in Australia each month, for a total of 732 separate novels published in Australia each year (although in 2005, more lines came on to the market, thereby increasing the total number of published novels, with two more lines expected in 2006). Added to that total is a range of single-title romances published under various other Harlequin imprints, such as Red Dress Ink and Mira. These single-title romances take the total number of Harlequin novels published in Australia to over 900 titles in a year.

Clearly, romance is just as popular as it has ever been, if not more so. With that as a starting point, this project analyzes the motivations readers have for reading romance, and, as an extension of that, examines the ways in which publishers seek to meet the reading needs of romance consumers. I would say at the outset here that I regard romance reading as a question of consumption; these are popular texts that are sites of specific reading pleasures. To investigate readers' preferences, a series of focus groups was assembled, and the views of regular romance readers were sought on their reading and purchasing habits.

These focus groups comprised regular readers of romance between the ages of 20 and 60. All participants were female, despite efforts to attempt to recruit male romance readers. There were some initial problems in the recruitment of participants for the focus groups. The opening appeal was carried out through several media outlets, such as the Brisbane ABC radio station (a rough equivalent to the BBC); local commercial radio stations; the daily Brisbane newspaper, *The Courier Mail* (a Rupert Murdoch-controlled outlet), as well as other national newspapers, such as the Melbourne *Age*; and flyers in local public lending libraries and in bookshops that specialize in romance fiction. These initial appeals were largely unsuccessful in that they yielded very few prospective participants. The lack of success in recruiting participants in this manner required a different approach. The second round of appeals for participants was made more personally through e-mails to workplace bulletin boards. A free advertisement was run in various government departments, asking for participants and encouraging people to pass on the request. This method generated more than a dozen extra participants in under two days and then a continual trickle of respondents for the next fortnight. Each volunteer was then asked to pass on the request to any friends or colleagues whom they believed may have fitted the profile of a romance reader. This generated an additional half dozen participants.

Participants who attended the groups were asked informally why they had chosen to volunteer to participate. Interestingly, some of those who volunteered after reading the public service advertisements had seen and heard the previous publicity. However, they had chosen not to act on it because they assumed the researchers would not need extra people, or they were suspicious of the nature of the research. Many saw the electronic message board notice through their work as a safe and easy thing to respond to because it required an individual to make personal contact with someone at work and then left it up to the individual to e-mail an expression of interest. This also explains why the personal approach through QUT Creative Writing & Cultural Studies yielded a comparatively large number of responses when compared with media publicity. Respondents attached extra credibility to requests that came from someone they knew, and felt safer knowing that a colleague had been in personal contact with the researcher. The same issues occur when commercial research firms attempt to recruit participants for focus groups. This does suggest that romance readers are reticent about contacting strangers about their reading habits, which may well suggest that romance readers feel they will be subject to mockery.

Participants in the focus groups were initially asked about their major motivation for reading romance novels. Some participants were disarmingly frank enough to admit that there was no romance in their lives, so they read romance novels as a substitute, but these responses were in the minority. The key response here is that romance novels are perceived to be pure escapism. Participants used words such as "escape," "my time," and "relaxation" to describe their reasons for reading romance. It seemed to be generally agreed that the romance world was one they could enter and leave on short notice, and was not demanding of the reader. Conversely, though, there was a strong sense that the narrative had to be believable, in that the reader needed to be able to empathize with the heroine of the novel. There was no such discussion of the hero, however, which suggests that, as the data indicate, this is a female-centered genre. Some typical responses included:

I do specifically read romance novels when I'm stressed because it's an escapism thing

If I just want to totally unwind and not have to think about something I might just go and buy like a cheap one that's like a hundred pages in you know a couple of hours and, yep, you're done.

This question of empathy with the heroine is of some note, given the tension between the readers' expressed desire for escapism on the one hand, yet on the other their desire for a narrative that they felt was believable. Further discussion with the participants suggested that the issue of empathy was one of being able to empathize with the heroine on an emotional level rather than anything else. All the participants agreed that the actions and plots of the novels were highly unrealistic, in that the heroes tended to be fabulously wealthy (often without having to work overly hard for such wealth), be extremely good-looking, and exhibit behaviours that the participants said they would often find annoying or bizarre (such as the hero buying the heroine a new dress for their first date without first consulting her).

Given that the bulk of romance heroines tend to face some form of dilemma as a central feature of the plot of romance novels, this question of emotional empathy suggests that one of the pleasures of romance reading is the combination of the heroine's romantic or emotional uncertainty coupled with the familiarity with the genre that readers possess, namely in the knowledge that the narrative will almost certainly have a happy ending (which is, after all, one of the key determinants of romance being considered formula fiction). Participants suggested that the most satisfying narratives were those that were of extended length, the kind of book that a reader could "get into." One of the drawbacks of the category romance novels was that they were seen as being too short: those who avoided category romance tended to do so for this reason (as seen, for instance, in comments such as "you just get into it and it's over" or "I want something a bit more substantial"). In sum, then, the dominant pleasure of reading romance, for these groups at least, was associated with an extended narrative where the reader could empathize with the heroine, while at the same time knowing that there would be a positive resolution to the dilemmas or problems that the heroine faced.

Another aspect that came out of the focus groups was the degree of awareness that participants had for the marketing and sales of romance novels. One element that dominated my discussion with the sales and marketing team at Harlequin was the depth of understanding that marketers of romance possessed of the ways in which romance novels are perceived by readers and consumers. The participants in the focus groups were quick to deride category romances on the grounds that they were old-fashioned and probably favored by women of little education and experience. The participants described the "typical" Mills & Boon reader as follows.

> She would be quite older, big glasses that hadn't been changed since 1970 with one of those chains and a big straw bag.
> — participant, aged mid-30s, describing her perception of a "typical" M&B reader

> The person who reads this is someone with a simplistic lifestyle, hasn't traveled much, not much education, would never think to read a classic. Someone who thinks Jane Austen is a big stretch.
> —participant, non tertiary-educated public service worker, aged mid-40s describing her perception of a "typical" M&B reader

It would seem that there is a hierarchy of romance novels and romance readers, one in which category romances come in at pretty well the bottom of the scale. Curiously, perhaps, this is of little concern to those who publish and sell these novels. Harlequin marketers acknowledge that the image of the Mills & Boon imprint is at best staid. Harlequin Australia has most recently responded to this perception by redesigning the covers of its novels. Previous re-banding has altered the color schemes of the various lines, so that the different lines are now color-coded (for instance, the Blaze line, which is the most sexually explicit of the Mills & Boon novels, is published with a cover dominated by a black and ochre color scheme; Sweet Romances, which have virtually no sexual content, are pale blue). Instead of seeking to remake the image of the novels, Harlequin has sought to expand its range of offerings in order to capture a greater segment of the market. To this end, Harlequin Australia has lifted its sales of single-title romances from about 5% of total sales five years ago, to nearly 30% of total sales in 2004. The marketing strategy here is one that will consolidate the existing success of the Mills & Boon lines, while at the same time expand the readership in other directions, targeting those readers who would prefer not to be seen with a standard Mills & Boon novel. As one participant put it,

> This is going to sound really snobby of me, but I'm going to look a lot better carrying that out of the store (holds up Red Dress Ink book) than carrying that out of the store (holding up a Blaze novel). I wouldn't be seen reading something like that, not in a million years.
> — participant, aged mid-30s

What participants noted in their discussions is that they are aware of the way in which Harlequin markets its publications. Participants tended to refer to "they" when referring to the publishers of romance, as in "they want to you to sign on to buy books every month." Those who read Mills & Boon imprints frequently were well aware of the manner in which the image has been changed:

> You used to read Mills & Boon in my days, when I was a kid, and they were clean. Basically, there was nothing sexy at all – everything stopped at the bedroom door. Today, they're more explicit. And then they went through a stage of really, really over the top and now they've toned back off a bit."

> The difference is, when I was a kid, I would have been reading in those days they used to be called 'romance.' What happened with Mills & Boon is as we, the readers, grew older, so did the stories. And so they kept the reader moving with them. So now we're reading special editions, the intrigues, they are designed for, you know the characters are usually 35 up. It's basically the tender moments that you're talking about where the kids are late teens early 20s. They're very clever in the way they're taking the mature audience with them, so they're not cutting us out.

Inherent in both these responses is the idea of the publisher growing with the reader. The Mills & Boon brand is seen as a guarantee of a consistent form of novel and experience, yet what the responses here show is that readers are also aware that the company has changed both the image of its novels and its editorial content over time. The latter respondent's awareness of the twin demands of maintaining the readership base, while at the same time attracting new readers, highlights one of the major issues in romance publishing at present. Romance publishers need to attract younger audiences while simultaneously not alienating their established readership base. Harlequin Australia's own extensive market research highlights this issue: the average age of a romance reader in Australia is 46, although some lines have a higher average age (the average age of Medical Romances readers, for instance, is 52). The line with the youngest readership is the sexually explicit Blaze, with an average reader age of 39.

Clearly, then, romance novels must change with their readership, while not alienating readers' tastes, yet at the same time attract new readers. To achieve this end, Harlequin world-wide forms what they term "innovation teams" to study various aspects of popular culture in order to determine how women's preferences are changing. The most recent outcome of the work of these innovation teams is the launch of a new line of category romance, Harlequin Bombshells. This new line was launched in the United States in August 2004 and appeared in Australia in January 2005. The tag line for the Bombshells line is that they feature "kick-ass women"; these are heroines who seek out trouble and then use their (often formidable) skills to fix up the trouble that they have found. This new line is a direct response to the popularity of televisual heroines seen in *Buffy the Vampire Slayer* and *Alias*, television programs that have featured strong and independent women who can hold their own in a fight and are not intimidated by men.

This is an obvious and contemporary example of how Harlequin will adapt its lines to fit current popular culture. Bombshells will indirectly compete with the existing Intrigue line, which also features women in dangerous situations. A key difference, though, is that the women in Intrigue novels tend to be involved in danger through accident or coincidence, whereas the Bombshells women actively seek danger and trouble. Romance novels are therefore not isolated from contemporary popular culture, but rather will use popular culture as a barometer of where the (potential and current) readership preoccupations lie. In this sense, then, romance producers and publishers will engage with their readership to determine what kind of entertainment the readership is seeking and what kinds of women in popular culture are attracting the readership's attention. When a new line is to go into production, Harlequin will specifically commission established authors to write for the new line, then gradually ease in other authors if the line is successful. This has been the pattern with other lines such as Sexy Romances and Blaze.

It should be stressed, though, that these changes in characterization are predominantly a feature of the heroine of the novels, rather than the hero. The male characters in Harlequin romances have not changed significantly in the past thirty years, except that they are less violent and more communicative with the heroines. This lack of interest in the hero is most evident in the aftermath of the September 11 attacks in the United States: in conversation with one of the editors of Harlequin Australia, I suggested that there would have been a sharp decline in the number of the highly popular "sheikh" novels commissioned and sold (a not unreasonable thought, given that the Middle East had become a perceived site of war and terrorism). This, though, was not the case. Harlequin did, in fact, delay the release of some of their sheikh novels after September 11, but in the time since then there has been no marked diminution in the popularity of these kinds of romances. Sheikh novels, it seems, will continue to sell, despite wider socio-political conditions.

I use the sheikh issue deliberately here, as it brings me to the final element of this paper: at the Romance Writers of Australia annual conference in 2003, Jane Porter, a highly successful US-based romance author, advised the aspirational writers at the conference to follow the demands of the line to which they are pitching their stories; as Porter phrased it, "If my line likes Greeks and Sheikhs, I'm going to write Greeks and Sheikhs." Enough said: for romance authors and prospective authors, the demands of the line and the marketplace are considered to be supreme. A curious fact that did emerge from the focus groups was the number of participants who stated an ambition to become a romance writer. At least 20% of the 40 participants expressed such a desire, or stated that they knew a romance writer personally and wished to emulate her (one participant brought her daughter who writes for Harlequin with her to the session). As I have suggested in a quantitative study of romance authors,[1] romance authorship is the site of many and enduring stereotypes, namely that there is a set formula to romance novels, that it is easily done, and that writers are all millionaires. The focus group participants who wanted to be romance writers did not, though, hold these stereotypes, although some did hold perceptions that they could do a better job than some of the published authors they had read. Those who wanted to be authors were most aware of the market conditions and the associated demands of the different lines.

Those who wanted to be authors also tended to be involved with the Romance Writers of Australia (RWA). The RWA is the dominant body for romance authors in Australia, which runs both an annual conference as well as a series of smaller workshops at various locations throughout the year.[2] The RWA provides the ideal nexus between romance readers and writers. One of the key recommendations for aspiring authors is that they both enjoy and read romance. (Conversely, a frequent stricture for aspiring authors is that they should not do it for the money.) Organizations such as the RWA provide the perfect creative industries milieu for those who seek a career in romance. RWA sessions include discussion of market trends, the legal and taxation aspects of writing for a living, editorial feedback, and training sessions for authors on how to develop

---

[1] Thomas, Glen & Bridie James. "The Romance Industry: A Study of Reading and Writing Romance." *Inflections of Everyday Life*. Ed. Howard McNaughton and Adam Lam. Canterbury: U of Canterbury P, 2006.

[2] An Australian chapter of the Romance Writers of America is also active, but it does not attract the same membership levels as the Romance Writers of Australia. The American organization hosts an annual conference in the United States, which for Australian members is much more difficult to attend than a local conference. Many established authors are also members of both organizations.

plot, character, or sexual tension. Harlequin is a partner in the sponsorship of the RWA annual conference, as a means of both remaining in contact with their established authors and contacting aspiring authors. Prospective authors are provided with advice and guidance through the opportunity to meet with a Harlequin editor at the conference, which allows the author to pitch book ideas to the visiting editor and receive feedback on the line that would be best to target for the work the author is producing.

The desire to become an author, as well as attending conferences such as this, emblematizes the manner in which romance readers are engaged in a form of dialogue with romance publishers and romance fiction more generally. Romance is in this sense a "pure" creative industry, in that it brings together both producers and consumers who interact with one another, thereby shaping the direction of the industry. Authors of romance novels are, in a sense, independent producers of creative content that is then consumed by readers, many of whom then seek to become producers themselves. That the tastes of these consumers/aspiring producers are taken as a gauge of the direction in which the readership is going completes the cycle.

In conclusion, there exists an almost symbiotic relationship between the producers and consumers of romance fiction. The attitude often taken in critical studies of romance, namely that the content is handed down to a highly passive readership who then simply absorb what is given to them, is quite misplaced. In fact, romance publishers will seek to integrate elements of contemporary popular culture into the texts of the novels in order to better meet the desires of the readership. These desires may not be entirely associated with the genre of romance as such (like *Buffy* or *Alias*), but the depictions of women within these texts will have an effect on the way romance is produced. Romance is continually being updated as tastes within the wider culture change; these updates are largely consumer driven, rather than producer driven. In terms of category romance, as lines become less popular, they will be phased out of production and new lines will be introduced (for instance, Harlequin Flipside, which featured romantic comedy narratives, ceased publication in 2005). In creative industries terms, this represents an industry that is fully flexible and adaptable in the face of wider social change, rather than a static producer of formulaic narratives. It also suggests that the innovations in romance fiction tend to be consumer driven, an element that warrants further examination and discussion.

Works Cited

Bright, Laurey. *Life With Riley*. Chatswood: Harlequin-Mills & Boon, 2002.
Dubino, Jeanne. "The Cinderella Complex: Romance Fiction, Patriarchy and Capitalism." *Journal of Popular Culture* 27.3 (1993): 103-18.

Fielding, Liz. *City Girl in Training*. Chatswood: Harlequin-Mills & Boon, 2003.

Halldorson, Phyllis. *Professor and the Nanny*. Chatswood: Harlequin-Mills & Boon, 2000.

Modleski, Tania. *Loving with a Vengeance: Mass-Produced Fantasies for Women*. 1982. New York: Routledge, 1990.

Owen, Mairead. "Reinventing Romance: Reading Popular Romance Fiction." *Women's Studies International Forum* 20 (1997): 537-46.

Radway, Janice. *Reading the Romance: Women, Patriarchy, and Popular Literature*. 1984. Chapel Hill: U of North Carolina P, 1991.

Snitow, Ann. "Mass Market Romance: Pornography for Women is Different." *Women and Romance: A Reader*. Ed. Susan Ostrow Weisser. New York: UP, 2001. 307—22.

Thomas, Glen, and Bridie James. "The Romance Industry: A Study of Reading and Writing Romance." *Inflections of Everyday Life*. Ed. Howard McNaughton and Adam Lam. Canterbury: U of Canterbury P, 2006.

Glen Thomas

Glen Thomas teaches in the Creative Industries Faculty at the Queensland University of Technology. His research interests include romance fiction and publishing, technical communication, and American literature.

CHAPTER THREE

FORMS OF PLEASURE IN THE READING
OF POPULAR ROMANCE:
PSYCHIC AND CULTURAL DIMENSIONS

EVA Y. I. CHEN

With its perceived repetitive, formulaic plots, emotional excess and predominantly female readership, popular romance has always occupied the lowest echelon in the already devalued category of popular literature. Classic Marxist critique has exposed its complicity with the dominant bourgeois ideology that dopes the reader into an illusionary acceptance of the status quo, while early feminist critics decried the genre's patriarchal agenda that seduces women into "cherishing the chains of their bondage" (Firestone 180). Such critical disapproval on grounds of ideology, coupled with the traditional dismissal of romance on grounds of literary value, its perceived emotional excess and lack of reasoned control, is in stark contrast with the genre's enthusiastic reception among popular readers. Annual sales of popular romance easily surpass the total of all other popular genres added together (according to Paul Fleming's romance website, 2003 sales of romance fiction, standing at over US $1 billion, exceeded 50% of all popular fiction sales). The critical dismissal has not been able to answer the question of why the predominantly women readers[1] should love and cherish works that obviously seem to preach a passive

---

[1] Based on a 1983 survey by a US popular romance magazine, *Boy Meets Girl*, published in the Chicago area, Kay Mussell points out that out of the 22 million readers of popular romance, only 1% to 2% identified themselves as male. Though some male readers may not wish to disclose their gender, the number of male readers may not be significant enough to impact materially on marketing and editing considerations by the publishers (6). Another 1969 survey by the British researcher Peter Mann, upon request of the biggest publisher of popular romance, Mills & Boon, found that out of the 2000 readers investigated, the number of male readers is "negligible"; while women readers between

and restrictive femininity, with punishments along the way for transgressions. Does this merely confirm women's perceived masochistic nature? Are women readers really just easily manipulated dupes? And if so, what does this say about the feasibility of feminism, whose avowed agenda is for the change of gender reality and the increase of female consciousness?

A sea change has taken place in the study of popular romance since the 1980s with the intervention of feminist cultural critics in the field. Their scholarship in romance and other popular women's genres, like TV sit-coms and women's magazines, has contributed importantly to the study of popular culture (Turner 222). Departing from previous critical focus on the text and the production of meaning, this recent feminist cultural scholarship emphasizes the reader and the consumption of meaning. Rather than exclusively attacking popular romance's conservative textual ideology, recent critics have turned to questioning why the readers should find romance pleasurable and whether, in their uses and consumption of the text, they do more than just passively accepting the preferred textual meaning. While all this critical probing is going on, one concept begins to assume an increasingly crucial and transcendental significance, the concept of pleasure. Pleasure is now no longer the opiate, sugar-coating, conservative ideology but is instead celebrated as resistive, transgressive and utopian. Amid all this critical righting of the wrongs the genre has traditionally been subject to, there is a tendency to over-emphasize and romanticize the positive potential of pleasure, so that pleasure has increasingly become a magical concept encompassing all forms of complex reader behavior in the consumption of meaning, a concept standing for reader's agency that is divorced from power politics and textual control. This paper attempts a detailed analysis of this important concept by tracing and commenting on its application in the critical study of popular romance. While applauding most of the new work on pleasure, this paper also points out the risks of over-optimism and argues that celebrating pleasure as necessarily resistant may risk another form of essentialism. It also seeks to link this cultural-studies-informed feminist work with developments in psychoanalysis and especially their utilization in feminist film criticism, so that both the social and psychological dimensions of the concept can be exposed.

---

the ages of 15 and 34 constitute 60% of all the readers, most come from a lower-middle class background while very few are from the upper class (6). More recent statistics provided by Romance Writers of America Online show that figure was 93% in the 2002 survey and 91% in the 1998 survey.

The Nature of Pleasure

As an important psychic phenomenon, pleasure is a concept commented on by both Freud and Lacan. In *Beyond the Pleasure Principle*, Freud points out the crucial links between pleasure, repetition and the death instinct. He sees all drives as subject to a principle of constancy or inertia that searches for a diminution in the tension of desire and a return to "some early state" (Freud 1920: 37). Such a return is itself repetitive, and since the reduction of tension produces pleasure, the means of pleasure is thus through repetition. Freud further points out that repetition stands for a more primitive, more basic and more instinctual drive behind the pleasure principle (23), which is the ultimate state of inertia represented by the death instinct (36). As such, the repetitive pleasure, which reduces tension and stimulation and seeks a return to stability and inertia, basically reflects the operation of the death instinct. Yet on the other hand, there is a certain ambiguity to Freud's related ideas. Although *Beyond the Pleasure Principle* is often perceived to have established a sort of binary opposition between the death instinct (Thanatos) and life instinct (Eros) (Gallop 100), the two are not absolutely mutually exclusive. The life instinct, as a type of drive that escapes the principle of constancy and is the disturber of sleep, the "breaker of the peace" (40, 55), is also realized through "return" and repetition and aims similarly at "inertia" and release. Thus, repetition in the pleasure principle could articulate the two opposing instincts in interlocking ways, and the aim of repetition or what lies "beyond" the pleasure principle may not necessarily be death.

In his revision of Freud, Lacan points out that the death instinct is not separate but part of all drives (Lacan 1977: 257) and that the death instinct, instead of Freud's biological emphasis, is located in the symbolic order (Lacan 1954-55: 326). The death instinct is only the "mask of the symbolic order" (Lacan 1954-55: 326), reflected in the symbolic order's fundamental nature of endlessly producing repetitions. Yet such repetition is less a result of the total release of tension and gratification of desire than a result of the failure to understand the true nature of such pleasure and desire (itself already including dissatisfaction and lack). In other words, what is "beyond" the pleasure principle and the aim of repetition is a repetitive attempt at an earlier state of plenitude and oneness. Only when such an earlier state is irretrievably and forever lost, is there a *sense* of this pleasure. Thus repetition seeks pleasure and release of tension but already involves a gap between the signified, an ideal earlier experience, and the signifier, sense or knowledge of this experience. This gap leads to the realization of and search for pleasure but also necessarily produces tension that can never be completely satisfied; this forever residual sense of dissatisfaction, tension and frustration is where *jouissance* is located

(1964: 31). Thus to Lacan, *jouissance* both lies within and is an extension of pleasure. And the act of repetition, arising from the subject's failure to see that ideal pleasure could never be attained again, is thus a process of endless repetitive attempts wherein both pleasure and *jouissance* coexist.

Popular Culture and Pleasure

Pleasure is a universal psychic phenomenon, but in the field of culture, pleasure has been mostly linked with popular culture. This can be attributed to a significant extent to the influence of the Frankfurt School and their views on popular pleasure. Though the issues of pleasure, repetition and the death instinct are complex, it is Freud's views linking pleasure to inertia, closure and death that have largely influenced Adorno and, through Adorno, a significant part of critical evaluation of popular pleasure. Adorno argues that modern capitalist forms of popular culture, or "pleasure industry," are popular because they offer a closed pleasure that is repetitive, familiar, conservative and mechanical, an extension of the rhythms and structures of industrial production (Adorno and Horkheimer 137). Popular pleasure's addictive and instantly satiated nature dopes the populace into a satisfied acceptance of the status-quo and is unable to produce, like high art, utopian desires for a higher level of individuality and freedom (137-41). The nature of popular pleasure is thus "complicit" with the dominant capitalist ideology.

Adorno believes that pleasure is linked only to popular culture while high art, original in content and refusing to provide an easy or happy ending to gratify the readers, leads not to pleasure but sublimation. Such an idea of sublimation as arising out of dissatisfaction and an indefinite deferral of gratification sounds close to the Lacanian *jouissance*, but the problem lies in Adorno's definite polarization between pleasure and sublimation. If, as Adorno himself admits, the culture industry always promises the consumers a pleasure that it perpetually cheats them of, "the real point will never be reached," thus necessitating the endless cycle of repetitive consumption (139), then popular pleasure, as Connor puts it, must already contain frustration and dissatisfaction (209). A further question that needs to be asked is why and what lies behind such a rigid separation. Why is gratification and release of pressure perceived as having low value and exclusive to popular culture, while tension and rejection of gratification is seen as having high value and linked to high art? This leads to the class dimension behind the pleasure issue. Pleasure is obviously seen as mostly a passive physiological response to sensual stimulation where the mind plays no role, whereas sublimation needs conscious effort and active working of the mind. Here at play is obviously the dichotomy between mind and body, and the class constructions equating body with the lower classes. A derogatory view of pleasure is thus innately linked to an elitist class construction.

If popular pleasure is constrained and devalued to reinforce the established class structure while at the same time deliberately given some degree of free rein because of its perceived complicity in the distribution of dominant ideology, then it probably follows that a celebration of sensual pleasure to the excess, which transcends or breaks through the constraints, could embody a liberatory potential. Such a view is eloquently set out in both Bakhtin's and Barthes's ideas on pleasure. In his study of Rabelais, Bakhtin celebrates the carnival tradition and its elevation of sensual, bodily pleasures, as contributing to the development of Renaissance humanism away from the repressive control of medieval religious ideology. For Barthes, *jouissance*, or erotic pleasure, is valuable because it entails a fracturing of the familiar system of signification and challenges the reader's historical, cultural and psychological assumptions (14). Barthes's ideas have proven more useful to the study of popular literature because of their emphasis on textuality and because they firmly locate valuable pleasure on the sensual and bodily level. In addition, Barthes's theory shifts focus to the reader and the reading process, a focus coinciding with the developments in cultural studies itself, which also helps to explain the quick adoption of the Barthesian resistive pleasure by scholars of popular culture in the late 1980s and early 1990s.

One has to bear in mind, though, that Barthes distinguishes between two kinds of pleasure, one, *plasir*, for the conservative, familiar and comfortable pleasure that does not break with culture, and the other, *jouissance*, that breaks and fractures the established system. An important point is that Barthes links *plasir* specifically to mass popular culture, which is unable to give rise to *jouissance*. Though he also stresses that the line of division between the two pleasures is hazy, "the distinction will not be the source of absolute classifications" (4), this still poses problems for scholars of popular culture in their efforts to utilize Barthes's resistive pleasure to stress the positive values of the sensual pleasure brought by popular culture. It must be noted that to argue that sensual pleasure is available for transgressive discursive construction does not mean that the pleasure itself is necessarily progressive. Popular pleasure may just be a popular blow-off or an example of deliberate manipulation by the dominant class, to "give 'em what they want" (Mercer 54), so that it becomes a safety valve that both facilitates a smoother return to the status quo once tension is released and reinforces the existing class division that sees the popular as irrational. This danger is somewhat insufficiently heeded in the 80s' revival of interest in popular pleasure.

Feminism and Resistive Pleasure

Feminist cultural scholars' intervention into popular women's genres since the late 80s has become an important phenomenon in the field of popular culture. Feminist cultural scholars have battled for the value of popular romance and other women's genres, both as a form of popular culture against traditional dismissal of the field in general, and as part of women's culture against the emphasis on male subcultures within cultural studies itself (Shiach 333). The forms of pleasure women readers/users experience on an everyday level have become an important subject of research. Thus, popular pleasure, generally celebrated as resistive and utopian since the late 80s, is given a special gender dimension as particular forms of pleasure unique to women are elevated as proof of female agency and resistance. The focus has also moved away from text-oriented research that stresses the text's dominant power in distributing pleasure and implies a passive, ideal reader, to reader-oriented investigations that treat the readers as actual social subjects and romance reading as situated in a series of related social activities deriving meaning from its everyday cultural context. Hence, the prevalent use of ethnography that is also a distinguishing feature of research on women's genres within cultural studies. Using ethnography that seeks to find the historical reader located in specific socio-political contexts, critics such as Radway find women's pleasure in romance reading as positive and "combative" (7).[2] It is a woman's special gift to herself, a gift that allows women to focus on a single object that provides pleasure for themselves alone, while taking them away from the caretaking role of mother or wife imposed by patriarchy (91).

Later feminist critics of the early 1990s tend to be more celebratory of the particularly female forms of pleasure. Women readers' pleasure in reading the romance, traditionally dismissed as excessively emotional and marginalized as feminine and irrational, is now seen as a way of subverting the dominant logocentric language system and of constructing a positive, resistive female identity. The trivial, gossipy and often serial nature of women's genres also facilitates the communicative pleasure women experience in being part of a fan network of interaction, gossip and mutual reassurance, a network resistive of the dominant cultural system, which tends to suppress or denigrate the female voice (Brown 1990, 1994; Geraghty 1991, 1996; Livingstone; Nochimson).

---

[2] Tania Modleski's 1982 work, *Loving with a Vengeance: Mass-Produced Fantasies for Women*, also importantly defends the positive potential in the popular women's genres, including romance and soap opera, and criticizes the Frankfurt School for its exclusive emphasis on the production process. Modleski's approach is, however, mainly textual and differs from the ethnographic approach of later feminist studies on popular forms.

A close analysis of this feminist scholarship shows that, though worth applauding for its original disclosure of various forms of readerly pleasure and its emphasis on pleasure as a crucial site in its own right, this new scholarship, in too readily equating pleasure with positive resistance, may risk another form of reductive essentialism. As has been pointed out above, popular pleasure may also merely serve as a popular blow-off and may be manipulated by the dominant class for conservative ends. The popular readers are actual social subjects susceptible to discourses and power politics, which also inform the ideology of the texts they read. To disregard the shaping role of the text or the meaning-producing mechanism is to dislocate meaning consumption or reader agency out of its historical context and to, as Turner so well puts it, rationalize the status-quo, since reader activism can always be counted on regardless of how conservative a text may be (112).

Pleasure, Identification and Fantasy

Up until now, the thrust of feminist cultural scholarship on romance reading and pleasure has focused on social-cultural considerations and not enough on the psychic dimension of reading and the reading subjectivity. This absence is probably due to what David Morley terms as a reaction in cultural studies against psychoanalysis's traditional emphasis on drives and their determination of pleasure, which rules out any possibility of individual agency (43). Romantic genres have traditionally been criticized as engaging readers in false and illusory fantasies that offer escapist pleasure away from harsher reality. This, at least indirectly, confirms that fantasy, though perceived as illusory and passive, is an important source of pleasure during reading. One of the first critics to argue that the pleasure from fantasy is not false but "real" is again Janice Radway, who perceptively sees the need to incorporate a psychoanalytical as well as cultural analysis of the concept of pleasure (100). For this end she uses Nancy Chodorow's theory of female identity formation to argue that the pleasure women readers experience in witnessing vicariously the happiness of the female protagonist arises from women's universal desire for regression to an early, pre-oedipal state of nurturance. Feminist scholarship on popular culture has demonstrated a preference for Chodorow in analysis of female readership and spectatorship, and has largely bypassed the spectatorship theory of the seventies feminist film scholarship—especially that centering around the film journal *Screen*—because of the latter's perceived over-emphasis on the male oedipal gaze that excludes an active female spectatorship (Mayne 158). Chodorow argues that the infant's relationship with its nurturing parent supplies an early model of a "self-in-relationship," and that girls reproduce the mother's perceived identity of nurturance and tenderness while boys, in an effort of distinguishing from the mother, reject the mother's perceived nurturance. Since patriarchy enforces on women a primary relationship with men, women's essential needs for nurturance are never met. Radway uses Chodorow to argue that the pleasure of romance reading is thus derivable from a satisfaction of this regressive desire for a pre-oedipal state of nurturance and tenderness, out of a vicarious identification by women readers with the female characters (14).

Radway's perspective emphasizes the distinctive subjective position and fantasy pleasure peculiar to women readers as a result of the formation of female identity. Though this position is indeed true for a significant part of the pleasure during the reading process, such a perspective seems to be based on a somewhat linear identification between the female reading subject and the female protagonist or the female child in the pre-oedipal process of identity formation. But does identification also include other possibilities? Is there just one form of identification (the pre-oedipal stage) and one sort of regressive desire and pleasure? May the reader also identify with the position of the mother in the pre-oedipal, mother-child relationship or with a position of vacillation between the mother and the female child? Or even with a reading position not bound by the reader's own biological gender? Does pleasure in fantasy also arise from multiple, vacillating identificatory positions? These questions are worth further exploration, and recent feminist film scholarship on spectatorship, identification and fantasy has offered valuable insights into these issues.

Feminist film theory has itself come a long way as regards spectatorial identification. Seventies feminist film theory emphasizes a monolithic identification model based exclusively on biological gender. Thus, the male audience experiences pleasure out of identification with the patriarchal male characters in classic Hollywood films while the female audience experiences passive, masochistic pleasure out of identification with the subjugated female characters (Mulvey 3-10). More recent criticism, however, has come to see identification as more complex, involving approximation but also fragmentation and continual flux (Fuss 51). The new approach to identification is especially given a boost by the fantasy theory of LaPlanche and Pontalis, which, deriving from Freud's ideas on spectatorship in "A Child Is Being Beaten" (Freud 1919), emphasizes fantasy as the *setting* or structure for desire rather than its object. In "Fantasy and the Origins of Sexuality," LaPlanche and Pontalis argue that fantasy has nothing to do with the opposition between reality and illusion, but is instead concerned with a third concept, psychological reality. In fantasy, the viewing subject identifies with multiple and fluid positions, like that of the child being beaten, or the father beating the child, or even in a de-subjectivized form, "in the very syntax" of the fantasy, like the verb "beating" (LaPlanche and Pontalis 22-8). Thus identification in reading or viewing, instead of being straight and uniform, also involves multiple and fluid positions, and the viewing subjectivity, instead of chasing after or seeking to realize a target or sign in a linear fashion, is itself entangled in a series of constantly changing images. This idea of fantasy and identification has proved useful to feminist film scholarship, since the film viewing process would thus entail more than the monolithic identification traditionally constructed along the lines of gender, race or class. Instead, there is also the possibility that women viewers may identify with the hero or the narrative process, and experience active, multi-levels of pleasure (Williams 1: 706-11).

If we use film scholarship to analyze the reading process of popular romance, we may find that a similar fluid and multiple position is a key to the pleasure experienced by female readers, entangled as they are among a series of vacillating subject positions between the poles of loving and being loved. Cora Kaplan's analysis of the 1970s romance, *The Thornbirds*, is an early example that uses fantasy theory to discuss the pleasure of the text. Kaplan argues that the huge appeal of this romance lies in the fact that the reader is able to fantasize about multiple and fluid identifications between the male and female protagonists (161-62). While Kaplan's use of fantasy can be limited, in that she stresses the role of the text (through constructing an androgynous male protagonist) in offering and guiding the reader's fantasy pleasure, the romance reader may take on a variety of positions in multiple identifications with the heroine, the hero, or the process of loving, and therefore experience pleasure through each position. In fact, the process of fantasy and love, and the much-indulged-in process of seduction and courtship, is, as Ang points out, the more important source for pleasure rather than the final realization or target of desire (528-29). This may also explain why romances all deal briefly with the eventual happy ending of marriage but prolong the courting process, which could take on myriad different forms. Some romances may actually have the marriage first (often not as a result of free love) and then courtship later, but still the courting process takes up the bulk of attention before the couple finally moves toward a marriage, not just in name but also of real happiness (for more, see Pamela Regis's 2003 *A Natural History of the Romance Novel*). How do multiple subject positions during fantasy, such as that of the courting process, give rise to pleasure? This is because such fluidity has allowed the possibility of transcending a socially transcribed or fixed subject position that the reader normally experiences in real life. Pleasure is produced when the old fixed boundaries are eroded and new possibilities are tried on. A discussion of these differing subject positions involves an awareness of the real-life subjectivity of the historical reader, which could allow the critic to better avoid universalizing the subjectivity in question. Cultural studies scholars have long been wary of the essentializing tendencies of classic psychoanalytic frameworks, but the new theory of fantasy should be better able to cover both the cultural and the psychoanalytical sides of the concept of pleasure.

Finally, to argue that the reader's pleasure at least partly derives from fluid and multiple positions of identification does not mean that the reader can exercise unlimited agency. Reading as fantasy indeed allows the staging of conflicting desires and multiple performances, and it is indeed a site of excess not subject to any exclusive or fixed boundaries, but this does not necessarily translate into a political meaning of positive resistance. In the same way that the text's prescription of pleasure to the readers may not always be successful, the readers, despite their possible active use of the text, are still social subjects located in forms of discourse that also powerfully shape their use or pleasure. Thus, pleasure, an important psychic activity containing multiple possibilities of identification and fluid positionings of subjectivity, is also affected by specific socio-cultural contexts and as such, cannot be divorced from the cultural and political.

Works Cited

Adorno, Theodor and Max Horkheimer. *Dialectic of Enlightenment.* Trans. John Cumming. London: Verso, 1986.

Ang, Ian. "Feminist Desire and Female Pleasure: On Janice Radway's *Reading the Romance: Women, Patriarchy and Popular Literature.*" *Camera Obscura* 16 (1988): 179-90.

Bakhtin, Mikhail. *Rabelais and His World.* Cambridge: MIT Press, 1968.

Barthes, Roland. *The Pleasure of the Text.* Trans. Richard Miller. Oxford: Basil Blackwell, 1990.

Brown, Mary Ellen, ed. *Television and Women's Culture.* London: Sage Publications, 1990.

———. *Soap Opera and Women's Talk: The Pleasure of Resistance.* London: Sage Publications, 1994.

Burgin, Victor, James Donald and Cora Kaplan, eds. *Formations of Fantasy.* London: Methuen, 1986.

Chodorow, Nancy. *The Reproduction of Mothering: Psychoanalysis and the Sociology of Gender.* Berkeley: University of California P, 1978.

Connor, Steven. "Aesthetics, Pleasure and Value." *The Politics of Pleasure: Aesthetics and Cultural Theory.* Ed. Stephen Regan. Buckingham: Open University P, 1992. 203-220.

Cowie, Elizabeth. *Representing the Woman: Cinema and Psychoanalysis.* London: Macmillan, 1997.

Firestone, Calamity. *The Dialectic of Sex.* New York: Morrow, 1970.

Fleming, Paul. *Romance Homepage*. 15 Jan. 2004:
    <http://www.splumonium.com/DIR_romance/romance.html>.
Freud, Sigmund. "'A Child Is Being Beaten': A Contribution to the Study of
    the Origin of Sexual Perversions." 1919. *The Standard Edition of the
    Complete Psychological Works of Sigmund Freud* (*SE*). Trans. and Ed.
    James Strachey. Vol. 17. London: The Hogarth Press, 1955. 175-204.
————.*Beyond the Pleasure Principle*. 1920. *Standard Edition*. Vol. 18.
    1955.
Fuss, Diana. *Identification Papers*. New York: Routledge, 1995.
Geraghty, Christine. "Soap Opera and Utopia." 1991. Rpt. John Storey. 319-
    27.
————."Feminism and Media Consumption." *Cultural Studies and
    Communications*. Eds. James Curran, David Morley and Valerie Walker
    Dine. London: Arnold, 1996.
Kaplan, Cora. "*The Thorn Birds*: Fiction, Fantasy, Femininity." Burgin,
    Donald and Kaplan. 142-67.
LaPlanche, Jean and Jean-Bertrand Pontalis. "Fantasy and the Origins of
    Sexuality." Burgin, Donald and Kaplan. 5-28.
Livingstone, Sonia M. "Audience Reception: The Role of the Viewer in
    Retelling Romantic Drama." *Mass Media and Society*. Eds. James Curran
    and Michael Gurevitch. London: Arnold. 1991. 285-306.
Mann, Peter. *The Romantic Novel: A Survey of Reading Habits*. London: Mills
    & Boon, 1969.
Mayne, Judith. "Paradoxes of Spectatorship." *Viewing Positions: Ways of
    Seeing Film*. Ed. Linda Williams. New Brunswick: Rutgers University
    Press, 1994. 155-83.
Mercer, Colin. "Complicit Pleasures." *Popular Culture and Social Relations*.
    Eds. Tony Bennett, Colin Mercer and Janet Woollacott. Milton Keynes:
    Open University P, 1986. 50-68.
Modleski, Tania. *Loving with a Vengeance: Mass-Produced Fantasies for
    Women*. Hamden: Archon, 1982.
Morley, David. *Family Television: Cultural Power and Domestic Leisure*.
    London: Comedia, 1986.
Mulvey, Laura. "Afterthoughts on 'Visual Pleasure and Narrative Cinema',
    Inspired by *Duel in the Sun*." *Framework* 10 (1979): 3-10.
Mussell, Kay. *Fantasy and Reconciliation: Contemporary Formulas of
    Women's Romance Fiction*. Westport: Greenwood, 1984.
Nochimson, Martha. *No End to Her: Soap Opera and the Female Subject*.
    Berkeley: University of California Press, 1992.

O'Connor, Barbara and Elisabeth Klaus. "Pleasure and Meaningful Discourse: An Overview of Research Issues." *International Journal of Cultural Studies* 3.3 (2000): 369-87.

Radway, Janice A. *Reading the Romance: Women, Patriarchy, and Popular Literature.* London: Verso, 1984.

Regis, Pamela. *A Natural History of the Romance Novel.* Philadelphia: University of Pennsylvania Press, 2003.

Shiach, Morag. "Feminism and Popular Culture." In Storey, 333-41.

Storey, John, ed. *Cultural Theory and Popular Culture: A Reader.* 2nd ed. London: Prentice Hall, 1998.

Turner, Graeme. *British Cultural Studies: An Introduction.* 2nd ed. London: Routledge, 1992.

Williams, Linda. "Film Bodies: Gender, Genre, and Excess." *Film Theory and Criticism: Introductory Readings.* Eds. Leo Braudy and Marshall Cohen. Oxford: Oxford University P, 1999. 701-15.

———.*Hard Core: Power, Pleasure, and the "Frenzy of the Visible."* Berkeley: University of California Press, 1999.

Eva Y. I. Chen

Eva Yin-I Chen received her PhD in English from the University of Sussex and is currently Associate Professor in the English Department of National Cheng-Chi University in Taipei, Taiwan. She has published a book on D. H. Lawrence and a number of refereed papers on urban modernity and British literature of the modern period. A Chinese version of this paper appeared in a Taiwanese journal, *Chung-Wai Literary Monthly*, Vol.32, No. 12 (May 2004): 149-74.

CHAPTER FOUR

BOUND TO LOVE:
CAPTIVITY IN HARLEQUIN SHEIKH NOVELS

EMILY A. HADDAD

We don't mind surrendering provided it's to the rule of love.
—Valerie Parv, *Royal Spy*, 2002, p. 6

How to keep a resistant heroine and her future husband together long enough for both to realize and acknowledge that they are in love? This is a central structural challenge facing writers of category or formula romance novels such as those published by Harlequin. An extended episode of captivity easily resolves the problem, enforcing proximity when the man refuses to let the woman go. Where the male protagonist is a sheikh, such an episode also serves to reaffirm the cultural stereotype of the dominant Arab man holding "his" women in virtual enslavement. This stereotype is supported as well by the other principal incarnation of the captivity scene in Orientalist romance fiction: the heroine falls into the grip of a villain or sandstorm and must be rescued by the male lead. In either case, captivity is crucial both to the plot outcome and to the narrative's participation in contemporary Orientalist discourse.

Captivity is a widely used trope in romance novels regardless of their setting. Anne Kaler's 1999 essay, "Conventions of Captivity in Romance Novels," for instance, points out that "captivity is a prime plot device in romance" (86). Despite her opening reference to Edith Hull's *The Sheik* (1919) and her mention of several other novels with Middle Eastern settings, however, Kaler does not address the manifestations or implications of captivity there with any specificity. Pamela Regis comments more extensively on *The Sheik* in her 2003 book on romance fiction and foregrounds the "abduction, assault, and imprisonment of [Diana Mayo] the heroine" in Hull's novel (Regis 115). However, Regis identifies Diana as "the prototypical twentieth-century popular romance novel heroine" (119), universalizing her rather than seeking to particularize the significance of her captivity in Algeria. Similarly, the hero, Ahmed, is for Regis an "extreme" version of the "alpha-male heroes in twentieth-century popular romance novels" (120); Regis does not explore further the implications of his ethnicity or nationality.

The aim of Regis's analysis is to justify her identification of *The Sheik* as "the ur-romance novel of the twentieth century" (115), and in this context it is understandable that she would insist that "defining [this novel] solely by its exotic setting threatens to obscure its universality as a romance" (123). Nor do other critics contend fully with the exotic as a matrix for romance captivity. For example, Gabriele Linke's 1997 article comments usefully on a "contradiction" between primitivist nostalgia and the civilizing mission in romances with Middle Eastern settings (207), but does not discuss captivity. Also relevant is Stephanie Burley's argument, from an essay published in 2000, that romance fiction's conventional

> associations of heroes with darkness and heroines with whiteness are indeed connected to culturally current ideologies of race, ethnicity, and otherness in 20th century America, and . . . that these chromatic associations are central to the way that white audiences make sense of and desire these texts. (324)

The novels Burley discusses are set in America and do not involve Arab characters, although some of her conclusions about "a wider racial economy of representation" (328) would be applicable to books with Middle Eastern settings as well. That a current Harlequin (originally Pinnacle) romance series featuring African American characters is called "Arabesque" is emblematic of such a connection. Lynne Pearce and Jackie Stacey include several essays on interracial romance in *Romance Revisited* (1995), but none of these articulates a racial dimension to romance between British or American white women and Middle Eastern men.

"From Sahara Sands to Shangri-La," a 1994 chapter by Mary Cadogan, is one of only two essays I have encountered that is dedicated to this subgenre of the romance. Cadogan's selective overview of sheikh romances centers as much on the desert as on the protagonists' relationships; she sees these romances as characterized by "violent, erotic escapism" (126). Although she makes several references to captivity as a plot element, she does not investigate its significance as a trope, either per se or in relation to marriage. The other essay on this topic, "Lust and Dust" (1997) by Julia Bettinotti and Marie-Françoise Truel, surveys the early development of the subgenre and relates it particularly to the conventions of nineteenth-century travel writing. Captivity is mentioned only once in their analysis; they assert that

> [w]hat originally appeared to be a story of captivity and enslavement turns out to be a story of resistance and female liberation. As for marriage, [it] would not

imply female submission to an established order, but rather . . . a type of catharsis. (192)

As this comment ends their article, there is no elaboration. I hope that my essay will show that a more thorough investigation of captivity and its relationship with marriage in sheikh romances is warranted, especially given that in Anglo-American popular culture, the Arab world is persistently associated with captivity, as John Eisele has observed in his 2002 essay on the "eastern"—movies about "the wild east." Eisele lists "abduction," "enslavement," and "imprisonment" first among the "narrative devices" characteristic of Hollywood films about the Middle East (68). (Indeed, one of the films discussed by Eisele is the 1921 movie version of Hull's *The Sheik*.)

Even if we follow the lead of Regis and others in recognizing the universality of *The Sheik* and its descendants, we should also acknowledge their specificity, for one cannot safely assume that all captivity in romance is functionally or morphologically uniform. Given the pop-culture identification of Arabs with abduction, it seems especially necessary to consider how captivity scenes work in the Orientalist romance novels that incorporate them. My chapter will begin by documenting the manifestations of captivity in this particular subgenre of category romance—a subgenre that a prolific contemporary Harlequin writer, Alexandra Sellers, calls the "sheikh fantasy" (*Born Royal* 6) and others have termed "'sand' books" (Seidel 166) or "desert fabula" (Bettinotti and Truel 184). Primarily through analysis of selections from two Harlequin miniseries—Sellers's "Sons of the Desert" and Susan Mallery's "Desert Rogues"—I will show that captivity in these contemporary Harlequins not only enables the development of the plot, but also precipitates an ideological shift, which dissipates the heroine's feminist dedication to the ideals of personal liberty. In the end, as liberty pales in comparison to the delights of love, bondage gives way to bonding. Yet the framework of captivity remains, transmuted into a vision of marriage that has been channeled specifically through the motif of the harem. Finally, I will argue that while sheikh romances may or may not join with other romance subgenres in providing women readers with a way to relieve the stresses and worries of their own lives, they also offer something more distinctive: the opportunity for women readers to address their anxieties about otherness, and specifically Arab otherness.

Captivity in Contemporary Harlequin Sheikh Fantasies

Harlequin dominates the field of series romance fiction, of course, and Harlequin has consistently incorporated travel to exotic locations, as numerous critics have observed. In particular, Harlequin has promoted captivity, or at least the threat of captivity, as a selling point for fiction set in the Arab world.[1] Novel titles from the 1970s, 1980s, and 1990s signal the attraction of captivity for readers: consider for instance Violet Winspear's *The Sheik's Captive* (1979), Rebecca Stratton's *The Silken Cage* (1981), or Sara Wood's *Desert Hostage* (1991).[2] The cover blurbs of earlier Harlequins reflect attention to captivity even more sharply. For example, the blurb from the back cover of Charlotte Lamb's 1978 novel, *Desert Barbarian,* reads in part:

> On the moonlit sands of a desert oasis, they were utterly alone.
> "Why have you brought me here?" Marie's voice was husky with alarm. Did this arrogant stranger want only the ransom her wealthy father would pay ... or was there something more?
> Her captor gave her a mocking smile.

The captivity scene at issue is not central to the novel's action, yet the novel is promoted as if it were, suggesting again the appeal of captivity for Harlequin readers, at least in the eyes of Harlequin publicists. The "voice husky with alarm" also makes an appearance in the blurb for Margaret Pargeter's *The Jewelled Caftan*, another 1978 Harlequin promoted as a captivity narrative:

> "You can't keep me here as your prisoner!" Rosalind's voice was husky with alarm. Sidi Armel ben Yussef had saved her from death at the hands of an unscrupulous band of desert barbarians. What would he expect in return?
> "In my own way I shall extract all the gratitude I desire. Be very sure of that!" The soft, savage emphasis in Armel's peculiarly threatening words told Rosalind that she had to leave—and quickly. But would he let her go?

The blurb from Margaret Mayo's *Stormy Affair* (1979) calls upon captivity in much the same way:

> Only in dreams did dark, handsome strangers carry off the woman of their choice.
> But the dream was all too real when Amber, on vacation in Tunisia, was kidnapped and made a prisoner of the wealthy Hamed Ben Slouma.

---

[1] For overviews of Harlequin's history as a publisher, see Radway 39-44 and Regis 156-60. Current information on romance publishing may be found at www.rwanational.org, the website of the Romance Writers of America, a national organization ("Industry Statistics").

[2] One might also cite the tagline on the front cover of Alexandra Sellers's 1997 novel, *Bride of the Sheikh: "Kidnapped by her husband!"*

There was no means of escape from his secluded home; no ally among
his servants. But Amber had only four days in which to get away—four days
until Hamed made her his wife!

Similarly, the back cover of a 1993 novel, Emma Darcy's *The Sheikh's
Revenge*, announces that the male lead, Kader, has "abducted" the heroine,
Leah: "Imprisoned in his lavish palace deep within the desert, Leah braced
herself to fight the merciless assault of this powerful man—against her body,
her will and her very soul."

The more recent novels analyzed in this essay are usually presented with
greater subtlety, but even if captivity is less blatantly advertised, it is no less
important to many of the novels themselves. As a plot device, captivity prompts
much of the action and thereby supports the development of an emotional
relationship between heroine and hero. It also provides an ideological point of
reference for both characters; it represents simultaneously what they desire and
what they abhor.

I will begin my analysis by articulating the role of captivity in romances in
the "Desert Rogues" and "Sons of the Desert" miniseries.[3] The author of
"Desert Rogues," Susan Macias Redmond, writes under the name Susan
Mallery and also goes by Susan Macias and Susan Macias-Redmond. She
received a master's degree in Writing Popular Fiction from Seton Hill
University in January 2004. Harlequin has published more than fifty of her
novels. Mallery's *The Sheik's Secret Bride*, a 2000 novel, gives us our starting
point. The protagonist is American single mother Liana Archer, who takes a job
teaching math in the fictional gulf nation of El Bahar in part because of "her
love of sheik romance novels" (9). On arrival, she is overcome by "her instant
and overwhelming attraction" to the country's crown prince (12). As if to reify
her emotional response, the prince actually takes her captive, arranging for her
and her young daughter to be driven to his palace without her permission.
When she asks him, "Have we been kidnapped?" he answers: "Of course not. ...
I am Crown Prince Malik Khan of El Bahar. I bestow on you the honor of being
my guest at the royal palace" (22)—as if his identity obviated the possibility that
Liana has been abducted, whereas in fact it merely confirms it. Liana finds out
that she cannot leave the palace without risking the loss of her job, and she

---

[3] I am excluding three of the twelve novels I have read in these two miniseries. Although
captivity is a significant motif in Mallery's *The Sheik and the Virgin Princess* (2002), I
omit it because the male lead is not an Arab but an American given the title of "sheik"
for his service to the Bahanian royal family. Sellers's *Sheikh's Honor* (2000) deals with
the aftermath of a hostage-taking, and the characters in *Undercover Sultan* (2001) spend
most of their time attempting to avoid capture, but neither precisely fits within the pattern
reinforced by the other novels in her miniseries.

concludes that "[S]he was trapped. Well and truly trapped" (47; see also 53). Liana and her daughter are later allowed to move out of the palace, but when Liana unknowingly marries Malik during a visit to a nomad encampment, her actual captivity is replaced by a marriage figured as captivity. Liana feels that "Malik had let her go, only to trick her into marriage" (135; see also 202); both the stay at the palace and the marriage are described as "against her will" (112, 202).

In Mallery's *The Sheik and the Runaway Princess* (2001), the half-Bahanian, half-American princess and art specialist Sabrina Johnson is rescued from certain death in the desert by Kardal, a bandit prince to whom she has been betrothed by her father, unbeknownst to her. Kardal's first words to her are "I have want of a slave girl" (12). (Like Bahar, Bahania is a fictional country on the Arabian peninsula.) Sabrina realizes quickly that "[t]here was no way she could escape" (14). "[K]idnapped, blindfolded and left with her wrists tied" (41), she is brought to Kardal's castle, where he puts antique gold slave bracelets on her arms and keeps her as she falls in love with him. When he finally asks if she wants to leave, she declines, even though it means remaining Kardal's possession: "You had your chance at freedom," he reminds her (172). Not until twenty pages from the end of the novel is the secret of her betrothal revealed, at which point Sabrina realizes, "I hadn't been kidnapped at all" (225). At their ultimate reconciliation, Sabrina places a set of slave bracelets on Kardal's arms, thus once again equating marriage with captivity, and allowing Sabrina to celebrate enslavement as choice. Although she rejects the idea of wifeliness as "[p]leasure in service" (228), the bracelets on her own arms remain intact.

Mallery's *The Sheik and the Princess in Waiting* (2004) covers much the same ground. The heroine, Emma Kennedy, a delivery-room nurse in Texas, is invited for a vacation in Bahania at the behest of its king. Her first thought is to wonder, "Was she being kidnapped?" (11). She soon reassures herself that "[o]n the bright side, if she *was* being kidnapped, it was by someone with money and style" (13). Once in Bahania, she finds out that she is already married to Reyhan, the country's crown prince, with whom she had had an affair while in college. At this point, she feels a "need to bolt for freedom" (29). But she cannot, and her enforced stay in Bahania continues for weeks. Falling back in love with him but doubting that he cares for her, Emma describes the experience as "torture—a prison sentence that trapped her with a man who wanted nothing to do with her" (194). But when she is actually taken prisoner by saboteurs, she and Reyhan each realize each other's worth. After he rescues her, she confesses her love, but he refuses to recognize his: "How could he be a man if he was controlled by a woman?" (246). In the end, he admits to being "humbled" (248), and they agree to live happily ever after. Emma does not tell

Reyhan, however, that "she loved her work too much to give it up," and she wonders silently "[w]hat Reyhan was going to say" (249). There can be no doubt that Emma, like Liana and Sabrina, understands marriage as restraint, if not true imprisonment.

Given the conventions of category romance, we would expect to find similar plot outlines in Alexandra Sellers's books.[4] Like Mallery, Sellers is a successful author, having published about thirty novels with Harlequin. Her page on the Harlequin website claims that she has a degree in Persian and Religious Studies from the School of Oriental and African Studies in London, and that she has been "dreaming about exotic locales [since] the age of 10" ("Alexandra Sellers"). Although she seems to have more academic background than Mallery, we find in her work not only plots framed like Mallery's, but also, and perhaps more surprisingly, a nearly identical set of Orientalist captivity elements. In Sellers's *Beloved Sheikh* (1999), for instance, Canadian archeologist Zara Blake first encounters her beloved, Prince Rafi, when he stares at her and she can barely "break out of the prison of his gaze" (16). Soon his bastard nephew, Jalal, captures her and holds her hostage for political purposes. Rafi declares her his wife and mounts an elaborate rescue scheme, meanwhile getting to know Emma through clandestine visits while she remains a "prisoner, chained like an animal to the wall" (84). Even though Rafi is cast as her rescuer rather than her captor, he demands her obedience just as he would that of a "minion" (91). His wedding gift to her is a jeweled "collar" (169), a term that resonates more with enslavement than with the free love both believe they have.

Like Mallery's *The Sheik and the Princess in Waiting*, Sellers's *Sheikh's Woman* (2001) has a multiple captivity plot. In fact, almost every relationship in the book appears governed by captivity. The hero's sister Nadia, who is missing for most of the novel, had been kept "a prisoner in her own home" by her abusive husband (180). The hero, Sheikh Gazi, abducts the heroine, English artist Anna Lamb, from the hospital after a car accident because he is convinced that she has kidnapped Nadia's infant daughter, Safiya, whom he also then removes from the hospital without permission. Although technically he does not "force" Anna to stay with him after the abduction (85), he arranges the circumstances so that she has no alternative but to stay, in her words, "against my will" (117). To protect Nadia, he also persuades Anna to pretend that she is his mistress and that Safiya is their baby. After they learn that Nadia has

---

[4] See Radway for a discussion of the "recipe" for romance plots (29; see also 134, 150); Regis and Cynthia Whissell provide other versions (Regis 19-50; Whissell 92-106). Kay Mussell's 1984 monograph, *Fantasy and Reconciliation*, offers perhaps the most detailed description of romance formulae.

reached safety, they acknowledge their love. Their marriage thus continues the roles each assumed during the long period of Anna's enforced stay. In each of these novels, captivity initially promotes the expression of freedom as an ideal, as the heroines rebel against their imprisonment. When they fall in love, however, their attraction to their future husbands becomes more compelling than freedom. Bondage gives way to bonding. Love originates within captivity for each of these heroines—regardless of whether the husband is captor or (more rarely) rescuer—and the structure of captivity remains, transmogrified as marriage.

Thus far, my analysis is largely consistent with that provided first by Tania Modleski in a 1980 essay in which she argues that Harlequins "neutralize women's anger and ... make masculine hostility bearable" ("Disappearing Act" 448). But both Janice Radway and Pamela Regis are right to observe that romance fiction offers something more positive than the neutralized and bearable. In her comprehensive 1984 analysis of how and why women read romance novels, Radway concludes that the books "actively assuage unstated fears and simultaneously provide [women] with the emotional sustenance they require" (16). Romance fiction is "compensatory literature"—the "emotional release" it enables helps to compensate women for their restricted and sometimes onerous daily lives (95). Radway's interviews with readers showed that most viewed their reading as informative as well, especially to the extent that it provided details about unfamiliar locations and customs. She argues that the novels are "compensatory" not only emotionally but also intellectually; they "fill . . . a woman's mental world with the varied details of simulated travel and permit . . . her to converse imaginatively with adults from a broad spectrum of social space" (113). Regis focuses less on readers' responses and more on the content of the novels, but agrees with Radway that romance fiction is potentially therapeutic, not just analgesic; it is less about "bondage" than it is about "women's freedom" (xiii), she observes, in that the heroines are liberated from a variety of obstacles—including captivity—on their way to union with their beloved.

It is important to recognize, though, that captivity does not truly disappear: rather, as both anger and hostility are converted into love, captivity is allowed to morph into marriage. This transformation is epistemological, not ontological, in that it depends far less upon any alteration of the two protagonists' behavior than upon change in the hermeneutic framework within which each interprets the other's behavior. Radway defines this "activity of reinterpretation" as the heroine's "mental process of trying to assign particular signifieds to [the hero's] overt acts" (157, 139; see also 216). But the heroes are also engaged in this process—a process in which there are really only two signifieds available: "he/she loves me" and "he/she loves me not." Moreover, none of these three feminist critics—Modleski, Regis, and Radway—investigates the extent to which the trope of captivity per se enables a novel to promote its heroine's apparent liberation through union. Initially, I would propose, the relationship between captivity and liberation is, as one would naturally presume, oppositional: in captivity the heroine is motivated to identify herself ideologically with freedom. However, once she begins to fantasize about marrying the hero, that fantasy becomes enmeshed with her desire for liberty. By the time the marriage occurs, it already has an automatic affiliation with freedom, in that the heroine desires both marriage and freedom more than anything. Thus a fundamental conflict in these novels—between the feminist position that a woman can and should take care of herself, and the traditional patriarchal assumption that a woman should be subject to a man—is neatly resolved through captivity as a trope, because it brings women to associate liberation and self-determination with captivity's successor and opposite number, marriage. A woman who has been subject to a man in captivity thus appears automatically to have achieved liberation when she is married, even if marriage is functionally a continuation of captivity: literally, wedlock.

The Harem, between Captivity and Marriage

It is important, however, to specify the dynamics of this continuation, and for that we must look particularly at the fantasy of the harem. In standard Orientalist fashion, the harem is perversely attractive to several of the Mallery and Sellers heroines, and their ventures into harem fantasy help to facilitate their acceptance of captivity as a constituent of both courtship and marriage. In Mallery's *The Sheik and the Princess in Waiting*, for example, Emma invites the topic during a tour of Reyhan's palace, asking him:

> "Were many women captured and held against their will?"
> Reyhan smiled. "It is a time-honored tradition for sheiks to take that which they admire."
> How comforting. "So there's a harem there in the palace, too?"
> "Of course." (87)

Within a couple of paragraphs, Emma has begun to imagine herself as an inmate of the harem, wondering "what it would be like to be captured by him. Would he be kind? Demanding? She shivered at the thought of either" (87). In a similar fashion, Liana, the heroine of Mallery's *The Sheik's Secret Bride*, finds herself both enticed by and horrified at the institution of the harem. She worries that Malik might "expect her to sleep with him" but reassures herself that "[i]n this day and age women were not kidnapped to be placed into a harem" (54). Like Emma, Liana soon discovers that in fact her future husband's palace does have a harem, a separate living space for the women of the household. The only resident now is Fatima, the crown prince's "elegant" grandmother, who explains that "none of the princes" have ever "kept any women for [themselves]." Somehow her explanation does not foreclose the possibility that one of them might—and indeed Fatima herself implies that possibility by claiming to be "lonely" (65). It is in the harem that Fatima helps Liana get dressed and made up in preparation for the desert visit that proves to be Liana's wedding night. The stereotypical connotations of the harem are confirmed during the preparation when Fatima teases her "that Prince Malik could get two or three dozen camels for you" (98). In the sexual encounter that follows the wedding, Liana realizes "that her body was no longer hers to control," but has no regrets (123). Metaphorically transformed by her preparation in the space of the harem, the math teacher and mother who had fought for her own autonomy is now content to abandon it at the most fundamental level. Later, when she is distressed that "[m]y entire life is out of control" because Malik is "the one doing the controlling" (153), she takes refuge in the harem, where she is comforted by Malik's sisters-in-law, who temporarily reproduce the homosocial female community of the harem. As Liana continually projects onto the largely vacant space of the harem her own fantasy of harem life, her ventures into the harem catalyze her transformation from captive to wife.

In Sellers's *Sheikh's Woman*, the fantasy of the harem is elaborated when Anna dreams that her lover, Sheikh Gazi, asks for her father's name so that he can gain permission to marry her. In the dream, she declines, saying, "I am no better than a slave. Do not seek to know my father, but only know that I willingly give up all for one taste of thy love" (106). This dream marks an important turning point in the narrative, as Anna begins to affiliate herself with her surroundings independently of her feelings for Gazi. The paragraphs after the dream record Anna's strengthened bond with the baby Safiyah, her appreciation for the palace gardens, and her growing knowledge of Arabic. In short, the harem fantasy that dominates her dream seems to precipitate the beginning of her cultural assimilation, and thereby paves the way for the merging of her captivity into her marriage in much the same way as it does for Liana in Mallery's *The Sheik's Secret Bride*.

Sellers's *Beloved Sheikh* offers the most fully developed harem fantasy of any of the novels, again initially in the form of a dream. While she is Jalal's captive, Zara dreams that "she was newly entered into the harem, that she had arrived only today, ... when the Sultan of All the Worlds had accepted her as a gift" (105). He "commands" her presence (105), and so she is exhaustively bathed and readied for his pleasure. She dances for him and then they have sex. At the moment of entry, she recognizes him as Prince Rafi, her beloved. This dream becomes an important source of comfort to her as her imprisonment continues. At the same time, Rafi himself begins to envision her as an odalisque. Having brought her a kitten as a gift, for example, he enjoys watching her play with it and muses that "[j]ust so might the favourite of the harem have toyed with a kitten, in decades and centuries past" (120). For these two lovers, then, the harem provides a paradigm for their relations with one another, a way for both to recuperate captivity as connection. The ending of the novel—the triple wedding of three princes and their brides—neatly suggests the communal sexuality of the harem while denying its polygamy. Thus while the harem is originally—in this novel and elsewhere—posited as a mode of captivity, it is reincarnated as a space of sexual satisfaction. Along the way, once again, bondage gives way to bonding.

My argument takes a different tack here than Christopher Castiglia's in his more comprehensive analysis of captivity narrative in the American context. Contemporary mass-market captivity romances featuring Indians as captors, he suggests, "demonstrat[e] that Indian 'captivity' is a relative freedom compared to the slavery imposed on women by white men, [and the novels thereby] make explicit [a] critique of white patriarchy" (191). One mechanism of this critique is "the interracial and mostly female communities [the heroine] develops while crossing cultures" (192). The harem is of course an archetypal female community, but it seems to me that in the sheikh romance it functions more commonly to recuperate than to critique patriarchy, and that white patriarchy is not singled out for criticism in any specific way. In Sellers's *Sheikh's Woman*, for example, Anna's British (and presumably white) ex-boyfriend, Jonathan, is depicted as an unsympathetic narcissist, but his flaws are insignificant compared to those of Yusuf, Nadia's brutal and treasonous Barakati husband; white patriarchy per se is evidently not the primary ideological target in this novel. Similarly, in both Sellers's *Beloved Sheikh* and Mallery's *The Sheik and the Runaway Princess*, the demonized patriarchs are neither American nor British men but rather the hero's Barakati nephew (Sellers) and the heroine's Bahanian father (Mallery). Like Jonathan in *Sheikh's Woman*, Chuck, the (again, presumably white) American ex-husband in Mallery's *The Sheikh's Secret Bride*, is irresponsible and selfish, but for much of the novel the hero Malik appears no less so. Liana and Malik fall out as a result of Liana's realization that "I have to feel as if I'm an equal partner in my marriage" (241). She was never able to achieve this with Chuck, and she refuses Malik's offer of marriage on the grounds that she will "never be on an equal footing" with him either (242). Clearly, neither her American partner nor her Bahanian one is exempt from this critique of patriarchy. Although Malik moderates his patriarchal harshness with the help of his grandmother, Fatima, in the end he announces his love in a form that connotes mastery more than equality: "Your place is at my side. Stay" (250).

It is difficult to read such a novel according to Castiglia's model, for the harem serves the purpose of patriarchy rather than standing as an alternative to it. This is the case even if one adopts Suzanne Juhasz's view:

> The marriage ending is less cooptation, as some would have it, with success contingent upon submission of self to that patriarchal institution . . . than it is *reward* for self-realization, for a maturation that derives from relationship rather than separation. (239; emphasis hers)

Juhasz does not discuss novels with Middle Eastern settings, but one could extend her argument to encompass the harem as a space (albeit attenuated) of homosocial female connection; the heroine achieves "self-realization" within this setting, and is rewarded with the opportunity for heterosexual union. Patriarchy is sustained here both by the primacy of that union and by the construction of the harem as a transitional place rather than a destination.

The Fear of the Sheikh

In their analyses of romance fiction, Tania Modleski, Janice Radway, and Pamela Regis assume—rightly, I think—that romance novels perform some sort of service for their readers. I would suggest, however, that there is more to the subgenre of the sheikh fantasy specifically than either palliation of women's pain (Modleski), or escapist pleasure (Radway), or cheerleading for women's liberation (Regis). The analyses offered by writers of romance have, overall, even less explanatory value. Jayne Ann Krentz, a prolific and best-selling writer of romance, announces, for instance, that romance novels both "celebrate female power" and "invert . . . the power structure of a patriarchal society because they show women exerting enormous power over men [and] portray women as heroes" (5). Krentz's view is shared by another highly successful romance writer, Alison Hart, who "see[s] the genre as . . . exuberantly pro-women" (96). Of course the genre is pro-women, and of course women are the heroes of the novels, yet that does not prevent these books from reinforcing the power of patriarchy—even if only by showing how very difficult it is to oppose it. All of these critics and authors reach their conclusions by considering the novels mainly vis-à-vis gender. The question of romance fiction's value for women might, however, also be asked vis-à-vis racial or ethnic otherness. If Harlequins can make heterosexual women feel better about their relations with men, could they not also make white, western women (Harlequin's primary readership) feel better about inter-cultural or inter-ethnic relations?[5]

Linke's essay on mass-market romance takes a step in this direction, presuming that "the popularity of romances . . . rests [in part] on the value of romantic fiction as a means to confirm group identity, to enforce a feeling of belonging along national, regional, ethnic, gender and class lines" (198). Such a sense of belonging is often predicated upon a differentiation of self from other, as Linke points out (196). I would propose that it also entails some form of (psychological) defense against the threat implied by the other. In his classic book, *The Uses of Enchantment* (1975), Bruno Bettelheim suggests that children use fairy tales to externalize their fears; they are comforted because the tales allow them to work through those fears in a fantastical context that is safely removed from the child's physical world (62).[6] Thus by hearing "Hansel and Gretel," for example, a child can confront his or her fear of parental abandonment without trauma. A romance novel could serve its reader in much the same way, providing a means for her to sort out and come to terms with racially inspired fears of Arabs.[7] If so, the anxieties manifested in these novels are essentially those of white slavery—put bluntly, the fear implied is that an Arab man will abduct her and take advantage of her sexually. Thus the novels' constant troping on both captivity and, more specifically, the harem is fundamental to the cultural work that they appear to do.

Radway mentions a related aspect of Bettelheim's argument, bringing it to bear on matters of gender rather than ethnicity (100; see also 141). Yet if she is right that "romance reading is . . . an activity that takes place within a specific social context," it is important that this context be understood to extend beyond what she identifies as women's "common social condition" (212). Radway argues that

---

[5] For an overview of the demographics of romance readers, see "Reader Statistics."

[6] Alan Dundes's 1991 critique of *The Uses of Enchantment* reveals Bettelheim's disregard for the work of his predecessors in both folkloric studies and psychoanalysis, and shows that he borrowed concepts and even phraseology from another scholar, Julius E. Heuscher, without attribution. Dundes effectively destroys Bettelheim's credibility as a scholar, but at the same time admits the "legitimate and worthwhile contribution" made by his book's argument (81).

[7] My argument here is consistent with Linke's suggestion "that national and regional aspects of identity as well as class and ethnic groups are reinforced through the way category romances present history, places, foreign cultures and their population, and their rituals of everyday life" (199), but again places more emphasis on the importance of threat.

an ideal romance . . . deal[s] convincingly with female fears and reservations by permitting them to surface briefly during a reading process that then explicitly lays them to rest by explaining them away. (158)

Those fears are not simply "female," however, despite their specific manifestation in a heavily gendered context. Rather, they derive also from the larger cultural and political circumstances that inevitably impinge upon women's personal lives. As Modleski observes in *Loving with a Vengeance* (1982): "mass-cultural texts both stimulate and allay social anxieties" (28). Yet the anxieties at issue in her treatment are primarily those produced by sexism, and her subsequent analysis focuses almost exclusively on matters of gender, largely disregarding the questions of ethnicity with which the novels I am discussing are indubitably concerned as well.

As I write this, America has, with the help of Britain, been pursuing its war in Iraq for nearly three years, since 19 March 2003. The so-called insurgency, a movement consisting almost entirely of Arab men, has resisted Anglo-American occupation with a range of tactics, including the taking of captives or hostages. Earlier in the conflict, the Iraqi army also captured members of the occupying forces. On 12 June 2005, National Public Radio reported that forty-four foreign hostages were known to be held in Iraq, and that another four dozen had been killed in the preceding year. Most hostages have been men of various nationalities, including Iraqis as well as Americans, Canadians, Australians, and others ("French Reporter"). Women captured include the Italian journalist Giuliana Sgrena; Italian aid workers Simona Pari and Simona Torretta; French journalist Florence Aubenas; Teresa Borcz-Kalifa, a Polish woman who had lived in Iraq for a long time; and most recently Jill Carroll, an American journalist captured on 7 January 2006. Perhaps the two captives best known in the United States are Margaret Hassan and Jessica Lynch. Hassan, the director of the international charity Care in Iraq, was an Irishwoman married to an Iraqi; she had been resident in Iraq for thirty years and held dual citizenship. She was abducted and then killed in October 2004. Lynch, an American soldier, was taken prisoner in March 2003 following a motor vehicle accident and later rescued. The extraordinary attention to Lynch's case seemed predicated on her appeal as a young, single, white woman. Some media outlets at the time observed, for example, that Shoshana Johnson, who was in the same unit as Lynch and suffered similar injuries, received far less media coverage and a much lower Army disability benefit; Johnson was eleven years older than Lynch, a mother, and black (Hockstader).

Emblematic of the sexualization of Lynch is a report from the less-than-reputable *New York Daily News* on 6 November 2003, headlined "Fiends Raped Jessica." The story, written by Paul D. Colford and Corky Siemaszko and prompted by the publication of Rick Bragg's authorized biography of Lynch, begins with the statement that "Jessica Lynch was brutally raped by her Iraqi captors." As journalist John Kampfner reported for the BBC and the *Guardian* in May 2003, there is no credible evidence that Lynch was physically abused during her captivity, let alone raped. Yet the *Daily News* story presents her rape not only as factual but also as inevitable:

> A pretty, blond 20-year-old from the hollers of West Virginia, Lynch knew what could happen to her if she fell into Iraqi hands. A female pilot captured in the Persian Gulf had been raped.
> "Everyone knew what Saddam's soldiers did to women captives," Bragg wrote.

Although poorer than most Harlequin heroines, Lynch nonetheless meets the other criteria: young, pretty, white, and apparently unattached. The fate presumed for her by the *Daily News* betrays the sexual vulnerability entailed in her status; essentially the same sexual vulnerability is exemplified in Harlequin sheikh novels' manipulation of the motif of the harem, and indeed of the trope of captivity generally.

Based on Bettelheim's theory, we might expect that as real threats began to approximate fantasized ones, the therapeutic effect of the fantasy would diminish. The events of the last three years would, then, militate against the continued publication of sheikh novels in which the white American or British heroine is taken captive by an Arab man. But in 2004 and 2005, Alexandra Sellers published two books and Susan Mallery three; also published were at least eight novels by other writers. A new Harlequin miniseries called "Surrender to the Sheikh" even premiered in 2005 with titles by Jane Porter and Susan Stephens. Captivity remains a prominent trope and even a selling point: one of Mallery's books is called *The Sheik's Kidnapped Bride* (2004), and Susan Stephens has written *The Sheikh's Captive Bride* (2005).[8]

In reading these books and others published in 2004 and 2005, it seemed to me that despite the persistence of the captivity trope, there had been a change in its deployment that could confirm my intuition that sheikh novels have been doing a particular kind of cultural work—although I must of course remain mindful, as Radway says, of "the difficulty of proving [the] accuracy" of claiming such a cultural effect (158). Typically, these most recent novels moderate the captivity experience in some way. In other words, the way in which they implement this particular romance convention appears to have responded to its societal context by evolving or undergoing a "mutation," to

---

[8] *The Sheik's Kidnapped Bride* was originally copyrighted in 2000, but was reissued in August 2004 in the "All-time Favorites" miniseries—hence my consideration of it as a 2004 rather than a 2000 publication.

borrow the term used by Jackie Stacey and Lynne Pearce, who argue that the "capacity for mutation" or "re-scripting" is responsible for "the continued success of romance as a cultural institution" (12). For example, although Sellers's new books draw on the harem fantasy, two differences are notable: both heroines are Arabs, though English-speaking, and neither plot line relies on a conventionally framed episode of captivity. Jalia, the heroine of *The Ice Maiden's Sheikh* (2004), is a Bagestani princess raised in exile in England. Her exile had been a kind of imprisonment, but by nature it lacks the intensity of the captivity experiences narrated in the other books I have discussed. The heroine of *The Fierce and Tender Sheikh* (2005) is another princess, Shakira, who had been lost following the assassination of her parents, and is at the beginning of the book living as a boy in a refugee camp. Her imprisonment in the camp ends early in the novel, and (in part because of her cross-dressing) is not continuous with her marriage, thereby diverging from the pattern established in the Sellers and Mallery books overall.

Closest to the pre-2004 paradigm is Susan Mallery's 2005 contribution to the "Desert Rogues" series, *The Sheik and the Bride Who Said No*, in that the hero's imprisonment of the heroine plays an essential role in the plot, and in that the harem facilitates captivity's conversion into marriage. In this novel, American veterinarian Daphne Snowden is confined to the otherwise unoccupied harem of Murat, the crown prince of Bahania and her former boyfriend, after she successfully prevents him from marrying her teen-aged niece. But her struggles against this confinement seem muted by comparison with those in earlier novels. By the second page of chapter three she has already admitted to herself that she is "enjoying" her stay (31), and four pages later she tells Murat that "the harem is beautiful" and that she is "comfortable" there, "[a]side from the whole idea of being kept against my will" (35; see also 86). Murat's sisters-in-law (all Americans) provide a kind of harem community for Daphne, but their jokes about her being a prisoner further weaken any impression that her imprisonment places her at risk (68). When she tells them her story, one exclaims, "That's kidnapping," but the other immediately points out, "he must really love her" (74). Daphne's own family also denies that she is being unduly restricted (82). Even Daphne's escape attempt implies her own complicity; she evades the harem guards but runs straight for Murat's office. It turns out later that Murat's father has masterminded the entire affair in collusion with Daphne's niece, with the aim of inducing Daphne and Murat to resume their relationship.

After this revelation Murat appears less a powerful captor than another victim trapped in the (admittedly benevolent) machinations of his father, and the original captivity plot loses much of its already limited potency. In short, while the conventional elements of the captivity-based romance plot remain in place, their significance is consistently downplayed. Captivity plot elements are even more understated in another recent Mallery book, *The Sheik's Kidnapped Bride*; indeed, this novel is so very sparing in its use of captivity as a trope that the title appears a misnomer. Heroine Dora Nelson, an American executive assistant, does end up confined in the harem, but at the initiative not of the hero, Prince Khalil Khan of El Bahar, but rather of his grandmother, Fatima (familiar to us from Mallery's *The Sheik's Secret Bride*). Fatima advises Dora not to let Khalil "dominate" her (110). Indeed, long before Dora and Khalil have resolved their differences, Dora acquires an important administrative position in the palace; her sojourn in the harem clearly does not imply her subordination. In Mallery's most recent "Desert Rogues" novel, *The Sheik and the Virgin Secretary* (2005), the heroine is bound to the hero only by a compact that she herself initiated; captivity in the conventional sense is nearly absent.

Recent books by other writers generally follow a similar pattern, with captivity deemphasized as a plot device and/or as a theater for the display of power relations. In Jane Porter's *The Sheikh's Virgin*, for example, the imbalanced cross-cultural power relations typical of captivity in the earlier novels are largely absent, though captivity remains important to the plot. Like the heroine of Alexandra Sellers's *The Ice Maiden's Sheikh*, Porter's heroine is bi-cultural: Keira Gordon was born Keira al-Issidri, and the narrative returns obsessively to her confusion over her half-English, half Barakan heritage until Keira finally realizes that "[s]he loved the Barakan part of her" (132). (Baraka is a fictional North African country.) Keira is repeatedly subject to imprisonment, first by men loyal to her father, then by her future husband, Sheikh Kalen Nuri, and then by her father himself, who releases her to Kalen only as Kalen is coercing her into marrying him. Captivity and marriage do coincide within this novel, but each new version of the heroine's captivity is also an actual (not figurative) escape. Moreover, because it turns out that both Kalen and Keira's father were acting under duress, intimidated by the threat of a political enemy, they are largely absolved of guilt in their various entrapments of Keira, much as Murat, from Mallery's *The Sheik and the Bride Who Said No*, is absolved when his father's conspiracy is revealed. Finally, while there is in Porter's novel a brief episode in which Keira plays an Ottoman "slave girl" (152), she does not share the harem fantasy so commonly expressed by earlier heroines—and in any case, her Barakan heritage keeps at bay any implication of white slavery. Thus despite the recurrence of captivity as a plot device, the significance of captivity as a trope is significantly reduced in this novel.

In several other recent novels, captivity is not even a prominent plot device. Despite its title, Susan Stephens's *The Sheikh's Captive Bride* (2005) contains only a thin captivity plot: the English heroine, Lucy Benson, is constrained only by the fact that her son's father, Prince Kahlil of Abadan, refuses to let the royal baby leave Abadan (another fictional country, of unspecified location but probably on the Arabian peninsula). Although Lucy resents the security guards who protect the infant prince and feels that "[s]he had to get away" (66), her only escape attempt fails. She quickly capitulates when Kahlil explains that because their son was conceived during a one-night stand, they must marry for six months in order to ensure his legitimacy as an heir to the throne. Lucy is already in love with Kahlil by this point and cannot convince herself to look forward to her divorce when she "will be a free woman again" (144). While this novel joins its predecessors in overlaying marriage upon captivity, the captivity element is far less substantive and involves no physical containment.

The captivity plot in Kristi Gold's *Challenged by the Sheikh* (2004) is even more shadowy. American Imogene Danforth needs to learn to ride in order to clinch a business deal, so she approaches Sheikh Rafi ibn Shakir about lessons at his stables in Georgia. He agrees to teach her but only if she will stay at the stables for three weeks to concentrate on her riding. This period serves the same narrative purpose as captivity, in that it enforces proximity between the hero and the heroine at the behest of the hero, but there is really nothing coercive about it—in fact, Imogene spends much of her time fending off her employer's attempts to get her back to the office. Although apparently troping on captivity, the novel has no more than a ghost of a captivity plot. Moreover, because the book is set on the heroine's home turf rather than the hero's, and because she too is quite wealthy, the imbalanced power relations that underlie many of the other novels do not develop here.   In the same vein, Laura Wright's *The Sultan's Bed* (2005) is set outside the Middle East and exhibits only a very diluted version of the captivity plot. Mariah Kennedy, a California lawyer, sprains her ankle and is immobilized while the injury heals. Her new neighbor, Sultan Zayad Al-Nayhal, volunteers to assist her. Not only does he help at home, but he also tracks down information for her current legal case and drives her to an important social visit. Thus although Mariah is confined during this period, Zayad is not the agent of her confinement, and indeed provides what mobility she has during her healing. Wright is also the author of *A Bed of Sand* (2004), which does little more than allude to captivity in narrating the love affair of Sakir Al-Nayhal (Zayad's brother) and his assistant, Rita Thompson. The same could be said of Sharon Kendrick's *Exposed: The Sheikh's Mistress* (2005).

Nearly all of these recent novels find some way to evoke the captivity plot as a narrative structure without either demonizing or empowering the hero as captor. Although these homeopathic doses of captivity remain effective as a precondition for marriage, they do not entirely share the two fundamental characteristics of their predecessor novels: captivity does not drive the novels' plot with the same force, and the harem is only rarely and incompletely developed as a transition from the captive to the married state. Further, where the novels that appeared before 2004 typically wallowed in the exoticism of their orientalized settings, the newer novels often minimize or even eliminate the Arab world as a setting, or diminish cross-cultural conflict by ascribing a Middle Eastern identity to the heroine. In only one of these ten recent novels (Mallery's *The Sheik and the Bride Who Said No*) is a white American or British woman actually taken captive in the Middle East. The various elements that might have served the pre-war novels' readers as a way to work out their fears of Arabs have thus been largely abandoned.

Unlike the traditional folk tales discussed by Bettelheim, Harlequin novels have no witches or trolls available to make a real-life situation seem bearable by comparison with its fantasized counterpart—and in fact, as Radway observes, much of the novels' appeal and potency lie in their apparent realism (186-92).[9] The conventional hyperbole entailed in the trope of captivity serves much the same purpose as the folktale's supernatural villain; the heroines' imprisonment does not violate the novel's insistence on the "real," yet it is extreme enough to remain potentially therapeutic. When such hyperbole begins to appear more likely than fantastic, captivity loses its tropic, figurative character and instead acquires an imminence that must prevent it from fulfilling its previous function. Events in Iraq since March 2003 have forced captivity out of the realm of the hyperbolic; fears engendered by the threat of Arab men's aggression may have therefore exceeded the reach of the captivity-based romance plot. My analysis of Harlequin novels from 2004 and 2005 suggests that they continue to address these fears, but by different tactics. Instead of exaggerating the threats through fantasy in the manner of a folktale, they downplay them, shielding the reader from what scares her: foreign locations, still-populated harems, overly powerful Arab men. Such a shift of tactics may, I have suggested, be compelled by current circumstance: the possibility of a white woman being taken captive and harmed seems quite immediately real, as we all learned with horror following the kidnapping and execution of Margaret Hassan—and there is no comfort to be had, Bettelheim would remind us, in the depiction of the real.

This essay is dedicated to Sandra Naddaff, with whom I read my first romance, and to Josette Haddad, with whom I read them still.

---

[9] Writing about American captivity narrative as it figures in contemporary historical romance, Kate McCafferty also points out the complex way in which reality and fantasy inform each other, but she sees it primarily as a means to enhance "the domestic reader's capacity to identify with the possibilities of a romantic love that transcends mundane reality" (43).

Works Cited

"Alexandra Sellers." *eHarlequin.com*. 2005. 30 Sept. 2005:
<http://www.eharlequin.com/cms/authors>.

Bettelheim, Bruno. *The Uses of Enchantment: The Meaning and Importance of Fairy Tales*. 1975. New York: Random, 1977.

Bettinotti, Julia, and Marie-Françoise Truel. "Lust and Dust: Desert Fabula in Romances and Media." *Paradoxa* 3.1-2 (1997): 184-94.

Burley, Stephanie. "Shadows and Silhouettes: The Racial Politics of Category Romance." *Paradoxa* 5.13-14 (2000): 324-43.

Cadogan, Mary. *And Then Their Hearts Stood Still: An Exuberant Look at Romantic Fiction Past and Present*. London: Macmillan, 1994.

Colford, Paul D., and Corky Siemaszko. "Fiends Raped Jessica." 6 Nov. 2003. 30 Sept. 2005:
<http://www.nydailynews.com/front/story/134264p-119598c.html>.

Darcy, Emma. *The Sheikh's Revenge*. Harlequin Presents. Toronto: Harlequin, Nov. 1993.

Dundes, Alan. "Bruno Bettelheim's Uses of Enchantment and Abuses of Scholarship." *Journal of American Folklore* 104 (1991): 74-83.

Eisele, John C. "The Wild East: Deconstructing the Language of Genre in the Hollywood Eastern." *Cinema Journal* 41.4 (2002): 68-94.

"French Reporter, Aide Released in Iraq." Narr. Jennifer Ludden. *All Things Considered*. Natl. Public Radio. 12 June 2005. 21 Oct. 2005 <http://www.npr.org/templates/story/story.php?storyId=4700297>.

Gold, Kristi. *Challenged by the Sheikh*. Silhouette: Desire: Dynasties: The Danforths. New York: Harlequin, June 2004.

Hart, Alison. "The Key Formula in Romance: A Woman's Quest." *North American Romance Writers*. Ed. Kay Mussell and Johanna Tuñón. Lanham, MD: Scarecrow P, 1999. 93-99.

Hockstader, Lee. "Ex-POW's Family Accuses Army of Double Standard on Benefit." *Washington Post* 23 Oct. 2003: A3. *LexisNexis Academic*. LexisNexis. I. D. Weeks Lib., U of South Dakota, Vermillion SD. 5 Nov. 2005 <http://80-web.lexis-nexis.com.proxy.usd.edu/universe>.

"Industry Statistics." *Romance Writers of America*. 2005. 4 Nov. 2005 <http:www.rwanational.org/statistics/industry_stats.htm>.

Juhasz, Suzanne. "Texts to Grow On: Reading Women's Romance Fiction." *Tulsa Studies in Women's Literature* 7.2 (1988): 239-59.

Kaler, Anne K. "Conventions of Captivity in Romance Novels." *Romantic Conventions*. Ed. Anne K. Kaler and Rosemary E. Johnson-Kurek. Bowling Green, OH: Bowling Green State U Popular P, 1999. 86-99.

Kampfner, John. "Saving Private Lynch Story 'Flawed.'" *BBC News* 18 May 2003. 30 Sept. 2005 <http://newsvote.bbc.co.uk/mpapps/pagetools/print/news.bbcco.uk>.

————."The Truth about Jessica." *Guardian* 15 May 2003. 30 Sept. 2005 <http://www.guardian.co.uk/Iraq/Story/0,2763,956255,00.html>.

Kendrick, Sharon. *Exposed: The Sheikh's Mistress*. Harlequin Presents: For Love or Money. Toronto: Harlequin, Sept. 2005.

Krentz, Jayne Ann. Introduction. *Dangerous Men and Adventurous Women: Romance Writers on the Appeal of the Romance*. Ed. Jayne Ann Krentz. Philadelphia: U of Pennsylvania P, 1992. 1-8.

Lamb, Charlotte. *Desert Barbarian*. Harlequin Romance. Toronto: Harlequin, Oct. 1978.

Linke, Gabriele. "Contemporary Mass Market Romances as National and International Culture: A Comparative Study of Mills and Boon and Harlequin Romances." *Paradoxa* 3.1-2 (1997): 195-213.

Mallery, Susan [Susan W. Macias, Susan Macias Redmond, Susan Macias-Redmond]. *The Sheik and the Bride Who Said No*. Silhouette: Desert Rogues. New York: Harlequin, Feb. 2005.

————.*The Sheik and the Princess in Waiting*. Silhouette: Desert Rogues. New York: Harlequin, Apr. 2004.

————.*The Sheik and the Runaway Princess*. Silhouette: Desert Rogues. New York: Harlequin, Nov. 2001.

————.*The Sheik and the Virgin Princess*. Silhouette: Desert Rogues. New York: Harlequin, Mar. 2002.

————.*The Sheik and the Virgin Secretary*. Silhouette: Desert Rogues. New York: Harlequin, Dec. 2005.

————.*The Sheik's Kidnapped Bride*. 2000. Silhouette: All-time Favorites. New York: Harlequin, 2004.

————.*The Sheik's Secret Bride*. Silhouette: Desert Rogues. New York: Harlequin, June 2000.

Mayo, Margaret. *Stormy Affair*. Harlequin Romance. Toronto: Harlequin, Apr. 1980.

McCafferty, Kate. "Palimpsest of Desire: The Re-Emergence of the American Captivity Narrative as Pulp Romance." *Journal of Popular Culture* 27.4 (1994): 43-56.

Modleski, Tania. "The Disappearing Act: A Study of Harlequin Romances." *Signs* 5.3 (1980): 435-448.

————.*Loving with a Vengeance: Mass-Produced Fantasies for Women*. New York: Methuen, 1982.

Mussell, Kay. *Fantasy and Reconciliation: Contemporary Formulas of Women's Romance Fiction*. Westport, CT: Greenwood P, 1984.

Pargeter, Margaret. *The Jewelled Caftan*. Harlequin Romance. Toronto: Harlequin, Nov. 1978.

Parv, Valerie. *Royal Spy*. Silhouette: Intimate Moments: Romancing the Crown. New York: Harlequin, June 2002.

Pearce, Lynne, and Jackie Stacey, eds. *Romance Revisited*. New York: New York UP, 1995.

Porter, Jane. *The Sheikh's Virgin*. Harlequin Presents: Surrender to the Sheikh. Toronto: Harlequin: June 2005.

Radway, Janice. *Reading the Romance: Women, Patriarchy, and Popular Literature*. Chapel Hill: U of North Carolina P, 1984.

Regis, Pamela. *The Natural History of the Romance Novel*. Philadelphia: U of Pennsylvania P, 2003.

"Reader Statistics." *Romance Writers of America*. 2005. 4 Nov. 2005 <http:www.rwanational.org/statistics/reader_stats.htm>.

Seidel, Kathleen Gilles. "Judge Me by the Joy I Bring." *Dangerous Men and Adventurous Women: Romance Writers on the Appeal of the Romance*. Ed. Jayne Ann Krentz. Philadelphia: U of Pennsylvania P, 1992. 159-79.

Sellers, Alexandra. *Beloved Sheikh*. Silhouette: Desire: Sons of the Desert. New York: Harlequin, June 1999.

————.*Bride of the Sheikh*. Silhouette: Intimate Moments. New York, Harlequin, Mar. 1997.

————.*The Fierce and Tender Sheikh*. Silhouette: Desire: Sons of the Desert. New York: Harlequin, Jan. 2005.

————.*The Ice Maiden's Sheikh*. Silhouette: Desire: Sons of the Desert. New York: Harlequin, Dec. 2004.

————.*Sheikh's Honor*. Silhouette: Desire: Sons of the Desert. New York: Harlequin, May 2000.

————.*Sheikh's Woman*. Silhouette: Desire: Sons of the Desert. New York: Harlequin, Jan. 2001.

————.*Undercover Sultan*. Silhouette: Desire: Sons of the Desert: The Sultans. New York: Harlequin, Aug. 2001.

Stacey, Jackie, and Lynne Pearce. "The Heart of the Matter: Feminists Revisit Romance." *Romance Revisited*. Ed. Lynne Pearce and Jackie Stacey. New York: New York UP, 1995. 11-45.

Stephens, Susan. *The Sheikh's Captive Bride*. Harlequin Presents: Surrender to the Sheikh. Toronto: Harlequin, Aug. 2005.

Stratton, Rebecca. *The Silken Cage*. Harlequin Romance. Toronto: Harlequin, Oct. 1981.

Whissell, Cynthia. "The Formula behind Women's Romantic Formula Fiction." *Arachne* 5.1 (1998): 89-119.

Winspear, Violet. *The Sheik's Captive.* Harlequin Presents. Toronto: Harlequin, Nov. 1979.

Wood, Sara. *Desert Hostage.* Harlequin Presents. Toronto: Harlequin, Nov. 1991.

Wright, Laura. *A Bed of Sand.* Silhouette: Desire. New York: Harlequin, Sept. 2004.

————.*The Sultan's Bed.* Silhouette: Desire. New York: Harlequin, June, 2005.

Emily A. Haddad

Emily A. Haddad is the author of *Orientalist Poetics: The Islamic Middle East in Nineteenth-Century English and French Poetry* (Ashgate 2002) and of several essays, including "Body and Belonging(s): Property in the Captivity of Mungo Park" (in *Colonial and Postcolonial Incarceration*, ed. Graeme Harper, Continuum 2001). Her most recent publication is an article on the Suez Canal in *Victorian Studies* 47.3 (Spring 2005). She is Associate Professor of English at the University of South Dakota.

CHAPTER FIVE

DETAILS: HITCHCOCK READS *REBECCA*

ANDREA AUSTIN

It seemed a match made in heaven: producer, David O. Selznick, fresh from the success of *Gone with the Wind* (1939); the screen adaptation rights to Daphne du Maurier's best-selling novel, *Rebecca* (1938); and director, Alfred Hitchcock, come to Hollywood to make his first big-budget, American picture. What could go wrong? From the very beginning, however, conflicts erupted over the production of the film, *Rebecca* (1940)—conflicts fundamentally about textual ownership. Du Maurier, disappointed with Hitchcock's 1939 adaptation of her previous novel, *Jamaica Inn*, cited the director's "cavalier attitude towards source material" and refused to write the screenplay for *Rebecca* (Turner 11). Meanwhile, Selznick and Hitchcock progressed from disagreement about who should play the lead female role to an all-out, knock-down feud over the script before shooting even began.[1] Selznick angrily declared the first screenplay, prepared under Hitchcock's supervision by Philip MacDonald and Joan Harrison, "a travesty" and "an abomination" and drew a line in the sand: "we bought *Rebecca*, and we intend to make *Rebecca*" (Turner 12). Far more than mere backstage buzz, these struggles mirror a preoccupation with aesthetic value and artistic control central to the text itself. In fact, several of Hitchcock's major deviations from the original novel stage the tensions between the

---

[1] Auiler includes the director's, the producer's, and Mrs. Hitchcock's comments on the screen tests for contenders for the role of the narrator; Margaret Sullavan was considered "too big and sugary" for the part, and Ann Baxter too voluptuous. Even Fontaine was appraised as "too coy and simpering," though she did win the part (307-310). Olivier's choice was Vivien Leigh, but both Hitchcock and Selznick were adamant that she was all wrong for the part. Interestingly, Olivia de Havilland, Fontaine's sister, was Selznick's first choice, but she refused to test for the part when she learned that Fontaine was also being tested (Turner 14).

principal characters directly through scenes of artistic/authorial production and in so doing, reveal a gender-inflected aesthetics as the film's subtext.

Robin Wood, commenting on *Rebecca*'s textual contestations, offers this graphic suggestion: Hitchcock's film "fails to either assimilate or vomit out the indigestible gothic core of the original" (22). Interestingly, Hitchcock ultimately disowned the film. In spite of his determination to set his own stamp on the story, he confided to Truffaut, "Well, it's not a Hitchcock picture" (Wood 65). Critics have been quick to construe the comment as a veiled reference to Selznick's interference. Yet Hitchcock is more specific as he continues the conversation with Truffaut. He hints at an essential femininity that marks the source material as resistant and unyielding. "There was a whole school of feminine literature at the time," he goes on; "The fact is, the story is lacking in humour" (Wood 65). The "indigestible core" would seem to be not merely generic—the Gothic—but also gendered. Moreover, Hitchcock implicitly conflates the romance novel (the "school of feminine literature") with the popular film genre of the 1930s and 40s, the woman's film ("at the time").

The romance novel as a genre has been particularly associated with women writers and readers since at least the eighteenth century. Although academics have variously suggested women's romance as inherently regressive in its encouragement of women's dependence on men and conformity with patriarchal codes, or progressive in its portrayals of strong and unconventional women who defy sexual prescription, critical concensus has come more recently to rest on a combination of both, on a kind of textual subterfuge that allows romance writers to, in the words of novelist Rebecca West (and Emily Dickinson), "tell the truth, but tell it slant" (qtd. in Gilbert and Gubar 281). The woman's film, on the other hand, emerged from the male-dominated movie studio in and around the era of the second World War. Molly Haskell argues that its ideological agenda was primarily a function of backlash. The woman's film was designed to convince its female viewers to be wary of any wartime independence they might be enjoying (27-28). Haskell notes, "women might have better jobs, largely as a result of the war and the shortage of male personnel, but they would pay heavily for it in the movies. Naturally" (29). Hitchcock's conflation of the genres, though, signals that the textual conflicts of *Rebecca* are as much a collision in gendered aesthetics as they are embedded in a reactionary wartime agenda.

Indeed, the film's insistence on art as a motif attests to its investment in the aesthetic as a category. Details of architecture, painting, and writing punctuate primary plot tensions. At the same time, Hitchcock's renunciation of *Rebecca* not only conveys his discomfort with the aesthetic value of both the source material's genre and that of its adaptation but also reveals his suspicion that his own text has somehow become aesthetically contaminated. In the following pages I suggest that the source of that contamination—the "indigestible core"—

is precisely the feminized detail, and I contrast du Maurier's with Hitchcock's treatment of architecture, including the represented built environment and architectures of plot; the imagistic arts, including cinema and painting; and writing, including the textual trace of letters, signatures, monograms, books, and other representations of the written word within the film. Where du Maurier's novel valorizes the aesthetic role of the detail and its contribution to the textual strategies that underpin women's romance as a genre, the film presents a counter-aesthetics, working feverishly to contain and neutralize the feminine agency of the detail.

The Frame

Truffaut considers the filming of *Rebecca* an important watershed in Hitchcock's career and notes that du Maurier's material spurred the director to devise some of his signature techniques (Auiler 26-32). Some of these techniques, I would add, are also born of the need to address fundamental conflicts of genre and aesthetics. Hitchcock's shift from the original's emphasis on the ghost story to a preoccupation with the minutae of the psychological thriller suggests the degree to which his film, too, like the romance, must rely on the detail. However, his revisions work to subsume and transmute the feminized and insurgent detail, re-coding it as an obedient prop in a masculine genre. Again and again in this film the detail is "manhandled." Abstracted, projected, totalized, and framed, it comes to support and serve the purpose of the artistic whole.

Eschewing du Maurier's consistent and sustained use of the Gothic, the film is a deliberate generic amalgam, its plot constructed to fit neatly into three distinct categories. The first section is nearly all romantic comedy and consists of the Monte Carlo scenes. The humor Hitchcock felt lacking in the original has been added all in a lump in these early scenes by making comic butts of the narrator (played by Joan Fontaine) and of her employer, Mrs. Van Hopper (Florence Bates). The young woman's awkward naivete and the older woman's vulgar aggressiveness are not only presumed comic in and of themselves but also in their contrast and provide the romantic comedy's parallel of the Gothic contrast between the narrator and Rebecca. The second section is the most Gothic and of the three, follows the novel most closely. The third section is pure detective story, containing the largest amount of added material, as well as the major plot change of Rebecca's accidental death rather than her murder at the hands of Maxim (played by Laurence Olivier). Hitchcock's redistribution of the material amongst three popular genres may have derived from a desire to appeal to a wider, more diverse audience, but such a desire also implies that the Gothic is too specific, too restricted—and too feminine. Romantic comedies of this period, which could boast hits such as *Bringing Up Baby* (1938) and *The Devil and Miss Jones* (1941), appealed to both men and women, while the detective story was already becoming firmly entrenched as men's fare. Consequently, the film's broadened focus not only partakes of a certain disparagement of the Gothic in its implied judgement of insufficiency, or "smallness," but also brings *Rebecca*'s particularity of genre to heel under a supposedly more comprehensive, "larger" cinematic whole. Such deliberate architecture of scale is Hitchcock's strategy throughout.

Hitchcock's overall engineering of genre is mirrored in the very methods by which he creates Gothic atmosphere within Manderley during the middle portion of the film. On set, the director had physical ratios altered in order to make the narrator seem very small and to play up her insufficiency (Nesbit 12; Auiler 116). Set construction and camera angles combined to create this portrayal, with door knobs on the Manderley set raised, furniture made over-sized, and cameras placed to shoot from very high or very low perspectives so as to exaggerate the size difference between the narrator and her surroundings. A scene from the narrator's first morning in the mansion, for example, is shot from a camera placed just behind Fontaine and tracking up to take in the grand staircase, cathedral windows, and numerous doors opening from passageways above and below, then panning back to reveal Fontaine dwarfed in the center of the screen. Similar shots depict the narrator's first meeting with Jack Favell (George Sanders), her first entries into the morning room and Rebecca's bedroom, and her contemplation of the paved terrace when she considers jumping from the window in the wake of the disastrous fancy dress ball. Wide exterior shots of the grounds of the estate take advantage of natural scenery to augment the effect, particularly filming of Fontaine on the beach and outlined against the massive rocks and the sea beyond. Despite the centrality of her role as narrator, the second Mrs. de Winter is trivial and insignificant, a mere detail lost against the panoramic expanses, interior and exterior, that are Manderley.

Materially, the house also stands as a map of the relationships between the main characters. Hitchcock follows the novel in allowing the two wives' physical placement at Manderley to underscore apparent contrasts between them. Rebecca presided over the east wing, overlooking the sea, while the narrator is given a room in the west wing, overlooking the rose garden. The narrator's room contains only functional, generic items bought for non-specific female guests long before she arrived. Sparsely furnished, it markedly lacks the lavish ornamentation that identifies Rebecca's. Nor is the bedroom Rebecca's only province. Her things spill over, cluttering the morning room with an elegant though ostentatious display, threatening the masculine comfort of the library with bowls of flowers, lining the drive with the blood-red rhododendrons of her own choosing, and creeping down to the beachfront cottage and the dock where her boat is moored. In the film, as in the novel, Rebecca is entirely represented by all the small details of her physical existence at Manderley—her scented handkerchiefs, her date book, her gossamer nightgowns—all the excess things that stand in for her and haunt the narrator with their too close and too strong femininity. The housekeeper, Mrs. Danvers (played by Judith Anderson), is Rebecca's proxy and cements the association between the dead woman and the objects by preserving them undisturbed.

A number of scholars, including Tania Modleski, Mary Anne Doane, and Kaja Silverman, read the imprint of Rebecca's things as an equation of the house with an essential femininity or a feminized, labyrinthine subconscious (Modleski 41-42; Doane 76-79; Silverman 139-41). The power of the house to bewilder and terrify the narrator rests, however, only in part on its association with Maxim's deceased wife. We should not forget that Manderley is the de Winter family estate and, as Alison Light argues, Rebecca's supposed crime is her threatened usurpation of the estate from the established line of patriarchal inheritance (47-49); she taunts Maxim with the spectre of a bastard. An apt name, "Man"derley stands as well for Maxim. The narrator's terror in both the original and the adaptation is as much of her new husband and his aristocratic lineage as it is of Rebecca's memory and of Danvers. The film conveys this terror perhaps nowhere so well as in the sequence illustrating the narrator's dramatic first arrival on the estate. The camera cuts between the narrator, Maxim, and Manderley as the music builds to a crescendo and Fontaine's face reveals the narrator's absolute awe of both the husband and the house.

Fundamentally, Manderley embodies an aesthetic conflict between the detail and the neo-classic Ideal, a conflict arising from its association with both Maxim and Rebecca. The neo-classic Ideal adheres to a valorization of the organic and/or constructed whole and prizes the total effect—symmetry of form, balance rather than excess—over individual features. Rebecca's definitive style poses a significant challenge to that Ideal. Her lavish ornamentation of the rooms to which she has laid claim threatens to overwhelm Manderley with a mutant and mutinous superfluity of detail. In fact, Rebecca is the detail, the particular, within Manderley rather than being representative of Manderley as a totality, so that her menace to the estate consists equally in her aesthetic offense of refusing to consign the detail to its inferior place and in her threat of bastard offspring. Hitchcock's repeated staging of the narrator's reluctance to even sit in the furniture at Manderley emphasizes, by contrast, her inability to make an impression on her environment. As her first glance at the estate implies, the narrator appreciates the whole and will not attempt to interfere with its formal austerity. She will not attempt to "put her stamp" to the place. She knows that her own smallness and triviality equip her to play at best only a supporting role.

In the *Aesthetics*, Hegel places architecture at the top of a hierarchy of art forms distinguished by their relative proportions of detail and Ideal. He notes:

> Everything is lost in the greatness of the whole. It has and displays a definite purpose; but in its grandeur...it is lifted into an infinity in itself. This elevation above the finite, and this simple solidity is its one characteristic aspect. It is precisely where particularization, diversity, and variety gain the fullest scope but without letting the whole fall apart into mere trifles and accidental details. (2: 685)

Here, he aligns the detail and the Ideal with the physical and the abstract, and it is the role of the detail to prop up, to lift, the whole into an abstract absolute ("infinity"). The mansion can thus be seen as the ground of a war over proportions. In the novel, du Maurier carries the issue further, moving beyond hierarchies of relative weight to destabilize the very endeavor of such categorization. Rebecca straddles the abstract/physical divide, her haunting of Manderley both an abstract effect of the uncanny and a material effect of her previous residence there. She is, as Silverman phrases it, an "absent presence" (139). Du Maurier's formulation of the detail/Ideal relationship defies conventional aesthetic categories like Hegel's, and the memory of Rebecca is never put to rest in the novel, as her boat's name foretells: Je Reviens. The narrative, too, refuses conventional resolution and does not offer to resituate the detail; it begins in limbo and ends there with the narrator's revelation that she and her husband have been physically expatriated from their home and now wander from hotel to hotel, avoiding the memory of Rebecca's murder by immersing themselves in the details of cricket matches, boxing bouts, dog racing, "even billiard scores"—any small, unrelated thing to prevent remembering the past (6).

Rebecca's threat to the system of aesthetic difference does not go unresolved in the film, though, as it does in the novel. Hitchcock's handling of the introductory and concluding sequences functions as both frame and gloss for the intervening material. The introductory sequence, a set of establishing shots, presents us with a view of the road, the front gate, the overgrown rhododendrons, a wall, a window, a window pane, and continues to track in, closer and closer, as the narrator moves through the nightmare dreamscape. With an almost architectural logic, the scenes identify the increasingly proximate detail as the source of terror. The concluding sequence, in which Mrs. Danvers sets fire to the estate, reverses this motion. Tightly focused on the embroidered "R" of Rebecca's monogrammed pillow, the camera pans back to reveal flames encompassing the bed, then the room, and finally, the entire house aflame. Swinging out and back, the concluding shots re-assert the primacy of the whole over the part. Although in this last panorama of the house, Danvers destroys it, ostensibly in an act of revenge, the primary visual effect is the burning of Rebecca's things and along with them, the housekeeper. In truth, Manderley is sacrificed through the logic of its contamination by Rebecca's proxy details.

II. The Portrait

It is, of course, the kind of sacrifice that throws the baby out with the bath water, much as Hitchcock preferred to throw *Rebecca* from his body of work in spite of its critical acclaim and awards.[2] Attempts to contain the detail end by eradicating it, by burning it from the screen, which in turn brings the entire edifice of the film's implicit aesthetic theory toppling down around it. Several scenes specifically involving sketching, painting, and cinema are either revised from the original or entirely interpolated by Hitchcock and metafictively illustrate the film's aesthetic theory.

To begin with, du Maurier's narrator has a "very unusual and very lovely" name (32), a fact with which we are tantalized because her name is withheld from us throughout. Indeed, we really learn very little about the novel's narrator except that she herself has a talent for observation—an apt eye for details. She begins her story with the dream of Manderley, the same dream sequence Hitchcock renders as his introduction, and moves to the description of her present "hotel existence" before taking us back in time to Monte Carlo. Instead, Hitchcock deletes the material that treats the present and interjects in its place a short scene in which a girl (the narrator, as we later discover) intently surveys a man (Maxim) against the background of an ocean cliff. The girl believes the man about to jump, but when she calls out to him, he rounds on her angrily and frightens her away. This scene reminds me strongly of Hitchcock's later work in *The Birds* (1963). As Constance Penley has argued, *The Birds* dramatizes women as a presumptive and punished spectators. Melanie, the lead female character, wrests spectatorship from male control at several points in the film rather than accepting her prescribed place as object of the gaze. Melanie is punished for this presumption, as *The Birds* concludes with her combined catatonia and blinding (381-386). Like Rebecca, she is a defiant and sexually aggressive woman. However, in the scene from *Rebecca*, it is the narrator who holds the power of the gaze and provokes an angry response from the male as a result. One might say it is the narrator's strongest moment in the entire film, her most emphatic act of personal assertion, when she walks alone to the cliff tops of Monte Carlo to view the sea. Her presumption as an observer here parallels

---

[2] *Rebecca* won the 1940 Academy Award for best picture, and Olivier, Fontaine, Anderson, and Hitchcock were all nominated for Oscars in 1940 for *Rebecca*.

her presumption as a female artist, for in this scene she has brought her pencils and sketchpad.

The narrator's competitive assumption of the role of artist provokes a hierarchization of art forms in *Rebecca*, more or less in line with Hegel's, and concomitant with the film's handling of the detail. Sketching and painting come to have a lower, feminized status with architecture and, as Hitchcock construes it, cinema occupies a higher status and is associated either with male authority or with the male artist. In Hegel's system, painting is a less Ideal art than architecture and necessarily involves a greater reliance on the detail since

> artists [must] call attention to the painted surface, or to the contrast between real and represented space, by . . . noticeable marks, by a flattening of the canvas, by reversal of rules for occlusions and other anomalies. (Goldman 195)

Because it is only a two-dimensional representation, a painting requires more detail in order to render a likeness. Hegel further suggests that portraiture is even lower down in the hierarchy, lending itself less to abstraction than landscape painting. "The portrait-painter," he writes:

> has least of all to do with the Ideal of art...in the sense that all the externals in shape and expression, in form, colour, features, little hairs, pores, little scars, warts, all these he must let go [if] he is to [approach] the Ideal. (1: 155)

Hitchcock's narrator will experience a progressive diminishment as artist after that first encounter with Maxim until she is required to relinquish her claim to that role entirely. In the novel, although the wind proves "too high for sketching" the day she returns to the cliffs of Monte Carlo in Maxim's car, the narrator describes the harbor—"a dancing thing, with fluttering paper boats"— with the eye of a practiced artist (28). When she returns to the cliffs, her object has changed as well. She has become a portraitist and sketches not the landscape but Maxim. That he, rather than the wider world, has now become her object suggests a narrowing of her field of vision, but further, her sketching has been reduced to the attempts of a mere amateur, for her activity a second time provokes his disdainful response. He pulls the sketches from her and tosses them aside, saying, "They don't look a thing like me, why don't you just keep me company?" He denigrates her skill and asks her to give up her work so that her role has shrunk from landscape artist to portraitist to mere companion before she is even married. The relationship will require her to relinquish her power as artist and to become simply a supporting detail for Maxim.

Once at Manderley, their Monte Carlo days prove to be an interesting source of nostalgia for Maxim. Another addition of Hitchcock's with no correlative in the novel is the honeymoon home movie sequence. Hitchcock condenses the novel's narrative of a broken cupid by combining it with Maxim's screening of the home movies, but condensation alone cannot account for the treatment of the source material here. The home movie scenes actually lengthen this portion of the story. In addition, Hitchcock adds a fashion display by the narrator while the movies are being shown. As Maxim watches the films, the narrator enters the room in a new dress and new hairstyle, attempting to look uncharacteristically glamorous and "grown up." Bringing these elements together (the cupid, the movies, the fashion show), the sequence in fact comments on Maxim's role as artist and makes of the feminized detail a powerfully overdetermined display of fetishism.

Fontaine conveys all the fear and awkwardness of du Maurier's original narrator when she accidentally knocks a porcelain cupid off the desk in the morning room. In both versions, the narrator hastily shoves the statue into a drawer and hides the pieces by covering them with paper. The smashed cupid, an *objet d'art* of extravagant ornamentality, also serves as an oblique reference to Rebecca's broken and surreptitiously hidden body. When the narrator joins Maxim to watch the honeymoon reels, he is so immersed in the details of his film that he barely notices her. Not until Danvers enters the room with the broken cupid in her hands does Maxim turn to look at the narrator, dressed in the designer gown and pearls she supposes more like Rebecca's. He trivializes the women and their quarrel along with the cupid by saying simply, "I never liked it anyway." His comment echoes the confession he will make about Rebecca later in the film: "I never loved her." The troublesome material detail, whether porcelain, velvet, or flesh and blood, is a victim of patriarchal contempt. And yet Maxim delights in the details of the screen. His appreciation of the detail—for he can appreciate it—is bestowed on its displaced and projected representation in cinema. He delightedly points out the ducks, the flowers, the narrator's sweater, as he re-starts the film. The detail has been transmuted by its projection onto the screen, controlled, contained, and enjoyed by the male filmmaker.

A logic of substitutional equivalence at work throughout the film is particularly condensed in this sequence, operating on several levels at once to bind the women together in a metonymic chain of fetishism. Things stand in for women, and women stand in for other women in a representational displacement that moves the detail from particularity to universality. In *The Fashion System*, Roland Barthes discusses the way in which the detail masquerades as an item of unique style. The reality of the fashion detail, he argues, is its support of a system of mass production; a small selection of trifles pretends to differentiate between essentially interchangeable ("the same") garments (121-35). Sut Jhally makes a similar argument about music video and describes the result of the metonymic logic that drives the video displays of countless women draped around a central, male artist: one woman is as good as another because they are "all the same," essentially interchangeable in their supporting roles. In du Maurier's text, this metonymic logic is part of the Gothic menace that surrounds the narrator. Horror attends her discovery that patriarchy reduces women to a sameness, a sameness perhaps nowhere as humiliating as in the substitution of the naked Jane Doe's body for Rebecca's. With Hitchcock's version, horror evolves through the narrator's frustrated efforts to prove her dissimilarity from Rebecca—a small change in emphasis but one that makes a world of difference.

The difference between the novel's treatment of the portrait of Caroline de Winter and the film's perfectly illustrates this shift. Clearly, the portrait extends the series of metonymic substitutions and in du Maurier's text, it confirms the narrator's increasing obsession with Rebecca. Her obsession verges on seduction as her self-conscious passivity begins to dissolve through the first wife's alluring influence. The narrator begins to assert herself. To start, she authors the reinstitution of the Manderley ball (not, as in Hitchcock's version, Mrs. Danvers). Second, no longer struck dumb with terror at the choice of a sauce, as in her first week at the mansion, she finds the courage to command Mrs. Danvers on the menu. Most significantly, for the first time since Monte Carlo, we read of her sketching. She resumes her role as artist and produces several sketches of potential costumes for the ball. Ultimately, Mrs. Danvers suggests to the narrator that she copy the clothing in the life-sized portrait of Caroline de Winter. Her desire to see the narrator don the exact costume Rebecca wore the last time the Manderley ball was held may further the housekeeper's own schemes, but the narrator's susceptibility to the advice is owed both to her seduction by the image of Rebecca and to her artistic knowledge and perfectionism. Other costume ideas were discarded because their sketches, according to her critical eye, "did not please," not being of the same quality as "the reproductions of Rubens and Rembrandt" (198). At the same time, the narrator's positive assessment of the portrait of Caroline illustrates her professional background because it derives in part from the fact that the painting is "a Raeburn" (203), a piece of knowledge that would be out of character for Hitchcock's narrator who merely gives a schoolgirl clap of her hands when Danvers points out the portrait and then rushes off to order the costume.

That du Maurier's narrator becomes Rebecca most precisely when Rebecca had become Caroline makes a point of patriarchy's fetishistic reduction of women, yet the context of artistic proficiency within which this collapse of identity occurs also allows us to read the women's equivalence subversively. The narrator's delighted appraisal of the represented details of Caroline's clothing ("those puffed sleeves, the flounce, and the little bodice" [203]), coupled with Caroline's status as an entitled female owner of Manderley, highlight the attractiveness of the insurgent detail. The real struggle of du

Maurier's narrator consists of how to integrate her simultaneous identification with the feminized detail, whether subservient or insurgent, and the controlling agency of the artist. This integration is precisely the seduction Rebecca offers as she defies the traditional aesthetic system, its distinguishing categories, and its polarized roles.

Hitchcock's subtle changes to this portion of the story skew the seduction dynamics in a different direction. Again, condensation is an ostensible factor, but the effect of the changes runs beyond practical motivations. Hitchcock chooses to depict the narrator's difficulty in selecting a costume with only one scene, that where Danvers finds the narrator's sketches in the wastebasket. The housekeeper repeatedly thrusts them back at her, and she as repeatedly refuses them, conveying not critical judgement of her own efforts but complete and utter terror of Danvers. Confronted by the housekeeper, she is afraid to own her work. Hitchcock thus highlights Mrs. Danvers's agency rather than the girl's. Nor does his narrator experience a surge of self-assertion as her identification with Rebecca grows. Her pursuit of Danvers on the evening of the ball illustrates a lamb-like naivete as the narrator, cringing against the wall in her curls and white ruffles, discovers herself to have been deliberately lured into Rebecca's room. In the novel, there is no sense of deliberate entrapment in the room. Du Maurier's narrator follows Mrs. Danvers with increasing command, enters the room quietly to find her crying, and realizes that the older woman is still inconsolable over the loss of Rebecca. Although Danvers will still urge her to jump at the close of their conversation, the narrator sees the housekeeper's venom as the childish, uncontrolled grief of "an old woman who [is] ill and tired" (241), not the exultance of a devil, and a fall from the window as an escape from Maxim's disdain and supposed preference for his first wife.

In the film, though, Danvers grows to satanic proportions during this scene, terrorizing the narrator with the luxuriance of Rebecca's furs, the exquisiteness of the lace on her nightgowns, the elegant stitchery in her monogram, the silver hairbrushes at the boudoir table, the profusion of Rebecca's sexual conquests— in short, with the promiscuous excess and proximity of the feminized detail. Hitchcock's Danvers is irredeemably villainous and her malice unmitigated. The film's narrator is brought to make a clear choice of distance from Rebecca and to see identification with her, and with her synonymous details grown excessive and uncontrollable, as a form of suicide. Were she to jump to her death from the window, the narrator would in effect be "killed into art,"[3]

---

[3] The phrase is from Gilbert and Gubar; they discuss the nineteenth-century motif of a heroine made into an aesthetic object, an *objet d'art*, by her untimely death (150-57). In death, she is perfect, a wax or marble model who passively fulfills the ideals of beauty of the male artist/creator, in accordance with the Pygmalion myth. In this way, the heroine is always an art object rather than artist and creator in her own right.

rendered instantly as ornately inanimate as her doubles, the porcelain cupid or the portrait of the long-dead Caroline. On the other hand, in rejecting Danvers and Rebecca, she also rejects the agency they offer and dwindles into the wife we see during the trial, supporting her husband, biting her lips in silence. Although only Danvers, as Silverman points out, is burnt as a witch at the end of the film (147), the narrator, too, is put to the classic witch test, and she is damned either way. Du Maurier's narrator, by contrast, never fully resolves her simultaneous fear and fascination with Rebecca so that ultimately, she makes no choice between the test's alternatives; Rebecca continues to be "in some manner unforeseen. . . a living companion" long after the burning of Manderley (5).

My own fascination with the film began, I confess, with a short and apparently trivial addition of Hitchcock's that occurs early in the first segment. The addition is a scene, on the face of it, meant to round out the edges of the romantic comedy with small talk and light banter. While breakfasting at the hotel in Monte Carlo, the novel's narrator tells Maxim about her artist father. She says simply, "It was not easy to explain my father and usually I never talked about him. Twenty-four hours afterwards my family history was mine no longer, I shared it with a man I did not know" (24). We never know what she shared since the intervening material is a blank. The film, however, interpolates the rest of the conversation. The narrator chatters happily, "Father was a painter." Maxim responds, "Good lord! What did he paint?" She answers, "Trees. Well, one tree." Maxim again responds with a question: "You don't mean to say he painted the same tree over and over again?" The narrator offers this intriguing answer: "Father always said if you found one perfect thing, you should stick with it." This light conversation carries significant weight; it encapsulates the film's entire aesthetic theory. If the terror of the Gothic portion derives from the excessive detail, its insurrection threatening to overwhelm the whole and submerge it in chaos (from not being able to see the forest for the trees), then the patriarchal dream that the narrator shares with Maxim is that of the artist's attempt to perfect both nature and the detail until they have transcended their individual status and become an abstract totalization. Or, as Hegel put it, until they reach infinity. The tree becomes perfected with repetition and is thus able to symbolize the neo-classic Ideal of the organic whole, such as it does in so many mythological systems as the tree of life and the whole of creation. It is worth noting that this scene is also the only moment in the entire film when Maxim finds the narrator captivating; it is the only moment in which he is truly paying attention to her words.

III. The Writing (On the Wall)

The truly correlative scene in the novel is not the conversation about the narrator's father, but her recollections immediately preceding it. She is thinking about a postcard of Manderley, but she does not share these thoughts with Maxim. Like the father's tree in the film, the narrator's memory of the postcard illustrates the novel's aesthetic theory in miniature, one quite different from the screen version's. At breakfast "we sat," she remembers, "for a while without talking," and

> I thought of a picture post-card I had bought once at a village shop, when on holiday as a child in the west country. It was the painting of a house, crudely done of course and highly coloured, but even those faults could not destroy the symmetry of the building, the wide stone steps before the terrace, the green lawns stretching to the sea. . . . Perhaps it was the memory of this post-card, lost long ago in some forgotten book that made me sympathise [with him]. Maybe there was something inviolate about Manderley that made it a place apart; it would not bear discussion. (23)

The postcard is a deft touch, insinuating the similarity between Maxim and Manderley as representative of the classical Ideal and at the same time, connecting the novel's recurrent motifs of text and image. The narrator here adopts the role of artist and critical observer in providing an aesthetic assessment of the picture ("crude") while the postcard format and its mixture with the book blend the two media. The narrator's recollection succinctly symbolizes an overturning of classical aesthetics. It allies her with Rebecca, with Rebecca's ability to defy absolute categories, and with a dissolution of hierarchy between graphic image and text. In the *Aesthetics*, Hegel relegates writing to the lowest point in the hierarchy of art forms. The written text, he reasons, is representationally more distant from its subject than is an image and thus necessarily needs more detail. Written text is able to represent only by parts that give an impression of the whole:

> It can bring before our minds only in isolated traits one after another what we see at one glance in the real, and therefore in its treatment. . . it cannot spread itself so far as the total view. (2:982)

Rebecca's writing is a central motif in both novel and film. Just as Rebecca's boat, or the cupid, or the silver brushes identify her synecdochically, so too does the written text, particularly in modes that also emphasize its visual impact: monogram, signature, appearance on the page.

Rebecca's authorship is central to the Gothic atmosphere of the story. The "bold, slanting strokes" of the "R" in Rebecca's signature, for example, at once fascinate and repel the novel's narrator. They manifest the will and power of the woman writer. Later, in the morning room, she compares her handwriting to that of Rebecca's and reveals a grudging admiration as she pronounces her own "that of a second-rate pupil in a third-rate school" beside Rebecca's elegant script (57). Even early on, in Monte Carlo, when Maxim gives the narrator a book of poetry that Rebecca had earlier given him, the signature on the flyleaf disturbs her, causing her to excise it and throw it in the fire. She puts from her the temptation of the power of the woman writer and the seduction of authorial control. That this power is correlative with that of the visual artist is suggested not only by the imagistic nature of Rebecca's described writing but also, more obliquely, by the narrator's costume research. She turns first to the library at Manderley for inspiration for her sketches. In this activity, she moves adeptly between text and image, transcribing written description into visual rendering.

Hitchcock retains Rebecca's textual trace, providing close-ups of the flyleaf, the date book, signatures, letters, monograms, and the lettering on the boat. Yet he employs this trace in a strategy that again runs counter to du Maurier's. The film opposes text and image and couches this opposition in terms of the aesthetic conflict between the detail and the whole. Writing, Rebecca's most powerful remnant, is aligned with the detail not only through its association with the first wife but also in the repeated extreme close-ups of bits of text throughout the film. Although the film's medium makes it impossible to avoid the visual impact of her writing, Hitchcock's insistence on Rebecca's monogram in the concluding shots is evocative. Rebecca's insistent textual presence is thoroughly demonized, suffering the same fate as Danvers in the concluding sequence's close-up of the elaborate and fetishistic "R" on the pillow as it is engulfed in flames. Indeed, Modleski has argued that the textual trace of du Maurier's novel haunts Hitchcock's picture just as Rebecca herself does Manderley (43). The director's desire to "burn" her text out of his picture, literalized in the burning of the monogrammed pillow that represents the eponymous heroine, suggests his imposition of cinematic and imagistic control over both text and detail. Maxim supports this agenda through his relationships with Rebecca and with the narrator and, pointedly, through his role as filmmaker.

If, as Haskell suggests, the "wet, wasted afternoons" the woman's film offered its female viewers encouraged them to accept "the gradual dribbling of self-esteem, and self, down the drain of meaningless triviality" (22), then Hitchcock may indeed have fulfilled Selznick's wishes and made *Rebecca* a woman's film. That his *Rebecca* also functions in part as a manifesto on aesthetics is more curious. After all, he had made it clear that he felt the genre beneath him, as did Selznick's first choice for Maxim, Robert Coleman, who flatly refused to play the leading man in "a woman's picture" (Turner 12).

Hitchcock invests a very slight vehicle with the hugely important task of explicating a theory of art if we believe his casual dismissal of the film's genre, du Maurier's novel, and the women's romance the novel exemplifies. The gesture is as ironic as the investment of the film's central aesthetic statement in miniature in the conversation about the narrator's father and the tree. Ultimately, the genres of the woman's film and the women's romance novel hold enough weight to carry a deliberate, compelling aesthetic theory precisely because of their subversive use of the trivial—of the detail.

Jane Austen's characterization of her art as a kind of painting on two inches of ivory is a thoroughly appropriate summary of gendered aesthetics. Likewise, Judy Chicago presents a feminine aesthetics as "ivory work"with her multi-media installation, "A Dinner Party." Combining painting, needlework, glass, ceramics, and text in a reclamation of women's contributions throughout history, the installation defies the conventional relationship of part and whole, of text, image, and frame, and refuses either to subsume the detail as a support for the whole or to foreground the detail itself as insupportable excess. Women's romance, with its strong predilection for the detail, enacts a similar quiet revolution of style. And *Rebecca* is the genre's "poster novel," stitched together entirely of every small and haunting thing, from lace handkerchief trim, rhododendron petals, and pieces of porcelain, to the smell of white azalea after the rain.

Works Cited

Auiler, Dan. *Hitchcock's Notebooks: An Authorized and Illustrated Look Inside the Creative Mind of Alfred Hitchcock.* New York: Spike, 1999.

Barthes, Roland. *The Fashion System.* Trans. M. Ward and R. How. New York: Hill and Wang, 1983.

Doane, Mary Ann. "*Caught* and *Rebecca*: The Inscription of Femininity as Absence." Thornham, 70-82.

Du Maurier, Daphne. *Rebecca.* New York: Avon, 1971 (1938).

Gubar, Susan and Gilbert, Sandra. *The Madwoman in the Attic: The Woman Writer and the Nineteenth-Century Literary Imagination.* New Haven: Yale UP, 1979.

Goldman, Alan. "Representation in Art." *The Oxford Handbook of Aesthetics.* Ed. J. Levinson. Oxford: Oxford UP, 2003. 192-210.

Haskell, Molly. "The Woman's Film." Thornham, 20-30.

Hegel, Georg and Wilhelm Friedrich. *Aesthetics: Lectures on Fine Art.* Trans. T.M. Knox. 2 vols. Oxford: Clarendon Press, 1975.

Hitchcock, Alfred. *Rebecca.* prod. David. O. Selznick. Clarion, 1940.

80   Andrea Austin

Jhally, Sut. *Dreamworlds II: Sex, Power, and Music Video.* Media Education
Foundation. Videocassette. 1994.

Light, Alison. "Returning to Manderley." *Forever England: Femininity,
Literature and Conservatism Between the Wars.* New York: Routledge,
1991. 45-63.

Modleski, Tania. "Woman and the Labyrinth." *Women Who Knew Too Much:
Hitchcock and Feminist Theory.* New York: Methuen, 1988. 27-43.

Nesbit, John. "Hitchcock on a Tight Leash." *Culture Dose* 1.23: 2002. 12-16.
[review]

Penley, Constance. "A Certain Refusal of Difference: Feminist Film Theory."
Art After Modernism: ReThinking Representation. Ed. Brian Wallis. New
York: New Museum of Contemporary Art, 1984. 375-390.

Silverman, Kaja. "Fragments of a Fashionable Discourse." *Studies in
Entertainment: Critical Approaches to Mass Culture.* Ed. Tania Modleski.
Bloomington: Indiana UP, 1986. 139-152.

Thornham, Sue, ed. *Feminist Film Theory: A Reader.* New York: UP, 1999.

Turner, George. "Du Maurier+Selznick+Hitchcock's Rebecca." *American
Cinematographer* July 1997, 10-15.

Wood, Robin. *Hitchcock's Films Revisited.* New York: Columbia UP, 1989.

Andrea Austin

Andrea Austin is an Assistant Professor in the English and Film Studies
Department at Wilfrid Laurier University. She teaches popular culture,
cybercultures, and women's writing, and has been researching in the areas of
gender and the built environment, including aesthetics, architectures, and virtual
realities.

CHAPTER SIX

THE HAUNTED SPACE OF THE MIND: THE REVIVAL OF THE GOTHIC ROMANCE IN THE TWENTY-FIRST CENTURY

DEBORAH LUTZ

To say that there has been a revival of the Gothic romance is to gesture back to the rich and complex history of an ever-changing genre. At the same time, it is to say nothing particularly surprising or new: the term "Gothic" has always included the "revivified" in its very meaning. Indeed, when the term itself was originally coined, it referenced a long-dead people—the Goths—and the idea of the "Gothic" was a romanticization of the people and their time, an aestheticization that had little to do with their actual historical existence. Similarly, in mid-eighteenth-century England, when the Gothic architectural style became all the vogue again after centuries of being out of fashion and when the Gothic novel emerged soon after, we see this new sense of the Gothic constructed out of what was thought to be "medieval": a people, time, and architecture primitive, irregular, non-enlightened. Thus it was thought that "medieval" meant a visible, tangible spirit world where ghosts wandered about ancient abodes, where unquiet and lost souls would travel the earth eternally, where the demonic still held sway over the living. To set a story in the middle ages meant, to late-eighteenth-century Gothic writers, to have as a backdrop a less "civilized" society where kidnap, rape, imprisonment, and torture were far more prevalent.

When the Gothic romance reappeared in the 1950s in England and America and swept the paperback fiction market, spurring thousands of novels influenced by *Rebecca*, *Jane Eyre*, and *Wuthering Heights* to be written and voraciously read by a large and eager public, the Gothic referred back to an undeterminable time, "historical" but never really historical—a kind of anytime, anywhere where violence and magic lay just beneath the surface of magnificent and sinister scenes.[1] Hence, while the Gothic always appears to be a representation of the past, to be a casting back to a particular time and place with its own unique atmosphere, it really reinterprets the past according to present preoccupations; it creates a world of desire, danger, and fantasy that speaks about the present rather than past truths. The Gothic is then, by its very nature, a fantasy of a fantasy, an amorphous spirit wafting in front of a mirror. At the heart of the Gothic we thus find ourselves, following shadows, trying to make absence present, trying to draw out the darkness from the light. The two movements driving the revival, as I will argue in the following, involve a desire to retain a sense of the mind as a sacred space and a post-feminist openness to a wide range of representations of women's erotic desire.

The new Gothic romance dates to around 2001 when Dorchester publishing started its "Candleglow" Gothic series, the second series since the mid 1970s to follow closely the rules of the Gothic. There was also a line of Gothics in the 1990s put out by Zebra, and from 1991-1998 a journal on Gothic romance was published (another resource is RWA's website on the Gothic romance: GothRom). But Dorchester's line is still quite active, with a new title put out this year. However, in a number of ways, the Gothic romance never did fully die out: many Gothic themes could be found in other popular romance lines, particularly "romantic suspense," "paranormal romance," and various types of historical romances, particularly those set in the Victorian and Medieval periods. We must pay attention to a line of romances that calls itself Gothic and purports to follow all the major themes of the genre because this shows us that the Gothic, *as Gothic*, sells, and no longer needs to go "underground" as it has had to do since the 1970s. It is not just in this line of romances that we can locate the Gothic today. The aspect of the Gothic that involves the closeness and accessibility of the spirit world has become a central theme on television, with shows like "Medium," "Supernatural," and "Ghost Whisperer." Eighties goth music has become a real force again, with many new and emerging bands reinterpreting the dark chords and atmospheric melancholy of such groups as Joy Division and the Smiths. The neo-Victorian movement in design and architecture has many Gothic elements, including the ornamental qualities of

---

[1] For a detailed history of the mid-twentieth-century Gothic romance and its relation to the mystery and the erotic historical, see Radway, *Reading the Romance*, especially page 31; Thurston, *The Romance Revolution*, especially pp. 41-44; and Pamela Regis, *A Natural History of the Romance Novel*. For a discussion of Harlequin's move from mysteries, westerns, and thrillers to romance, see Kay Mussell and Johanna Tunon, eds, *North American Romance Writers*. The obvious historical relatedness of the plots of *Jane Eyre* and *Rebecca* and *Jane Eyre*'s influence on the contemporary Gothic romance has been discussed by many; see particularly Thurston, chapters 1-2 and Tania Modleski, especially chapters 1-3.

antler horns, taxidermy, and animal skin rugs. And just a quick glance through an Anthropologie catalogue proves the Gothic's influence on hip fashion.

One central tenet of the Gothic, which has carried through all its revivals, is the Gothic sense of space and presence. The term "Gothic" has always been associated with a certain style of architecture, one that creates spaces that feel darkly embattled: thick-walled, small-windowed, obscure-cornered.

> It rose up out of the mountainside, part rock, part marble, a huge, hulking palazzo, impossibly large and sprawling. It looked evil in the gathering dusk, staring with blank eyes, the rows of windows frightening in the lashing wind. The structure was several stories high, with long battlements, high, rounded turrets, and great towers. (Feehan 4)

A moment supersaturated with meaning in the Gothic is when the heroine approaches the Gothic space, radiant with dark menace and secrets needing to be disclosed. She faces the enigma, the pure mystery. Approaching the castle or mansion as one would come upon a cipher, she knows there is something to be uncovered there, some unknown that must be plumbed. Crossing that threshold, she enters a realm tense with the dark violence of the past.

> Like the clang of the bell, the walls of the entryway whispered a mournful welcome. She was certain of it, though the exact words were not clear. They brushed across her skin like the passing of warm air, or the movement of spirits made restless by her unexpected presence. A sense of foreboding gripped her, warring with a feeling of anticipation. (*The Grotto* 21)[2]

The Gothic denies the domestic, the "home," the sense of resting in comfort; its cold draftiness lends itself to ever severer discomforts, such as imprisonment, deprivation of basic bodily needs and the possibility of rape. The sublimity of the gloomy mansion means it cannot be truly touched with the warmth of

---

[2] Compare the two contemporary descriptions quoted above to the very similar one from Ann Radcliffe's *The Mysteries of Udolpho* (1794), when Emily approaches the castle which will soon become her prison:

> Emily gazed with awe upon the castle, which she understood to be Montoni's; for, though it was now lighted up by the setting sun, the gothic greatness of its features, and its mouldering walls of dark grey stone, rendered it a gloomy and sublime object. As she gazed, the light died away on its walls, leaving a melancholy purple tint . . . Silent, lonely, and sublime, it seemed to stand the sovereign of the scene, and to frown defiance on all, who dared to invade its solitary reign. As the twilight deepened, its features became more awful in obscurity . . . (216).

humanity; the presence of death feels irrevocable, incessant, unquiet. The Gothic space often holds a palpable sense of regret and sadness.

When the Victorians appropriated the Gothic, the forbidding sense of space remained as one of its hallmarks. Mid-nineteenth century, Charlotte and Emily Brontë recreated the wind-torn and tormented Italian castle as the English country homes of Thornfield and Wuthering Heights, still holding the terrors of the demonic. Gothic rooms call on the unconscious and the shadowy ghosts that knock around there, causing terrors from childhood to start up in the dark recesses of the mind. Many have read Gothic spaces in just such symbolical ways: either standing as a figure for the body that might be penetrated or raped or representing the interior of the mind in its vast unknown reaches or cramped imprisonment (and both these representations can be true at the same time). In fact, Terry Castle and Marshall Brown both argue, boldly and quite convincingly, that the original Gothic novel (of the late eighteenth and early nineteenth centuries) is responsible for the invention of the narrative representation of consciousness.

We could read this in an ontological way: the heroine approaches the mystery of existence itself, and it is terrifying. The fear here is of the life-and-sanity-threatening forces that might exist and be uncovered, but the even more terrifying possibility is to find nothingness, an empty abyss. Heidegger argues that the moment when our essential selves are truly confronted, we are faced with the terror of endless possibility. *Angst* comes from uncovering our authenticity and seeing the indeterminacy of what might be, of fully realizing the true singularity of each existence, of standing utterly alone in the world.

With the Brontës we already see that an important shift in the Gothic space has happened: the heroine enters the house in order to master it, to open its doors, to absolve the evil of the past. In the Gothic proper, the heroine must escape the space altogether, before she is killed by its horrors. Thornfield's imprisoned madness is set free through death; it is cleansed through its destruction. While Catherine dies, her daughter redeems Wuthering Heights and makes it present, airy, open to the light of the future. Catherine haunts her Gothic house, yearning so terribly to get back in (rather than to get *out*, a brilliant rewriting of Gothic imprisonment). In Daphne du Maurier's *Rebecca* (1938), Manderlay's deceits and hatreds are exposed and then are burned away by fire; Camilla in Phyllis Whitney's *Thunder Heights* (1960) discovers the murderer and his violent past and casts him out; in Mary Stewart's *Touch Not the Cat* (1976), Bryony saves and absolves Ashley Court by disclosing its tortured history.

In the new Gothic we see the heroine approaching the dark and hulking abode with similar trepidation but with an even stronger desire to step into the unknown and with a real, willful strength of mastery. In Penelope Neri's

Obsession (2003), Caitlynn arrives at the fortress-like Huntington Square mansion hoping to discover her cousin who mysteriously disappeared from the house two months ago. Isabella arrives at the legendary palazzo of Christine Feehan's *Lair of the Lion* (2002) and knows that the evil she feels there must be remedied; she is the only one who can cast it out. Rather than merely escape the haunted house as in the Gothic proper (mid-eighteenth century to beginning of the nineteenth century) or require a wholesale destruction as means of salvation as in the nineteenth and twentieth-century Gothic, in all of these contemporary narratives the heroine remains in the Gothic house because she has made herself a part of it through confrontation, honesty, and mastery.

Evelyn Rogers's Gothics feature the heroine's masterful approach to the haunted space, as well as a number of other Brontë-influenced elements. Caterina, in *The Grotto* (2002), returns to the cursed Villa, which belonged to her dead husband—whose sadism and misogyny made his death a relief—in order to revive its winery and find a new direction for her empty life. She must uncover the force behind the curse and face her traumatic past with her husband. In *The Ghost of Carnal Cove* (2002), Rogers sets up the cliff-clinging Windward House and the cove near it as haunted by a female waif. Makenna is drawn to these mysteries of the past, and she must understand them in order to finally escape their murderous attempts on her life and those of the ones she loves. Blackthorne Hall beckons enigmatically to Lucinda, in Rogers's *Devil in the Dark* (2001), and she finds herself compelled to explore the violence and pain that surround it. A good deal of Rogers's success with the Gothic romance genre (she wrote three of Dorchester's Gothics) is her masterful use of *Jane Eyre* elements (as well as *Rebecca* ones): a hallmark of a good Gothic. To name just a few: in *The Ghost of Carnal Cove*, her heroine, like Jane, paints and draws figurative pieces that often have dark, disturbed subjects. She is asked by the handsome but too-prim rector to teach the children of the village. Captain Saintjohn is the Rochester who lives in the Thornfield-like Windward House, where the attic contains some mystery. His wife is dead: did he kill her? He has a young son he wants Makenna to teach. Similarly, the "devil" of Evelyn Rogers's *Devil in the Dark* (2001) descends directly from Heathcliff and Rochester, as the author herself makes explicit in her introduction. Rogers's Duke of Ravenswood haunts the Yorkshire countryside on his huge black stallion.

From the Brontës to the present, the heroine steps immediately into the role of detective; she must disclose the way into and out of the labyrinth; she must uncover a past that holds unspeakable horrors. Like a child coming out of trauma, she must find a way to speak, to represent the terrible, to tell its story. Much of the experience of dwelling in this darkness comes from the conventional truism of the romance: discovering that the most important part of the self resides in the other, even an unknowable, terrifying one. Herein lies the essential difference between the Gothic proper and many later manifestations of the Gothic, culminating in the Gothic of today: in facing the Gothic mansion or castle, the heroine begins an exploration that finally leads to the most mysterious unveiling: that of her own interior spaces, her own darknesses, her own lost past.

Makenna in *The Ghost of Carnal Cove* finds not only that she is in love with a man haunted by an accursed and hidden past, which she must unveil and assist him in facing, but also that the ghost of a woman haunts the beach, a ghost only she can witness. She comes to discover that her recently dead mother didn't exist, according to the name and story Makenna was always told. "She had no past; she did not even have a name she could honestly call her own" (239). Left to ask essential questions, such as "Who am I; what do my memories, my past mean?" she realizes the ghost is somehow the access to meaning. In confronting the ghost, she is face to face with herself. "Staring at the ghost was like staring into a mirror. She was looking at herself" (337). While she learns that the ghost is her real mother, who committed suicide in the cove when she was betrayed by her lover and then cast out by a censorious father, we read this as the uncanny moment of the self facing the double, realizing the mystery of the fragmented self, the self in pieces. Catching a momentary view into the unknown interior, the vast unconscious space, she finds the dark house of the mind—the most terrifying sublime space with its perilous chambers, dark dungeons, and dizzying turrets. With this calling forth of the haunted mind, the Gothic romance taps into ideas dear to the Modernists: the impossibility of ever knowing the self. However, Makenna finds a sense of mastery over her own haunted self; she finds a way to claim it and tell its own story, while yet always holding onto the mystery of the unknowable. This is the central attraction of all Gothic literature: revisiting the nescience of the everyday.

Thus the history of the Gothic romance as a genre represents a general movement from the heroine initially mapping exterior puzzles—the floor plan of the castle in order to find a woman bricked into a small declivity; the endless series of labyrinthine hallways in order to escape the castle; the whereabouts of a missing painting that will explain who the master of the house really is—to turning inward, discovering the castle of the self. Emily Jane Cohen creates a related argument about the Gothic proper, which she calls "a manifestation of a desire to create personal histories, in which all of life is experienced as a kind of museum" (883). In contrast, the new Gothic heroine must be able to narrativize not only the cavities and underground rooms of the castle, but she must also be able to find out her own tale and wrest control of her own history. As she approaches the Gothic abode, she faces a reflection of her own secret reaches.

At the same time she asks, what lost worlds does this mansion embody? She also asks, what is hidden inside my own interior?

Vivian Gornick argues that romance is dead today because love is no longer the deeply transformative experience it once was thought to be; we must do for ourselves what love used to be able to do for us.

> Romantic love now seems a yearning to dive down into feeling and come up magically changed; when what is required for the making of a self is the deliberate pursuit of consciousness. (162)

Self-knowledge is more important than love, she argues, and this understanding comes from the examined life—the inward and solitary activities involved in such popular means of excavating the layers of the mind as memoir writing and therapy. Readers of romance could never agree with Gornick, and one could argue that the investigation of the self appears as a theme in much contemporary romance, not just the Gothic type. The Gothic romance manages to provide the idea that transformation on both levels might happen (through love *and* self-revelation), and that these revolutions of the self can be dependant on one another. Of course, the fantasies that draw the reader to the romance novel are just that—fantasies—and Gornick writes of the real mind. Yet on the level of fantasy, it is interesting to note that the desire the new Gothic romance works to satiate involves dwelling in the dark reaches of one's own mind. With the new Gothic, readers have the pleasure (and terror) of seeing the mind as a sublime space, as haunted and endlessly mysterious.

In an age peculiarly engaged in arduously knowing the self, in uncovering and illuminating all the dark demons, the Gothic provides a countermovement. The excessive popularity of the self-help book, the soul-searching memoir, the therapeutic relationship, shows a need in our culture, of the last twenty years or so, to *know* the mind, to shine a bright light on interiority. The Gothic draws on another desire, one that crosses boundaries of historical periodization, gender, and class—that of peering into darkened rooms, stepping into haunted spaces not merely to expose them and banish all their mystery, but to keep the darkness in play, to fall in love with it even. Robert Hume makes a similar argument about the popularity of the Gothic in the late eighteenth century: "Gothic and Romantic writing spring alike from a recognition of the insufficiency of reason or religious faith to explain and make comprehensible the complexities of life" (290).

The heroine investigates the secrets of lost spaces, but she also revels in the very secretness of these places. She has a kind of "negative capability," to use Keats's famous term: "that is when a man is capable of being in uncertainties, Mysteries, doubts, without any irritable reaching after fact & reason . . ." (quoted in Motion 217). The eroticism of the Gothic resides in the pulling back of layers while always knowing that more layers will exist to be pulled back. Cohen argues that the Gothic proper "is part of a search for the sacred" (883), and we can see the same spirit with the contemporary Gothic—a sense of seeing the self as a space spiritual, transcendental, even messianic. To see a space as sacred is to revere its obscurity, to believe in its invisible powers. The Gothic reasserts the sacredness of the sublime interior as a place that can be mastered but also can still retain its darkness.

The new Gothic tends more and more toward holding onto this magic, this mystery, through an increasing use of the supernatural and the fantastic. The eighteenth- and nineteenth-century Gothic (and even most of the Gothic romances of the mid-twentieth century), tended in the other direction: the novel sets up the haunted space only, in the end, to explain the supernatural elements empirically. Radcliffe was notorious for this, for having ghosts and mummies start forth only to later explain how they were merely injured, moaning servants, or life-like waxworks. The Gothic elements of *Jane Eyre*, most of Dickens, and other Victorian canonical works, are merely atmospheric or are eventually, as the plot progresses, explained away. Bertha's imprisonment in Thornfield is a good example. Her haunting of the upper reaches of the mansion and her nighttime appearances throughout the house seem to prove that the house is haunted by an evil spirit. When her story is told, all supernatural elements are dissipated. In probably the most Gothic Victorian novel, *Wuthering Heights*, the house of the title *might* be haunted by Catherine's spirit, but she could also be an illusion from Lockwood's anxiety dreams and Heathcliff's crazed love. In the Gothics of DuMaurier, Holt, and Stewart, malevolent presences become only the work of criminal and violent minds. Yet in a number of the contemporary Gothics, the characters believe in actual haunting, in invisible evil spirits, in mythological creatures, such as the manticore and the werewolf. In Feehan's novel, set vaguely in medieval Italy (unusual for the contemporary Gothic, which is usually set in the Victorian period), the hero's cursed state involves appearing to some as part man, part lion and sometimes transforming fully into a lion (a retelling of "Beauty and the Beast" as well as Angela Carter's "The Tiger's Bride"). In the end the heroine accomplishes a lifting of this curse, but believing in these magical states is never questioned. In Dawn Thompson's *The Ravencliffe Bride* (2005), the hero, akin to a werewolf, becomes a wolf whenever he feels passion or sexual arousal. Here we see the Gothic romance sharing in a general tendency today for a crossing of genres, such as a mixing of romance and fantasy. There is also an increased popularity of "vampire" romances, futuristic ones, and those that fall under the general heading "paranormal" (Dorchester publishes many such cross-genre romances). This tendency further supports the need today to keep open the enchanted world, the world that always maintains its magic.

A second essential tenet of the Gothic that dates back to the nineteenth century and still plays an important role in the new Gothic is the demon lover or villain who becomes the hero. The two distinct entities of the villain and the lover in the Gothic proper (this is particularly clear in Radcliffe) are brilliantly combined by Byron and then the Brontës into the tormented, self-exiled man who lashes out in his pain and whose spiritual homelessness can only be appeased by the heroine. The dangerous lover of many contemporary romances, not just the Gothic, has his roots in the Gothic mode through his link to madness, the doppelganger, Satanism, the Wandering Jew and Cain.[3] But clearly it's the Gothic romance that posits the lover as truly dangerous, as possibly even fully demonic. Rogers's "Devil Duke" of *Devil in the Dark* is surrounded by menacing rumors: "a man's life is in danger when he is around" (13). As she faces the hero of *The Ghost of Carnal Cove*, Makenna wonders, "if he would harm her" (76). In *Obsession* the heroine suspects, for much of the novel, that the hero is Jack the Ripper. Caterina, in *The Grotto*, worries that the hero is the one making attempts on her life; she thinks: "Did the beauty hide the threat of a viper?" (82). And in both *The Ravencliff Bride* and the *Lair of the Lion*, the hero cannot control his transformation into a wild and possibly savage creature that might unwontedly kill the heroine. It is in this very danger that the eroticism of these heroes resides: their attraction comes from a hint of sadism, of physical power, of their uncontrollable passion that might turn into a deathly rage.

Cynthia Griffin Wolff describes the romance reader's attraction to the dangerous lover as part of what she calls the devil/priest conflict, a fairly common phenomenon in female sexuality, named after the virgin/whore thought to beset men. The fantasy the Gothic plays with is not so much that of rape as we often see in the "erotic historical" (Thurston's term), but rather that of murder. Their love and their sexual consummation might cause her death. The linkage of love and death stretches back to *Romeo and Juliet*, to the *liebestod* of the Germans, to the orgasm as the *petit mort* of the French. To die for love, to save the other through death of the self—these are all concepts familiar to the reader of the Gothic romance. Yet at some point around the beginning of the nineteenth century, when Romanticism began to shift into Victorianism, self-sacrificing impulses became gendered, became female-coded. The general societal understanding of womanhood involved their passive role in romantic and sexual relations. Influenced strongly by Evangelicalism, the ideal model of the middle-class woman was as a wife and mother who sacrificed herself for her husband and children. After the 1960s and 70s feminist revolution, many

---

[3] The history of the Byronic hero as romantic lover has been traced by many; see especially Modleski, Thurston, and David Richter. See also my *The Dangerous Lover: Gothic Villains, Byronism, and the Nineteenth-Century Seduction Narrative*.

feminist theorists pointed, disapprovingly, to the masochistic qualities of the heroine's self-renunciation in the dangerous lover romance; Modleski called this "the desire to obliterate the consciousness of the self as a physical presence" (37). Many women who enjoy dangerous lover romances of varying types have experienced embarrassment in light of the feminist view of annihilation fantasies as disempowering; they worry others might feel that they are participating in a fantasy that supports violence against women (both Radway and Thurston discuss romance readers' embarrassment with their romance reading habits).

The willingness of women to embrace death fantasies in this resurgence of the Gothic today comes from two impulses. The first involves an important shift in the character of the heroine. The protagonist of the new Gothic has a good deal of agency, much more than the narrator of *Rebecca*, of many of Stewart's and Holt's Gothics, of the old-fashioned Harlequin that Modleski read and wrote about. Rather than young, inexperienced virgins, most of the heroines of the new Gothic are in their late twenties, early thirties. They have had at least one sexual relationship with a man and they have dark and complicated pasts of their own. Rogers is especially good at creating heroines who are themselves dangerous lovers. Makenna in *The Ghost of Carnal Cove* has just been jilted by her lover and fiancé, and she arrives at the cove in a somewhat heartbroken state, with a misanthropic desire to be utterly solitary and paint. When she finds out that her mother's identity is a mystery to her, she takes on the Byronic quality of having a secret wound, which she keeps hidden from the hero. She is the one who is haunted, who has a tormented interior, and the hero desires to plumb her secret reaches, to save her from herself, to redeem her back into a life among people. Hence the moments of sexual danger become gender neutral: both the hero and heroine desire a self-immolation in love. "She stood to face him, wondering if he would harm her; and wondering, too, though the possibility lay beyond all reason, if she had the power to harm him" (76). We find ourselves back in the time of the German and English Romantics when the artist and the man of true feeling were one who could swoon into self-dissolution.[4]

The dangerous lover's reemergence as a popular force comes in a post-feminist climate. Post-feminism, while recognizing the advances of the feminists that have come before it, loosens some of the tight holds of early feminism and is willing to re-appropriate certain paradigms that were earlier deemed dangerous to feminism. Willing to live in the present and to find a place within patriarchy, post-feminism can be likened to the post-Marxism of

---

[4] We see such masochistic men especially in the poetry of Shelley and Keats, as well as much of Goethe's writings. Mario Praz is an especially good source for this movement. He also has a chapter on the eighteenth and nineteenth-century *femme fatale*.

Gilles Deleuze and Felix Guattari: a need to find pleasures and freedom with what exists now. Desiring the dangerous lover openly and without remorse and humiliation belongs to a post-feminist historical moment, one where women are more willing to admit to a whole range of sexual desires (allied to such theorists as Judith Butler, one of post-feminism's first arguments was to create both a hetero- and homo-sex positive environment for pornography).

The Gothic romance follows transgressive impulses as the Gothic always has. The transgressions we are seeing today are enmeshed in this particular historical moment and expand the boundaries of our understanding of the mind and of female sexuality. They rebel against excessive desires to know and against narrow definitions of women's eroticism. The Gothic yearns for the mystery of the self, for erotic darkness, but finally the deepest mystery the Gothic romance keeps alive is still that of all romance: the transformative experience of love.

Works Cited

Brown, Marshall. *The Gothic Text*. Stanford, CA: Stanford UP, 2005.

Carter, Angela. *The Bloody Chamber*. London: Penguin, 1979.

Castle, Terry. *The Female Thermometer: Eighteenth-Century Culture and the Invention of the Uncanny*. New York: Oxford University Press, 1995.

Cohen, Emily Jane. "Museums of the Mind: The Gothic and the Art of Memory." *ELH* 62.4 (1995): 883-905.

Feehan, Christine. *Lair of the Lion*. New York: Dorchester, 2002.

Gothic Romance Writers Incorporated. Romance Writers of America: GothRom. 16 October 2005. www.gothrom.org.

Hume, Robert. "Gothic versus Romantic: A Revaluation of the Gothic Novel." *PMLA* 84.2 (1969): 282-290.

Lutz, Deborah. *The Dangerous Lover: Gothic Villains, Byronism, and the Nineteenth-Century Seduction Narrative*. Columbus, OH: Ohio State UP, 2006.

Modleski, Tania. *Loving with a Vengeance: Mass-Produced Fantasies for Women*. New York: Routledge, 1994.

Motion, Andrew. *Keats*. London: Faber and Faber, 1997.

Mussell, Kay, and Johanna Tunon, eds. *North American Romance Writers*. London: Scarecrow, 1999.

Neri, Penelope. *Obsession*. New York: Dorchester, 2003.

Praz, Mario. *The Romantic Agony*. New York: Meridian, 1956.

Radcliffe, Ann. *The Mysteries of Udolpho*. 1794. New York: Penguin, 2001.

Radway, Janice. *Reading the Romance: Women, Patriarchy, and Popular Literature*. Chapel Hill: U of North Carolina P, 1991.

Regis, Pamela. *A Natural History of the Romance Novel*. Philadelphia: U of Pennsylvania P, 2003.

Richter, David. *The Progress of Romance*: *Literary Historiography and the Gothic Novel*. Columbus, OH: Ohio State UP, 1996.

Rogers, Evelyn. *Devil in the Dark*. New York: Dorchester, 2001.

———.*The Ghost of Carnal Cove*. New York: Dorchester, 2002.

———.*The Grotto*. New York: Dorchester, 2002.

Stewart, Mary. *Touch Not the Cat*. New York: William Morrow, 1976.

Thompson, Dawn. *The Ravencliff Bride*. New York: Dorchester, 2005.

Thurston, Carol. *The Romance Revolution: Erotic Novels for Women and the Quest for a New Sexual Identity*. Chicago: U of Chicago P, 1987.

Wein, Toni. *British Identities, Heroic Nationalisms, and the Gothic Novel, 1764-1824*. London: Palgrave, 2002.

Whitney, Phyllis. *Thunder Heights*. New York: Ace Star, 1960.

Wolff, Cynthia Griffin. "The Radcliffean Gothic Model: A Form for Feminine Sexuality." *Modern Language Studies*. 9.3 (1979): 98-113.

Deborah Lutz

Deborah Lutz is an Assistant Professor at Long Island University. She has written widely on Victorian sexuality and eroticism, and her book—*The Dangerous Lover: Gothic Villains, Byronism, and the Nineteenth-Century Seduction Narrative*—traces a literary history of the lover whose eroticism comes from his remorseful and rebellious exile, from his tormented and secret interiority. She is currently working on a book about Victorian sexual radicalism.

CHAPTER SEVEN

HOPE, FAITH AD TOUGHNESS: AN ANALYSIS OF THE CHRISTIAN HERO

REBECCA BARRETT-FOX

What is the ideal man—the man you wish you were or the man you wished you had married? Is he strong? Handsome? Capable? Nurturing? Intelligent? Self-sufficient? Self-sacrificing? Tender? Gentle? Great with children? Passionate? Righteous? Moral? Self-made?

A list of impressive demands, indeed! Where can such a man be found? Based on my research on conservative, born-again, evangelical Protestantism, the answer, my friends, is in one place alone: the Bible.

But that doesn't mean that the answers can be easily found, which is why an entire industry devoted to defining, clarifying, protecting, nurturing, defending, promoting, and teaching biblical masculinity has erupted among Christians in the United States. As seen in cultural phenomena from conferences to self-help books, from peer support groups to professional counseling programs, from Christian romance novels to popular films, the question of what a godly man is—and how his beset masculinity can survive in today's world—is a central concern of Christians.

Though Promise Keepers, an all-men organization aimed at, among other things, what they define as the proper place of the male in the family and the church (that is, at the head), began only 14 years ago, concern with the lack of male "headship" is an ancient issue—at least to judge from the concerns that the Apostle Paul was hearing from the churches he visited. Since the 1600s, female worshippers have outnumbered male worshippers in American churches—and, after all, there weren't many churches in the U.S. before the 1600s. The "feminization" of the church has been a threat to male dominance in Christian church structure and theology for a long time, but the 1970s marked, according to many contemporary Christian writers, a particularly troubling time. Seeing themselves and the mythical American way of life, which involved nuclear families in which the mother served the family by bearing and rearing children and the father served by earning money, as threatened by cultural changes such as no-fault divorce, legalized abortion, and feminism, fundamentalists led a cultural backlash. Sex was everywhere, from innuendo in television programs such as *Three's Company*, now a regular in the Nick at Nite line up on children's cable network Nickelodeon, to the sex education classroom in public schools. In language that is echoed by those militating against gay marriage today, the family was under attack by the apparently evil, secular forces of feminism and secular humanism and, in a few years, multiculturalism. Tim LaHaye, now perhaps best known for co-authoring the *Left Behind* series, even blames increasing reports of erectile dysfunction on feminism, writing in 1985:

> Our world is far more insecure than it was twenty to thirty years ago. Men are less sure of themselves in their traditional role as head of the household. This self-doubt has led several writers to analyze the phenomenon of the 'feminized male.' With the women's liberation movement still generating sex-role confusion, we may expect even more sexual dysfunction among men in the years ahead. (188)

More than ten years later, Ed Young echoes this complaint when he writes in *Expression of Love: A Plan for Pure Relationship Intimacy* that frustration with sexual relationships is "at least partly due to our culture's relentless blurring of the lines between true masculinity and true femininity" (73).

In this context, writers such as Marabel Morgan, author of *The Total Woman* and coordinator of hundreds of workshops devoted to maintaining "traditional" households in the face of the rising employment of women, and Dr. James Dobson, founder of Focus on the Family Ministries, fought back. Their strategy was not to scream for a return to traditional values (though certainly some took this more aggressive stance) but to employ proven marketing strategies and appeal to a mass market through popular culture in order to bring the mainstream toward values of the increasingly politically savvy Christian Right.

Railing against "the increasing prevalence and acceptance of hermeneutical oddities devised to reinterpret apparently plain meanings of Biblical texts," the Council on Biblical Manhood and Womanhood in 1988 released the Danvers Statement, which outlined their concerns about "the widespread uncertainty and confusion in our culture regarding the complementary differences between masculinity and femininity" (writers of the Danvers Statement do not consider the idea that masculinity and femininity are anything except biologically assigned according to one's genitalia) (para. 1). The group affirms ten principles, including the equality of men and women before God and distinctions between manhood and womanhood, distinctions that include male leadership at home and in church and female "willing, joyful submission" to this leadership. When these roles are questioned, only disorder results, including, for men, "a worldly love of power or an abdication of spiritual responsibility" and for women, resistance to "limitations on their roles." This passage from the Danvers Statement articulates two concerns: first, a concern that men will abandon their leadership role and, second, a concern that women will take up this leadership role. In other words, the church and the family (the two institutions that, for these Christians, are the foundation of Western Civilization and thus every good thing in the world) will fall into the control of women.

When stated this baldly, the Danvers Statement's thesis is a bit difficult to accept, much less enforce, even to Christians, especially considering the increasing number of women attending theological schools and working as pastors and the even larger number of single mothers who identify as Christians. The good news for the Council on Biblical Manhood and Womanhood is that their message is being communicated in a more palatable manner through popular culture, including two areas under discussion in this paper: paramilitary Christian romances aimed at men and Christian romance novels aimed at women.

The Christian romance novel, a bustling subgenre published by both secular and religious presses, is aimed at women. Whether in shorter serial novels or longer trade editions, the books tell the same story over and over again: a man and a woman, one usually a Christian and one not, conflict over some issue before realizing that their mutual love of God draws them into a monogamous, heterosexual, reproductive marital relationship. Since these books are generic fiction, they abide by relatively strict rules regarding character development, plot, and writing style. Based on my analysis of hundreds of these books as well as on feedback regarding the books from hundreds of readers and writers of the genre, I have summarized a few notable patterns that illuminate what a godly man is. Not surprisingly, these qualities are echoed in paramilitary Christian romances.

While the main concern of Christian romance novels is the development of a love relationship between a male and female character, the main concern of paramilitary Christian romances is the development of male leadership of home, community, and country. "Paramilitary" because they often take on the rhetoric of a hero physically battling and suffering in the protection of those in his realm of responsibility, these tales romanticize leadership and death in an appeal to what their creators see as an intrinsic element of masculinity—the need to defend one's clan. On film, they include Mel Gibson's recent *The Passion*, in which Jesus is depicted as a suffering servant (but not one who suffers as women suffer, which is to say that he suffers with strength, not with submission). In literature, they include the best-selling *Left Behind* series, read by both men and women but focusing mainly on the exploits of two men—

Rayford Steele, a pilot, and Buck Williams, a journalist—as they and other members of the Tribulation Force fight against the anti-Christ when they discover that they have been "left behind" after the Rapture. Like romance novels aimed at women, these paramilitary Christian romances aimed at men firmly articulate a belief in God-ordained, inviolate masculinity.

Perhaps Promise Keepers best summarizes what this masculine model is in the "Seven Promises" that form the core of their beliefs. As the name says, Promise Keepers is aimed at renewing male commitment to the values the group holds, including fraternity and the building of "strong marriages and families through love, protection and biblical values"—the biblical values that the Danvers Statement lists. Currently, the group is reaching its mission through the implementation of "The Platoon Challenge," a plan that uses military jargon to organize men's groups. Mixing military rhetoric with biblical language, romantic love, and conservative politics, the group defines masculinity in a way that appeals to both men and women.

This wide appeal is necessary in order to garner support for what might otherwise be seen as the same old male dominance. Christian romance novels, for example, are read by women who seek a wider definition of love than secular romances, with their focus on sexual compatibility, offer. Says 'Nessa, who quit reading secular romances because of the explicit sexuality, "I ask you, does sex make romance? No, it doesn't" (e-mail to the author; name of the writer has been changed). Focus on sexual intercourse draws attention away from what 'Nessa and others see as the more valuable and enjoyable parts of love: romance, wooing, talking, and cuddling. Not surprisingly, Christian romance novels depict such scenes frequently. In this way, Christian romance novels provide sensuality without explicit sexuality, offering a traditionally "female" version of romance that many women find comforting and appealing. The result is "guilt-free reading," says Joanne Heim, an assistant editor at NavPress (Bearden 16).

That women enjoy books that promote traditionally female variations of love—that is, romance, snuggling, care-taking, and verbal exchanges—is not surprising. What might be more of a surprise is that the men in the novels, in addition to not being the typical sexual predators of steamy romances, are caretakers. More often than not, they are devoted Christians, caring fathers, workers in the helping professions. They are tender musicians, thoughtful listeners, sensitive, wounded souls. They pray—and readers hear their prayers in internal monologues. They care about their relationships with God and with women. In *Family for Keeps* by Margaret Daley, the hero, a former football star healing from the death of his wife, forms a relationship with Tess, a pediatric nurse. As is typical in these novels, the hero, not the heroine, is the emotionally mature character. In one scene, Mac recalls his first encounter with Tess, in which she was dressed like a clown to amuse the sick children in her ward. The plight of one young cancer victim had moved her to tears, and Mac discovered her crying.

> He remembered the helplessness he'd felt when he'd seen Tess crying in the waiting room, her face streaked black with the evidence of her tears. A strong urge to comfort had drawn him into the room before he could stop himself. Her vulnerability had moved him, causing him to forget his own losses.
>
> He wanted to know what had put that look in her eyes that declared she'd seen more than her share of pain and suffering. He wanted to get to know her. He wanted to ease her burden.... (210)

Mac, like secular heroes, is tough—an athlete, strong and capable. At the same time, he is a wounded soul, searching for answers about the death of his wife and his father. He is a tender father himself to his two children. He is a caring emotional rock, a leader in the relationship with Tess. He is sympathetic, earnest, vulnerable—but his vulnerability is not grounded in weakness but in his faith in God. It is his love for Tess, a patient, pure, romantic, nonsexual love that leads her to renewed faith, faith not just in the power of love but in God.

Women readers enjoy depictions of men like Mac—and nearly all the heroes in these books are like Mac—because they posit a new hero, one who retains all the rugged individualism, toughness, and power of secular heroes but combines this traditional masculinity with gentleness, patience, and attention to female needs, from snuggling to child-rearing. The result of this kind of love is a blooming of the heroine, a movement from mistrust, low self-esteem, and disbelief in God to security, confidence, and faith. In this way, the books put responsibility for the success of a relationship on the hero and contribute to the heroine's dependency upon the hero for her identity. Women are especially vulnerable to this kind of loss of self, perhaps because, as Jan Cohn points out in her Marxist readings of romance novels in *Romance and the Erotics of Property: Mass-Market Fiction for Women*, women have traditionally had to bargain their love for security. Colette Dowling, in *The Cinderella Complex: Women's Hidden Fear of Independence*, posits that women feel this way because they . . .

> are taught that they have an out—that someday, in some way, they are going to be saved. That's the fairy tale, the life message we have introjected as if with mother's milk. We may venture out on our own for a while. We may go away to school, work, travel; we may even make good money, but underneath it all there is a *finite* quality to our feelings about independence. Only hang on long enough, the childhood saying goes, and someday someone will come along to rescue you from the anxiety of authentic living. (4)

Christian romance novels, with the guarantee of a happy marriage, contribute to this "finite quality to our feelings." The books thus provide a model for relationships in which women's worth is located in men and men, as leaders, bear a heavy responsibility.

The desire for this responsibility is intrinsic for the hero in Christian romances. In paramilitary Christian romances aimed at men, the struggle to accept responsibility is a bit more difficult. Even Christ, after all, asked that the cup of suffering pass him by. But real men accept their leadership role, which means that they are to act like the heroes in Christian romance novels. Focus on the Family, Promise Keepers, and other Christian ministries encourage men to maintain traditional gender roles while being open, sympathetic, and emotionally responsive. They are to be more than breadwinners, though they are to be this too. They are to be coaches, teachers, lovers, leaders.

The Christian hero is seductive. He loves you tenderly, monogamously, thoroughly, patiently, passionately, purely, and with attention to your needs. He raises his own children, does his own laundry, gives you foot massages, meets your needs before you even articulate them. He brings home the bacon, fries it, and serves it to you in bed. He is, as Stu Weber, a leader of the Promise Keepers movement, says in the title of his best-seller, a "tender warrior." While one might be able to read Christ as this model of masculinity, does it exist anywhere else?

No, argue many Christian writers. Women are naturally more romantic than men, goes one common argument, but they must live with men, so they force themselves to be less romantic, to lower their own expectations. For these women, argue Tim and Beverly LaHaye in their best-selling marriage advice book, *The Act of Marriage*, "it seems better to suppress that desire [for romance] than to become disappointed over the lack of romanticism in their husbands" (41). While the LaHayes encourage husbands to be more romantic in order to meet their wives' desires, other Christians suggest that a better plan is to discourage romantic feelings in women. Patrick Hurd, for example, pastor of a fundamentalist Baptist church, says that youth in his congregation "are prohibited from boy/girlfriend speculation or gossip even to the extent of Christian romance novels or other various movies and stories," for "romance novels only serve to waste time and stir the hearts of young girls" (para. 28). To "stir the hearts" means to create inappropriate or unreasonable desires—not only sexual desires (since, after all, Christian romance novels do not contain sexually explicit or even suggestive material), but desires for romance, desires for men to be a certain way. "These books," writes Crystal Rae Nelson, a married Christian woman who read many of the novels prior to her marriage, "encouraged me to build up an expectation of love" that was inappropriate (para. 3). This caused her considerable heartache, for it meant that her expectations were different than the reality God had planned for her, she realized later. That striving for an unrealistic goal creates unhappiness in a marriage is the major complaint that Christians have about Christian romance novels. Says one woman regretfully:

> I quit reading all Christian romances when I noticed my discontent with my husband was increasing. He was nothing like the men in romance novels, and the harder I tried to make him 'perfect' the more miserable we both became. (Morris para. 7)

According to Nelson, women believe that they are "benefiting from absorbing these idealistic examples of what 'falling in love' should be like," but, instead, she now believes she was only creating a gap between what she wanted and what she had (Nelson para. 1).

This gap, says Christian online commentator Grantley Morris, is similar to the one that pornography creates for men. Pornography, he says, fosters in men desires that cannot be fulfilled by women.

> Both erotica [a term that Morris uses interchangeably with "pornography," or "the visual side of sex," as he defines the term] and romantic fiction create images of, and a longing for, things that no normal partner could ever match, with the result that both sexes end up wishing their partners were more like those portrayed on the screen. (para. 4)

The dissatisfaction increases when partners are unable to or refuse to live up to these new expectations. Just as "women feel uncomfortably about such things as giving their partner a private strip show," so do "men typically feel uncomfortable about romance," says Morris (para. 3). In fact, according to Morris, women should realize that men feel "effeminate" when they are romantic; Morris reminds women that "[e]xcept in romantic fiction, what lights *your* fire, probably puts *his* fire out" (para. 12, notes and bold in original). Ultimately, men's failure to be "comfortable about romance" leads women to become "dissatisfied with their lives because their husbands don't measure up to the hero, and the romance isn't there as it is in the story," says an anonymous woman who responded with agreement to Morris's article (para. 10).

Romance "as it is in the story" is absent from real-life relationships not only because men are naturally unromantic but also because romance requires much effort—more than is available for most men—goes the common wisdom. As a romance-reading friend of Beliefnet writer Deborah Belonick said:

> They are not going to light candles and carry you up the stairs. Today's man not only holds a job but also has child-rearing and household responsibilities, like the woman. (para. 6)

Real-life men do not have time or energy to perform as well as fictional men. Simply, they do not know the discourse. "Novelists and script writers devote enormous effort to getting the man saying the perfect thing in just the right romantic setting," Morris observes. He humorously notes:

> They are experts in knowing what appeals to women....In real life situations not even the writers themselves could equal the charm of their fictional characters. Normal conversation, for instance, would not allow them enough time to get their lines right. (para. 4)

Here Morris agrees with Linda Barlow, a secular romance writer, who suggests that the hero is "*not* the feminine ideal of what a man should be. The romantic hero, in fact, is not a man at all" (49, italics in original). This gender confusion worries many Christians. "The more longings [for romance] are fanned by romantic fiction," warns Morris, "the more women end up virtually craving women in men's bodies" (para. 11). Morris links this to lesbianism, for what romance novels encourage women to want is the kind of love that women give—in other words, men who love women as women might love women (para. 10).

Women's experiences as the object of "woman-love"—that is, what Morris calls "romance"—has transforming potential for women and for men, and, I believe, this is the good news of the Christian romance novel experience for women and the paramilitary Christian romance experience for men. These cultural artifacts provide models of men that may currently be unrealistic, as Morris says. Perhaps few men do act as nurturing, caring, and concerned as men do in the novels or are supposed to according to the self-help books, seminars, and masculinity ministries. Christian romance novels, though, provide opportunities for men to change. Indeed, transformation is central to the novels, for the characters must move from self-centered people to God-centered people, and out of this change comes love. The change begins in fear—in, to use Christian discourse, recognizing that one is a sinner and needs to change. Heroines and readers are "boldly lifting the veil on the phallus," says secular scholar Tania Modleski, "and are finding mortal men standing behind it, somewhat sheepish, perhaps, at having been exposed, but maybe a little relieved as well" (26). The novels can be liberating for men, who are freed, at least within texts, to be emotional, nurturing, and loving.

"The transformative promise holds out possibilities of change, progress, and escape," write Jackie Stacey and Lynne Pearce (18). The opportunity for heroes to change—in fact, the generic requirement that they do—may influence how women see men in real life. "Perhaps women are less likely to settle for so little from men and are increasingly demanding that they change their emotional behaviour accordingly," suggest Stacey and Pearce (36). Rather than comparing real-life lovers to fictional lovers and then criticizing real-life lovers for their failures to "measure up" to heroes, readers might instead use the novels to encourage their husbands to be more like heroes, to be more emotionally considerate and sensitive. This can enrich a romantic relationship, provide a safe environment for a man to experience himself as a true lover (that is, one who loves as a woman wants to be loved), and allow women to be loved in new ways. One woman, responding with agreement to Morris's article, criticizes the novels for making women selfish because "[t]hrough these fantasies [women] focus on how everyone should be treating them but never see how they are treating others" (para. 8). This "focus on how everyone should be treating them" does not necessitate insensitivity to others, though, and, in fact, such focus on their desires allows women to ask for new relationships with their romantic partners, relationships that can be transforming for men.

According to the formula of the Christian romance novel and the paramilitary Christian romance, a formula built into the Danvers Statement, a happy relationship depends upon the man taking responsibility for the happiness of the woman. While this means, for women, neck massages and foreplay and thus opens new forms of emotional expression for men, the tradeoff is continued subservience to male "headship" within the relationship. Whether this is a step forward in the sense that at least women and men are increasing some of their expectations for men or a step back in the sense that it creates a happy complacency about female submission perhaps depends upon the position one is in to begin: husband or wife. Whether one ends up a well-cared-for wife under strong male leadership or a husband with a wider emotional range and more developed empathetic capabilities (still ordering his household under his authority), at least men and women move away from patterns that rob women both of authority in the home and emotional support from their spouses and toward a model that places emotional responsibility at least partly on men, who can only benefit from such a shift in thinking about marriage.

Works Cited

Barlow, Linda.   "The Androgynous Writer: Another Point of View." *Dangerous Men and Adventurous Women: Romance Writers on the Appeal of the Romance*.   Ed. Jayne Ann Krentz.   Philadelphia: U Pennsylvania P, 1992.   45-52.

Bearden, Michelle. "When Romance Gets Religion." *Publisher's Weekly* 242 (1995): 57.

Belonick, Deborah. "The Bold and the Biblical: What Do Some Romance Novels Have in Common with Scripture? Both Celebrate Female Wisdom." n.d. *Beliefnet*. 15 February 2002. <http://www.beliefnet.com/story_3381.html>.

Daley, Margaret. *Family for Keeps*. New York: Steeple Hill, 2002.

The Council on Biblical Manhood and Womanhood. 2004. "The Danvers Statement." 15 March 2004. *The Council on Biblical Manhood and Womanhood*. <http://www.cbmw.org/about/danvers.php>.

Dowling, Colette. *The Cinderella Complex: Women's Hidden Fear of Independence*. New York: Pocket Books, 1981.

Hurd, Patrick. "The War Over Sexual Purity." 1998. *Wisdom's Gate*. 24 February 2002. <http://www.homeschooldigest.com/PH.htm>.

LaHaye, Tim and Beverly. *The Act of Marriage: The Beauty of Sexual* Love. Grand Rapids, MI.: Zondervan, 1976.

LeHaye, Tim. *Sex Education IS for the Family*. Grand Rapids, MI.: Zondervan, 1985.

Modleski, Tania. "My Life as a Romance Reader." *Paradoxa: Studies in World Literary Genres* 3. 1997: 15-28.

Morris, Grantley. "Romantic Fiction and Christians: The Hidden Enemy: Surprising Insights: Romantic Fiction: The Female Equivalent of Porn?" n.d. *Net-burst.net*. 15 February 2002. <http://net-burst.net/help/fiction.htm>.

Nelson, Crystal Rae. "A Warning Against Christian Romance Novels: The Dangers of Romanticism." N.d. *Young Women Stepping Heavenward*. 15 February 2002. <http://www.goodmorals.org/crystal.htm>.

'Nessa. E-mail interview. 4 February 2004.

Promise Keepers. "Seven Promises." 2003. *Promise Keepers*. 10 March 2004. <http://www.promisekeepers.org/faqs/core/faqssore24.htm>.

Stacey, Jackie and Lynne Pearce. "The Heart of the Matter: Feminists Revisit Romance." *Romance Revisited*. Eds. Lynne Pearce and Jackie Stacey. New York: New York U P, 1995. 11-45.

Weber, Stu. *Tender Warrior: God's Intention for a Man*. Sisters, OR: Multnomah, 1999.

Young, Ed. *Expression of Love: A Plan for Pure Relationship Intimacy*. Sisters, OR: Multnomah, 1997.

Rebecca Barrett-Fox

Rebecca Barrett-Fox is pursuing a doctoral degree in American Studies at the University of Kansas, where she is focusing on contemporary conservative Protestants and issues of family life, reproduction, and sexuality.

CHAPTER EIGHT

HOW DARE A BLACK WOMAN
MAKE LOVE TO A WHITE MAN!
BLACK WOMEN ROMANCE NOVELISTS
AND THE TABOO OF INTERRACIAL DESIRE

GUY MARK FOSTER

> He cupped my face and his eyes seemed to plead with mine. "Are you
> willing to give us a try, then?"
> I thought for only a second, then said, "Yes."
> He breathed a sigh of relief. "I didn't know if you were going to say
> yes or no."
> "Actually, I think I knew the answer to that question a long time ago."
> His expression was tender, as he said, "I love you so much."
> "I love you, too. I really do," I returned as he bent his head and kissed
> me again and I wrapped my arms around his neck without a second thought.
> I was deeply happy and deeply in love and despite all of my
> reservations before, I no longer felt as if a line had been crossed. The difference
> in our color was not an issue to me and at that moment I didn't think or care
> about the consequences that might come our way. I just wanted to be with him.
> And that's all that mattered. (Carter 340)

The above passage serves as the closing lines to Lizzette Carter's recently
published interracial romance, *The Color Line* (2005), in which the novel's
black female protagonist is depicted in the final stages of an emotionally
draining journey. After surviving a series of stiff oppositions to her effort to
admit to family, friends, and co-workers alike, but also to herself, that the man
she has fallen in love with is white instead of African American, this woman is
finally able to be at peace with her decision. But such peace is not easy to come
by. For many contemporary heterosexual black women, white men continue to
be, in terms of the psyche, virtually indistinguishable from white males in the

historical past. The latter were men who imposed themselves on black women's bodies with impunity, and who made every attempt to strip these women of their dignity and self-worth through rape and other forms of physical and psychological abuse. For some scholars, contemporary black women's psychological anxieties about the role this horrific past continues to play in the present is the real reason why couple relationships and marriages between black women and white men remain outnumbered two to one by those between black men and white women, and not because white men are failing to choose black women as lovers and wives (see hooks 69; Dalmage 62). This anxiety is captured vividly by one contemporary black woman who, faced with the prospect of dating just such a man, wonders aloud: "Am I the strong, comely wench with the good teeth that the slave master looked for in a black woman back then? Am I the hot Sally that turns him on?" (Romano 237). Because Americans as a group have never properly confronted this history, nor adequately resolved the devastating political and economic disparities that history left in its wake—i.e., chronic structural inequality between blacks and whites, disproportionate life expectancy rates for the two groups, the cultural devaluation of blackness in general, and black womanhood in particular, racially gendered stereotypes, and the list goes on—white men continue to present specific challenges for heterosexual black women to overcome if they are ever to view these men as potential object-choices rather than oppressors.

Although we can discern traces of a similar psychological struggle having been waged in the mind of the narrator in the above passage, the fact that the novel ends with this woman and her lover finally reunited after being estranged for much of the book suggests that she has somehow resolved many of these challenges—at least for the time being. What the narrator's concluding affirmation suggests (an affirmation that was a long time in coming in the narrative) is that she did not always feel as she now does, neither about this relationship, nor about this man in particular. Quite the opposite, in fact. The narrator's resistance to taking a white man as her lover and confidant—to transgressing the imaginary "line," as she puts it, between the socially constructed racial categories of "black" and "white"—was evident from the first pages of the novel, a plot feature that is endlessly repeated in numerous contemporary interracial romances. Conceptually, this recurring feature, or trope, of these texts recalls a similar "line" of sexual transgression, one which, in Western societies, separates such culturally normative desires like heterosexuality from its stigmatized counterpart, homosexuality; curiously, most theorists have tended only to identify and map the latter imaginary "line" *as* sexuality per se, but not the former—a point to which I will return later. This essay suggests that such narrative emplotments, symbolized by transgressions of the color line, as well as their enormously satisfying endings, are emblematic of such texts, which have become a growing sub-genre within the romance market. A brief sampling of these texts, in addition to Carter's *The Color Line,* includes: Dyanne Davis's *The Color of Trouble* (2003), Margaret Johnson-Hodge's *The Real Deal* (1998), two by Sandra Kitt: *The Color of Love* (1995) and *Close Encounters* (2000), and Monica White's *Shades of Desire* (1996). In most of these novels, just as in the above excerpt, the emotional and psychic release the protagonists enjoy by the narrative's final page leaves readers with the distinct impression that something dramatic has changed in our society to bring about such a complete reversal of affect for such women. But what exactly?

If we take what Peter Brooks has said about plot to be true, namely, that "[p]lots are not simply organizing structures [but] also intentional structures, goal-oriented and forward-moving" (12), we might say then that the plot of the interracial romance novel *purposely* reproduces and repeats within its narrative structure some of the same anxieties and fears that are often associated with black-white intimacy among contemporary blacks and whites who exist in the world *outside* the text. This is an anxiety that these men and women have inherited as a result of the horrors of the past, and which some believe continue to hinder any productive resolution of those past events in the present. What is useful to note, however, is that interracial romances reproduce this anxiety and fear only to short-circuit it by the novel's final page, so that ultimately the black female protagonist and her white male companion get to enjoy having their formerly tabooed union embraced by some of the very same individuals who would have been happy to see that relationship aborted. In the end, the types of "narrational strategies" to which I am alluding, "serve to cast doubt upon the presumed 'naturalness' of a conceptual model" of heterosexual desire that would insist on viewing race and sexuality through rigidly segregated frameworks—one made legible to us by the centrality of the color line (qtd in Abelove 604). These narrational strategies therefore call into question common-sense assumptions about the strict oppositions that "race" and "sexuality" are supposed to encompass: in this case, I suggest, such segregation results in black same-race heterosexuality and homosexuality, on one side of the color line, and white same-race heterosexuality and homosexuality, on the other. This *analytical* color line, one which separates race, gender, and sexuality into what is putatively regarded as "equal" halves, remains a central problem of much of contemporary theoretical discourse. It is one that often renders illegible the complex sexualities of people of color in general and those of black women in particular. In many of these analytical accounts, the three categories are understood as separate rather than categories that are themselves mediated by all the others to produce the conditions of legibility. For example, little of this work thus far has managed to tell us, in any consistent way, just how, to use Allan Bérubé's formulation, gender is "lived through" race and sexuality, or

how sexuality is itself "lived through" race and gender, and therefore
experienced differently for different subjects at different times and places (243).
This takes us to black women writers, their readers, and the romance genre.

Black Women Readers and the Romance Genre

According to industry analysis, the romance fiction market enjoyed annual
sales of $1.41 billion worldwide at the end of the last millennium. Of this total,
approximately 10 to 30 percent of these sales were attributed to African
American consumers, many of whom, but not all, appeared to buy primarily
from the growing niche market of romance imprints that specialize in black-on-
black heterosexual coupling (see Dyer C1; Osborne 61). These figures suggest
that black women have been readers of popular romances since the genre first
emerged with the appearance of Harlequin in the late 1940s. Unfortunately, the
storylines that Harlequin generated at the time did not include African
Americans or any other people of color as protagonists, only whites. It would
not be until a black female journalist published the first ever black-themed
romance novel, *Entwined Destinies,* under the pseudonym of Rosalind Welles in
1980, that heterosexual black women would be able, to invoke the specialized
language of Freud's developmental theory of human sexuality, to bring their
identificatory and desiring identities into the type of "same-race, different
gender" alignment that was culturally sanctioned as normative at that time by
both blacks and whites (see Collins 247-278).

Because of this dearth of published romantic fiction with black heroines
prior to the 1980s, black women who chose to read romances often had to
engage in Herculean feats of imagination just to find pleasure in them. For a
politically engaged black reader (that is, someone who came of age imbibing the
nationalist rhetoric that proclaimed "black is beautiful" along with her mother's
breast milk), this meant having to find white men sexually desirable by one of
several means: either by (1) transforming themselves, at the level of fantasy,
into white women, in which case they could pine over and lust after white men
safely within the confines of a "proper" same-race, different-gender
identification; (2) transforming both the novel's hero and heroine into blacks,
and therefore maintaining the integrity of their own raced identification; or (3)
such readers could bracket out race altogether and consume the narratives as if
racial identification, whether black, white, or other, and the myriad cultural
issues that routinely circulate around those identifications, were not a factor in
the lovers', or in the reader's, subjective experience of the text. Whichever
strategy these readers decided upon, they could not desire white men *as* black
women, since doing so was socially proscribed both in the white community
and, increasingly through the 1950s and 60s, in the black community as well.

Engaging in such covert pleasure was not always without a corresponding price, however. Some women who eagerly consumed these works during an era when it was not taboo to identify and desire cross-racially would experience a jarring reality when, virtually overnight it seemed, all such practices were deemed a form of betrayal of other blacks, if not self-hatred against oneself for being black. Whether these reading habits became a matter of public knowledge or not, I suggest in this essay that the black female reader of these romances would often police her own desires if no one else did. However, one thing this individual would *not* do apparently is to stop reading these narratives altogether.

The contemporary black romance author Evelyn Palfrey confirms my analysis on this point. In her revealing article, "The Writing Life," Palfrey explains what it was like to read these early romances in which none of the main characters were African American:

> There was a time when I had to *pretend* that the heroine had short, nappy hair like mine, instead of long, flowing and blond tresses. A time when I had to *pretend* that the tall, dark and handsome hero really was dark. I guess I was too young and hungry for romantic images to realize how ridiculous it would be for this heroine to be chased across a Scottish moor, or through the streets of London. (Palfrey 16; emphasis mine)

On the one hand, the author's reliance on the distancing language of "pretense" reveals the extent to which she found her consumption of these novels psychologically troubling, so troubling that today she feels the need to qualify her past identification with the novels' characters as a willful, even youthful, act of imagination. Indeed, Palfrey's need to read these narratives was so insistent, she tells us, that she was willing to suppress her own corporeal identity as a black racial subject in order to satisfy that need. However, on the other hand, she does this by disavowing knowledge of the fact that not all heroines of romance novels have, as she puts it, "long, flowing and blond tresses," or the fact that black women actually *do* live in places like Scotland and London today. Moreover, the author chalks up these disavowals to the fact that she was too immature to know any better. But was she?

For what Palfrey does *not* say in her article is that those early romance novels she read so feverishly were actually "historical" and not contemporary romances—the dead giveaway being her sly reference to "Scottish moors." Therefore, these narratives were already removed from herself, both in terms of temporal distance and geography. I want to suggest that these misleading statements function to convey the author's profound discomfort, even shame, with reading white-themed romances at all. In other words, Palfrey is trying to convince her readers as much as she is trying to convince herself, retroactively, of the historical integrity of her "politically" correct, same-race heterosexual desires: that is, as a black woman she has *always* desired black men and never desired white men, even if the white men she desired had to be transformed first into black men before she would desire them. Indeed, as Palfry puts it, she must have only *pretended* to identify with the heroine and to desire the hero; she couldn't have really had those feelings. After all, to have really had those feelings would have meant that at some level Palfrey hated herself for being black. She must have also hated all black people because they too were black, especially, as a self-avowed heterosexual woman, black men. And for a black woman like Palfrey, living in the U.S. in the aftermath of the Civil Rights and Black Power movements, such a self-image was particularly difficult to reconcile.

Amazingly, this double bind of sorts would persist for most black female readers of mainstream romance narratives until 1994 when a major publishing house established an entire line devoted exclusively to African American romances. Kensington Publishing became the first major publisher to back an African American romance under its imprint, Arabesque. Palfrey remembers the first time she came across one of these titles:

> I will never forget the day another mother at my daughter's school gave me an Arabesque paperback. I could see the cover from across the room. So being the shy person I am, I walked right up to her and said, "Where'd you get that?" She had just finished the book and gave it to me. Well, I took it home and read it that night. The very next day, I was at the black bookstore when it opened. Talk about a kid in a candy store! Rochelle Alers, Maggie Ferguson, Gwynne Forster, Donna Hill, Beverly Jenkins, Francis Ray. I bought one of each. And I was just as happy as a pig in slop. Those writers brought me so much joy. *I no longer had to pretend.* The heroine not only looked like me, but she acted like me. And thought like me. And the heroes—they were like the men I knew. (Palfrey 16-17; emphasis mine)

While Palfrey's exuberant language shows that she clearly over-identifies racially with some of the characters and scenarios in the romance fiction she reads, I would say that her over-identification speaks more to her eagerness, as a politically-engaged, heterosexual black woman, in wanting to consume *psychically* satisfying images of black-on-black heterosexual intimacy, than it does to the fact that the black male and female characters in African American-themed romances all look, act, and think like herself. More important to the author, it seems, is that these are images of heterosexual intimacy that do not require her, as a condition of her readerly pleasure, to consider the psychologically displeasing notion that she may be self-hating because she is black and the characters in the narratives are not. The feminist critic Tania Modelski rejects the easy slippage some people believe readers of romances make between themselves and the characters in these novels. Writes Modelski:

Since the reader knows the formula, she is superior in wisdom to the heroine and thus detached from her. The reader, then, achieves a very close emotional identification with the heroine partly because she is intellectually *distanced* from her and does not have to suffer the heroine's confusion. (41)

Modelski's insight about readerly identification and distancing is useful not only for understanding how contemporary white female consumers of romantic fiction engage with these texts, but it is just as useful, I think, for coming to some understanding of how contemporary black female consumers engage these works as well. After all, black female readers of black-themed romance novels live in a society they recognize daily as racist as well as misogynist. Moreover, this is a society in which they know that black same-race heterosexual relationships have been historically maligned as a matter of course. A prime example of this maligning can be seen reflected in the lasting influence of Daniel Patrick Moynihan's 1965 controversial study, "The Negro Family: The Case for National Action." In this document Moynihan characterizes black male-black female couple relationships as matriarchal rather than patriarchal and casts the gendered dynamics of such bonds in pathologized terms when compared with the gender and sexual dynamics of white same-race families. For this reason, an African American woman romance writer's depiction of black male and female lovers serves to portray an idealized imaginative space within which black women readers can contain their fears of racism—which frequently distorts black same-race heterosexual bonds—and therefore project their private (hetero)sexualized longings without having to be concerned about how those bonds will be portrayed. In other words, as Modelski suggests, black female readers of these works are already distanced enough from the plots of these novels to be able to see them for what they are: fictional correctives.

Another reason why contemporary black women writers may have turned to the romance genre to tell their own stories is that in romances the subject of racial politics and group struggle against whites in general is not required to be the *raison d'etre* of the genre. After all, in romances such conflicts are subordinated to, but not erased from, issues of personal longing and sexual fulfillment. As the critic B. Ruby Rich has suggested, "The advantage of romance as a launching pad for political engagement is that it carries built-in optimism, just possibly enough to move ahead in these times of race-hatred and scapegoating" (336). Quite frankly, readers of romances do not generally place the same political demand on their authors to contest societal inequalities as is the case with most so-called "serious" literary texts that make up the core of such oppositional discourses as the feminist and African American literary traditions. For instance, says black romance author Beverly Jenkins,

Romance is a necessary part of life. But so many books about black people are studies in survival. Not everything has to be about the civil rights movement. I'm very proud of [the] "heaving bosoms" and "throbbing manhoods" [that I offer] to black women all over America! (qtd in Israel 153)

What Jenkins's remarks suggest is that, while many contemporary black women see themselves within a racially divided society, not all of these women's needs can be met through texts with only a racial focus. As evidenced by the imaginative reading strategies to which black women like Evelyn Palfrey resorted in the decades before explicitly black-theme romances were widely available, for most black women their psychological and emotional needs often *exceed* those directly related to racial politics. This is certainly the case with (hetero)sexual needs. But what about those black women readers of pre-black-themed romances who had learned to suppress their sexual attraction to white men as a condition of proving their loyalty to the race in general, and to black men in particular? Must these women once again repress that desire as a condition of their membership in the racial collective? And if so, what does this say about the state of their freedom as contemporary black women?

"But nobody had the right to question her love for him": Redefining Freedom for Black Women

This brings me to Patricia Hill Collins, who writes in her 1990 landmark volume, *Black Feminist Thought: Knowledge, Consciousness, and the Politics of Empowerment*, that "traditionally, relationships among black women and white men have long been constrained by the legacy of black women's sexual abuse by white men and the unresolved tensions this creates." Because of this extensive and brutal history, Collins argued at the time that "freedom for black women has meant freedom *from* white men, not the freedom to choose white men as lovers and friends" (191). Historically, black women who have chosen white men as lovers and companions have been vilified and often punished by the black community. We can see this over time in the verbal and physical retribution that has been visited upon black women who were perceived to violate the racial collective's unspoken, sometimes spoken, gender and sexual norms (see hooks 67-70; Mitchell 218-239). However, in a more recent book, *Black Sexual Politics: African Americans, Gender, and the New Racism* (2004), Collins identifies a "double standard" that, while present in earlier eras, has re-emerged in the post-civil rights era for black men and black women who date and marry interracially with whites. This double standard is a result of the contrasting ways in which black men and black women have been positioned historically in relation to narratives of racial progress. For while freedom for black women has been defined by their freedom to reject white men sexually rather than to embrace them, freedom for black men has been defined as the freedom for these men to *choose*, without fear of white male retaliation, white women as lovers and wives. As Collins explains it:

> African American men were forbidden [under pain of death] to engage in sexual relations with all white women, let alone marry them. In this context, any expansion of the pool of female sexual partners enhances African American men's standing within the existing system of hierarchical masculinities. (262)

Collins's remarks dovetail neatly with Devon Carbado's analysis regarding the central role that race and gender played in high profile controversies involving such diverse black male figures as Mike Tyson, Clarence Thomas, and O. J. Simpson. Carbado argues that when blacks are perceived to be perpetrators of crime and must prove their guilt or innocence, for many African Americans the status of black men as "black" assumes a greater importance to them than whether or not the men are actually guilty of the crime with which they are charged. This is especially the case if white men and women are the victims of black men's alleged crimes. Hence, writes Carbado:

> O. J. Simpson's gender matters but Nicole Brown Simpson's does not. As a black man defending himself against the criminal justice system, Simpson represents what is black, and blackness is essentialized to represent who and what he is. He became, as it were, "the race"–and a symbol for racial injustice. In this context, black people view Simpson as *another black man being put down by the system,* or *another* famous *black man being put down by the system.* (165-166)

For some black women writers, deeply cognizant of this double standard for interracially coupled blacks, the act of affirming black women's freedom by simply depicting same-race heterosexual relationships between black women and black men is perhaps too limiting. This is the case because such depictions only amount to black women's *partial* freedom, since they accept the black communal norms that restrict black women's sexual choices in relation to the broader latitude allowed to black men. However, in choosing to author non-pathologized portrayals of mutually consenting romantic and sexual bonds between black women and white men, black women writers explicitly challenge the gendered sexual assumptions that Collins singles out as being so central to contemporary black civil society. In other words, these writers grant to their fictional heroines the same type of broad desiring prerogatives that black men assumed in the wake of the Civil Rights and Black Power movements.

As bell hooks has suggested, the historical and cultural taboo against interracial heterosexual intimacy on the part of the white dominant society, but too on the part of black communities, has functioned in part to control and manage black women's freedom overall. According to hooks:

> Just as sexist white folks used the idea that all black men were rapists to limit the sexual freedom of white women, black people employ the same tactic to control black female sexual behavior. For many years, black people warned black females to beware involvement with white men for fear such relationships would lead to exploitation and degradation of black womanhood. While there is no need to deny the historical fact that white men have sexually exploited black women, this knowledge is used by the white and black public as a psychological weapon to limit and restrain the freedom of black females. (67)

As a consequence of such communal scare tactics, many contemporary black women have historically shied away from forming close personal as well as professional relationships with white men, and therefore they frequently experience a sense of discomfort, even crippling terror, when in the presence of white men in the workplace, at school, as well as in other everyday venues. Indeed, hooks has found that "[t]here are many black women who have as phobic a fear about white male sexuality as the fear white women have traditionally felt towards black men." However, as the author astutely reminds us, "Phobic fear is not a solution to the problem of sexual exploitation or rape. It is a symptom" (68).

Freud reminds us that, among other things, symptoms are the result of a compromise, in particular, as he puts it, "a compromise between the need for satisfaction and the need for punishment" (*Inhibitions* 98). As such, symptoms function primarily as "substitutions" for some traumatic experience that the unconscious deems too troubling and therefore bars from conscious thought, that is, represses (30). However, closely related to symptoms, for Freud, is anxiety—in fact, "these two represent and replace each other," but they are not interchangeable (*New Introductory* 83). Rather, Freud makes it clear that, in terms of chronology, anxieties predate symptoms, which function as their substitutes. In Freud's view, anxiety is closely situated to either a real or perceived danger, while the symptom that replaces it primarily comes about as a consequence of the subject removing him- or herself, or being moved, from this danger. As usual, Freud illustrates his creative speculations by way of real or hypothetical examples from his own and other analysts' clinical practices. In this case, he turns to the example of a patient who suffers from agoraphobia: the fear of open spaces. For Freud, agoraphobia initially begins for the patient when he goes outside. It is being outside that produces an anxiety attack, one that he knows would repeat "every time he went into the street again." Hence, as a result of this foreknowledge of anxiety, the agoraphobe develops the "*symptom* of agoraphobia" as a way of protecting himself from the anxiety he knows he will suffer if he does venture outside. Freud therefore concludes that "the generation of anxiety is the earlier and the formation of symptoms the later of the two, as though the symptoms are created in order to avoid the outbreak of the anxiety state" (*New Introductory* 83-84; emphasis mine). What I find provocative about Freud's discussion of symptoms as they relate to the anxieties they replace is the role the former plays in the formation of the ego's borders—as Freud puts it, symptoms lead to a "restriction of the ego's function"; in other words, an "inhibition" (83). As such, symptoms are not necessarily temporary psychic structures the way Freud sees them; rather, because they replace that which was already present, they acquire a morphological integrity that the subject internalizes and takes on in establishing his or her bodily character. Indeed, in discussing this process, Freud relies on a military metaphor that invokes the mental image of a fortress, "They [symptoms] are a kind of frontier-station with a mixed garrison," he writes. In elaborating on the seeming intransigence of a symptom, Freud goes on to state:

> The ego now proceeds to behave as though it recognized that the symptom had *come to stay* and that the only thing to do was to accept the situation in good part and draw as much advantage from it as possible. It makes an *adaptation* to the symptom—to this piece of the internal world which is alien to it—just as it normally does to the real external world. (*Inhibitions* 99; emphasis mine)

Here, Freud suggests that in adapting to the symptom and deriving an "advantage" from it, the subject accommodates him- or herself to the symptom in a way that is not only unreflective but also—and this is crucial to the argument I'm trying to make—self-preservative. In a word, the symptom is quickly naturalized as part and parcel of the subject's own identity formation as a way to ward off further anxiety. In fact, the symptom becomes indistinguishable from that identity so that, eventually, the symptom *is* the identity. The reason Freud gives for why this is possible has to do with the ego's belief that the symptom offers "protection" of some sort—as Freud puts it when discussing a patient who was prevented from creating a symptom to replace an obsessive washing ritual: "he falls into a state of anxiety which he finds hard to tolerate and from which he had evidently been *protected* by his symptom" (*Inhibitions* 83).

How, then, borrowing Freud's analysis, might we come to see contemporary black women's phobic fear of white men as lovers and companions—especially when that fear is rendered semiotically, through plot, character, and dialogue—as operating through a similarly unreflective and self-preservationist logic of protection? If it is true that, as bell hooks has suggested, black women's rejection of white men today (a rejection anchored in phobic fear) functions as a "symptom" that has come to replace the historical "anxiety" of sexual exploitation and rape—a symptom that these women perceive as *protecting* them from having to suffer a similar trauma and which therefore has become a permanent part of their identity as black women—how would such an obsession ultimately be resolved, assuming of course that one *wanted* to resolve it, someone like, say, a character in a literary text, for instance? For his part, Freud suggests that an individual might resolve this obsession by "find[ing] the path back to the memory of a traumatic experience" ("The Aetiology of Hysteria" 195). Lest we forget, the characters in the vast majority of black-authored literary texts are figures that acknowledge rather than deny "the material circumstances of racial oppression" and its psychological effects on black subjects, effects that are frequently experienced as traumatic memory—their own or someone else's (Tate 4). Likewise, plots of black-authored novels are signifiers of those events as filtered through the very acknowledgment of such trauma. Indeed, as Claudia Tate puts it, "the modern black text functions like a racially sensitive psychotherapist"; in other words, such works teach black readers to recognize "the parameters of the negative, racist and patriarchal boundaries which traditionally define [black people]" and to dare "to step outside of them" so as "to understand their own individuality, worth and ability [and] utilize inner strengths in the service of growing and coping" (Tate 17-18).

Regarding the plots of *interracial* romances in particular, I would say that the black female protagonist's rejection of white men as suitors is structured by this same textual knowledge. This means that black female characters, like many black women in real life on whom these characters are modeled, are vested textually with the memory of racist white men sexually abusing black female bodies with impunity, a memory many of these characters experience as traumatic. It is this memory that is debarred from consciousness, as in: "That can't happen to me." However, once repressed, the memory returns in the form of a symptom, causing these female characters to behave and speak in ways that textually demonstrate their *a priori* rejection of white men as possible lovers and companions, as in: "This *won't* happen to me." As if following to the letter Freud's suggestion about self-healing through an imaginative restaging, rhetorically the text reenacts the trauma of rape and sexual exploitation through the displacement of that trauma onto the protagonist's active avoidance of white men, a rejection that then gets renarrativized as the black female character's strong racial identification, rather than what it is at base: fear. When another black female character shows Lacie of Lizzette Carter's *The Color Line* photos of her family, for example, complete with white husband and mixed-race children—the clear implication being that Lacie too might consider such a relationship—the protagonist's fear (a fear masked as disgust) is evident: "Carrie, you have a lovely family and I'm very happy for you, but I can't do this. That's not for me. I date black men. I always have" (Carter 55). In order to resolve this psychic dilemma of neurotic avoidance, the text of the interracial romance is driven, as a motor drives an engine, to hurl these characters along a vertiginous path that will deliver them straight to the very source of their anxiety in order to resolve it: white men themselves.

Because the formulaic structure of the romance novel is primarily rooted in conflict—and usually conflict that is gendered rather than gendered *and* raced, which I suggest is the case with these novels—the genre offers contemporary writers a ready-made literary form upon which to engage the pain and degradation that such relationships have historically caused for black women outside the text. Hence, the novels are structured, i.e. plotted, to be therapeutic in that they are organized in such a way as to enable a cathartic release on the part of their protagonists, as well as, if successful, on the parts of their faithful readers—whatever these readers' race, gender, or sexual identities may be. Such texts allow the protagonist to confront the stigma of interracial desire where contemporary black women are concerned. But then they also enable these women to turn what may be experienced as a stigma into an occasion for self-affirmation and independence. How these novels achieve this, I've tried to argue, is by redefining the notion of black women's freedom in terms of their relationships to white men. Instead of freedom for black women being defined, as Collins puts it, by the fact that black women successfully manage to *elude* the sexual interests of white men, these characters come to redefine their freedom by embracing the knowledge that they are just as free to reject or accept the sexual interests of white men as they are free to reject or accept the sexual interests of black men. The decision to do so is entirely their own. It neither belongs to their parents, to their brothers, to their close friends, to their co-workers, nor to society. If, as Janice Radway writes, "the romance . . . is never simply a love story, [but] also an exploration of the meaning of patriarchy for women" (75), then I would say that the *interracial* romance is both a love story and an exploration of the meaning of patriarchy *and* racism specifically for *black* women living in radically changed times in which the past is not easily repressed.

Homophobia vs. Mixophobia:
The Same-Race, Different Gender Rule

Like their same-race counterparts, black-authored interracial romances all involve black female protagonists as they search for love and wholeness in a world that is not only hostile to women, but that is also hostile to black people in general.   A defining feature of these narratives is that the black female protagonist is not only psychologically unprepared to become sexually and emotionally involved with a white man over the long term, no matter how handsome and charming this man may be, but that she is also at some level psychologically *unwilling* to become involved with him in this way as well. The reasons for this unwillingness are both personal and collective. While one of the implicit goals of such narratives is to break down the protagonist's strong, personal resistance to interracial intimacy so that she may finally confront and overcome her fears about white men as intimates, certainly another goal of these novels is to assist this character in overcoming any additional fears she may have about letting down the racial group to which she feels an abiding responsibility.

For example, in Monica White's 1996 debut novel, *Shades of Desire,* the protagonist expresses her personal resistance to black-white coupling in the book's very first paragraph. In this novel, a professional black woman, Jasmine Smith, goes out one night to a mixed-race dance club with three of her closest African American girlfriends to celebrate her twenty-sixth birthday. One of these women, Taylor, who is also the protagonist's roommate, has been in a long-term but rocky relationship with a white man whose parents disapprove of his committed relationship with a black woman. As the novel's first-person narrator, Jasmine quickly distances herself from her roommate's sexuality by informing the reader that although she likes Cameron well enough and can understand what Taylor "sees in him," she nonetheless concludes that "the problems black woman/white man [relationships] cause are [too large of a] price to pay for love." As she puts it, "*personally,* I didn't think I could do it" (1; emphasis mine). Interestingly, Jasmine does not clarify what she means when she admits to understanding what it is that Taylor "sees" in Cameron. Does this mean that *she* also finds Cameron to be sexually attractive? Or does it simply mean that she thinks he is a nice person? The fact that Jasmine does not explicitly *say* what she means points up the extent to which she may feel constrained in being able to admit, even to herself, whether or not she finds Cameron attractive because he is white.

I suggest that the discomfort the protagonist exhibits in being unable to acknowledge if she finds a particular white man handsome or not is structurally similar to, though ultimately different from, a type of discomfort some heterosexual men, regardless of race, may feel when they are asked if they find another *man* attractive. After all, in a heterosexual man's mind, to admit to someone that he finds another man attractive is tantamount to admitting that he would like to sleep with that man. Obviously, if he were to admit to such a thing, then he would be leaving himself open, in a heterosexist society, to the culturally damning charge that he is a "homosexual." And this would be the case even if he is *not* homosexual but resolutely heterosexual. By the same logic, if a contemporary black woman were to admit to someone, especially to someone black, that she found a particular white man attractive, it would be tantamount to admitting that she would like to sleep with him, or at the very least that she would like to date him. Such an admission would therefore open her, in a racially divided society, to the culturally damning charge, at least within the black community, that she is an "interracialist," i.e. a person of color who dates whites. In contemporary black antiracist discourse, a black person's admission of attraction to a white person can often lead to questions about what "kind" of black person he or she is. This is because in such discourse to admit, if you are black, to finding even a *single* white person attractive encourages people to suspect—and these "people" are always other blacks—that, on the one hand, you find *all* white people attractive and, on the other, that you do not find *any* black people attractive (see Barnard 47-51; Scott 299-300). In other words, the same dichotomous logic that operates in our society to prevent a heterosexual man from verbally acknowledging that he finds another man attractive can be seen to structure the erotic situation between a black heterosexual woman and a white heterosexual man. This would explain why Palfrey felt that she had to "pretend" the white protagonists of the historical romance novels she read as a youth were black, since had they been white, which they were, her enjoyment of these texts would have targeted her as both self-hating and sexually deviant.

For Collins, such constraints serve to illustrate what she refers to as the "same-race, different gender rule." These are largely unspoken rules that establish societal norms for romantic and sexually intimate bonds within the contemporary U.S. In relation to race and gender, these rules work through a "logic of segregation" that requires black and white men and women to choose intimate partners in ways that are in keeping with our culture's heterosexist and racially homogamous norms (248). For example, for black men to satisfy these norms they must choose black women for partners and neither other black men, white men, nor white women, whereas white women, on the other hand, must choose white men for partners over black men, black women, or other white women. I suggest that the practice of giving voice to such "rules," as Jasmine does when she tells the reader that *she* personally could not date a white man, serves another function as well. After all, as any reader of interracial romances knows, the protagonist *will* become involved with just such a man—in fact, she will eventually fall in love with him, to the surprise and dismay of her friends and family alike. Therefore, this preemptive rejection of any possible cross-racial, heterosexual attraction must be seen to serve a purpose other than simply voicing her "true" desires. This statement can be interpreted not as a declaration of the protagonist's impossible attraction to a white man (after all, such an attraction is certainly possible physiologically), but rather as her effort to assert at the outset a strong racial identification as a contemporary black woman to "protect" herself in the same way that Freud describes the hypothetical patient's obsessive washing ritual serves as protection. While the two things are not necessarily mutually exclusive—a black woman with a strong racial identification can certainly be attracted to a white man without necessarily compromising that identification—the cultural mythology that circulates about interracial intimacy, especially in the black community, is so overdetermined as to make the two *seem* mutually exclusive, even if they are not.

Therefore, in order for her to affirm her identity as a proud black woman in culturally intelligible ways, and most importantly not to be punished by the racial collective for that attraction (which she knows she will be if she does not give up, i.e. repress, that attraction), the protagonist must eventually repudiate the compromise she struck when she first acquired the symptom of preemptively repudiating white men as possible lovers and confidantes. She does this within interracial romances by asserting strong "I" statements, such as, "personally I didn't think I could do it." For clearly the protagonist *can* do it; she just *won't*. Because she insists on taking this stance and holding to it so firmly, the protagonist of the interracial romance must be made to suffer, as Jasmine suffers, through a series of trials in which she eventually proves that the two things—being a proud black person and loving someone white—are not incompatible. Some of these trials, which we find represented as part of the plot of interracial romances, include the protagonist having to endure public scrutiny of her relationship through unwanted stares; criticism and possible rejection from family and friends; the protagonist's own concerns as to how her own racial identity will be affected by being interracially coupled; the fear of discrimination in the workplace as a result of her relationship, which may lead interracially coupled blacks to conceal their relationship from co-workers; random acts of verbal hostility and violence from disapproving others; and potential parenthood to mixed-race children—all of which are experiences that revisionist social science researchers have associated with the challenges faced by contemporary interracial couples (see Childs 2005; Dalmage 2002; Killian 2002; Rosenblatt 1995).

In *Language and Sexuality* (2003), Deborah Cameron and Don Kulick would call speech acts like Jasmine's "performative," in that speech of this type functions most often to secure the boundaries of the speakers' own identity in relation to the identity of someone they deem to be sexually different from themselves. For example, in their discussion of a group of five fraternity brothers, all of whom regard themselves as heterosexual, gossiping about the potential homosexuality of other men they suspect of being gay, Cameron and Kulick write that in addition to this gossip being homophobic, it also serves to help these men negotiate "a danger that cannot be acknowledged: the possibility of homosexual desire within the speakers' own homosocial group." Hence, by invoking homosexuality as something dissimilar from rather than like themselves, these men are able to "locate homosexual desire outside the group, in the bodies of absent others" (122). In so doing, they manage to contain, if only temporarily, the threat homosexuality poses to their own fragile sense of identity as heterosexual. According to Judith Butler, setting up contrasts of this type outside the subjective self "requires the simultaneous production of a domain of abject beings, those who are not yet 'subjects,' but who form the constitutive outside to the domain of the subject," in this case, gay men. To the five fraternity brothers, the absent gay men "constitute the site of dreaded identification against which—and by virtue of which" they are able to stake their "own claim to autonomy and life" as privileged heterosexuals, i.e. as *not* abject but normative. In other words, the fraternity brothers are able to claim they are straight precisely because, to them, the other men are gay or are perceived to be. But the solidity of these subjective boundaries turns out merely to be illusory. "In this sense," writes Butler:

> the subject is constituted through the force of exclusion and abjection, one which produces a constitutive outside to the subject, an abjected outside, which is, after all, 'inside' the subject as its own founding repudiation. (3)

Put differently, the subject is simultaneously the person he thinks himself to be *and* the person he most loathes; the former is made possible, buoyed up even, by the ghosted presence of the latter.

What I have been suggesting is that we can see evidence of a similar dialectic of exclusion and abjection at work, with race as the privileged term instead of gender, within interracial romances as well. In *Shades of Desire* this dialectic reveals itself in Jasmine's insistence that although Taylor is willing to transgress societal norms by dating interracially, it is not something that she is "personally" willing to do. By separating herself from what she perceives to be her roommate's racialized sexual difference (i.e., Taylor dates white men, the narrator does not), Jasmine hopes, in Cameron and Kulick's words, to "know [herself] as normal" (122)—and for African American heterosexuals "normal" sexuality involves adhering to the "same-race" portion of the hegemonic rule of desire to which Collins refers. Jasmine does this by repudiating what she believes to be an historically dangerous form of desire (black women coupled with white men) in favor of embracing what she believes to be its contemporary corrective (black women coupled with black men), which she views as not only self-affirming, but also group-affirming. While this last point is invoked but quickly dismissed in White's novel—the book is after all only 134 pages and moves rather swiftly, almost mechanically, through the range of challenges that contemporary interracial couples often endure on its way to a happy conclusion—this dual dilemma is treated with far more narrative complexity in other interracial romances, such as in Dyanne Davis's *The Color of Trouble* (2003) and Lizzette Carter's *The Color Line* (2005). In the former, the black female protagonist, Kari Thomas, ends her long engagement to her white fiancé ostensibly because of what she believes to be his infidelity, but really because of her deep, psychological fear of giving birth to mixed-race children, who represent to her a permanent estrangement from black people and from blackness itself. As the novel puts it:

> She [Kari] summoned up the image of her perfect circle of brown-skinned babies. And she prayed those babies would help her forget Jonathan Steele and her love for him. (224)

On the other hand, in Carter's *The Color Line,* the novel's protagonist, Lacie Adams, manages to keep her strong feelings for her white male boss at bay by cultivating a serious relationship with a black male entrepreneur who is every bit as successful as his white male counterpart, but whom she does not love. A key refrain in this novel at least—uttered by other characters, never by the protagonist herself—is the following: "Why would [a black woman] want to go with a rich white man when [she] can have a rich black man?" (100, 296). What is implied in such crude formulations is the black cultural belief that, all things being equal, heterosexual black women are better off with black men as opposed to white men. The problem with such thinking of course is that it acquiesces to the dominant cultural logic of segregation in maintaining rigid and exclusionary boundaries between "black" and "white" people, against which scores of African American and white antiracist activists fought so long and hard during the 1950s and '60s, and for which many of them gave their lives. This belief reinforces rather than challenges the racist ideology of "separate but equal" by essentializing differences between blacks and whites, that is, characterizing such differences as immutable and based in biology rather than culture. Furthermore, such an ideology is chiefly responsible for generating a host of deforming effects upon the lives of African Americans in ways that exceed the merely "racial," such as the cultural belief that black men have greater sexual stamina than white men, or that black women are naturally more fertile than white women.

By insisting that black women confine their sexual and romantic relationships to black men only, advocates of the same-race, different gender rule seek to reshape historical knowledge of just how the identity categories "black" and "white" were forged in the first place through a host of concerted disciplinary practices, including socially constructed laws against black-white sex and intimacy, elaborate and highly variable models of racial classification, and through the regulatory use of terrorizing violence. As a way to challenge such discourse, a crucial point that writers like Alice Walker and James Baldwin, among others, have often tried to impress upon Americans is that the relationship between blacks and whites is one of blood kin and not of indifferent strangers (see Baldwin, *Collected Essays* 32; Walker 540-541). But thus far such a lesson has been a difficult one for most of us to learn. Cameron and Kulick, in regards to gender, not race, reach a similar conclusion as Walker and Baldwin. Referring once again to the five fraternity brothers, the authors write:

> the way the straight men talk about the bodies of the despised/disavowed gay men suggests that what they claim to be repelled by is also (as a psychoanalyst might predict) a source of fascination. (122)

Moreover, this fascination can further be unmasked as an anxiety that what these men repudiate as outside themselves, same-sex desire, is, in actuality, both inside and outside simultaneously. Although Cameron and Kulick, and to a lesser extent Butler as well, privilege a hetero-homosexual binary model of desire and identification in their formulations, we might be led to wonder if similar "exclusionary logics" can be said to structure the cultural opposition between interracial and intraracial sexuality as well. While references to "race" frequently fall out of Butler's often brilliant efforts to theorize the psychic displacements that structure sexual subjectivities within a society organized around an imaginary belief in oedipalization, she nonetheless is astute enough to recognize that complexity of the symbolic exceeds gendered affiliations. In other words, can what these theorists have to say about homophobic straight men also be said, or at least be thought, about "mixophobic" heterosexual black women like Kari Thomas from *The Color of Trouble,* Lacie Adams from *The Color Line,* and to a lesser extent, Jasmine Smith from White's *Shades of Desire*? Certainly the black British filmmaker and theorist Isaac Julien would say so. In a provocative 1994 essay, Julien states the following, "The upholding of an essential black identity is dependent upon an active avoidance of the psychic reality of black/white desire" (125). Might the same be true of the black women in these novels as well? After all, it is not long after the narrator of *Shades of Desire* rejects interracial intimacy as a personal option for herself, while hesitatingly approving of it for her roommate, that she first meets the white man who will eventually become her husband. However, instead of rejecting this man's sudden invitation to dance, she practically throws herself into his arms. Indeed, given the narrator's strong rejection moments earlier to white men as romantic partners, it comes as something of a surprise to find that Jasmine does not vehemently refuse his invitation. What is it that accounts for the contradictory behavior the black female protagonists all exhibit in these narratives?

In her article, "Dating White: When Sisters Go There," Rachel Blakely argues that contemporary black women do not primarily reject white men because these men are white. In fact, black women are just as sexually curious about white men's whiteness as white men are curious about black women's blackness. Rather, what presents the greatest stumbling block to large numbers of black women willing to forge intimate bonds with white men is what Blakely calls the almost "schizophrenic" array of conflicting emotions many of these women continue to have where white men are concerned (149). As I stated at the outset, for many black women today, white men as a group still remain a risky proposition. As a black female character in a James Baldwin novel puts it when asked if she hates white people (ironically, this character is interracially involved at the time), "If any *one* white person gets through to you, it kind of destroys your single-mindedness. They say love and hate are very close together. Well, that's a fact" (Baldwin, *Another Country* 350). In other words, many contemporary black women feel the necessity of being constantly on their guard with white men; this is the case even with white men they may be sleeping with. And although it is certainly true that white men today hardly represent the monolithic cabal they once did in previous eras, at least as far as blacks are concerned, they are nonetheless various enough in their politicized astuteness regarding racial inequities to be a wildly unpredictable bunch. Therefore, it can be dangerous for any black woman to trust any white man too easily or, for that matter, too quickly. This point is echoed by Blakely, who writes, "In all the conversations I have had with black women, the strongest feeling they seem to conjure up about white men isn't love or hate. It's ambivalence" (149).

For Freud, the term "ambivalence" is often a code word for a deviation in the normative sexual aim. The central deviance within much of psychoanalysis is, of course, homosexuality. The notion of "ambivalence" is therefore intimately tied up with the very human process of sexual differentiation that Freud saw reflected in the Oedipal complex, and which Steven Angelides has referred to as an "allegory for the universalized account of human psychosexual development" (54). Although Freud does employ the concept of ambivalence elsewhere, the term seems to be most often identified with the tortuous path all human beings must travel before ideally taking up stable and fixed identity positions in the interlocking binary sex/gender system governed by the dyads male/female, masculine/feminine and heterosexuality/homosexuality. Ambivalence emerges for Freud at the precise moment when, in this case, the little boy begins to transform his polymorphous desires for his parents by distinguishing between at least two forms of desire: (1) his desire-for (his mother) and (2) his desire-to-be (his father). In making this distinction, the little boy becomes dimly aware that somehow he has managed to retain dual and contradictory attachments to his father, but not his mother. The attachments come in the form of affection and aggression, its diametric opposite. "Here, then," writes Freud, "we have a conflict due to ambivalence: a well-grounded love and a no less justifiable hatred directed towards one and the same person" (*Inhibitions* 102). However, Rachel Blakely's use of the derivation "ambivalence" in her discussion of the contradictory feelings some contemporary black women have about the white men in their lives cannot be properly explained by turning to Freud's gender-centric, though race-neutral, understanding of the subject's psychosexual development. In other words, his is an allegory that produces no meaning for this particular narrative account of sexual development, which is both gendered and overtly racialized.

Or does it?

As my earlier discussion of the Herculean strategies to which some black women resorted in order to enjoy reading romances before black-themed romances were widely available would suggest, black women *have* loved white men in the past, just as the polymorphous perverse little boy had loved his father as much as he had loved his mother; they just have not done so *openly*, or, in Palfrey's case, self-knowingly. For these black women, their love for white men was already present from the start, set up, as it were, as a "founding repudiation," one that forms the "constitutive outside" of their identities as strong black women. But might the same be true of a great many other black women, and for people of color in general, who did not hungrily consume romance novels as young people? For as Isaac Julien laments, "in this Western culture we have all grown up as snow queens—straights, as well as white queers." This is the case, Julien argues, because "Western culture is in love with its own (white) image" (125). While Julien may overstate the case somewhat, his point is certainly thought-provoking and worth some consideration, especially his claim that this "love of whiteness" is not to be associated with people of color exclusively, that white people themselves are narcissistically attached to whiteness *qua* whiteness. However, with the arrival of the discourses of black affirmation, such cross-racial affections were no longer politically tenable for people of color. Black women's desires for white men had to be repressed or risk punishment, even if indulged privately, just as the little boy's desire for his father, in his journey toward normative masculinity and heterosexual manhood, had to be repressed or else the boy would be subject to a similar rebuke. And just as the little boy developed "ambivalent," i.e. love/hate, feelings for his father, so too, I argue, have contemporary black women similarly developed love/hate feelings for white men—feelings that they are not socially sanctioned to vocalize without enduring the corresponding and character-assassinating charge that they are "interracialists," and therefore "unblack," traitors to the race, self-haters, the list goes on.

In depicting modern-day black women as they wrestle with the societal constraints of the "same-race, different gender rule," contemporary interracial romances remind us all of the socially constructed nature of desire, the point being that we are not free to desire whomever or however we would like; we have to carve out that freedom against a host of constraints. There are always consequences for desires that "cross the line" between what is considered normative and non-normative at any one time and place, a point that most theorists have not always pursued as expansively as they might. After all, writes Judith Butler, every subject is

> constrained by not only what is difficult to imagine but what remains radically unthinkable: in the domain of sexuality these constraints include the radical unthinkability of desiring otherwise, the radical unendurability of desiring otherwise, the absence of certain desires, the repetitive compulsion of others, the abiding repudiation of some sexual possibilities, panic, obsessional pull, and the nexus of sexuality and pain. (94)

While most readers in the West are generally accustomed to seeing such struggles played out within the context of a heterosexual-homosexual binary model of desire, I have been arguing in this essay that such struggles take place elsewhere as well, especially when black subjects are centered.

Conclusion

I'd like to close by returning to Peter Brooks, who reminds us that "[m]ost viable works of literature tell us something about how they are to be read, guide us toward the conditions of their interpretation" (xii). If this is so, then it is not difficult to imagine that many of these romances have something to teach us about how to accommodate ourselves to this sudden shift in the reconceptualization of racialized sexual freedom in a post-civil rights world, and not only as this freedom pertains to black women, but, really, as it pertains to all of us. After all, the total sum of sexual options for any one human being does not fall neatly between the poles of *either* heterosexuality *or* homosexuality. Such a belief only obscures the sheer complexity of human sexuality as it is constructed and lived out in a heteropatriarchal society also structured by racial hierarchies. It becomes just as important, then, for scholars to focus our efforts on making visible forms of sexuality that exist *within* these binary oppositions themselves. Put differently, just as there is not only one form of heterosexuality but heterosexualit*ies* (i.e. same-race, mixed-race, cross-class, multicultural, intergenerational, interfaith, etc.), there is not only one form of homosexuality but homosexualit*ies*. The tendency for contemporary scholars to privilege a heterosexual-homosexual binary model for making sense of sexual diversity unfortunately keeps whiteness at the center of what is nonetheless highly productive critical work, while continuing to marginalize and other the experiences of large numbers of people of color for whom racial identification comprises a significant part of their sense of self. When scholars revise our critical paradigms for thinking about sexual diversity in this way, we open the door for posing the types of questions that help us to more accurately comprehend the sexual lives of people of color, and not just "whites."

While I would say that every black woman suffers from the historical devaluation of black womanhood that bell hooks has argued is a legacy of the transatlantic slave trade, not all black women experience this legacy in the exact same way. While some black women choose to respond to this race/gender devaluation by forming powerful, restorative heterosexual bonds with black men, other black women choose to form fulfilling same-sex romantic relationships with other women of color. Still, some black women defy historical precedent even further by entering into romantic partnerships with white men and white women, as if directly confronting the fear of whiteness somehow reverses the degradation and stigma that black women have inherited as a result of these historical wrongs of the past. However, black men and women who choose to enter into intimate relationships with whites have been vilified by other blacks for being race traitors at best and self-haters at worst. Unlike lesbians and gay men of color, who since the late 1970s have developed a rich literary and cultural tradition of validating their unique desiring identities, blacks who are interracially coupled with whites are in the early stages of developing a "reverse discourse" with which to validate and affirm their own sexual object-choices; these choices are based also on race rather than on "just" gender. As a result of this ongoing work, scholars need to devise more nuanced interpretive frameworks. Although the contemporary romance novel may initially seem an unlikely textual site upon which to analyze one set of black women's responses to traumatic historical events, this essay has argued that no other literary form has thus far attempted to take up the vexed question of interracial sex as it relates to black women with the commitment and purpose of some of the novels I have explored here. With the exception of a handful of black women's literary texts that appeared in the post-Civil Rights era, and that explored the subject of interracial intimacy in unconventional ways, the subject of contemporary black women's sexual relationship to white men largely comprises an unmapped terrain within the mainstream African American literary canon. The emergence of interracial romances, especially those written by black women, makes it incumbent on scholars of black literature, as well as scholars of human sexuality, to rethink their founding paradigms so as to include variables that recognize the complex dimensions of black women's lives in particular and black people's lives in general.

Works Cited

Abelove, Henry et al., eds. *The Lesbian and Gay Studies Reader.* New York: Routledge, 1993.

Angelides, Steven. *A History of Bisexuality.* Chicago: U of Chicago P, 2001.

Baldwin, James. *Another Country.* 1962. New York: Vintage Books, 1993.

———.*Collected Essays.* New York: The Library of America, 1998.

Barnard, Ian. *Queer Race: Cultural Interventions in the Racial Politics of Queer Theory.* New York: Peter Lang, 2003.

Bérubé, Allan. "How Gay Stays White and What Kind of White It Stays." *The Making and Unmaking of Whiteness.* Eds. Birgit Brander Rasmussen et al. Durham: Duke UP, 2001. 234-265.

Blakely, Rachel. "Dating White: When Sisters Go There." *Essence* July 1999.

Brooks, Peter. *Reading for the Plot: Design and Intention in Narrative.* Cambridge: Harvard UP, 1984.

Butler, Judith. *Bodies that Matter: On the Discursive Limits of "Sex."* New York: Routledge, 1993.

Cameron, Deborah, and Don Kulick. *Language and Sexuality.* Cambridge: Cambridge UP, 2003.

Carbado, Devon, ed. *Black Men on Race, Gender, and Sexuality: A Critical Reader.* New York: New York UP, 1999.

Carter, Lizzette G. *The Color Line.* Columbus: Genesis Press, 2005.

Childs, Chito Erica. *Navigating Interracial Borders: Black-White Couples and Their Social Worlds.* New Brunswick: Rutgers UP, 2005.

Collins, Patricia Hill. *Black Feminist Thought: Knowledge, Consciousness, and the Politics of Empowerment.* Boston: Unwin Hyman, 1990.

———.*Black Sexual Politics: African Americans, Gender, and the New Racism.* New York: Routledge, 2004.

Dalmage, Heather. *Tripping on the Color Line: Black-White Multiracial Families in a Racially Divided World.* New Brunswick: Rutgers UP, 2000.

Davis, Dyanne. *The Color of Trouble.* Columbus: Genesis Press, 2003.

Dyer, Ervin. "Happy Endings: Black-Themed Romance Novels Start Small, but Now Sales Are on Fire." *Pittsburgh-Post Gazette* 12 June 1997. C1.

Freud, Sigmund. "The Aetiology of Hysteria." 1896. *The Standard Edition of the Complete Psychological Works of Sigmund Freud, III.* London: Hogarth Press, 189-221.

———.*Inhibitions, Symptoms and Anxiety.* 1926. *The Standard Edition of the Complete Psychological Works of Sigmund Freud, XX.* London: Hogarth Press, 75-156.

————.*New Introductory Lectures on Psychoanalysis.* 1933. *The Standard Edition of the Complete Psychological Works of Sigmund Freud,* XXII. London: Hogarth Press, 7-182.

hooks, bell. *Ain't I a Woman: Black Women and Feminism.* Boston: South End Press, 1981.

Israel, Betsy. "Heat in Another Color." *People* 13 February 1995. 153.

Johnson-Hodge, Margaret. *The Real Deal.* New York: St. Martin's Press, 1998.

Julien, Isaac. "Confessions of a Snow Queen: Notes on the Making of *The Attendant. Critical Quarterly* 36.1 (Spring 1994): 120-126.

Killian, Kyle. "Dominant and Marginalized Discourses in Interracial Couples' Narratives: Implications for Family Therapists." *Family Process* 41.4 (2002): 603-618.

Kitt, Sandra. *Close Encounters.* New York: Signet, 2000.

————.*The Color of Love.* New York: Signet, 1995.

Mitchell, Michele. *Righteous Propagation: African Americans and the Politics of Racial Destiny after Reconstruction.* Chapel Hill: University of North Carolina P, 2004.

Modleski, Tania. *Loving with a Vengeance: Mass-Produced Fantasies for Women.* Hamden: Archon Books, 1982.

Osborne, Gwendolyn. "How Black Romance—Novels, that is—Came to Be." *Black Issues Book Review* Jan-Feb. 2002. 50.

————."'Women Who Look Like Me': Cultural Identity and Reader Responses to African American Romance Novels." *Race/Gender/Media: Considering Diversity Across Audiences, Content, and Producers.* Ed. Rebecca Ann Lind. New York: Pearson, 2004. 61-68.

Palfrey, Evelyn. "The Writing Life." *Black Issues Book Review* (January-February 2005): 16-17.

Radway, Janice A. *Reading the Romance: Women, Patriarchy, and Popular Literature.* 1984. Chapel Hill: U of North Carolina P, 1991.

Rich. B. Ruby. "When Difference is (More than) Skin Deep." *Queer Looks: Perspectives on Lesbian and Gay Film and Video.* Eds. J. Greyson & P. Pratibha. New York: Routledge, 1993.

Romano, Renee C. *Race-Mixing: Black-White Marriage in Postwar America.* Cambridge: Harvard UP, 2003.

Rosenblatt, Paul et al. *Multiracial Couples: Black & White Voices.* Thousand Oaks/London: Sage Publications, 1995.

Scott, Darieck. "Jungle Fever? Black Gay Identity Politics, White Dick, and the Utopian Bedroom." *GLQ: A Journal of Lesbian and Gay Studies* Vol. 1. No. 3 (1994): 299-321.

Tate, Claudia. *Psychoanalysis and Black Novels: Desire and the Protocols of Race.* New York: Oxford UP, 1998.

Walker, Alice. "In the Closet of the Soul." *Words of Fire: An Anthology of African-American Feminist Thought.* Ed. Beverly Guy-Sheftall. New York: The New Press, 1995. 538-547.

White, Monica. *Shades of Desire.* Columbus: Genesis Press, 1996.

Guy Mark Foster

Guy Mark Foster is an Assistant Professor in the English Department at the University of California, Santa Barbara. He earned his PhD from Brown University in 2003. His central interests include racial and ethnic literatures, theories of sexuality, and contemporary US fiction. He is currently working on a book project, entitled *Waking Up with the Enemy: Critical Re-readings of Interracial Desire in Postwar African American Texts.*

CHAPTER NINE

"I FIND SOME HINDU PRACTICES LIKE BURNING
WIDOWS, UTTERLY BIZARRE": REPRESENTATIONS
OF SATI AND QUESTIONS
OF CHOICE IN *VEILS OF SILK*

MAURA SEALE

I no longer want to read about anything sad. Anything violent, anything
disturbing, anything like that [...] real life is bad for you, hold it in your hand
long enough and you'll get pimples and become feeble-minded. You'll go blind.
I want happiness, guaranteed, joy all round, covers with nurses on them, or
brides, intelligent girls but not too intelligent, with regular teeth and pluck and
both breasts the same size and no excess facial hair, someone you can depend on
to know where the bandages are and to turn the hero, that potential rake and
killer, into a well-groomed country gentleman with clean fingernails and the
right vocabulary. *Always*, he has to say. *Forever.* I no longer want to read
books that don't end with the word *forever*. I want to be stroked between the
eyes, one way only. (Atwood 98)

Margaret Atwood answers the question of "What is a Woman's Novel?" by
satirically describing romance novels, which she positions within the realm of
whimsy and in opposition to real life, which is distressing, brutal, and dismal.
To her, these novels are soothing and offer comfort to readers, unlike books that
depict reality, which are capable of harming both the body and mind. In her
seminal study on the romance genre, *Reading the Romance*, Janice Radway
concurs with Atwood's construction of the romance novel as essentially
fantastic:

Romance reading supplements the avenues traditionally open to women for
emotional gratification by supplying them vicariously with the attention and

nurturance they do not get enough of in the round of day-to-day existence. (Radway 212)

Similarly, Tania Modleski suggests that romances open up a fictive space in which "female readers [can...] believe in the possibility of transcending the divided self" and thus "achieve that state of self-transcendence and self-forgetfulness [that is] promised by the ideology of love" yet denied by the necessity for women to continually survey themselves in Western societies, while Kay Mussell argues that romances organize, idealize, and make significant the "chaos of daily life" in order to create a "fantasy world" (Modleski, "The Disappearing Act" 436; Mussell 188).

Each of these critics proposes that romances act as fantasies that supplement, conceal, and thus to some extent disavow the existence of inequalities within patriarchal societies and the psychological difficulties inherent in female subjectivity. Despite the potential for subversion in Harlequin novels in Modleski's reading, she contends that "the reader is encouraged to participate in and actively desire feminine self-betrayal," as the heroine can only achieve happiness and win the love of the hero through "self-subversion" ("The Disappearing Act" 435). According to Mussell, the fantasy worlds created within romance novels ultimately

> work to preserve within the reader's imagination the illusion of choice, to reopen the possibilities of doing it better the next time around, and to maintain received definitions of reality that seem impervious to a direct challenge. (173)

Radway as well argues that romance reading "may well obviate the need or desire to demand satisfaction in the real world because it can be so successfully met in fantasy" (212). John Cawelti and Rita Hubbard suggest that all generic forms and the romance genre more specifically "resolve tensions and ambiguities" in Western culture by creating a fantasy world in which women's needs can be met, thereby leaving reality untouched (Cawelti 35; Hubbard 177).

Romances, then, tend to reaffirm conventional roles and values, particularly around gender, of the social formations in which they are produced and read. For these scholars, most of whom identify as feminist, "[t]he romance's narrative structure embodies a simple recapitulation and recommendation of patriarchy and its constituent practices and ideologies" (Radway 210). These analyses all take for granted that fiction is essentially concerned with the real; the ways in which women's lives are represented within the romance genre can be either realistic, and accurately depict patriarchy, or unrealistic, and create an unattainable dream world in which women are always fulfilled. In Modleski's, Mussell's, Radway's, Cawelti's, and Hubbard's readings, as well as in the work of Mariam Darce Frenier and Carol Thurston, the antifeminism of the genre can be directly located in readers' inability to recognize the textual worlds of romance novels as untrue and incorrect depictions, since it is this perception that "acts for many women to obviate the imperative to construct alternatives that might lead to threatening change" (Mussell 173).

More recent scholarship on the romance genre and its relationship to gender ideologies and feminism, including newer work by Tania Modleski and Kay Mussell, has challenged this conclusion but not its grounds. Mussell, in a 1997 interview with Laurie Gold, the founder of the website, *All About Romance*, discussed how and why her views on romance novels changed:

> [R]omances have changed with the times. The newer romances incorporate feminist themes while still reaffirming more traditional notions about love and family. Moreover, many romance writers have openly claimed feminist values and, in the process, rejected easy stereotypes about themselves and their work. [...] More difficult to illustrate, but I think equally important, is change in feminist thinking itself. [...] [C]onventional romantic relationships, widely assumed to be discriminatory toward women, were not part of [a feminist agenda]. Thus romances were seen as threatening to female autonomy. But as feminism has matured—and as feminist scholars have come to recognize a broader range of female experience—some scholars have challenged those earlier notions in productive ways. I don't know how you can read many romances today as anything but feminist. To take just one issue: Heroes and heroines meet each other on a much more equal playing field. [...] I think that's clear evidence of the influence of feminism on romances and of the ability of romance novels to address contemporary concerns that women share.

For Mussell, then, the romance genre has become explicitly feminist due to changes in both feminist thinking and the genre itself. Modleski, too, moderates her criticism of romance novels as antifeminist by observing that there are "both progressive and regressive elements in popular texts" while scholar Pamela Regis contends, "the romance novel does not enslave women but, on the contrary, is about celebrating freedom and joy" as "romance heroines make their own decisions, make their own livings, and choose their own husbands" (Modleski, *Old Wives' Tales* 67; Regis 207). By the early 1990s, romance authors, most notably in the collection, *Dangerous Men and Adventurous Women: Romance Writers on the Appeal of the Romance*, also began arguing that their work was feminist. These authors suggest that romance emerges from a sense of "female empowerment," that these novels "celebrate female power," "acknowledg[e] the female gaze" and "invert the power structure of a patriarchal society because they show women exerting enormous power over men [... and] as heroes" (Krentz 5; Asaro). In these readings, romance novels have become feminist as they now are seen to accurately depict real feminist goals and ideals, such as female equality and the validity of women's choices; explicitly acknowledge the partial integration of feminist ideals into larger

American society, such as the redefinition of rape; and address the real-life changes women have experienced since the 1970s, such as the increase in the percentage of women who work. These scholars, in contrast to earlier romance scholars, deemphasize the fantasy of the romance genre and argue instead for its accuracy in depicting reality. Romance novels no longer act as supplements to reality but instead reflect and validate women's achievements; they do not articulate a fantasy of equality, but its enactment. In her 1991 introduction to the reissue of *Reading the Romance*, while acknowledging the influence of feminist thought on romance novels and this contemporary debate, Radway disputes this conclusion and maintains that

> even the most progressive of recent romances continue to bind female desire to a heterosexuality constructed as the only natural sexual alliance, and thus continue to prescribe patriarchal marriage as the ultimate route to the realization of a mature female subjectivity. (16)

As contemporary scholarship on the romance genre remains preoccupied with the relationship between feminism and romance, the racial and imperial politics of the romance genre have not received much scholarly attention. Indeed, the whiteness of the authors, characters, and readers generally goes unquestioned and unexamined. For example, in *Reading the Romance*, Radway describes the demographics of the Smithton readers in terms of current age, age at which they first began to read romance novels, marital status, number and age of their children, employment status, educational attainment, religious identification, and family income level, but not race (55-59). While Radway does acknowledge that "the Smithton group cannot be thought of as a scientifically designed random sample" and that "The conclusions drawn from the study, therefore, should be extrapolated only with great caution to apply to other romance readers," she does base her analysis of the romance genre largely on the responses of the Smithton readers (48). Whiteness is likewise invisible in the analyses of Modleski, Mussell, Cawelti, Hubbard, Regis, and the romance authors collected in *Dangerous Men and Adventurous Women*; the debates around the status of the genre as fantasy vs. reality, feminist vs. antifeminist have thus presumed a white, female reader (who is also assumed to be middle-class and heterosexual).

Representations of race and imperialism are, however, pervasive within the romance genre. For example, four of the "ideal romances" that Radway explores in detail explicitly address racial difference: Kathleen Woodiwiss's novel, *Shanna*, is set in the antebellum Caribbean, while *Ashes in the Wind* takes place during the American Civil War, as does Margaret Mitchell's *Gone with the Wind*; Celeste De Blasis's *The Proud Breed* examines the conflict between

Anglos and Californios in historic California (Radway 121).[1] Although Radway neglects to consider the connection between racial and gender ideologies in these texts and the Smithton readers' reception of them, other scholars have begun to incorporate race into studies of the romance genre. Stephanie Burley has recently argued that the "racially encoded language, trope, and ideology" of Silhouette romances "are indeed connected to culturally current ideologies of race, ethnicity, and Otherness in twentieth century America" (Burley 324). Her analysis takes as its subject the metaphoric associations of lightness/whiteness and darkness/blackness, or what Toni Morrison refers to as the "Africanist presence" (5), which occur in these texts around white characters. Burley argues that

> the employment of racial tropes of blackness as solvable intrigue, as sexuality, as the savage other who constructs triumphant and powerfully mysterious white heroines [...] reinforces normalized notions of powerful and mysterious whiteness. [...] They reflect the white-centered discursive landscape of American popular culture and create romantic fantasies out of the same racial language codes used to demean Black people and culture in the real world. (339)

The white heroes of romance novels, Burley contends, are portrayed as black or dark to emphasize their enigmatic and occasionally antagonistic nature and masculine virility, whereas white heroines are depicted using images of lightness or whiteness so that the eventual triumph of the heroine in winning the hero's love is concurrently "a symbolic victory of whiteness over darkness," a victory that is explicitly related to social, economic, and political inequalities (336). In her analysis, representations of race and gender are implicitly connected, as racial metaphors are deployed in the construction of masculinity, femininity, and heterosexual love.

The relationships between representations of race and gender are also taken up, albeit in a less complex way, by Evelyn Bach in "Sheik Fantasies: Orientalism and Feminine Desire in the Desert Romance," which takes as its subject the "desert romance" of the twentieth century. Bach argues that within feminine desire, Orientalism is refigured; specifically, the "desert romance destabilizes perceptions of the Orient as the West's feminized Other" (9). The generic and Orientalized desert is experienced by the heroine as "a transformative environment [that enables] her to discover and delight in the genre's ideal of true femininity," as she moves from being an initially independent and somewhat asexual figure to a woman subdued by the love of her sheik (Bach 31-32). The hero makes a similar journey, from overtly

---

[1] *All About Romance* also keeps and regularly updates a lengthy list of romance novels set in "exotic locations," many of which directly and indirectly discuss racial/ethnic difference, colonialism/imperialism, slavery, etc. See www.likesbooks.com/set.html.

masculine Orientalized stereotype to a racially hybrid, "partially civilized," and thus marriageable man (Bach 32). The setting of such novels in the desert allows the evocation of Eastern "fatalism" or "destiny," which Bach suggests "carries the potential for continuing desire" in female readers (36). Bach's essay does not, however, examine the reasons for or implications of the use and refiguring of Orientalist representational practices, and views the genre and Orientalist discourse as static and unchanging as it conflates novels written by British and American women and men from 1919 to 1996.

This paper seeks to combine and complicate these two broad modes of scholarly investigation by examining the connections between feminisms of the early 1990s, concurrent debates about the gender ideologies employed in the romance genre, and representational practices around the issue of sati in Mary Jo Putney's novel, *Veils of Silk*. Putney's novel draws on tropes that depict the sati as heroine or victim and foregrounds the notion of the widow's choice within a culturally relativist framework; this parallels the focus of the "therapeutic" or "babe" feminism of the early 1990s, the reformulation of romance novels as intrinsically feminist that occurred at this time, and the concurrent emergence and popularization of a discourse of multiculturalism in conjunction with the Persian Gulf War.

In 1992, Mary Jo Putney, a romance author previously known for her Regency-set novels, published the final book in her "Silk" trilogy, set in the early Victorian era. *Veils of Silk*, set in India under British colonial rule, followed *Silk and Shadows*, which takes place in Great Britain, and *Silk and Secrets*, which is set in Central Asia. The Scottish hero of *Veils of Silk*, Ian Cameron, is brother to the heroine of *Silk and Secrets* and a former officer in the British army, while the Russian heroine, Laura Stephenson, lives with her stepfather, a colonial administrator, in India. Due to his imprisonment alongside Laura's uncle in the Muslim city of Bokhara, Ian incorrectly believes he is impotent and proposes a marriage of convenience to Laura, who fears her sexual nature due to her parents' tempestuous and disastrous marriage, which ended when her father committed suicide following her mother's infidelity. While retrieving some of Laura's uncle's belongings from the independent principality of Dharjistan, Ian and Laura uncover a plot to overthrow the British colonial regime and naturally, ingeniously thwart it while simultaneously finding true love and fulfillment in each other. Their relationship is paralleled within the novel by two Indian couples: Meera, a Hindu widow, and Zafir, a Muslim Pathan, who serve as maid and valet respectively for Laura and Ian; and the maharajah and maharani of Dharjistan, Rajiv Singh and Kamala.

Although Ian and Zafir were close friends prior to the commencement of the novel, Laura and Ian meet Meera, "an expensive indulgence that [her husband] had acquired to amuse his later years" as she is fleeing from being unwillingly immolated on his funeral pyre (Putney 197). Immediately following her older and higher-caste husband's death, Meera declares: "'I will not go to the pyre with my husband'" and in the face of her husband's family's insistence, argues, "[a] widow must become suttee voluntarily, or it means nothing. I do not consent, nor would Mohan have expected me to" (Putney 198). Despite this, "the women of the household did everything they could to coerce Meera to becoming suttee" and finally, "[d]izzy with exhaustion and confusion," she says, "'Perhaps, [...] perhaps I should.'" These "stumbling words [are] taken as the consent needed," and Meera prepares to go to the pyre with all of her jewelry in order to spite her husband's family. As she leaves her home, she wonders, "if those long-forgotten women had become suttee willingly, or whether, like her, they had been forced" (Putney 199). While in the procession to the pyre, she thinks:

> She would have run away if there had been any hope of escape, but there was no such hope. With her own eyes she had once seen a woman try to escape the pyre, only to be shoved back into the flames by her own son. No, there was no escape, and Meera was resigned to the fact that she must die. Who was she, a mere mixed-caste female, to rail against the unfairness of fate? [...] Numbly she endured the ceremonies, knowing that she should be praying or even desperately savoring these last moments of life. But all she could think about was the fire. If a man's wife must die at his side, why did it have to be so painfully? [...] The moment came for her to ascend the ladder to the top of the pyre. When she faltered, a hard hand shoved her upward. (Putney 200)

Once the fire starts, Meera leaps from the pyre and thinks, "[e]ven if she became a beggar and starved, it would be a better end than what she was fleeing" (Putney 202); her husband's family chases her, but she encounters Laura, Ian, and Zafir, who, upon hearing Meera's claim that "'[m]y husband's family is forcing me to become suttee against my will,'" fend off her pursuers with a combination of rifles, threats, and curses and escape with her on horseback (Putney 204-205). Once they are safe, Ian remarks to an appalled Laura, "'I've always suspected that much of the reason for suttee is to get rid of inconvenient women'" (Putney 206). The narrative then traces Zafir's courtship of Meera and their eventual marriage. The fact that Meera is Hindu and Zafir is Muslim is not explicitly addressed in the novel, with the exception of two exchanges between Meera and Zafir around veiling and purdah, which will be discussed later.

The escape episode stands in stark contrast to Laura's discussion about sati with Kamala, the maharani of Dharjistan, later in the novel; Kamala was able to choose her husband from an assortment, "a dozen princes of suitable rank," and when she speaks of Rajiv, wears an "expression of shining love" (Putney 248-249). Ian later observes that "Kamala and Rajiv Singh are one of the great

Indian love stories. Among the common people, it's said that they're the
reincarnations of Shah Jahan and Mumtaz Mahal" (Putney 251). After
quarreling with Ian, Laura seeks Kamala's advice; the conversation segues into
a discussion of Hinduism:

> "Aren't you disturbed by things like suttee?" Laura asked, thinking of
> Meera. "Many women are burned against their will."
> "That is wrong, of course," Kamala said firmly. "Anyone who forces
> a woman against her will is a murderer who will pay for it in the next life. But
> for a woman who chooses it, suttee is a rite of great holiness. If Rajiv Singh dies
> before me, I will certainly accompany him to the pyre."
> "You, Kamala?" Laura was so surprised that she stopped walking. It
> seemed impossible to reconcile such a terrible death with the serene, beautiful
> woman beside her.
> The maharani smiled gently, as if talking to a child. "When Rajiv dies,
> my spirit will die with him. What is the point of preserving my body when we
> can be together in death and also in our next lives? When the time comes, I will
> go without doubts."
> "I hope it doesn't come anytime soon," Laura said fervently.
> "Srinivasa [the court astrologer] says we have many years still." After
> a few more steps, she added, "There is an old tale of a Rajput princess whose
> husband was called to battle on their wedding day. He was killed, and the next
> day she went to the pyre with him, virgin, bride, and widow, her nuptial flowers
> on her breast." (Putney 292-293)

Although Rajiv Singh is initially involved in plans to oust the British due to
rumors that his adopted heir would not be recognized as legitimate by the
British, Kamala's pregnancy leads him to cease his support of the insurgents and
by the conclusion of the novel, Kamala and Laura, who returns to Scotland with
Ian, are corresponding through letters.

Veils of Silk, published five years after the highly publicized burning of
Roop Kanwar in Deorala, Rajasthan and set eleven years after the abolishment
of sati by the British colonial government, presents the reader with two
dissimilar representations of sati or widow immolation (Loomba 210, 212). In
The Karma of Brown Folk, Vijay Prashad argues that in popular American
Orientalism, India is not simply "romantic and beautiful; it also come across as
hideous and barbaric," as a place of "ghastly and beautiful mysteries" and is
thus "simultaneously desirable and undesirable" (22, 27). Representations of
sati in the early twentieth century embody this dichotomy by highlighting both
the spirituality of the practice and its barbarism; Putney's depictions of Meera
and Kamala are contiguous with these discursive practices, as each character
embodies one of the poles in this construction of India (Prashad 30). Meera, as
well as the nameless widow she watched burn, is presented as "an abject
victim," "the oppressed and victimized Indian [...] woman" or a "superslave,"

"thrown upon the heap, sometimes fastened to it by unscrupulous family members or pundits," the undesirable aspect of Orientalized India, the appalling and barbaric (Mani 97, 117; Loomba 209; Prashad 21-45). Kamala, in contrast, is "superhuman"; she is presented "as a woman with special powers to curse or bless, as one who feels no pain, and one who will be rewarded with everlasting extra-terrestrial marital bliss" and "the privileged signifier of [...] the devoted and chaste," the appealing and mysteriously spiritual India (Mani 97; Loomba 209; Prashad 21-45). Her recounting of the story of the virgin widow evokes a parallel between sati and "heroic male deaths," suggesting that the "sati [...] dies positively for something, instead of negatively to escape a miserable life" (Loomba 210).

Putney's dichotomous representation of the sati as either helpless victim or heroic sacrifice seems to emerge from what Lata Mani has identified as the "common discourse" around sati in colonial India, which was utilized by both the indigenous elite, colonial officials, and advocates for and against sati (Mani 109-110). This discourse relies on "the hegemony of religious texts, a total indigenous submission to their dictates, and the religious basis of sati," leading those who deploy it to search the brahmanic scriptures for instances of sati (Mani 95). Putney hints at this aspect through Kamala's evocation of the "holiness" of the ritual and the presence of a Brahmin priest at Meera's failed sati, who angrily tells Ian, "'[s]uttee is our ancient custom, Englishman," as well as the conflation of tradition with scripture that Mani contends is at the heart of this "modern discourse on tradition" (Putney 204, 292; Mani 116). This emphasis on the religiosity of the practice also powerfully evokes American notions of India as predominantly a site of spirituality that emerged within nineteenth century American transcendentalism and continues to exist today within countercultural and New Age discourses (Prashad 15-18, 47-53). Yet this is not the predominant theme running throughout these two disparate discussions of sati; although Mani suggests that this discourse precludes discussion of the widows, that "they are denied any agency" as they "are neither subjects or objects, but rather the ground of the discourse on sati" (Mani 117), the representations of sati in *Veils of Silk* are very much invested in notions of agency, choice, and will.

Ania Loomba notes that prior to its abolition in 1829, British officials "strategically divided sati into illegal and legal, voluntary and involuntary ones," resulting in a "narrative division [...] of satis into good and bad ones" that played into perceptions of women as victims, heroines, and sites on which to enact tradition or modernity (Loomba 211-212, 215). Discussions around sati following the Deorala incident in 1987 also drew on these discursive practices, but, as Loomba argues, due to the presence of the women's movement, "the question of the widow's choice was at the core of all debates" (Loomba 215).

The lack of choice Meera is given is continually emphasized by the text; she refuses, is coerced into ambiguously consenting, sees herself as and tells others that she is being forced into sati, and is eventually physically pushed onto the pyre. This lack of choice is verbally reaffirmed by Ian immediately following the incident and by Laura and Kamala in their later conversation, as well as through the actions of Ian, Laura, and Zafir as they rescue Meera from her husband's family. Kamala's decision to become a sati is similarly rendered through the concept of choice; for the woman who "chooses" sati without "doubts," Kamala notes, it can be an incredibly meaningful act (Putney 292-293).

Despite this textual validation of some satis—those that are voluntary—as acceptable, Laura remains perturbed by the rite, even after Kamala's explanation. She says of the story Kamala recounts, "'That is a story of great power, but I am too much of the West to truly appreciate it,'" and when Kamala relates that she is not upset by the presence of her husband's concubines, remarks, "'That is a very mature attitude. [...] I'm not sure I'm capable of that much maturity'" (Putney 289, 293). The text is pervaded by a sense of the intrinsic incommensurability of cultures, as Ian finds "'it bizarre that a soldier who would risk his life for me without a second thought would refuse to accept water from my canteen'" (Putney 94). Similarly, Laura, who is "'tired of being surrounded by an alien culture that I'll never fully understand,'" observes when her horoscope is drawn up that "'[a]s a European, I'm uncomfortable with the idea that the future is fixed and immutable'" (Putney 104, 286). The text embraces a culturally relativist position, wherein "differences between cultures are discrete and relative with no real connection or common basis for evaluation"; while there can be good and bad satis, the practice itself must implicitly be backed due to this essential untranslatability and hence implicit validation of all cultural formations (Mohanty, "'Under Western Eyes' Revisited" 520).

In this novel, sati is reformulated as an issue "of female and individual choice" within a culturally relativist framework that pushes for discursive closure by eliding questions of power (Loomba 222; Mohanty "'Under Western Eyes' Revisited" 520). The recuperation of sati as traditional, authentic, and legitimate by Kamala, a moment in which Putney succumbs to "its grotesque power and ideal authenticity at the expense of understanding how and why it is produced in the first place," moves toward a representation of the native or subaltern as "non-duped" or sanctified, a move that further erases the role of power by disembedding the native from history and "turning history 'upside down'" (Loomba 220; Chow 344). Cultural relativism operates within the sense of pure cultural difference that also grounds Orientalism, "in which objects are what they are *because* they are what they are, for once for all time, for ontological reasons that no empirical material can either dislodge or alter" (Said 70). Sati becomes a timeless, ahistorical symbol of the empowerment and subjectivity of Indian women and simultaneously their oppression and status as objects, thus acting to erase them:

> As the discourse of what the British perceive as a heathen ritual is sublated [...] into what the British perceive as crime, one diagnosis of female free will is substituted for another [...and the] figure of the woman disappears, not into a pristine nothingness, but into a violent shuttling which is the displaced figuration of the "third-world woman" caught between tradition and modernization. (Spivak 300, 306)

The representational and discursive practices around sati in *Veils of Silk* evoke the ideals of "babe" or "therapeutic" feminism, which entered popular discourse in the early 1990s (Quindlen 4; Sandell 24). This conception of feminism suggests that "thanks to feminists in the 1970s, women today are empowered social agents, captains of their destiny, so to speak, if only they would recognize it" (Gerhard 37). Individual choice is key, as "individual acts of transformation can transcend the power and influence of institutions" and "the problem of male domination and violence [is] at the level of individual men and women" (Sandell 23, 27). One variant of this therapeutic feminism is "power feminism," most famously articulated by Naomi Wolf in her 1994 work, *Fire with Fire: The New Female Power and How to Use It.* Jillian Sandell suggests that power feminism "seeks power for individual women to use for themselves and advocates women meeting their own needs in responsible ways" (Sandell 27). From this emerges a sense that individual female choice, unconstrained by ideological considerations, can address oppression; in this discourse, all choices are necessarily valid, as long as they meet the needs of individual women. Like cultural relativism, which "serves as an apology for the exercise of power," therapeutic, babe, and power feminism, by "focusing on individual acts of or responses to oppression [neglect] the larger picture of systematic and institutionalized patriarchal privilege" (Mohanty, "'Under Western Eyes' Revisited" 520; Sandell 27). The Indian women in *Veils of Silk* can thus be represented as always already freely choosing or not choosing sati as they are "captains of their desire." Meera's husband's family is not implicated in larger systems of gender oppression but is merely greedy and jealous on an individual level; indeed, it is her female relatives that push Meera into sati in order to inherit her jewels and wealth while her male relatives prepare for the funeral. Kamala can freely choose sati because her love for her husband is so complete and overwhelming. The decision to embrace sati is not depicted as expected of her by her family or by Rajput society.

Meyda Yeğenoğlu has recently criticized scholarly analyses of Orientalism for "fall[ing] short in recognizing how representations of cultural and sexual difference are constitutive of each other" (1). The emergence of babe, therapeutic, and power feminism in the early to mid-1990s is contemporaneous with the popularization and subsequent attack on the discourse of liberal multiculturalism and political correctness; both repertoires foreground the individual, freely choosing subject, and deemphasize systematic oppression and inequality (McAlister 245-246). Liberal multiculturalism also bears much in common with cultural relativism, as both operate on notions of discrete, unchanging, and hierarchized cultural difference; American multiculturalist discourse contends that some of these differences, be they gendered, sexual, racial, or ethnic, can somehow be incorporated into the nation-state but that others cannot. It is these unassimilable differences that mark the boundaries of the nation (McAlister 255-259; Prashad 110-113). In *Epic Encounters: Culture, Media, and U.S. Interests in the Middle East, 1945-2000*, Melani McAlister suggests that popular discourse around the Persian Gulf War relied on multiculturalism (250). Putney's 1992 use of a culturally relativist framework and her evocation of India as a space of religion and spirituality, which Prashad argues is the defining feature of American multiculturalist representations of India, echoes popular discursive practices around the Persian Gulf War (Prashad 113).

Although the novel is set in British Colonial India, its representations of non-white people in relativist and Orientalist terms and sense of British rule as generally benign—the hero, Ian, claims, "In British India, life is far less hazardous, taxes are more fair, and every peasant can have his day in court and receive justice"—parallel what McAlister calls "military multiculturalism" and more broadly, the narrative around the American response to Iraq's invasion of Kuwait (Putney 262; McAlister 235-236). This narrative, Marita Sturken argues, constructed the Persian Gulf War as a clean war: "Instead of images of man against man, these are images of weapons against weapons" (132). The erasure of human bodies and communities in popular representations of the Persian Gulf War is in some sense duplicated in Putney's unwillingness or inability to depict the ugliness and cost of British imperialism, which is instead displaced to narrow-minded and intolerant individuals. In a conversation with Ian, for example, Rajiv Singh notes:

> "You are tolerant, Falkirk. Because of men like you, the English yoke weighed lightly for many years. But more and more of your countrymen seek to 'improve' us, to change our heathen ways. They despise the gods and customs that make us what we are. The more such Britishers there are, the more Mother India will chafe at the harness." (Putney 262-263)

Through the similarity of its representational practices to military multiculturalism and the dominant perceptions of the Persian Gulf War, Putney's novel could also be understood as participating in the consolidation of a particular type of American national identity—a "respectful 'rainbow,'" rather than the melting pot, and the benevolent hero of the Persian Gulf War (McAlister 252).

The critiques of earlier scholarship on the romance genre that are emerging at this time are thematically similar to both babe or therapeutic feminism and cultural relativism:

> The fantasies are uniquely feminine and the story is essentially the heroine's. She is the one with choices to make, she is the one to take control, to triumph at the end. Yes, she finds love and the man of her dream (and mine), but the power of choice is ultimately hers. I put her center stage and give her all the heroic qualities usually given to the leading man—she is brave and free spirited, smart and strong willed, honorable and proud. Yet she retains her leading lady role as well, for she is loving and nurturing and sexually alluring. By the end of the book the power is all in my heroine's feminine hands—power over her enemies, over herself, and over the hero, her chosen man. It is her world, her triumph, her story. (Williamson 126)

Penelope Williamson, a romance author, frames the romance narrative around the issue of personal preference and suggests that the enactment of individual female choice can challenge systems of oppression and the workings of power. This articulation of the romance genre generally captures the critique of studies such as Radway's in the early 1990s; heterosexual marriage, which romance novels must incorporate in order to fit within the generic form, can and would be freely chosen outside of systems of patriarchal and heteronormative power and thus can only be a legitimate, unideological choice. The construction of female choice here as fundamentally unconstrained is the means by which romance is constructed as feminist, as emblematic of female empowerment. *Veils of Silk* embraces this discourse by figuring Ian and Laura's marriage as one of convenience, based on their needs for companionship. Laura is able to say, "'[i]f I had common sense, […] I would not be considering your proposal,'" yet she is essentially alone in the world, a Russian in British colonial India at the height of the Great Game, without discernible means of supporting herself (Putney 98). Her choice to accept Ian's proposal, then, is conditioned by the material realities of being a woman, just as Kamala's choice to become a sati or Meera's attempt to flee it are overdetermined by the social formations in which they live. As Loomba observes, "subaltern agency, either at the individual level or at the collective, cannot be idealized as pure opposition to the order it opposes; it works both within that order and displays its own contradiction" (223). She goes on to note that "identity is both self-constructed, and constructed for us" despite the insistence within the discourses of therapeutic feminism and cultural relativism and the representational practices of romance writers of the autonomy of female choice and identity (223).

The decontextualization and elemental equality of choice in *Veils of Silk* results in a move that parallels Chandra Mohanty's description of liberal feminism's tendency to rely on "women as a category of analysis" wherein "women are characterized as a singular group on the basis of a shared oppression" (Mohanty, "Under Western Eyes" 56). The main female characters of the novel, who seemingly have little in common—Laura, the Russian stepdaughter of a British civil servant; Meera, the mixed-caste widow of a merchant; and Kamala, the maharani of Dharjistan and a Rajput princess—are all represented as desiring basically the same things, namely, a loving husband, a secure home, and children. By the conclusion of the novel, Laura discovers she is pregnant and receives two letters:

> The week before, a letter had arrived from Dharjistan. Kamala had borne a son. [...] [B]abies seemed to be the order of the day. A month earlier, a letter from Meera had informed her that Zafir's confidence is his virility had not been misplaced. A little Pathan was expected in the autumn. (Putney 394-395)

Women are not characterized as a single group based on their oppression here, but rather based on their wish to bear children.

Despite the text's use of cultural relativism, there is a residual sense of uneasiness around some non-Western cultural practices that undermines this relativism and contributes to the construction of what Mohanty calls "third world difference" (Mohanty, "Under Western Eyes" 73). Similarly, Prashad perceives this discomfort as fundamental to American Orientalist representations of India, which are concurrently pleasing and repulsive (22). This uneasiness appears in Laura's continued consternation regarding Kamala's stated decision to become a sati if Rajiv Singh dies first and also around Meera and Zafir's discussions about marriage, conversion, and purdah:

> "Women need more freedom, not less," Meera retorted as she scooped up the sliced carrots and dropped them in the stew. "I suppose you think we should all be penned up like goats in a cage the way Pathan women are."
>
> "Our women have freedom and influence within the home, where it matters," Zafir said reasonably. And outside, the veil protects them from the advances of strangers."
>
> Meera knew that what she was doing was hazardous, like teasing a tiger but she couldn't resist saying, "Women wouldn't need protection if men weren't such beasts."
>
> "So we are," Zafir agreed. (Putney 237-238)

"Marrying me will mean giving up the life you know, and you will lose some liberties that a Hindu woman has. But you will gain other liberties, along with security and protection. Though Pathan women must be veiled when they venture into the outside world, within the compound they have influence and respect. If you accept me, I will do my best to make it easy for you to become one of us." (Putney 266)

In the first passage, it is worth noting that Meera has no response to Zafir, and, despite her disagreement with him and indeed, her likening of Pathan women to goats, she does eventually marry him and accept both purdah and veiling. The language in the second passage is one of loss—of life, freedom, identity—as any sense of gain is disputed by the very vagueness and non-specificity of terms such as "security," "influence," "respect," and "protection," all of which lack an object. Moreover, as Leila Ahmed suggests, "The peculiar practices of Islam with respect to women had always formed part of the Western narrative of the quintessential otherness and inferiority of Islam," and it is this otherness that these discussions between Meera and Zafir evoke (149).

This anxiety also emerges when Meera is awaiting her death on her husband's pyre:

Meera's resignation lasted until the first yellow flame shot upward, fed by the oil-soaked cotton. The hem of her sari flared and pain blazed along her lower leg, shattering her numbness. She screamed and hurled herself frantically away from the flames. Unable to wait passively for an agonizing death, she scrambled down from the pyre, even though she expected that remorseless hands would seize her and hurl her back into the inferno. (Putney 202)

The emphasis in this scene is on the bodily pain that cannot be dissociated from the act of sati, regardless of whether or not the widow chose to participate. The violence and horror of this moment is such that it undermines any rationalization of the practice that the text may attempt to articulate. Sati and purdah become oppressive "phenomena to be judged by Western standards," resulting in the creation within the novel of the "third world woman" who reinforces "assumptions about Western women as secular, liberated, and having control over their own lives" (Mohanty, "Under Western Eyes" 72-74). Laura's choice to marry becomes more reasonable, more rational, when compared to the choice of these women to burn themselves or veil themselves for heterosexual love. Laura and Ian's marriage is seemingly unbound by the absurd restrictions that Meera and Kamala face, an aspect of the text that is heightened by its interpellation of the reader as white through creating a sense of identification with the white heroine (Radway 64; Althusser 74).

These moments contradict the novel's reliance on a discourse of cultural relativism and reveal understandings of difference that emerge from white liberal feminism; as with cultural relativism, this construction of the dissimilarities between women's lives is predicated on the notion of a certain sameness that is related to biological sex. While cultural relativism suggests that this equivalence is grounded in free choice, the depiction of Meera and Kamala as "third world women" is tied to a sense that women around the world seek essentially the same thing, although in vastly distinct and differently valued ways. Their choices thus become incomprehensible to white readers, who ostensibly pursue identical goals. Ultimately, this move acts to consolidate a particular notion of white womanhood, deny white women's collusion in systems of oppression, and to reassure the white reader of her essential freedom (Winter 11). As Jacques Derrida argues:

> Each time ethnocentrism is precipitately and ostentatiously reversed, some effort silently hides behind all the spectacular effects to consolidate an inside and to draw from it some domestic benefit. (qtd. in Spivak 293)

The depictions of sati in Mary Jo Putney's 1992 novel, *Veils of Silk*, draw on a discursive repertoire that is similar to that of both "therapeutic" or "babe" feminism and white liberal feminism. Like therapeutic feminism, *Veils of Silk* emphasizes the notion of choice in discussing sati. In culturally relativist terms, all choices are valid and, to some extent, exist outside of systems of power; sati can thus be unproblematic if the widow chooses to participate because she does so freely. This idealization of choice within the novel evokes debates around the romance genre and the construction of it by some critics and authors as inherently feminist. In addition, the representations of sati and Indian women in *Veils of Silk* deploy the assumptions of white liberal feminism by evoking the stereotypical "third world woman," who desires the same things as white women but attempts to achieve her aspirations in an unfathomable, and hence irrational, peculiar, and Other, way. The representational practices of therapeutic, babe, and white liberal feminism that emerged in the early 1990s echo some of the same tropes as liberal multiculturalism, which entered popular discourse at approximately the same historical moment. Ideals of individual freedom and choice around gender and race could act to secure nationalism, especially during a conflict such as the Persian Gulf War. While most scholars have neglected to interrogate the relationship between the gender and racial ideologies of "escapist rot," the representations of both women and racialized individuals within novels such as *Veils of Silk* are fundamentally intertwined (Douglas 213). The significance of such ideologies lies not in whether they are realistic or fantastic, but in what political work they perform, which systems they legitimate, and which individuals they marginalize.

Works Cited

Ahmed, Leila. *Women and Gender in Islam*. New Haven, CT: Yale University P, 1992.

Althusser, Louis. "Ideology and Ideological State Apparatuses (Notes Toward an Investigation)." *Lenin and Philosophy and Other Essays*. Trans. Ben Brewster. New York: Monthly Review P, 1971.

Asaro, Catherine. "Feminism and Romance." *All About Romance*. http://www.likesbooks.com/quick16.html.

Atwood, Margaret. "What is a Woman's Novel?" *Ms*. Aug. (1986): 98.

Bach, Evelyn. "Sheik Fantasies: Orientalism and Feminine Desire in the Desert Romance." *Hecate* 1 (1997): 9-43.

Burley, Stephanie. "Shadows and Silhouettes: The Racial Politics of Category Romance." *Paradoxa* 5 (2000): 324-341.

Cawelti, John G. *Adventure, Mystery, and Romance: Formula Stories as Art and Popular Culture*. Chicago: U of Chicago P, 1976.

Chow, Rey. "Where Have All the Natives Gone?" *Displacements: Cultural Identities in Question*. Ed. Angelika Bammer. Bloomington, IN: Indiana UP, 1994.

Douglas, Susan. *Where the Girls Are: Growing Up Female with the Mass Media*. New York: Times Books, 1994.

Frenier, Mariam Darce. *Good-Bye Heathcliff: Changing Heroes, Heroines, Roles, and Values in Women's Category Romances*. New York: Greenwood Press, 1988.

Gerhard, Jane. "The Personal is Still Political: The Legacy of 1970s Feminism." *"Bad Girls" "Good Girls": Women, Sex, and Power in the Nineties*. Eds. Nan Bauer Maglin and Donna Perry. New Brunswick, NJ: Rutgers UP, 1996.

Hubbard, Rita C. "The Changing-Unchanging Heroines and Heroes of Harlequin Romances 1950-1979." *The Hero in Transition*. Eds. Ray B. Browne and Marshall W. Fishwick. Bowling Green, OH: Bowling Green U Popular P, 1983.

Jensen, Margaret Ann. *Love's $weet Return: The Harlequin Story*. Bowling Green, OH: Bowling Green State U Popular P, 1984.

Kishwar, Madhu and Ruth Vanita. "The Burning of Roop Kanwar." *Race and Class* 1 (1988): 59-67.

Krentz, Jayne Ann. "Introduction." *Dangerous Men and Adventurous Women: Romance Writers on the Appeal of the Romance*. Ed. Jayne Ann Krentz. Philadelphia: U of Pennsylvania P, 1992.

Loomba, Ania. "Dead Women Tell No Tales: Issues of Female Subjectivity, Subaltern Agency, and Tradition in Colonial and Postcolonial Writings on

Widow Immolation in India." *History Workshop Journal* 36 (1993): 209-227.

Mani, Lata. "Contentious Traditions: The Debate on Sati in Colonial India." *The Nature and Context of Minority Discourse.* Eds. Abdul Jan Mohamed and David Lloyd. New York: Oxford UP, 1990.

McAlister, Melani. *Epic Encounters: Culture, Media, and U. S. Interests in the Middle East, 1945-2000.* Berkeley, CA: U of California P, 2001.

Modleski, Tania. "The Disappearing Act: A Study of Harlequin Romances." *Signs* 5 (1980): 435-448.

————.*Old Wives' Tales and Other Women's Stories.* New York: New York UP, 1998.

Mohanty, Chandra Talpade. "Under Western Eyes: Feminist Scholarship and Colonial Discourses." *Third World Women and the Politics of Feminism.* Eds. Chandra Talpade Mohanty, Ann Russo, and Lourdes Torres. Bloomington, IN: Indiana UP, 1991.

————."'Under Western Eyes' Revisited Feminist Solidarity through Anticapitalist Struggles." *Signs* 2 (2002): 494-535.

Morrison, Toni. *Playing in the Dark: Whiteness and the Literary Imagination.* New York: Vintage Books, 1993.

Mussell, Kay. *Fantasy and Reconciliation: Contemporary Formulas of Women's Romance Fiction.* Westport, CT: Greenwood P, 1984.

————.Interview with Laurie Gold: "Are Feminism and Romance Novels Mutually Exclusive?" *All About Romance.* http://www.likesbooks.com/mussell.html.

Phillips, Susan Elizabeth. "The Romance and the Empowerment of Women." *Dangerous Men and Adventurous Women: Romance Writers on the Appeal of the Romance.* Ed. Jayne Ann Krentz. Philadelphia: U of Pennsylvania P, 1992.

Prashad, Vijay. *The Karma of Brown Folk.* Minneapolis, MN: U of Minnesota P, 2000.

Putney, Mary Jo. *Silk and Secrets.* New York: Onyx, 1992.

————.*Silk and Shadows.* New York: Onyx, 1991.

————.*Veils of Silk.* New York: Onyx, 1992.

Quindlen, Anna. "And Now, Babe Feminism." *"Bad Girls" "Good Girls": Women, Sex, and Power in the Nineties.* Eds. Nan Bauer Maglin and Donna Perry. New Brunswick, NJ: Rutgers UP, 1996.

Radway, Janice A. *Reading the Romance: Women, Patriarchy, and Popular Literature.* Chapel Hill, NC: U of North Carolina P, 1991.

Regis, Pamela. *A Natural History of the Romance Novel.* Philadelphia: U of Pennsylvania P, 2003.

Said, Edward. *Orientalism.* New York: Vintage Books, 1979.

Sandell, Jillian. "Adjusting to Oppression: The Rise of Therapeutic Feminism in the United States." *"Bad Girls" "Good Girls": Women, Sex, and Power in the Nineties*. Eds. Nan Bauer Maglin and Donna Perry. New Brunswick, NJ: Rutgers UP, 1996.

Sturken, Marita. *Tangled Memories: The Vietnam War, the AIDS Epidemic, and the Politics of Remembering*. Berkeley, CA: U of California P, 1997.

Spivak, Gayatri. "Can the Subaltern Speak?" *Marxism and the Interpretation of Culture*. Eds. Cary Nelson and Lawrence Grossberg. Urbana, IL: U of Illinois P, 1988.

Thurston, Carol. *The Romance Revolution: Erotic Novels for Women and the Quest for a New Sexual Identity*. Urbana, IL: U of Illinois P, 1987.

Williamson, Penelope. "By Honor Bound: The Heroine as Hero." *Dangerous Men and Adventurous Women: Romance Writers on the Appeal of the Romance*. Ed. Jayne Ann Krentz. Philadelphia: U of Pennsylvania P, 1992.

Winter, Bronwyn. "Fundamental Misunderstandings: Issues in Feminist Approaches to Islamism." *Journal of Women's History* 1 (2001): 9-45.

Yeğenoğlu, Meyda. *Colonial Fantasies: Towards a Feminist Reading of Orientalism*. Cambridge: Cambridge UP, 1998.

Maura Seale

Maura Seale received her MA in American Studies from the University of Minnesota in 2005. Her work focused on representations of race and imperialism in American mass culture in the latter half of the twentieth century. Currently she is a graduate student at the University of Michigan and will receive her MS in Information in 2007.

CHAPTER TEN

FEMALE ENFRANCHISEMENT
AND THE POPULAR ROMANCE:
EMPLOYING AN INDIAN PERSPECTIVE

JAYASHREE KAMBLE

[Marion Zimmer] Bradley goes on to argue that the bad influence of romance novels is so profound and pernicious that women, raised on "a steady diet of this kind of reading" and incapable of distinguishing between harmful fantasy and true reality, are unfit for the workplace, unfit for motherhood, and unfit for genuine love. In short, the modern romance novel, a meretricious and debased literary form, creates helpless, though willing victims.
—Alison M. Scott, reviewing anti-romance criticism

Rape fantasy, escapist literature, trashy novels, masturbatory fiction—the epithets that are used to refer to popular romances are almost always snide, if not completely sexist and puritanical. Condemned as soft porn that encourages women to accept and enjoy their subservient position in a patriarchal culture, romance fiction has been regarded as the epitome of masochistic desire. Germaine Greer referred to romance novels as "escapist literature of love and marriage voraciously consumed by housewives" (214). These novels are thus seen as sugarcoated patriarchal ideology, a hegemonic discourse that its female audience has internalized. Most critiques of the genre reveal two main objections to romances—that they are pornographic and anti-feminist. This paper contests this view by reexamining some of the assumptions on which it is based. Furthermore, it places the genre in the center of its global audience by bringing its readership in India into the discussion and presents the alternative subversive readings this audience could create.

The standard structure of the romance plot includes the meeting of a woman and a man, their tempestuous encounters—usually a result of strong sexual tension or of circumstances not conducive to a love affair—and an eventual acknowledgment of romantic feelings by both partners, leading to a wedding or plans for a prospective one. The emphasis romance novels place on heterosexual relationships that culminate in marriage appears to be antithetical to some of the principles of second-wave feminism. In fact, Joanne Hollows cites examples of writers who claim that romances are a conspiracy against feminism:

> [...] Ann Douglas argues that as the feminist movement grew so did the readership of Harlequin fictions in which "woman's independence is made horribly unattractive and unrewarding, her dependence presented as synonymous with excitement." (Hollows 72)

Some researchers even claim that these novels prompt women to tolerate abuse (Kloberdanz 50). Thus, not only are these books seen as a source of dangerously antiquated ideas but also as a discourse that has considerable power to affect the attitudes and behavior of women in the real world—all for the worse.

The first problem with such critiques is that they are either too early or simply fail to take into account the fact that the genre has evolved rapidly in the last thirty years and that it contains numerous sub-genres. Even when the latter is acknowledged, critics choose to focus on the series that validates their arguments. As Alison Scott notes, the variety of romance novels available in the genre is turned aside by the simple expedient of calling them all "Harlequins," treating the most formulaic texts as representative of the genre as a whole—including the works that do not prescribe to a formula beyond the structure mentioned above (214). Much of this criticism also stems from the stream of feminist thought that views this fiction as a part of mass culture and its readers as cultural dupes, weak recipients of the lies told by a culture industry shot through with patriarchy. Such an attitude patronizes the ordinary viewers/readers and claims for itself the insight that they supposedly do not have (Hollows 26). It almost appears as if romances are a convenient punching bag, seen to represent the combined faults of female authorship, pulp fiction, and literature on sex.

Even Janice Radway, who first studied the genre by surveying some of its readers in 1984, appears in her early work to think that the novels extol a conservative ideology that has a detrimental effect on the lives of readers. But not only is her 1984 analysis limited to middle-class American readers, she makes two more assumptions in arriving at this conclusion—that readers use these books as guides for living and that they will probably internalize the genre's "anti-feminist" moments (216). She and many other academics neither fully concede the potential feminist stance in these works, nor do they really believe that the readers of romances may be taking away a reading that is different from the one that seems obvious to them. The central weakness of this critical conviction is the fact that it rests on second-wave feminism, which assumes that it is making a universal statement for all women, but is in fact limited to the needs and beliefs of white middle-class women. So when a feminist reading of any cultural entity is done and the text (be it a movie, a book, or a practice) is pronounced as anti-feminist, the reading overlooks the communities of women (of other social classes, nations, or cultures) who might view the text in an entirely different light. This is precisely why I am arguing for a more nuanced understanding of popular romance fiction based on a yet unexamined romance readership—one in India.

A survey that I conducted in 2005 found that romance readers in India range from homemakers to teenagers in high schools, young women in college, and career women. Most of the respondents speak more than two languages; 20 out of 23 respondents have at least one college degree (and seven hold Masters degrees). While three said that they stopped reading romances because they found them monotonous, five considered them "light, easy reading." Three readers noticed that the genre has become more realistic over the years, and four believed that romance reading has made them more accepting of others. One respondent claimed to have a new perception of male-female relationships, and another felt able to relate to the problems experienced by "western" women. At least three readers felt that the genre had become less emotional and romantic and expressed a desire for less "graphic" descriptions of sex. The survey results not only challenge the belief of who is reading romances but also the misconception that they are only read for escapism or sexual gratification. For instance, Bridget Fowler, who does analyze a neglected section of romance fiction readership—working class women in Scotland and England—argues that the readership is comprised of childlike uneducated women who can never change the facts of their own subjugated existence and resort to these texts purely as if they were a sort of religious salvation fantasy (15).

Taking into consideration an untapped community of readers, of which my survey only represents a tiny fraction, shows how romances can create an empowering fantasy. It allows an interpretation of this genre as a study of the female psyche, one that is helping the impulse for a change in women's social status to emerge in different parts of the world. The narratives in these texts are subversive enough to allow women in a different culture to reassess the social structures that dictate their lives. My approach rests on the work of theorists who have argued against a bleak view of cultural reception, among them John Fiske. Building on Michel de Certeau's ideas of popular resistance, "making do with what the system provides," Fiske argues that there is a "culture of everyday life" in which the juggernaut of dominant ideology is opposed by the audience (25). This is the territory of popular culture. According to Fiske, viewers of media culture or readers of popular literature practice a selective style of apprehension, filtering out undesirable dominant ideology and adapting the original or obvious message for something that is more appropriate to their particular reality. This way of reading in order to focus on what is relevant to the reader's circumstances is termed as resistance to the flood of mass culture. One of my survey respondents demonstrated this behavior, professing a preference for romances in which heroines outwit heroes. Fiske further argues that the extreme machismo and sadistic desires of romance heroes actually serve to remind readers that in the real world they live in a similar environment that favors men, an environment that they have learned to accept as normal (114). Romances can thus denaturalize patriarchy and gender bias through the unpleasant treatment of the heroine at the hands of the hero. Fiske's analysis opens the door to the many interpretations romances offer their readers, provided that they wish to see them. The dual lenses of popular resistance and a different cultural perspective will further substantiate my argument that romances can lend themselves to a feminist reading.

The Reader in India

India is a country that mixes conservative traditions with liberalism. Women were awarded the same rights and freedoms as men when the Indian Constitution came into effect 55 years ago, but there is still social regulation and supervision of their actions, thoughts, and feelings, and unfortunately, a prevailing belief in the superiority of the male sex, in terms of both physical and intellectual capacity. The education of female children is on the rise, yet it is still considered secondary to the education of the males in the family, especially in rural areas. Furthermore, women's education is often treated more as a means of improving the marketability of daughters in the marriage mart rather than a path to personal development or a career. Meenakshi Gigi Durham illustrates this with her own experience of fellow Indian women at an exclusive school and college in India in the 70s and 80s:

> At both of these institutions, the majority of students were from affluent and orthodox Indian families. They expected to have arranged marriages (most of them, in fact, eventually did).

She further points out that while many of these students dressed to imitate western media images,

> ...the underlying assumption was always that these fashion experiments were geared to one thing only: finding a place as a housewife and mother, acquiring perfection in the domestic role while having a career, "if my husband will allow it," as they said without rancor. (201)

To a large extent, Durham's observations still hold true. Most families still consider marriage to be the most suitable occupation for a woman, a marriage that is arranged by the head of the family. Once married, a woman is expected to produce a child within the first year of marriage (or put up with nosy and snide comments from her new family). It is preferable if she gives birth to at least one boy child because that is imperative for carrying on the family name. It is more economical as well, since daughters have to be married off, and the money spent on raising them (not to mention the unofficial dowries many are given) is a drain on parents' finances. A recent *Times of India* article cited figures from the Indian census confirming the validity of the concerns expressed about the detrimental effect of such a social environment on Indian women in the United Nations Population Fund's 2005 State of World Population report ("Is the Window Closing?").

It is evident that even as western feminism argues about female power in relation to significant but abstract concepts such as a masculinized writing practice, there are places in the world where a more concrete struggle, related to the immediate reality of controlling one's daily existence, is still to be undertaken. Much of what western feminism considers a battle won, such as a woman's right to earn a living, live independently, or choose her acquaintances or husband, is not uncontested in a culture like mine. Again, this is not to argue that Indian society or law runs roughshod over women. Indian women live something of a double life—on one level, they have social, economic, and political rights in accordance with the highest principles of democracy, but on another level, all rights become secondary to the imperatives of tradition, a tradition that insists that women are wives and mothers first and must always put their own needs and desires last. Consequently, irrespective of what the law dictates, Indian women are often required to exist as relational entities, exercising limited authority over major life decisions. Any charge that such a life is unfair is met with a variation of the attitude that existed in England and the United States in the Victorian Age. Society defends its strait-jacketing of women by stressing the essential nature of the division of the sexes and claims that women do exercise power over their families through their roles as wives and mothers. While women have to be kept within the bounds of the home and traditional marriage because that is the "natural" way of things, they are also to be enshrined, put on a pedestal for their nurturing capacities and delicate sensibilities. It then follows that women must be restrained from living too "liberal" a lifestyle because this may invite rape. This ideology is ever present and directs the actions of most Indian women and their families.

An Early Stage of Feminism in Romances

While most romance readers in India live in urban areas and experience the pressures noted above somewhat distantly, even educated, urban women rarely escape them completely. To a woman in such a culture, contemporary romance fiction published by Harlequin-Mills and Boon, and Avon, to name a few, is not just a fantasy; it is the vision of a society in which—irrespective of whether the stories are true to life—writers can imagine a female protagonist who has the biggest say in the course of her own life. It was reading romances as a teenager in the early nineties in India that made me realize that my world was not conducive to achieving selfhood as a woman, and this initial impression of the feminist sub-text in romances was not overturned even after I discovered the scholarly arguments on the anti-feminist message of these books. (This critique admittedly has some basis in fact, but is largely applicable to some 1970s romances.) I read the novels employing de Certeau's "tactic," utilizing an alternative reading practice to combat the sexist nature of some of them. I honed in on, delighted in, and remembered only those aspects of romances that seemed feminist to me and helped me analyze and evaluate my own situation. In doing so, I did and still do make the texts relevant to me. When viewed through the lens of a culture that has never experienced a feminist movement, contemporary romance fiction can thus be seen to contain startlingly radical elements. What has in the past been considered only a vehicle for perpetuating gender stereotypes and encouraging bored housewives to stay barefoot, pregnant, and dependant, in fact has the potential to provide women in other cultures with tactics to recognize and contest patriarchy—*as it exists in their own contexts*.

What is it that can be read as feminist in these novels? For one, it is the woman's ability to choose her sexual and emotional partner. This may not seem very progressive since it is something that has been practiced for a century or more in Europe and the United States. Even when arranged marriages were the norm, courtship rituals that were aimed at acquiring a woman's consent were firmly in place. However, women in several cultures, if not actually forced into marriage with a virtual stranger, are brought up to think of such an arrangement as inevitable. Durham notes that her fellow students were "[a]ware that marriage was unquestionably their fate, and that it would be arranged by their parents in the Indian tradition [...]" (201). There has only been a marginal shift in this attitude in India.

Surrounded by such an all-powerful conservatism, a reader who comes across popular romance novels is hard pressed to see these stories, in which women live and work alone when they choose, as well as evaluating potential life partners on their own, as anything but ground-breaking. My initial acquaintance with the romance genre in the nineties included novels from Mills and Boon (UK) and Silhouette (US), both series that tell the story of a present-day female protagonist who meets a man she is strongly attracted to and with whom she forms a long-lasting relationship. Some of these romances were written in the seventies and early eighties and did employ many of the plot elements that romances are still trying to live down—such as overbearing heroes and meek, martyr-like heroines forced to marry them for social or economic reasons. Some critics argue that this is why romances are regressive, that their emphasis on marriage perpetuates conformity to traditional family structure. However, though my familiarity with such gender stereotyping (and marriage-making) in my own culture stopped me from questioning the teleology of such novels, it also made me turn to the romances that did contradict the marriage narrative I knew—by letting the heroines marry where they pleased. As far as I could tell, the claim that a woman could decide *whom* she wished to marry was a step forward, not back. My sustained interest in the genre rests on the fact that it continues to create heroines who make this radical—to a reader like me—choice.

In novels such as Sally Wentworth's *King of the Castle* (1978), the heroine evaluates the hero's worthiness as a potential mate and father, only marrying him after careful examination and analysis, testing not only her own feelings but his as well. Romance novels have always allocated space to such introspection on the heroine's part, allowing her to mull over her sexual as well as emotional compatibility with the hero. These passages dwell at length on the rush of feelings—a mix of love and desire—that the man evokes and are often accused of being purple prose. But these dialogues with the self are rich in content, revealing women's ideas about what makes a man attractive as well as capable. Furthermore, the freedom to spend time thinking about these issues also prepares the ground for the freedom to act on these thoughts. One need not automatically assume that these heroines think a great deal about the men in their lives because women have been indoctrinated to worship the phallus; their meditations can also be seen as revelatory of control and self-knowledge. Instead of being mere objects of exchange, commodities to be passed from the authority of one man to another, romance heroines demonstrate their right to judge the men around them in these internal debates, as is seen in this excerpt from best-selling writer Nora Roberts's *Cordina's Crown Jewel* (2002). In it the heroine, Princess Camilla, working on a dig with archaeologist Delaney Caine, analyzes her growing love for him. Notice that she articulates to herself the causes of her emotional attachment, studying how Delaney's characteristics have prompted her response rather than stopping the rumination at the first paragraph (which acknowledges her love). It is she who decides to make the first overture after she has finished her evaluation of him as a worthy partner:

Why she was in love with him, she thought with surprise. Wasn't that fascinating. Somewhere during this complicated and problematic interlude, she'd slid headlong in love with a bad-tempered, irritable, rough-mannered scientist who was more likely to snarl at her than smile.

He was rude, demanding, easily annoyed, impatient. And brilliant, passionate, reluctantly kind. It was a captivating mix that made him uniquely himself. She wouldn't change a single thing about him. More, she thought, leaning against the wall to watch him. He had one of the most essential traits she wanted in a friend, and in a lover. He had honor.

They were alone here, yet he'd never tried to take advantage of that. In fact, he rarely touched her even in the most casual way. Though he was attracted—she knew she wasn't wrong about that—his personal code wouldn't allow him to exploit the situation.

Her lips twitched in a smile. That made him, under it all, a gentleman. How he would hate to be termed so. So, she was in love with an ill-tempered gentleman who wouldn't allow himself to seduce his temporary assistant. That meant it was going to be up to her to seduce him. (123-24)

A heroine possessing such an interiority would undoubtedly appear path-breaking to readers like the Indian women mentioned earlier by Durham, who accept that their families would choose their husbands, leaving them with minimal decision-making powers:

They talked of marriage but not of romantic love or sex. Aware that marriage would be arranged by their parents, their discussions of men were pragmatic. "He should be quiet and fair-skinned." "I don't care if he is good looking or not, but he should have a good job." "If he wants to settle abroad, then he should be willing to come back to India every year to visit." (201)

Though some Indian women have begun to assert their right to have a greater say in selecting a bridegroom, many have been raised to believe that the demand is morally suspect. To such readers, heroines like Camilla are the introduction to a new stage in female enfranchisement within the arena of marriage because they dramatize the internal process of assessing oneself and one's prospective partner and treat the institution as only a desirable *possibility* rather than a given.

Not only do romances allow the heroine moments of rumination to examine what she feels, but they also afford her the opportunity to lock verbal horns with the hero; thus conversation contests dominate all the courtship rituals that are an integral part of the novels. The conversations can be seen as furthering the cause of female choice, too, though I suspect that most critics overlook them because they often confine themselves to the immediate needs of the narrative. Carol Thurston is in the minority in her focus on dialogue in erotic romance. She cites several examples in which heroines declare their need for independence or their disgust at the double standard to the hero (68-69, 76-77).

A further understanding of Indian attitudes may illustrate why I regard such repartee as a sign of liberation for women. In Indian culture, interaction between the sexes is carefully regulated, and there is no equivalent to the concept of dating. Young adults might see each other on a social basis, but there is no official social approval of the practice. The only way to do so is to hide the fact that one has a boy/girlfriend from one's family. Pre-marital sex is still unacceptable, and live-in relationships are rare. This does not mean men and women do not seek each other out, but society does not sanction any interaction outside wedlock. This puts limits on communication—verbal or otherwise—between the sexes. I recently received some e-mail spam titled "Convert Your Love Marriage into an Arranged One" from an Indian web-based firm. Since matrimonial classifieds—personal ads containing profiles of prospective brides and grooms—have become an acceptable addition to more traditional ways of arranging marriages, this firm offers couples a way to con their families into believing that they are complete strangers who have found each other's profiles online. The creation of such a service is a sign of how the current generation of Indians is straddling different social environments.

Even when marriages are being arranged, the two people involved get only a brief chance to speak with their prospective spouses. Traditionally, relatives or friends of the family recommend a match. Usually the prospective groom's family arrives at the woman's house to get a look at her and ask about her educational background and her culinary skills. On a few occasions, the couple is given a few minutes to get acquainted, and that is all the time the two get to decide if they will have a successful relationship. If the match is acceptable to both sides on the basis of that meeting, they get engaged. In some "liberal" homes, it is then acceptable for the couple to meet a few times before the actual wedding, but an excessive enthusiasm for these meetings is frowned on. As is evident, the bride and groom are joined in matrimony without having spoken to each other about any but the most superficial things.

Why is this system so firmly entrenched? Quite possibly because it is taken for granted that marriage is a social institution that is in place to perpetuate the family name, and wives are meant to don the role of child-bearer and nurturer in whichever household they are sent. Marriage is less about being in love or passion or even personal fulfillment—it is a means of maintaining the social framework. In this scheme of things, conversations (which could play an important part in testing a couple's mutual compatibility before the wedding) become redundant. Since it is every Indian woman's duty to make all the compromises needed to keep her husband and his family happy, it is considered needless for the bride and groom to talk to each other to decide if they will suit; she *has* to figure out a way for them to coexist. Conversations with a potential spouse are thus seen as possessing limited usefulness—as are, by extension, all casual conversations between unrelated men and women. If one is a reader used to this social environment, the conversations between the hero and heroine in romances acquire great significance. Not only do these verbal exchanges presuppose a certain freedom in interacting with the other sex, they portray a social set-up where a woman gets a chance to express who she is and learn more about the man before making a lifelong commitment. Witness this conversation from Roberts's novel—a debate over the interpretation of findings from a dig—between Delaney, the archeologist, and Camilla, a budding anthropologist, who challenges his theories of courtship in an ancient culture:

> "How do you know a man didn't woo a woman by bringing her wildflowers, or a cup of fresh elderberries?"
> "I don't. But I don't know he did, either. No evidence either way."
> "But don't you think there was a ritual of some sort? Isn't there always? Even with animals there's a mating dance, *oui*? So surely there has to be some courtship procedure."
> "Sure." He dipped the bread, grinned at her. "Sometimes it just meant picking up a really big rock and beating some poor sap over the head with it. Loser gets the concussion. Winner gets the girl."
> "Only because she either had no choice, or more likely, she understood that the man strong enough, passionate enough to smash his rival over the head to win her would protect her and the children they made together from harm."
> "Exactly." Pleased with the tidy logic of her mind, he wagged a chunk of bread at her. "Sexual urge to procreation. Procreation to survival."
> "In its own very primitive way, that's romantic. However, the remains you've studied to date don't show a high enough percentage of violent injury to support the theory that head bashing was this tribe's usual courtship ritual."
> "That's good." Admiring the way she'd spun his example back to prove her point, he gestured with his fork. "And you're right." (116-17)

The dialogue establishes the protagonists' common interest in social anthropology as well as their ability to have an intellectual disagreement. Delaney engages her in the conversation, thus making space for Camilla to express her assessment. She proves her point through a logical argument, and he concedes the validity of her logic rather than being patronizing or dismissive. Passages such as these establish a screening ritual, if you will, that helps the conversers discover mutual interests. They encourage a reader to regard marriage as the culmination of several such moments, not a developmental stage in one's social physiology that one must fall in with when one reaches marriageable age.

In several romances, such as the one in the above example, the men—not just the hero, but male characters in general—do not automatically assume that conversation implies a sexual invitation. While conversations are sometimes laced with sexual innuendo, they are often attractive because they *aren't* sexual. I find this appealing because conversations between men and women in my culture are often considered suspect, precisely because society regards every such encounter as unnecessary for its own sake—and thus possessing a dangerous sexual potential; this reinforces the barrier between the sexes and denies the possibility of any worthwhile platonic exchanges between them. Women especially are thus forced to follow society's dictates and restrict their conversations to other women because to do otherwise is to risk one's "reputation" and jeopardize one's relations with one's family as well as with a prospective or actual husband. To a reader only acquainted with this over-regulation of gender interaction, even a simple conversational gambit by the romance heroine becomes a liberating act.

Not only is this commonplace structural element striking to me for the reasons mentioned above, its content contributes to a feminist ethos. Conversations in romances usually follow a pattern. In the initial stages of the narrative, the heroine engages in verbal fencing matches with the hero, the exchanges relying heavily on devices such as mistaken identity and faulty information. In most of these cases, the dialogue plays out the conventional battle of the sexes. While the ghost of 1970s romance paperbacks, in which the hero threatens to obliterate the heroine verbally and physically, is resurrected, it is also exorcised by the heroine's refusal to collapse under pressure. In Linda Howard's *Dream Man*, police detective Dane Hollister is initially suspicious of Marlie Keene, who is a psychic. Their first meeting is far from cordial; he is overtly hostile, and she responds in a similar vein to his attack:

> She stood and faced him, squaring off with him as if they were two adversaries in the old West about to draw down on each other. Her face had gone calm and curiously remote. "I've told you what happened," she said in a clear, deliberate voice. "You can believe it or not; It doesn't make any difference to me."
>
> "It should," he replied just as deliberately.
>
> She didn't ask why, though he paused for her to do just that. Instead her mouth twitched into a tiny, humorless smile. "I realize that I just became your prime suspect," she murmured. "So why don't I save your time and mine by telling you that my address is 2411 Hazelwood, and my telephone number is 555-9909."
>
> "You know the routine," he said with sarcastic admiration. "I'm not surprised.... Or maybe you're just reading my mind, since you're psychic.... Maybe you can tell me what comes next, unless you need a crystal ball to tell you what I'm thinking."
>
> "Oh, that doesn't take a mind reader, but then you aren't very original...I have no intention of leaving town"... She wasn't backing down, and his stomach muscles knotted again. At first glance she had looked like a drab, a nonentity afraid of making herself more attractive in any way, but the first look

into her eyes had forcibly changed that opinion. The woman facing him didn't lack self-confidence, and she wasn't the least bit intimidated by him even though he was almost a foot taller. Something else stole into his awareness. Damn, he could smell her, a sweet, soft scent that had nothing to do with perfume and everything to do with female flesh. His involuntary reaction made him even angrier.

"See that you don't...Is there anything else you see in your crystal ball, anything you want to tell me?"

"Of course," she purred, and the sudden glint in her blue eyes told him that he'd walked right into that one. "Go to hell, Detective." (39)

The first encounter thus places the characters on an equal footing, albeit on seemingly opposing sides. Marlie withstands Dale's accusations of being a murderer, and once the initial misunderstanding is resolved—he receives confirmation that she is psychic and has an alibi—the sexual attraction becomes the driving force of their interaction. In this as well as other novels, the conversations then become verbal foreplay, building up to the moment of sexual intercourse. The liberating nature of this banter is well illustrated by another example from *Cordina's Crown Jewel*, in which Delaney and Camilla disclose why they are drawn to each other:

And she saw desire, the dangerous burn of it in his eyes. Felt it stab inside her like the fired edge of a blade.

"Why is this, do you think?" she murmured.

He didn't pretend to misunderstand. He didn't believe in pretense. "I haven't got a clue—other than you being a tasty treat for the eyes."

She nearly smiled at that and turned to rinse the razor again. "Even attraction should have more. I'm not sure we even like each other very much."

"I don't have anything against you, particularly."

"Why, Delaney, you're so smooth." She laughed because it eased some of the tension inside her. "A woman hasn't a prayer against such poetry, such charm."

"You want poetry, read a book."

"I think I do like you.... On some odd level, I enjoy your irascibility."

"Old men are irascible. I'm young yet, so I'm just rude."

"Precisely. But you also have an interesting mind, and I find it attractive. I'm intrigued by your work.... And your passion for it. I came looking for passion—not the sexual sort, but for some emotional—some intellectual passion. How strange that I should find it here, and in old bones and broken pots."

"My field takes more than passion and intellect."

"Yes. Hard work, sacrifice, sweat, perhaps some blood...If you think I'm a stranger to such things, you're wrong." (Roberts 93)

The sexual repartee simultaneously makes room for Camilla to analyze the contradictory nature of her emotions and verbalize her desires. Moreover, it lets her declare her interest in a career rather than just a man, as is seen in her application of the term "passion" to the former rather than the latter. She is also able to correct Delaney's misconceptions about her ability to work in the given field. The above example further exemplifies the startling honesty that romance heroines are increasingly displaying in their dealings with men. Thurston notes a similar trend as early as 1981:

> When a hero urges a wife or lover to be honest rather than using 'feminine wiles' and 'veiled ploys' to get him into her bed (Donna Comeaux Zide, *Lost Splendor*, Warner, 1981), we are seeing a change in the traditional meaning of feminine, which once excused all manner of devious behavior on the basis that it was in the nature of the beast—the female. (76)

Camilla's forthrightness dismantles the stereotype that women are insidious by nature, enticing men in order to gain power. It presages a world that offers greater social equality, eliminating the need for the traditionally dispossessed figures to resort to underhandedness to get what they want. The apparent simplicity of conversation in romances is thus remarkable because it gives the female protagonist a voice. This is notable not just because I employ a different cultural lens but also because it reflects the genre's contribution to the development of the female voice in the western narrative tradition. Vocal women in eighteenth- and nineteenth-century novels—for instance, Catherine Earnshaw in *Wuthering Heights*—were often portrayed as childish or selfish. They were rarely afforded the opportunity to converse with a man as his equal and were frequently punished with disgrace and death. In contrast, even the so-called doormat heroines in the romances get numerous chances to participate in a dialogue with male characters, especially the hero.

Critics such as Ann Barr Snitow, however, regard conversations in Harlequins as mendacious. As she puts it:

> Harlequin romances alternate between scenes of the hero and heroine together in which *she does a lot of social lying* to save face, pretending to be unaffected by the hero's presence while her body melts and shivers, [and scenes in which the heroine is essentially alone...] [emphasis mine]. (249)

Conversations in which the heroine tries to hold her own against the hero even in the face of her desire or love for him—and in which the power struggle of the first encounter hasn't developed into the banter of courtship—may at face value signal poor writing, or a reactionary character who either doesn't know her own mind or can't stick to her resolve to keep the man at bay. But the very see-sawing of the heroine's emotions and its effect on her speech is a marker of precisely what feminists hold that women need to be encouraged to do—reevaluate and reassess their notions of whether they need a man to make them happy. In Kim Lawrence's *Pregnant by The Greek Tycoon* (2005), Georgie and Angolos Constantine have met after a two-year separation, and Angolos wants her to give their failed marriage another try. Though angry at his abandonment and harsh treatment, Georgie agrees to return to Greece with him on a "trial basis" for the sake of their son. But the reconciliation is far from smooth, with her torn between memories of the powerlessness she experienced at the hands of the husband she loved, as well as of their sexual compatibility:

> Georgie's stomach flipped. Her covert glance at his hard, male, deliciously streamlined body resulted in an adrenaline surge of huge proportions. She inhaled deeply and nearly fell off the wall.
>
> "And you wanted me..." Her heart was hammering so fast she could barely breathe. Her knees had acquired the consistency of cotton wool.
>
> "And you wanted me." He said it again.
>
> A scared sound rasped in her throat and her eyes lifted. "Things change," she croaked defiantly.
>
> Angolos studied her flushed face, lingering on the softness of her trembling lips. "And some things don't."
>
> Silently she shook her head.
>
> He took her chin in his hand and tilted her face up to him. There was anger in the dark eyes that moved hungrily over her delicate features. "Why can't you admit it?" he rasped.
>
> "Because I don't want to feel this way...when you..." Without warning she slid off the wall and under his restraining arm. Eyes blazing, her breasts heaving, she stood defiantly glaring at him.
>
> "I'm not an impressionable kid. Getting me into bed won't change my mind."
>
> "It might make you feel less frustrated, however." Georgie was about to respond angrily to this supremely arrogant suggestion, when he added, "I know it would make me feel less frustrated. Where you are concerned I've never had any self-control..." He watched her eyes widen with shock and his lips twisted in a self-derisive smile. "You haven't the faintest idea what it does to me to be this close to you and not touch..." he said thickly.
>
> A surge of heat traveled through her body. "Tell me..." she demanded throatily, then almost immediately started to backtrack as though her life depended on it. "No...no, I didn't mean that."
>
> [Here Georgie remembers making love to him and is aroused by the memory. Angolos is pleased by proof of her desire for him, admitting that he was unsure of her feelings in the past.]
>
> "The flame that burns brightest does not always last the longest. You were very young—"

"And stupid," she cut in angrily. "Yes, a lot of people think that, and it just goes to show that a few more years on the clock don't necessarily make you any less stupid!" If anything she wanted him more now than she had then.
"So that aspect of being back with me does not fill you with disgust?"
"The sex was always pretty fantastic." She grunted, avoiding his eyes as though her life depended on it. "It was the other stuff we are terrible at."
"So, we will work on the 'other stuff', and enjoy the sex," he announced, sounding pleased with himself, which, considering she had just told him she fancied the pants off him, was not surprising. Why did her mouth detach itself from her brain when she was around this man?
"That remains to be seen," she replied… (108-111)

Such apparently illogical conversations that contradict everything we have seen the heroine do to keep the hero at bay (or what we know she feels) are in fact manifestations of a latent feminism. They assert that a woman need no longer be content to slide into a relationship purely because a man finds her attractive or even because she is attracted to him. If romances were just making a case for marriage, the novels would end the moment the heroine meets the tall, dark, handsome man. Instead romances are increasingly preserving the appearance of a fairy tale while subverting the marriage narrative and empowering the woman in question. Let's take a conversation from Linda Howard's *Angel Creek* (1991) to illustrate this development. In this novel, set in the American West in the early 1800s, the rugged and powerful hero Lucas Cochran wants Dee Swan's land as much as he wants her because it holds a water source. Even after he seduces her, though, her resistance to his demands and his bafflement at it mark most of their interactions. In this excerpt Dee dismisses Lucas's suspicions about Bellamy, his rival:

"I don't want him here again," he said flatly, just in case she was in any doubt.
"I didn't invite him in the first place." She added thoughtfully, "I didn't invite you, either. Isn't it strange? The poor men who could have used a homestead just wanted me for sex; you and Bellamy have plenty of land, but you want more. I'd have to say that Bellamy wants it more than you do, since he offered marriage."
Lucas tensed, every instinct alert. "Is that what it would take?" he asked, carefully feeling his way….Dee didn't look at him, but out across the land.
"Getting married would be even worse than selling out," she said, "I'd lose both my land and my independence. Of the two, selling it would at least let me stay independent." (173)

The dialogue documents Dee's refusal to enter the patriarchal economy, even though she has already admitted to herself that she is in love with Lucas. (She only consents to marriage after he decides to sign over his own ranch to her and draw up a contract to ensure that her land remains in her name.) These moments constitute a pattern in which romance heroines constantly remind readers of the problematic nature of the institution that is made to appear attractive through the presence of a loving man, an observation of great import to a reader from a culture that has never questioned patriarchal marriage.

Even dialogue that is less confrontational can play a role beyond establishing the compatibility of a couple. In many romances the repartee that is present after the first instance of "emotional intercourse" (as opposed to just sex) often takes on a new air of trust and mutual respect. In several novels the conversations that follow the acknowledgment of mutual affection, and sometimes an agreement of impending nuptials, are even more interesting because they establish the model for the interaction that will exist between the couple even after the novels end, i.e. when the romance settles into marriage. In a way the dialogue tells readers that a marriage based on meaningful pre-wedding interaction between the man and woman will assuredly not deteriorate into empty silences but remain as exciting and affectionate as the courtship was, and that the woman will not recede into the anonymity of wifedom after the initial sexual mystery has been dispensed with. They suggest that the ability to speak and be heard is as much a prerequisite for a marriage of true equals as sexual attraction. Many of Lisa Kleypas's novels are preoccupied with this idea, as demonstrated by the concerns that Addie Warner voices to Ben Hunter, her fiancé, in *Give Me Tonight*, a romance set in Texas in the 1880s:

> "I want you to listen to me in twenty years the same way you do now. As if my opinions matter to you."
> "They do. They always will. Anything else?"
> "Yes. I don't want to turn into a belonging of yours, an attachment like an extra arm or leg, someone who's expected to agree with everything you say. I won't be silent during the dinner conversations at our table." Now that she had started to open up to him, it was much easier to continue. "I need to be respected but not sheltered. I want your honesty, always, about everything, and to be given a chance to show I can do more for you than the cooking, the washing and the sewing. All of that can be done by any woman. I want to have a place in your life no one else can take, and I don't mean a pedestal."
> "I wouldn't try to put you up on one."
> "You wouldn't? You wouldn't want me to change after we're married, and do everything you say, and never argue with you?"
> "Hell, no. Why would I change the things that attract me to you the most? Let other men's wives play mindless fools if it pleases them. I'd rather have a woman who has some common sense. And why should I want you to agree with me all the time? It would bore the hell out of me to be with someone

who parroted everything I said. Put your mind at ease, darlin'. I'm not marrying
you in order to change you." (262-63)

The conversation is a verbal contract, promising the continuing existence of the
woman rather than her erasure by the fact of marriage. It ensures that one of the
ways the male will assist in this endeavor is by acknowledging the female's
voice. *Give Me Tonight* is an historical romance overlaid with a time-travel plot
because Addie is actually a nurse from the 1930s who finds herself living the
life of another Addie in the 1880s. The above conversation thus dramatizes the
grafting of twentieth century values on the world of the historical romance and
highlights the genre's desire to step away from traditional gender roles. Once
again, a reader from a culture dominated by an older patriarchal value system
may identify with the Addie of the nineteenth century and her desire for a more
progressive social structure, thus employing the text to denaturalize that system.
Simultaneously, Indian readers may identify with Ben's acceptance of Addie's
demands, even if they are unlike anything he is familiar with in his own
reality—once these demands are voiced, their rightness becomes self-evident
even to one who has never experienced a feminist movement.

   Along with freedom of speech, romance novels are increasingly giving
heroines more control over their own bodies. I am inclined to read a feminist
assertiveness in this phenomenon, especially in light of my knowledge of the
social pressure in India to conform to a particular body image (much greater
than in the US or Europe). A woman of marriageable age is regarded as having
a better chance of being accepted by a prospective groom's family if she has
perfect eyesight and fair skin, and isn't too short/too tall/too thin, and more and
more, too chubby. Contact lenses and laser surgery procedures that can correct
vision are much in demand because they improve a woman's matrimonial
options. Clothing is also regulated, usually by one's family and neighbors, who
act as conduits for the conservative views on the matter. Indian society frowns
on clothes that do not cover most of the body, especially where women are
concerned. Even when fully dressed, the kind of clothing one wears is marked
with different moral undertones. Durham recalls experiencing such marking
firsthand when she moved to India from Canada in the seventies. While she
opted to wear shirts and jeans as a protest against the demand to conform to an
Indian ideal of femininity, the behavior was interpreted as sexually provocative:

   I remember one of my friends telling me seriously when I was seventeen or
   eighteen years old, "You know, Gigi, if you wear jeans all the time like you do,
   people will think you are not a virgin." (201)

Thus, almost anyone feels free to comment on a woman's attire, either by
chastizing her for its "westernness"/skimpiness or propositioning her for her

apparent lack of morals. Thus, one has little say over how one's body is clothed, though this varies according to region and economic conditions. Women in urban areas are adopting non-traditional wear, but this is still not an unmarked act; whether a woman wishes it or not, any deviation from conventional Indian clothing or ideal body type labels her as transgressive or sub-standard. So in myriad little ways, Indian culture exercises a stranglehold on the female body, limiting a woman's autonomy over the self.

Conversely, romance novels (especially contemporary romances) often emphasize the casualness of the heroine's clothes. There are undeniable instances when she is described as being dressed in the height of fashion, but the authors also describe occasions when the heroine is all too human in her unmade-up state. Here is an example from Linda Howard's *Loving Evangeline*, in which the hero, Robert Cannon, and the reader see Evie Shaw for the first time:

> Evie Shaw, in contrast, [to the women he usually dated] evidently paid no attention to her clothes. She wore an oversize T-shirt that she had knotted at the waist, a pair of jeans so ancient that they were thread-bare and almost colorless, and equally old docksiders. Her hair, a sun-streaked blond that ranged in color from light brown to the palest flax, and included several different shades of gold, was pulled back and confined in an untidy braid that was as thick as his wrist and hung halfway down her back. (24)

Evie's disinterest in adopting a sophisticated dress code is highlighted by the contrast with the glamorous women that heroes like Robert date. She is one of the many heroines who are comfortable with their physical selves even if their bodies and faces do not resemble those of cover girls. They prefer to wear utilitarian clothing and have little time or inclination for elaborate beauty treatments. In Howard's *Mackenzie's Mission* (1992), Caroline Evans is a physicist with strong opinions on women's dressing styles:

> She had decided while still in adolescence that men had no idea how uncomfortable women's fashions really were and really didn't care, since they themselves weren't called upon to spend hours standing in tendon-shortening high heels, encased in sweltering hosiery, bound either by bras or dresses tight enough to take over the job of lifting and separating, or pushing together to create cleavage, according to the dictates of the occasion. [...] Fashion, in her mind, consisted of equal parts stupidity and lunacy. In a logical world, people would wear functional clothing, like jeans and loafers and sweatshirts. (30-31)

I thus see an increasing trend in the heroines toward being happy with an unglamorous appearance rather than yearning for an unrealistic ideal created by men. Several romances also go one step further in demystifying the heroine's once mysterious and picture-perfect body. Many of them star heroines with small breasts, large hips, freckled skin, unruly hair, cellulite and stretch marks and offer no apologies for this non-conformity to the media-created standard of beauty. They deal with menstrual cycles and the debilitating effects of a period on a woman's body and temperament. Coming from a culture that considers this topic taboo, I am always intrigued by this matter-of-fact attitude towards female physiology. In my home state of Maharashtra (Western India), women used to be considered impure when they had a period. They were to stay in a separate space in the home and refrain from touching anyone. Such extreme practices are mostly a thing of the past, especially in urban areas, but even today, women in many parts of India are unable to participate in religious rituals or visit temples if they are menstruating, or to even speak of it. In striking contrast to my experience, not only do women in romances talk about the workings of their bodies with other women, but they also do so with the men in their lives. They grumble over the bodily pains that women were traditionally never supposed to mention and expect their partners to be sensitive to their concerns. Howard, whose work shows a persistent interest in shattering the myth of the two-dimensional woman, tackles this issue with humor in *Heart of Fire*. The novel is an adventure story set in the Amazon, with Jillan Sherwood, an anthropologist, and Ben Drake, her lover, trying to get back to Manaus and avoid being killed by artifact thieves. Jill, consistently keeping the highly sexed Ben in line, bluntly tells him that she won't have sex with him during her period:

> "I'm always really tired and don't feel good on the first day of the period," she explained, keeping her eyes closed.
> The silence was thick. Then Ben said, "I'm learning. You didn't actually say you were having your period. You simply made a statement that you get tired and don't feel good on the first day of your period. You're still punishing me, aren't you?"
> "I'm having my period," she said flatly. "And I don't know any way I could have arranged that to coincide with your many transgressions."
> Ben looked at her again, this time noting the circles under her eyes. She wasn't kidding. He felt a moment's dismay, then concern. "Do you have anything to take? What can I do to make you feel better?"
> She did open her eyes then, and smiled at him. A real smile, not the angelic one that made him shudder. "I'm okay. I don't feel sick, just tired. If you really need me, wake me up. And I promise I'll be better tomorrow." [...]
> He said, "How long does this usually last?"
> "What, my period, or your strange delusion that everything I do is planned specifically to keep you from making love as often as you seem to think you should? My period will last four to five days. I've seen no break in your delusion at all."
> He grinned. Ah, he loved it when she talked sweet to him. "I don't know where you got the idea that having a period prevents making love."

"From the fact that I don't feel like it, don't want to, and won't let you."

"I guess that about covers the issue." (256-57)

In a way, heroines like Jillian are demanding recognition for a three-dimensional female body, one that is accompanied by its own aches and pains but needs to be accepted instead of being hidden behind images of skinny models or, in the case of my culture, behind yards of clothing. Surely this affirmation of the female body's reality—its de-fetishization—is an undeniable feminist move.

An extension of this concept is the sexual assertiveness of women in these novels, demonstrated by their ability to be an active participant in the sexual act, and to give or deny the hero access to their bodies. As I've noted earlier, an Indian marriage is often a union between people who are virtually strangers but are expected to have sex for the purpose of having children. The woman should be a virgin but must still allow her husband his conjugal rights as soon as he wishes to exercise them. This is not to imply that all grooms seduce or rape their brides, or that the latter feel no sexual desire, but women do feel obliged to accept a sexual overture when it is made by the husband. In romance novels, however, a heroine not only has the final say in whom she will marry but she also decides if and when she wants to share her body with the hero (as seen in the above excerpt). Erotic historical romances that were written in the seventies did contain instances of seduction or rape (Thurston 50-51). But the trend died soon, with readers unwilling to accept the episodes as anything but sexual assault. While heroines are still occasionally virgins (another thing for which feminists slam romances), their decision to end that state is an indication of a personal freedom that women in some countries still don't have. Also, increasingly more novels contain female protagonists who have had prior sexual relationships, either in or out of wedlock, and do not have to explain their past to indignant heroes. Thus, there is a trend toward asserting a woman's autonomy over her own life and her sexuality.

Romances are trying to challenge the glorification of phallicism that marks a patriarchal culture—and was evident in novels in the seventies—by making the heroine's sexual desires the center of the narrative. Women in more recent novels are not indiscriminate in their sexual lives, but they aren't silent about what they need from a sexual relationship either. They are active partners and unashamed of enjoying intercourse. They not only participate in sex but also initiate or reject it when they wish, appearing to sense the power dynamic involved in the act. Dee Swan in *Angel Creek* is one such woman:

> When they woke up he wanted to make love to her again. He was
> startled when she tried to squirm away from him. "I don't want to," she said
> fretfully.
>   "Damn if you aren't the most contrary woman I've ever seen," he
> muttered. "*Why* don't you want to?"
>   She shrugged, her mouth sulky. "I just don't want you holding me
> down again right now."
>   He ran his hand through his hair. God, why had he been surprised?
> The wonder was that she hadn't done something about it before now…
>   "Then you get on top," he said.
>   Interest sparked in those green eyes. He could see that she was
> intrigued by the idea of controlling their lovemaking, and therefore controlling
> him. (167)

Thus, though *Angel Creek* includes several instances in which Lucas coerces
Dee to make love, she retains her selfhood by placing her own conditions on
their sexual—and emotional—intimacy.

The sex in romances is verbal as well as physical with each partner asking
the other's needs instead of running for the finish line. The relationship that is
portrayed is thus one of equals who also care about the partner's pleasure as
much as their own. This is a revolutionary concept to a reader from India,
where sex is not openly discussed or even admitted to, and women's sexual
desire is not acknowledged as natural. This attitude towards women and sex in
Indian society was exemplified by the reaction to the 1994 movie, *Bandit
Queen*, a bio-pic about a female bandit from a remote region in the heart of the
country. While the movie's handling of a key theme—the caste system that
haunts rural India—incited strong discussions, what caused as much controversy
was a love scene in which the protagonist was shown to be on top of her lover.
Guardians of Indian culture insisted that it was a travesty of our traditions
because an Indian man never allows his female partner to be on top. Against
this background, reading about the kind of sex in which the woman not only
expects and receives pleasure—often from actively exploring and controlling
the male body—can afford an Indian reader a whole new perspective on female
liberation in the bedroom.

Much of what has been identified as sexual fantasy or pornography in
romances is a veritable database of complex female desire. These novels
express the sexual needs that tradition has dictated women do not/should not
have. They describe passion using terms that seem exaggerated and unrealistic,
but it is important to look at these passages as indicative of women's
unarticulated and unacknowledged needs—emotional and sexual. Witness the
conclusion of the love scene quoted above:

She loved it, too. By the time she settled astride him, sinking down to envelope his shaft, his hands were locked on the headboard above him as he strained to control himself. He was gasping, his eyes closed from the pleasure she had wrought. She had seduced him that time, her mouth tender in his mouth and chest, her breasts brushing against his stomach and loins as she swayed over him. He thought of other things he would teach her, but right now he had all he could handle. Of course she loved it; she was enthralled by having him at her mercy, if he could call it that. It was more like torment, delicious, searing torment.

Dee moved slowly, rhythmically, her eyes closing as her own hunger built. This was pure ecstasy, she thought, and she knew she would never regret these moments no matter what happened. It wasn't the physical pleasure that was so precious, but the link between them that was forged by the pleasure. (167-68)

Western feminists may scoff at this supposed liberation of female sexuality in romances over the last three decades, pointing to the limits imposed on the heroine's sexual activity through the authority of the hero and deriding her dependence on him. But for an Indian reader, the romance heroine's progress from someone who has little say in the act of sexual intercourse to one who can explore and control her sexuality is an empowering one.

When one employs an alternative cultural perspective, it thus becomes evident that the romance heroine is no pushover, nor is she exhorting readers to turn into a combination of virgin, whore, enabler, doormat, baby machine, and supermodel. She does fine on her own strength and doesn't need a[ny] Man to be fulfilled in life. She feels no frantic urgency to be the "traditional" woman who must have a boyfriend/husband in order to avoid being labeled unfeminine. But neither does she wish to sacrifice her sex life or emotional needs for ascetic individualism. When she does fall in love, it is not with the first available man she has met. That is partly why romance heroes seem to be paragons, both physically and emotionally—they fulfill the heroine's rigorous requirements. The hero is not Mr. Right because he is the standard "tall, dark, and handsome" romantic figure—his character is code for a man who the heroine has thought about, assessed, and chosen as a life-mate. Such a choice strongly argues individual self-knowledge and independence. It heralds an attitude that acknowledges a woman's sovereignty over the most private aspects of her self. This is the first step in fulfilling other demands, such as a woman's right to refuse sex to a previous lover, the right to expect sexual fulfillment and the right to decide if she wants to have a child. What could be more in line with the feminist agenda than romances that have and are presently laying the groundwork for women (especially those who aren't touched by academic feminism) to realize the legitimacy of these demands?

As I've shown here, the reading community of romance fiction is quite diverse and the implications of its changing composition for romance reading need to be examined further.   Since the act of reading is not identical everywhere, nor is patriarchy or the means of contesting it, romance criticism must move beyond the claim that all romance reading behavior betrays a desire to conform to patriarchy and that this universal subconscious fantasy must be eradicated by enlightening the ignorant masses.   The women's liberation movement that began in the West in the sixties did not translate exactly into countries like mine. (Thirty-five years ago, my culture could not have identified with bra burning as a feminist act since it did not associate bras—whose use was confined to some urban populaces—with femininity.) But the romance fiction genre may carry some of feminism's arguments to the thousands of readers who do not—and may never—have access to its scholarship or experience a full-blown feminist movement. My own romance reading made me conscious of the flaws of the Indian marriage mechanism—and of the institution in general—much before I came to academic feminism's more complex deconstruction of it.

The progressiveness of romance fiction thus becomes evident when the very narratives that appear reactionary are read through the perspective of readers whose social environments are markedly different from the post-feminist West. The genre's attachment to marriage does not preclude this audience from locating in these texts the moments that destabilize the institution (as it exists in its many avatars). Though the inevitable happy ending has been regarded as a way to indoctrinate readers to accept patriarchal marriage, in actual fact the narrative can work to remind them that the conclusion is unusual, quite a departure from the norm (this last being the marriages that people routinely enter into in the mistaken belief that everyone should marry as a matter of course).   To Indian readers, romance fiction can function as an extended discussion on what might justify the state of matrimony. While the genre offers romantic love as the only reason to marry someone (and is consequently labeled as an ideological construct), the heroine's love for the hero—and the love and respect she commands from him—may act as a means of resistance to the Indian ideology of marriage-as-inevitability.   Not only do romances thus contain subversive readings, even their manifest narratives can function to question other problematic grand narratives of marriage and family.

Works Cited

Bandit Queen. Dir. Shekhar Kapoor. Perf. Seema Biswas and Nirmal Pandey. 1994.
Durham, Meenakshi Gigi. "Out of the Indian Diaspora: Mass Media, Myths of Femininity and the Negotiation of Adolescence Between Two Cultures." In

Growing Up Girls: Popular Culture and the Construction of Identity. Ed.
Sharon R. Mazzarella and Norma Odom Pecora. *Adolescent Cultures,
School, and Society* Vol.9. New York: Peter Lang Publishing, Inc., 2001.
Fiske, John. *Understanding Popular Culture.* London: Routledge, 1989.
Fowler, Bridget. *The Alienated Reader.* Hertfordshire: Harvester Wheatsheaf,
1991.
Greer, Germaine. *The Female Eunuch.* London: MacGibbon and Kay, 1970.
Hollows, Joanne. *Feminism, Femininity and Popular Culture.* Manchester:
Manchester UP, 2000.
Howard, Linda. *Angel Creek.* New York: Pocket Books, 1991.
———.*Dream Man.* New York: Pocket Books, 1994.
———.*Heart of Fire.* New York: Pocket Books, 1993.
———.*Mackenzie's Mission.* New York: Silhouette Books, 1992.
"Is the Window Closing?" *The Times of India* 12 Oct. 2005. 15 Oct. 2005.
<http://timesofindia.indiatimes.com/articleshow/1260796.cms>.
Kleypas, Lisa. *Give Me Tonight.* New York: Onyx, 1989.
Kloberdanz, Kristin. "Don't Write Off Romance." *Book* 21 March/April 2002:
46-51.
Lawrence, Kim. *Pregnant by the Greek Tycoon.* New York: Harlequin, 2005.
Radway, Janice. *Reading the Romance: Women, Patriarchy, and Popular
Literature.* Chapel Hill: U of North Carolina P, 1984.
Roberts, Nora. *Cordina's Crown Jewel.* New York: Silhouette Books, 2002.
Scott, Alison M. "Romance in the Stacks; or, Popular Romance Fiction
Imperiled." *Scorned Literature: Essays on the History and Criticism of
Popular Mass-Produced Fiction in America.* Ed. Lydia Cushman Schurman
and Deidre Johnson. Westport, Connecticut: Greenwood Press, 2002. 213-
224.
Thurston, Carol. *The Romance Revolution: Erotic Novels for Women and the
Quest for a New Sexual Identity.* Urbana and Chicago: U of Illinois P, 1987.
Wentworth, Sally. *King of the Castle.* Toronto: Harlequin, 1978.

Appendix: Romance Novel Reading Survey

Please write N/A if the question is not applicable to your reading practices. You may add an extra sheet if you need more space for an answer. Please indicate the number for the question and answer clearly. Thank you for your time!

1. What is the highest educational degree you have obtained?
    ❏   High School (S.S.C., C.B.S.E., I.C.S.E. other state certificate.)
    ❏   Pre-College Degree level (H.S.C, 12th standard, etc.)
    ❏   Bachelor's Degree (B.A., B.Sc., B.Com, etc.)
    ❏   Master's Degree (M.A., M.Sc., M.Com, etc.)
    ❏   Doctoral Degree (Ph.D.)
2. What was your major or special subject in college?
3. How many languages do you know? Please name them.
4. Which language was the primary medium of instruction in your educational career?
5. What career are you pursuing (or trained for)?
6. Note some of your hobbies and extra-curricular activities.
7. On average, how many books do you read in a month?
8. Do you currently read romance novels?
9. How many romance novels do (did) you read each month? (Mills and Boon, Loveswept, Silhouette, historical or contemporary single titles, etc.)
10. When did you begin reading romance novels? (Note your age.)
11. How were you introduced to the genre? (Family member, friend, library, bookstore, or any other medium.)
12. Where do (did) you obtain romances?
13. How do you pick the next romance novel? (Tick all that apply)
    ❏   Author (Please name)
    ❏   Title
    ❏   Summary on the back
    ❏   Cover
    ❏   Series title (such as Mills and Boon, Silhouette, etc. Please name.)
    ❏   Other (Explain)
14. How long does it take you to finish reading a romance?
15. Do you discuss your reading with other romance readers?
16. Describe the attitude of people you know to romance novels.
17. Have you noticed any changes in romance novels since the time you began reading them?
18. Are you aware of any particular plotline or story element that you prefer to read in a romance? Please describe.

19. Is there anything in particular that you dislike or would like to see changed in the romances you read?
20. Do you know if reading romances has affected your attitudes or beliefs—political, social, economic? Please describe.
21. Please describe any other ways romance reading has affected you.
22. If you no longer read romances, can you describe when and why you stopped?

Jayashree Kamble

Jayashree Kamble is a doctoral candidate in the English Department at the University of Minnesota, Twin Cities, where she teaches courses on Shakespeare, British Literature, and Modern Fiction. Her research draws on the fields of popular culture and media studies. She is currently working on her dissertation, which explores the development of twentieth-century popular romance fiction and surveys the changes in the genre and its reception by readers and critics.

CHAPTER ELEVEN

FORMING A LOCAL IDENTITY:
ROMANCE NOVELS IN HONG KONG

AMY LEE

Hong Kong has always been presented to the world as an international city because of its location between the Mainland and the "rest of the world" and also because of its colonial past. But what does this internationality contain? For over a century, the official identity of it as a British colony has been enough to fend off any in-depth study of this internationality. Even the identity of a "cultural desert," mournfully coined by literary and cultural critics, has been accepted by most of its people. China's announcement of taking back Hong Kong's sovereignty in 1997, however, serves as a wake-up call, to start not only debates and reflections concerning Hong Kong's political and economic status, but also at different levels, its cultural identity. Thus, the literary history of Hong Kong, an almost uncultivated piece of land, received a lot of attention right after the early 1980s when the British Prime Minister, then Mrs. Margaret Thatcher, started talks with the Mainland Chinese government.

This paper, written in the early years of the twenty-first century, at a time when Hong Kong has celebrated its eighth year of return to the motherland and experienced the rule of its second chief executive, is intended to be an examination of its cultural identity, traced through the development of its most popular genre of reading—the romance novel. Although not many critics will find literary merit in the kind of readings discussed here, it is important to note that the rise in popularity of this writing coincides with the periods of Hong Kong's local identification. What I am suggesting in the following discussion is that the local romance novel shares the same history as Hong Kong's awareness to its complex identity, and the evolution of the romance novel in Hong Kong reflects quite accurately the change of attitude towards gender identity. In the following we shall first take a look at the context of the local literary history before we move on to an examination of some of the most popular romance novels through the last four decades.

The Prologue

There are different approaches to the mapping of the literary development in Hong Kong: as a branch of Mainland mainstream development; as a unique mutant from the East-West influences; as the oppressed nonentity desperately needing establishment of an identity away from the dominating influence of Chinese and British cultures; or as the new force capitalizing on the special position it inhabits in relation to China and Britain, among others. There is as yet no consensus as to what a Hong Kong identity contains, but the presence of different perspectives and standpoints has its merits in allowing an active exploration of a relatively new subject. The romance novel is a useful tool to empower oneself through an experience of self-construction, as a consideration of Hong Kong's cultural history will prove.

A Mainland Chinese scholar, Denghan Liu, regards Hong Kong as a direct descendant from China, thus Hong Kong literature becomes a branch of the Mainland development. In his introduction to *Xianggang wenxueshi*, he writes:

> [Hong Kong] is part of a Southern province, Guangdong, in China, is part of the framework of development of Chinese history; which also means that Hong Kong's ancient culture cannot be an independent culture, but only a wing of one of the Chinese National culture in the south—Lingnan culture (17).

Liu is situating Hong Kong's cultural root in the larger context of Mainland China and denying its independence. Liu also sees the cultural policy of the British colonial government as a strategy to develop Hong Kong through western culture, resulting in a hybrid city somewhere between the East and the West:

> This is the contemporary Hong Kong. It is neither a completely westernized modern city, nor a traditional Chinese feudal town; instead it is a Chinese city where the East and West mix and juxtapose, holding their own grounds and yet interacting with each other, and a colonized city functioning as a bridge for communication between China and the world for more than a century. The Eastern and Western cultures are distinct from each other and yet share blurred boundaries. Here is an upper society centralized around a completely westernized portion, existing side by side with a basically traditional Chinese population which has been influenced by some western ideas and cultural customs. (18).

What can be found in Hong Kong is basically a juxtaposition of both habits and practices imported by foreigners, as well as inherited traditions from Chinese culture. While the westernized lifestyle and practices manage to infiltrate into Hong Kong citizens, the old Chinese traditions stay and are gradually accepted by the western people here. This interesting hybrid Hong Kong culture is the subject of many studies, such as Hongzhi Wang's 王宏志book *Lishi de ouran: Cong Xianggang kan Zhongguo xiandai wenxueshi* 歷史的偶然 從香港看中國現代文 學史 [Historical Contingencies: A Study of Modern Chinese Literary Histories in Hong Kong]. Wang's book documents several major compilations of literary history in Hong Kong from the 1950s-70s. The major historians claim to have used an apolitical approach in dealing with modern Chinese literary history, which the author thinks is actually a resistance against mainstream politics. With the 1997 unification of Hong Kong and China, an attempt to explore Hong Kong's relation to China by writing histories of this kind is in line with the political and cultural attempt of identification.

While both the geographical proximity of Hong Kong to China and its dominantly Chinese population argue for powerful influence from Mainland writers, resulting in Chinese writing dominating Hong Kong's literary scene, it is interesting also to note factors leading to Hong Kong literature parting ways with the Mainland development. After the establishment of New China in 1949, Hong Kong has become a site where forces supporting and challenging the Communist Chinese government fight out their battles. On the one hand, the 1950s have seen the establishment of literary agents and venues supported by American funds, giving financial and other supports to literature against Communism. The term "American-Dollars Culture" was first coined in *Hong Kong Times* in 1956 to refer to this kind of anti-communist writing (Shi and Wang 4).

It has to be mentioned that the written language is different from the spoken language in Hong Kong. The written script is what is called "bai hua wen" 白話 文, and is the kind of modern Chinese script advocated by the May Fourth scholars, as different from the older scripts. Bai hua wen is more formal and follows a different set of rules from "Guangdong hua" 廣東話 [Cantonese], which is the spoken dialect in the southernmost part of China. Spoken Cantonese, when transcribed, will give very different characters from that of the written Chinese, and this split between the spoken and the written language is considered by many educationists as the biggest reason why the language proficiency of school children in Hong Kong is weakening. This fact is important especially in the Hong Kong context because from the 1960s onwards, when a more distinguished local awareness developed in the popular writing, one can see at the same time a change in the form of language used in the popular writing culture. In the 1980s when radio plays once again became a fad, the most popular plays were transcribed and published as written, "pocket size" books. Some of them are highly fashionable among secondary school students, the most active group of readers. Into the 1990s this kind of directly transcribed, written-Cantonese language declined in popularity, as the radio plays once again fell back into relative silence. Although the use of directly transcribed

Cantonese-Chinese has not claimed as big a market afterwards as when the radio-plays were popular, the written Chinese used in writings published in Hong Kong, particularly popular writing, is distinctly different from the kind of Chinese found in Mainland China.

Into the mid-1950s, however, when the reputation and the international recognition of the New China became more prominent, the voice of left-wing writers also become louder. This "green-back literature" (referring to the color of the American dollar notes) disappeared in the 1960s. But with the start of the Cultural Revolution in the Mainland in 1966, right-wing writers again gained more ground over the voice of the left wing. Thus the two decades of 1950s and 1960s can be seen as the foundation of the Hong Kong literary identity. As an extension of China, but under the political rule of a foreign power, Hong Kong enjoyed a unique quasi-detached, third-person identity, one that assumed association with China, yet politically independent from the Chinese mainstream.

The decade of the 1960s was a significant turning point in the history of Hong Kong literature in more than one way. Economically, the rapid development of manufacturing and commerce pushed urbanization to a high point. Readers expected new ideas, new approaches and new voices in the literature to reflect the reality of their lives. Western modernism was thus brought into Hong Kong by local writers who had a western-style education. Because of the rapid urbanization, the reading public also demanded easy-to-understand urban entertainment to fill their busy daily routine. Popular fiction started to be produced in massive scale during this decade, and the founding genres—martial arts fiction and romance fiction—remain to be the most prominent popular genres even today.

Famous martial arts fiction writer Yu-sheng Liang 梁羽生 started to serialize his works in the early 1950s, and Jin-yong 金庸 joined in later. Their works have remained popular today. Popular romance novels started in Hong Kong with Yi Da and Jack (both are pen-names used by male writers) in the 1950s, and became enormously popular in the 1960s, although literary critics do not share the same enthusiasm as the reading public. Jianwai Shi and Yisheng Wang comment in their article:

> This type of fiction specializes in the ups and downs of love and conflicts; it usually contains complicated relationships, or extra-marital relationships, overwhelmingly romantic. A common problem with this type is the stereotyping and formalistic framework. It never gets beyond depicting just the beautiful people, and love at first sight kind of plot. (6)

This view was shared by serious writers, such as Sima Changfeng 司馬長風. In his 1964 novel, *Li Ge* 驪歌, in the self-preface, he talks about romance fiction during the time:

> Nowadays popular fiction in overseas countries are usually romance fiction which have no connection to real life. They give a most restricted view of art, and what they describe in the books are nothing but male-female relationships. Those characters look as if they do not live on the earth nor in reality, but in an insubstantial mirage. (qtd. in Liangjun Yuan 339)

Some literary critics do not see literary developments in Hong Kong as a branch of Chinese literary development. Ackbar Abbas, viewing Hong Kong literary writing in the 1990s, calls it a culture of disappearance:

> The way the city has been made to appear in many representations in fact works to make it disappear, most perniciously through the use of old binaries like East-West 'differences.' (8)

Hong Kong disappears not because it is not represented, instead with 1997 approaching, representations of Hong Kong as it was before the reunification with Mainland China proliferated because the status of Hong Kong as a colony would soon come to an end. The unprecedented change means one face of Hong Kong will soon be no more. Attempts to represent the city are similar to people taking snapshots when they go traveling, as proof of the presence of fleeting moments. But what Abbas is saying is that representing Hong Kong within the parameter of an East-West difference is actually making Hong Kong disappear because the cultural phenomenon of Hong Kong cannot be understood merely by seeing it as a manifestation of the East, the West, or even as a mixture of the East and the West:

> [D]isappearance is not a matter of effacement but of replacement and substitution, where the perceived danger is recontained through representations that are familiar and plausible. (8)

Representations using the East-West parameter are only a make-do framework for talking about Hong Kong because they are easy to understand, but they are inadequate in representing Hong Kong.

According to Abbas, the problems of writing Hong Kong come from the unique position Hong Kong has in relation to both its colonizer and its sovereign power. When Hong Kong is returned to the Chinese government,

> we may expect to find a situation that is quasi-colonial, but with an important historical twist: the colonized state, while politically subordinate, is in many other crucial respects *not* in a dependent subaltern position but is in fact more

advanced—in terms of education, technology, access to international networks, and so forth—than the colonizing state. (5-6)

In certain aspects, Hong Kong the colonized state is more advanced than the colonizing power, whether it is Britain or China. Therefore, Hong Kong is already passing through a phase of special postcoloniality before its decolonization, a disturbance in the conventional understanding of chronology, which plays an important role in the composition of Hong Kong's culture of disappearance. This disturbance in the sense of time and the manifestation of certain Hong Kong cultural aspects can be seen in Abbas's interpretation of the "one country, two systems" formula, which is the device of the Chinese government to pacify the Hong Kong people's anxiety about independence in Hong Kong. He writes:

> [W]hat we will find will not be two systems (socialist, capitalist) but one system at different stages of development—a difference in times and speeds. (6)

That is to say, what can be found operating in Hong Kong will certainly be different from the political, cultural and economic mechanisms in Mainland China, but the difference is only a matter of different maturing speed. Abbas's view is a useful way to understand the difference between Hong Kong and China, particularly the uniqueness of Hong Kong culture. According to Abbas:

> Hong Kong has no precolonial past to speak of. It is true that in a sense Hong Kong did have a history before 1841 when it was ceded to the British. There are records of human settlement on the island going back at least to the Sung dynasty, but the history of Hong Kong, in terms that are relevant to what it has become today, has effectively been a history of colonialism. (2)

Hong Kong as a place of inhabitation certainly existed before 1840 when the Opium War was fought between China and Britain, but there was not much record of the activities going on, probably because of the unremarkable amount of resources on the island. Even the decision of the British government to have Hong Kong as a compensation for the loss of the opium burnt by Zexu Lin was not based on its resources. What the British had in mind was in fact the large Chinese market for her products, using Hong Kong as a door to the Mainland. This view is shared by Gengwu Wang, as he notes that "history" of Hong Kong existed before the colonial period, but it is not recorded carefully.   The unimportance of Hong Kong as a place for inhabitation perhaps can also be seen from Shuqing Shi's three-volume novel, *Xianggang sanbuqu* 香港三部曲 [Hong Kong Trilogy], in which the ancestor of some of the major characters is introduced, and the life habits, customary practices, and the way people thought are given a realistic representation. For the author, the desire to write the "epic" of Hong Kong comes with the first fire of gunshot on June Fourth of 1989. She "identifies with Hong Kong where she has been in sojourn for 10 years, willingly joins every demonstration with the 6 million population in Hong Kong," and she "should write as the witness of Hong Kong history" (preface). The awareness of time (1997 and the urge of June Fourth 1989) has marked a threat to the understanding of Hong Kong identity. Time and space together knit a particular narrative of Hong Kong. Discussing a film produced in 1984, *Yan zhi kou*,[1] which makes use of the ghost story genre to tell a story of Hong Kong, Abbas writes:

> Fifty years disappear into simultaneity while space in turn becomes heterogeneous and mixed. The result is that two periods of Hong Kong history are brought together in a historical montage. The paradox is that one of the most popular and fantastic of genres is used as a rigorous method of representing the complexities of Hong Kong's cultural space. (41)

Instead of the past slowly unfolding into the present, they are juxtaposed with each other in the same stroke; the sense of depth, which usually goes with the flow of time, disappears. This flattening of time also blurs one's mental image of the past and the present. The appearance of things, dress, and the mannerisms change, but apart from the surface difference, the mechanism of the past's representation is directly related to the logic of the present-day elusiveness of Hong Kong's identity.

A third way of understanding the literary development in Hong Kong is what has come to be called the In-Between Theory. In-Between Theory is my own translation of the Chinese term, "jiafeng lun" 夾縫論, loosely grouped perspectives on looking at Hong Kong's cultural position in relation to Mainland China and Britain. Disagreement and variation exist among the critics grouped, and at times this In-Between Theory also shows similarity to other schools of thought, just as it is possible to see overlapping beliefs between this group, such as Gaofeng Hong 孔誥烽 and what Abbas has written in his book. To put it simply, In-Between theory is an approach to understanding Hong Kong culture as an interaction between the British and the Mainland Chinese cultures. The different views of people, loosely grouped together under the In-Between Theory, bring out an interesting question about Hong Kong's position. Rey Chow and Ye Shi maintain that Hong Kong inhabits the weak position in between two very different cultures and needs to struggle for a right to speak for itself. On the other hand, Hong's reading of Fengyi Liang's work implies a

---

[1] Yan zhi kou 胭脂扣 [Rouge]. Dir. Stanley Kwan 關錦鵬 Perf. Leslie Cheung, Anita Mui, Facet, 1987.

strong Hong Kong position taking advantage of two different cultural associations. Whether it is a strong or weak cultural position is up to the reader, but not infrequently this kind of debate refers to Hong Kong's economic success. Hong Kong has become a center of attention because it is one of the most successful cities economically, though it started as a small fishing village. Is this success a direct result of the infrastructure and social system laid down by the British government? We are not trying to seek the answer in this discussion, but this is to show that the effect of colonial rule has a major impact on what Hong Kong is today. The mother and the surrogate mother have both left impressions on the formation of Hong Kong's character, which comes out an interesting hybrid.

However, the impact of this interaction on Hong Kong is different from the way Liu expresses it in his introduction to *Xianggang wenxueshi*, for he stresses the durable Chinese-ness Hong Kong inherits from China despite the cultural pressure exercised by British colonialism. In In-Between Theory, the impact of interaction between the two imperial powers on Hong Kong is a different story as told by Luo Feng:

> [Hong Kong culture] is a product belonging to neither the native Chinese nor traditional British. In fact, during the 150 years colonial history, Hong Kong has already nurtured her own unique and special cultural phenomenon through an encompassing inclusion. This culture includes both traditional Chinese cultural elements as well as nutrients and impact from the West, combining into an international cosmopolitan cultural frame. (qtd. in Hong 55)

One of the basic differences between this In-Between Theory, as in the words of Luo Feng and Liu's idea of cultural mixing, is in the orientation. Although Liu admits the powerful influence of British sovereignty over Hong Kong, he insists that the westernized features of this city are an intrusion from a foreign culture, underneath which one can see the Chinese city. Luo Feng, however, sees Hong Kong culture as a culture of her own, not belonging to either one or the other sovereign powers. Although in her words there is at times a falling back onto the Hong Kong-China orientation, generally her understanding of Hong Kong culture is as a discrete entity. In the original text, there is a slight contradiction in the way she explains Hong Kong culture. While she maintains that Hong Kong as a culture does not belong to either British or Chinese cultures, in the last sentence she regards the impact of western culture as "from outside," which is a way of putting Hong Kong's allegiance back to Chinese culture, Chinese as the "inside culture" and western as the "outside input." As Hong remarks, In-Between Theory is not yet a fully developed school of thought, and there are discrepancies among writers who are considered to be in the group, as well as within the individual discourses of each critic.

Rey Chow, and to a certain extent P. K. Leung, however, takes a lightly negative view of Hong Kong's relationship with China and Britain. Rey Chow says:

Take the question of language for instance: What would it mean for Hong Kong to write itself in its own language? If that language is not English, it is not standard Chinese (Mandarin/Putonghua) either. It would be the "vulgar" language in practical daily use—a combination of Cantonese, broken English, and written Chinese. (154-55)

Hong Kong is depicted as the oppressed party caught in between two oppressive powers, Britain and China, each trying to impose a different set of practices. That explains Chow's urging Hong Kong people to assert themselves by establishing their own set of values and systems. P. K. Leung (Ye Si) also says, "Everybody seems to want to prove that Hong Kong cannot tell its own story, that Hong Kong's affairs have to be narrated by others. Everyone is fighting for the right to tell the story" (4-5). The everybody in Leung's theory seems to include everybody but the people who are born and living in Hong Kong, who are expected to have the right and greatest knowledge to tell this story of Hong Kong.

What might make a person eligible to tell this story of Hong Kong, or what kind of story could be counted as a truly Hong Kong story? In thinking about this question, Abbas tries to distinguish between writing Hong Kong and Hong Kong writing. If Hong Kong is used as a qualifier to the subject of writing, then it:

might involve embarking on a critical survey of local authors and of texts produced in and on Hong Kong. It would be concerned with discussing a wide and representative number of works, written mainly in Cantonese, that would define a corpus and lead to the establishment of a tradition of Hong Kong literature. It might even pose questions of identity like, what is a Hong Kong writer? Or what constitutes an authentic Hong Kong text? (111)

This discussion focuses on some popular romance novels to see how these popular writings, although not written as serious records of objective life, offer themselves as authentic texts from which the readers can find identification and empowerment.

The Dialogue

As mentioned before, after the fight between the "greenback" culture and the left-wing writings, and the Cultural Revolution, which started in China in 1966, Hong Kong was left to develop its own culture and writing, which appeal to its population. In the mid-1960s, mass popular writing was just beginning, and Yi Da was no doubt one of the most representative figures of such an era. In a way, his works, although containing some prominent features of the local culture, continued the exaggerated and fantastic plots and characterization of what was referred to as "Hong Kong Legends" in the previous decade. He was in his twenties when he became a bestselling writer in the mid-1960s, and his novels were filled with fantastical features. They depicted a good life only possible in a place like Hong Kong, urban and comfortable, with characters enjoying the best of the world because of the good education and good money that most of them possess.

Unsurprisingly, this kind of romantic fantasy, although consumed eagerly by young people not only in Hong Kong but also in Southeast Asia, did not find sympathy in literary critics. Chuangui Sung, in his article, "Dissecting Yi Da," details why Yi Da could only be called a popular romance writer, but not a successful writer: the essential qualities of good writing are lacking in Yi Da's bestsellers. Those missing qualities include: expressiveness of words, coherence of thoughts and ideas, and expression of experience (4). While this is not the place to judge whether a popular romance writer should follow certain rules in his work, the way Sung characterized Yi Da's writing provides good insight into the psychology of the readers in the 1960s. He summarized Yi Da's works into the following features: stereotypical characters, standard occasions of how boy meets girl, how boy betrays girl, and how the girl's mother is always there to receive the fallen girl with open arms (4).

These standard components, which Sung finds repeated again and again in Yi Da's works, were gobbled up by readers in delight, for they fulfilled exactly the desires and the needs of the average readers—students, factory workers, ladies working at the dance halls. These novels, fantastic as they are, satisfied their vanity because the lifestyle mentioned in the novels was beyond their reach (The Repulse Bay Hotel, The Peninsula Hotel). Equally, all the major characters are only called by a foreign/English name, thus projecting a westernized or even elitist atmosphere to the stories. The uncontrollable passion and sexual desire, which lead to scene after scene of unrealistic and "romantic" behavior between the main characters, also help the readers to "live" during their reading what they probably dare not do in their real lives. Sung concludes his analysis by saying that it is finally laziness that explains the popularity of Yi Da's novels. The writer himself is lazy as his books are all narration and no reflection; the readers are lazy because they enjoy reading books that do not require them to think at all.

Despite criticism such as Sung's, Yi Da's novels were enormously popular for a long time, especially as he branched out to write other genres. Beginning from the 1970s, a new type of urban romance emerged with Yi Shu. Yi Shu 亦

舒 is a pen-name. Her real name is Yishu Ni; she was born in Hong Kong in 1949, completed her basic education here, and went to UK to study hotel management. She had worked as a reporter and editor before she started writing professionally. An enormously prolific writer, she has published non-stop since the early 1970s and is still maintaining a very active career. According to Dong Ge, special features in Yi Shu's novels include simple narrative structure, urban settings, and main characters as working women, depicting their lives and loves among the very busy daily routine. Many critics and literary historians regard Yi Shu's work as not depicting love, but actually describing a process of life and proving indirectly the impossibility and absence of love altogether. Yi Shu herself says:

> [I] have engaged in the writing of romance fiction for at least a decade, fortunately I am still writing. The themes are very narrow, they are just about love matters between men and women....Yet I am extremely suspicious about love; writing is one thing, living is another. Everyday people crowd in the ferries to go to work, yawning, wearing sport shoes and jeans. To live inside romantic fiction … that will be horrible, I am glad that I can distinguish between the two. (qtd. in Dong Ge 41-48)

Like many other writers in Hong Kong, Yi Shu started with writing columns in newspapers, and has since manipulated a different cultural space in constructing and reinforcing her writer's identity. Columns, a special literary space located on the threshold between a public and a private realm, have flowered in Hong Kong. In his two-volume *Xianggangshi xinbian*, Gengwu Wang talks about their value:

> There have always been debates as to whether column writing is literature. If we say "using words to express feelings and thoughts" is literature, then these columns are all literature; if we think that a reasonable artistry (figures of speech) should be present during the process of expression, then some columns are weak, or even not, literature. But, whatever the case may be, column writing in Hong Kong involves the most authors, readers, and biggest social influences, and therefore the most important genre in Hong Kong literature.
>
> […] Hong Kong possesses a lot of 'world's most' … I think we can add the eighth most: having the most number of columns and column writers in the world (553).

Aesthetic value aside, Wang calls columns the "most important genre in Hong Kong literature" because of its extent of influence.

The list of writers beginning their writing career as columnists include Nong Fu 農婦[The Farm Wife], Yanni Lin 林燕妮 Yi Shu 亦舒, Xiaoxian Zhang 張小嫻 Yi Da 依達 Cen Kailun 岑凱倫 Qiong Yao 瓊瑤 Lingling Zhong 鍾玲玲 Kuang

Ni 倪匡, Xi Xi 西西, Fengyi Liang 梁鳳儀, and the list can be longer. The flexibility of columns certainly allows writers of different kinds to have their work published, be it fiction or just personal observations and opinions. Even after writers have gained a name and moved on to publishing paperbacks, they keep on writing their columns, firstly because the newspapers like to have them there as attractions, and secondly because these writers can make use of the columns to maintain the readers' interest in the writer as a person, as opposed to just a voice on paper. Xiaoxian Zhang, one of the writers whose work will be discussed later, is one who operates columns side by side with her paperback publications. For details about how it is done, please refer to Jialing Chen 陳嘉玲, "Yi ge aiqing xiaoshuojia de chansheng: Zhang Xiaoxian de wenhua jiazhi" 一個愛情流行小說家的產生：張小嫻的文化價值 [The Birth of a Popular Romance Writer: Cultural Value of Zhang Xiaoxian]. Another example is Yi Shu, who has been enormously prolific, yet keeping columns in several newspapers.

The significance of the column in relation to the literary scene in Hong Kong can be surmised by the fact that many of the writers publishing today make their debut in writing columns, and many of them keep on writing columns even after becoming bestseller writers. The nature of columns embodies some of the most important qualities of writing in Hong Kong, as explained by Wang:

> Hong Kong is a busy industrial and commercial city, life moves very quickly, and short precise pieces are most welcome by readers. Different columns cater for a "variety" of tastes, and their handling emphasises "speed"; this is a "good" thing for the press because it "saves" a lot of editing time, which in turn saves a lot of expenses, being very cost effective—typical of industrial and commercial societies. (563)

Yi Shu's novels contain elements similar to those found in newspaper columns. As can be seen with a general survey of her works, her stories feature the same stereotypical characters, heavily loaded with an identifiable value system, moving in a cosmopolitan Hong Kong. The consistent urban atmosphere in her novels, as well as her character stereotypes, highlight a specific theme, which reconstructs the scenario of a Hong Kong story—the death of the mother. Yi Shu has created a vast collection of characters, but they usually fall into one or the other of her repertoire: the highly protected innocent and self-satisfied woman, the capable and knowing career woman who takes responsibilities for herself and very often others, the sphinx-like woman who selfishly makes use of others to advance herself. Characters may go through different stages of their lives, taking up different roles, thus complicating their personalities and experience, but in general the stereotypes do not prepare for a lot of subtleties in individual characters. In this discussion, an in-depth analysis of Yi Shu's characters will be avoided because of firstly, the rather repetitive nature of her writing, and secondly, the larger focus of this discussion.

There are mother characters in her large collection of books, but they do not play any role in their daughters' growth. Cheng Zhen is a journalist with a reputation in the fictional society of Hong Kong in *Juedui shi ge meng* [Definitely a Dream]. She is married and has an adopted daughter, Cheng Gong, whom she feels is not properly cared for by her own mother, an old school friend of hers. The biological mother is shown to be incapable of providing care for her daughter, either because she does not have the financial means or the maturity herself to become a good mother. Cheng Zhen, however, is a good surrogate because she sees herself as a friend. Time and again the nearly perfect relationship between the two is attributed to their compatibility as friends.

In contrast, Cheng Zhen's relationship with her own biological mother is described in a much more causal manner:

> A month after quitting, she is so bored that her bones ache. Her mother voices her complaints to Cheng Zhen every afternoon, covering her own misfortunes from when she was twenty and had to suffer the tantrums of her in-laws, up to the present when her children are unfilial. Cheng Zhen is sick of it. ("Juedui shi ge meng" 3)

This is no comparison to the way Cheng Zhen relates to Cheng Gong, who has no blood relations with her. The physical bond between the biological mother and daughter is shown as no advantage at all. Not only does one find a casualness in the biological mother-daughter relationship, but there is almost a deliberate downplaying of the importance of such a link over the development of the daughter's personality. The one who has the most long-lasting influence on the daughter is never the biological mother; it may be older women or total strangers from the previous generation, but not the narrator's own mother. Examples of such influence exerted by older and usually legendary women over a younger narrator can be found easily in Yi Shu's novels. In *Xiang xue hai* 香雪海 [The Mysterious Lady], it is the mysterious character of the title, the sick lady who has a particular attraction towards the young female narrator; in *Shiliu tu* 石榴圖 [The Paintings], it is the old aunt and the mysterious lady protagonist of the island called Illusion who capture the attention of the narrator and change her life. *You guoqu de nuren* 有過去的女人 [A Woman with a Past] and *Jiaming yu Meigui* 家明與玫瑰 [Ka Ming and Rose] also share this feature of a direct, strong impact from an older woman who has no relation with the narrator at all.

Certainly an in-depth, mother-daughter relationship may not be the first priority of the writer, especially when the majority of her readers will be young working women who look for entertainment, romance, and perhaps fashionable opinions in her novels. Yet the obvious appeal these books have for a major group of readers does reveal a link between the content of these stories and the readers' daily lives. After all, Hong Kong has a large population of working women who are reasonably independent financially because they are better educated on average than previous generations, and as a result the tie with the family is loosened. With mothers going out to work, daughters do not relate to mothers in the same manner as when mothers were always at home waiting for the children to return from school. This is not a unique phenomenon in the popular writing in Hong Kong. The writer's opinion in many cases may be upheld as an unconventional or knowledgeable opinion, especially when the writer has cultivated a particular image for himself or herself. Yi Shu started writing as an educated young woman, quick-witted, having traditional views on gender relationships but unconventional ideas on all other things. She has portrayed herself as a literary person, well-read in both English and Chinese, as shown in her *Liu Ying xuesheng rizhi* 留英學生日誌 [Journal of an Overseas Student in the United Kingdom]. She also assumes good taste in many aspects of life, for example, in clothing and appearance. Her narrators' voices are made to be felt throughout her novels, loaded with the same value system and making value judgments on other characters and situations accordingly. Some of the readers may be looking for value judgement of this kind when they read her novels; because of the process of identification, they would like to aspire to a status where their opinions are also valued by others.

Therefore, the fictional world where a mother plays only a minimal role in the daughter's life is a familiar world to the readers. Even a mother as famous as Cen Renzhi in Yi Shu's *Yuyan* [Prophecy] is not much help to her daughter in terms of the daughter's growth to individuation. She still has to depend on herself, thus her motto: "there is no one to depend on but oneself." In fact, one of the consistent themes throughout Yi Shu's novels and other writings is the need for women's independence, both financially and intellectually, because it is a matter of self-respect and dignity. This focus on the personal independence of women today comes hand in hand with the phasing out of the importance of the mother figure, as well as the male partner. The mother and the husband, who used to be the two biggest cornerstones of a woman's life, are phased out in the novels because the female today has only herself to rely on.

Liu introduces Yi Shu in his *Xianggang wenxueshi* by saying:

The city, city women, the bourgeois lifestyle of city women, form the basic elements of Yi Shu's novels. (388)

The ending of her stories are usually unhappy, this is a special feature in her works: real life, no dreams, but tears; no fantasy, but is still romantic. (387)

This sense of solitude is also a result of the urban environment of Hong Kong, as city life is represented as a race putting pressure on the individual's time, emotions and thinking space, so much so that people do not connect with each other anymore. The journalist, Cheng Zhen, in *Jeudui shi ge meng* describes her job as "a very demanding job. From early morning to late at night, running about, once relaxed, no one wants to pick up the equipment and dash about again" (164). The need to remain competitive puts pressure on human connection. Once the connection breaks down, the individuals become even more isolated and have to be more self-dependent by necessity.

Yi Shu is not the only writer using urban life in Hong Kong as the setting, but her romance novels have a special flavor true to a specific quality in Hong Kong culture. It is in her language. In an episode Cheng Zhen is discussing with her former boss, Liu Qun, her decision to emigrate:

> Liu Qun said with sympathy, "Cheng Zhen, people like you should stay [in Hong Kong]."
> Cheng Zhen was nonchalant, wiping her face with a dash of her hand, "Dong Xin has issued the final ultimatum,[2] it will be divorce if I don't go with him."
> Liu sneered, "Divorce then."
> Cheng giggled.
> "Why did you marry him in the first place?"
> Cheng leaned forward, "The truth or the lie?"
> "What about the truth?"
> "I never knew I would make my name, otherwise I would not have got married."
> "The lie?"
> "Everyone needs a home, time is eternal [the Chinese expression is "tian chang di jiu" 天長地久], at least there is someone to count the days together. Even the most glamorous banquet will end, there is no missing of good times" [the Chinese expression is "lian lian hong chen" 戀戀紅塵]. (9)

Cheng Zhen is a successful journalist who has already made a name for herself. One can see from the vocabulary that she is very much at ease with language, using Chinese idioms in an English structure. The two language systems are appropriated, mutated into a new way of speaking, a most colloquial Chinese language, though in written form, but much closer to the spoken Cantonese.

This mutant language style is not only a quality of this author, but is also a reflection of the literary and cultural forces at work in Hong Kong. A new force is born out of the interaction between the English language and Chinese culture,

---

[2] In Yi Shu's Chinese original, she has used the term, "哀的美敦" which does not mean anything in a Chinese context because it is a transliteration of "ultimatum."

giving birth to something neither one nor the other, but containing traces of both parents. Yi Shu's narrator speaks for her in *Liu Ying xuesheng rizhi*:

> Of course my English is up to standard, the standard of my English literature is also first rate. From Shakespeare to Dylan Thomas, Dickens to Joyce, Yeats to e. e. Cummings, Jane Austen to Agatha Christie—it is my duty to be even better. What else do I know? Apart from Chinese, I only know English (183).

With two major cultures exercising their influence on the social and cultural background of Hong Kong, competence in these two languages is not considered an achievement.

While Yi Shu continues to produce her urban romance novels, Xiaoxian Zhang started her writing career in the mid-1990s to construct another kind of female bond. The vertical mother and daughter link gives way to a lateral bond between peers. It is significant to see how Xiaoxian Zhang constructs her own image side by side with this new women-women bond. The following is a blurb on the cover of her book, introducing herself:

> Zhang Xiaoxian, from Guangdong Kaiping, graduated from the Department of Communication, Hong Kong Baptist College. Born in Hong Kong, her mind matures much faster than her body. When still a student, she liked to fight for justice, but soon she learnt the lesson, and hid away to write. She has been TV script writer and executive, and has written film scripts. Unfortunately she was too credulous and often cheated of her fees. Emotionally much wiser and it is the other party who always is cheated. Dreaming of retiring or getting married in the 1990s, but it seems chances are remote. (*Mianbaoshu shang de nuren* 麵包樹 上的女人[Woman on the Bread Tree]

As Jialing Chen mentions, the type of information given on the blurb is the result of calculation regarding the reader's reception (217-227). Zhang is constructed as an educated new woman, who may be credulous in other aspects but is definitely a shrewd character where romantic relationships are concerned. The details about maturity further reinforce her strength as a brain and not a body, and this image is important to the overall effects of her writing. The difference between the mind and the body is in the connotation given to the quality of the individual. In saying that Zhang projects a mind-image of herself rather than a body-image, what is enforced are certain qualities she has chosen for her public image. This public image has a significant role to play both in the identity of this writer and in the narrator's voice in her novels.

Except for her first novel, *Mianbaoshu shang de nuren*, all her later novels bear a photo of the author on the inside cover. The black and white photo presents Zhang as having long straight hair, in a white blouse, dark vest, and trousers. Zhang has a column in *Huangguan zazhi* 皇冠雜誌 [Crown Magazine], a literary-cum-entertainment magazine similar to *Reader's Digest*. Published by the big Taiwanese Publishing House, Crown Publication, it comes out every month, featuring major writers in Taiwan, as well as reports of literary and cultural activities in Chinese communities over the world, but mostly in Taiwan. It is also one of the major channels for spotting young creative writers because of the annual novel competition, for which the prize includes a writer's contract. Photos accompany her articles every time, and those photos also present the same quiet and intelligent-looking young woman. This image of an educated, thoughtful and capable young woman with taste is central to her writing career, as can be seen in the voice she assumes in one of her columns:

> In between love and contempt, there are several stages. Even if you miss them one by one, or you cheat yourself and will not admit, when it comes to contempt, there is no turning back. Because we can never despise someone we still love, but only despise those we do not. ("Ai yu bishi" 愛與鄙視 [Love and Contempt] 32)

This is a generalized observation regarding relationships. The important point is not whether this applies to any particular reader, but to show off Zhang as a rational and clear-minded sage when giving advice on romantic relationships.

Not only does Zhang assume this agony aunt role in her columns, but in her novels one of the women protagonists will always assume this role of the neutral narrator, who talks rationally and gives comments from a more rational point of view. One can see Cheng Yun in *Mianbaoshu shang de nuren* [Woman on the Bread Tree], Shen Yu in *Mai haitun de nuhai* [The Girl Who Sells Dolphin], Zhou Rui in *San ge A Cup de nuren* [Three Women of Cup Size A], and Qiu Huaner in *Zaijian ye youshu* [Goodbye Rodent], as alternative voices of the author because they represent a similar rationality in the face of romantic relationships despite the various frustrating experiences each of them has. In Zhang's fictional world, there are also young independent women who assume a similar role as her narrator in the column, young rational women who have the ability to analyze romantic relationships and generalize upon them.

These maxims, which are scattered about in her novels, on the covers of her books and in her columns, inhabit a central role in her writing. Here are a few examples:

> A woman can do for love what she normally cannot do. (*Zaijian ye youshu* 再見野鼬鼠[Goodbye Rodent] 237)

> There is no need to let a person know you love him, if you can give up everything else for him, that is only the minimum charge, that is your obligation. (*Hebao li de danrenchuang* 荷包裏的單人床[The Single Bed in the Wallet] 170)

He does not send me red roses any more. Maybe he has forgotten ever transforming into a nightingale before. Men are such people, once they have taken possession, they forget what they have done. (*San yue li de xingfubing* 三月裏的幸福餅 [Fortune Cookies in March] 161-162)

Content in these maxims is not so important as the form, for they have a specific function to serve in a commercial society like Hong Kong. Jialing Chen in her article writes:

Zhang Xiaoxian's soaring to fame is an example. Not only does she inherit the tradition of other intellectual female writers like Lin Yanni, but she successfully expands the role of 'intellectual female writer' to a professional stage of 'romance analyst'. Zhang is not only a popular romantic writer, but also an expert on handling contemporary romantic relationships. (219)

Yanni Lin 林燕妮 is a famous Hong Kong writer. Writing in the 1980s, she was one of the earliest intellectual female writers because she was highly educated and already a successful career woman before writing. Her image is of a romantic writer, who claims her novels are written with perfume. Zhang creates for herself a more "professional" image not only because professionalism is respected here, but obviously because there is a real need in the readership for such an authority. Since the 1960s when column writing became a popular form, there have been specific problem-solving columns in the papers and magazines encouraging readers' participation. Zhang's novels, as well as her columns, can be seen as another form of this advice-giving authority because she has set herself up as a professional.

It is not difficult to understand the emergence of a romance analyst such as Xiaoxian Zhang. With more married women joining the workforce, mothers and children cannot spend so much time together. Hong Kong society is producing new generations of young women who see their peers much more than their own mothers. The characters in Zhang's novels are a good illustration of this phenomenon. The young women are usually of similar age, either school friends or colleagues, and because of the time they spend together, they form a much tighter network than they do with their family members. This is an interesting development of female bonds, replacing the mother-daughter link in terms both of their power of influence and the individual's adherence to it.

The romance expert, who can be relied on to advise upon romantic relationships in contemporary society, has replaced the role played by the mother in previous generations of Chinese women. The young women's romantic encounters are all presented as individual worlds of their own, cut off from the past as well as the future. This isolation has created a strong sense of independence in both the young female characters and by extension the kind of world they inhabit. Not only is the mother-daughter vertical link of history flattened out into a lateral link among the young peer group, the overall sense of historicity is also eliminated in Zhang's fictional world, beginning with *Mianbaoshu shang de nuren* [The Woman on the Bread Tree]. The editor, Shuping Zhou 周叔屏, of Xiaoxian Zhang's novel introduces the book as, "This is an autobiographical novel, recording the youth, sadness and fall of the main character Cheng Yun and her good friends" (inside back cover).

The new generation of young women, who were born in the 1970s and came of age in the 1990s, enjoy a new independence totally non-existent in their mother's experience. This is the generation that is situated at a point in history when the past is irrelevant and the future too uncertain to foresee. In writing, this isolation from history becomes a flattening sense of time, not exactly compressing the flow of time into immediate moments following one another, but rather detaching the present moment from any sense of history. Plots unfold, characters move with the story, but the sense of time passing and its impact does not seem to leave an impression on either the development of the plot or the characters themselves. One vivid example of this "instantisation" of history can be found in *Hebao li de danrenchuang* [The Single Bed in the Wallet] when a gigantic poster is made based on the love story between Yunsheng and Su Ying to promote the restaurant (73-74).

The quality of this advertisement outside a department store has something in common with the quality of Zhang's novels, that of a snapshot, which captures a moment in time and freezes it into a permanent present. The story between Yunsheng and A Su has been turned into a huge two-dimensional image to be displayed. The private, emotional depth has been flattened to an image, used to attract totally unrelated people to come to a restaurant, which is not even the same establishment where the original couple met. The personal story of Yunsheng and A Su has become effective advertisement, and the degree of success is measured by the number of people visiting the restaurant, just as in *Mianbaoshu shang de nuren*, Lin Fengwen publicizes his feelings for Cheng Yun in the lyrics of popular songs.

Privacy seems to have been exploded by the penetrating media, which blows up the images, repeating the words so often and to such an extent that the emotional depth of the cultural products turns into a surface attractiveness. In *Sanyue li de xingfubing* [Fortune Cookies in March], finally Xu Wenzhi and Zhou Qingting have to accept their inevitable separation. Zhou Qingting says:

> On the evening of 30th June 1997, a new era was born. It was raining cats and dogs the whole day, the same rain when we first met. I was wearing the lemon yellow raincoat, walking alone outside Times Square. A song of farewell was broadcasting from the gigantic TV screen.
> "Separation is originally our shared helplessness." I heard Wenzhi's voice.

Looking back, his face was on the TV screen, he, in Beijing. (235-236)

What Wenzhi, a journalist sent to cover the reunification of Hong Kong to China, says on TV can be interpreted both as a public statement and as his personal message to the narrator. It is a moment of the clash between the historical and the fictional, for June 30th 1997 was the real historical moment when colonial Hong Kong was no more and the city's sovereignty was returned to China, and it interacts with the fictional scenario in this novel. The moment of Hong Kong's unification with its motherland coincides with the moment of separation between the narrator and her lover. The reunion with one's motherland does not help at all; her Wenzhi is far away in Beijing, voicing his helplessness on TV to his departed lover. The total solitude of both Wenzhi and Qingting at the moment of reunification with the mother is a manifestation of this paradoxical state of affairs. The mother's traditional role of providing a sense of orientation is not only lost, here to Qingting, there seems to be absolutely no need of the mother at all.

Zhang is not the only female romance novel writer in Hong Kong now, but she is one of the most sophisticated, in the sense that she is the chief editor of her own women's magazine (called *Amy*), that she owns the online version of the magazine, and that she has branched out into different types of romance novels, including the thriller-vampire type. Romance novels are a huge market in Hong Kong, and there are many current practitioners. The other writers are not all similar to Zhang, but the general atmosphere constructed in the works is toward the same direction—an emphasis on the aloneness of the women in love. Contemporary young women in Hong Kong are depicted as powerfully alone because the mother figure is no longer reliable as a source of support.

Epilogue: After the Millennium

The millennium marked another point of anxious identity search for Hong Kong people, just as it did for millions of others all over the world. This "march" into the new era, a cry for more demanding competitiveness, an awareness of the rise of other nations and stations, just a few years after the rejoining of the Motherland, is a big challenge for the still shaky Hong Kong economy as well as cultural identity. From the Mainland, we hear extremely individual, metropolitan voices, such as Wei Hui's *Shanghai Baby* (2000), and Mu Zimei, who puts her secret sex diary online for all to see. Urban and highly individualistic voices in China overwhelm not only the local readers, but also encourage and stimulate more energetic and more daring voices of the self. In 2004, Li Bihua's novel, *Jiao Zi* [The Dumplings], captured the Hong Kong readers via its ruthless self-centredness and its determination of not turning back.

Ai Qingqing, a middle-aged, retired actress, refuses to let time leave her behind, refuses to give up what is granted only to the young and beautiful, thus paying dearly for the rejuvenation of her face and her body. In Li Bihua's novel, we see how Qingqing ruthlessly takes her destiny into her own hands: eating fetus dumplings. We are not told whether she would be punished for her deeds, but the last image of the novel is a wonderful idyllic one. Qingqing remembers the day of her wedding, when all the best in the world was in her hands. Throughout the novel, we do not glimpse one moment of aging face, not one wrinkle, no slackening of sexual interest and pleasure, not one hint of betrayal by time. Even the casting of the film adaptation maintains this shyness from age. In fact, the actress (a teenage idol) is criticized for not convincing the audience; her middle-agedness is the best proof that this woman's world has no place for weakness, no place for the lagging behind, and will only ever be appearing in its best moments. This strange but popular romance novel of 2004, written by one of the most popular female writers, is the best illustration of what the Hong Kong romance novel has been trying to do all these decades, ever sharpening its power and proving its power by its presence.

Works Cited

Abbas, Ackbar. *Hong Kong: Culture and the Politics of Disappearance*. Hong Kong: Hong Kong University P, 1997.

Chen, Jialing 陳嘉玲 "Yi ge aiqing xiaoshuojia de chansheng: Zhang Xiaoxian de wenhua jiazhi" 一個愛情流行小說家的產生 張小嫻的文化價值 [The Birth of a Popular Romance Writer: Cultural Value of Zhang Xiaoxian]. *Wenhua xiangxiang yu yishixingtai: Dangdai Xianggang wenhua zhengzhi lunping* 文化想像與意識形態 當代香港文化政治論評 [Cultural Imagination and Ideology: Criticisms on Contemporary Hong Kong Cultural Politics]. Ed. Qingqiao Chen 陳青喬 Hong Kong: Oxford University P, 1997, 217-27.

Chow, Rey. "Between Colonizers: Hong Kong's Postcolonial Self-Writing in the 1990s." *Diaspora* 2.2 (1992) 151-70.

Dong Ge 冬戈. "Yi Shu yanqing xiaoshuo qianyi" 亦舒言情小說淺議 [Brief Comments on Yi Shu Romance Novels]. *Xiang jiang wen tan* 香江文壇 [Literary Scene in Hong Kong] 9 September 2002, 41-48.

Hong, Gaofeng 孔誥烽. "Chu tan bei jin zhimin zhuyi: Cong Liang Fengyi xianxiang kan Xianggang jiafeng lun" 初探北進殖民主義: 從梁鳳儀現象看香港夾縫論 [An Initial Exploration of Northern Colonisation: From Liang Fengyi to Hong Kong In-Between-ness]. *Wenhua xiangxiang yu yishixingtai: Dangdai Xianggang wenhua zhengzhi lunping* 文化想像與意識形態: 當代香港文化政治論評 [Cultural Imagination and Ideology: Criticisms on Contemporary Hong Kong Cultural Politics]. Ed. Qingqiao Chen 陳青喬 Hong Kong: Oxford University P, 1997, 53-88.

Li, Bihua 李碧華 *Jiao Zi* 餃子 [Dumplings]. Xianggang: Tiandi tushu youxian gongsi, 2004.

Liu, Denghan 劉登翰 ed. *Xianggan wenxue shi* 香港文學史 [Hong Kong Literary History]. Xianggang: Zhuojia chubanshe, 1997.

Liu, Yichang 劉以鬯 ed. *Xianggang wenxue zhuojia chuanlue* 香港文學作家傳略 [Biographical Notes on Hong Kong Literary Writers]. Xianggang: Xianggang shizhengju, 1996.

Shi, Jianwai and Yisheng Wang 施建偉; 汪義生 "Dangdai Xianggang wenxue de zhuxing - huishou wu liu shi niandai de Xianggang wenxue" 當代香港文學的鑄形——回首五六十年代的香港文學 [The Moulding of Contemporary Hong Kong Literature – Review of Hong Kong Literature in 1950s and 1960s]. *Xianggang wenxue* 香港文學 [Hong Kong Literature] 147, 1st March 1997, 4-7.

Sung, Chuangui 宋船歸 "Jiepou Yi Da" 解部依達 [Dissecting Yi Da]. *Pangu* 盤古 [History] 4, 27 June 1967, 28-32.

Wang, Gengwu 王賡武,ed. *Xianggangshi xinbian* 香港史新編 [Hong Kong History: New Perspectives], 2 vols. Hong Kong: Joint Publishing (Hong Kong) Ltd., 1997.

Wang, Hongzhi 王宏志 *Lishi de ouran: Cong Xianggang kan Zhongguo xiandai wenxueshi* 歷史的偶然: 從香港看中國現代文學史 [Historical Contingencies: A Study of Modern Chinese Literary Histories in Hong Kong]. Hong Kong: Oxford University P, 1997.

Yi Shu 亦舒. *Jiaming yu Meigui* 家明與玫瑰 [Ka Ming and Rose]. Hong Kong: Tiandi tushu youxian gongsi, 1980.

————.*Juedui shi ge meng* 絕對是個夢 [Definitely a Dream]. Hong Kong: Tiandi tushu youxian gongsi, 1996.

————.*Shiliu tu* 石榴圖 [The Paintings]. Hong Kong: Tiandi tushu youxian gongsi, 1988.

————.*Xiang xue hai* 香雪海 [The Mysterious Lady]. Hong Kong: Tiandi tushu youxian gongsi, 1983.

————.*You guoqu de nuren* 有過去的女人 [A Woman with a Past]. Hong Kong: Tiandi tushu youxian gongsi, 1988.

————. *Yuyan* 預言 [Prophecy]. Hong Kong: Tiandi tushu youxian gongsi, 1991.

————.*Liu Ying xuesheng rizhi* 留英學生日誌 [Journal of an Overseas Student in the United Kingdom]. Hong Kong: Tiandi tushu youxian gongsi, 1989.

Ye Si 也斯(Liang Bingjun, PK Leung). "Xianggang de gushi: weishenme zheme nan shuo?" 香港的故事: 為什麼這麼難說? [The Hong Kong Story: Why is it So Difficult to Tell?]. *Xianggang wenhua* 香港文化 [Hong Kong Culture]. Hong Kong: Hong Kong Arts Centre, 1995, 4-5.

Yuan, Liangjun 袁良駿 "Ershi shiji Xianggang xiaoshuo mianmianguan (ii) - Xianggang Xiaoshuo shi xulun 二十世紀香港小說面面觀 (下)——《香港小說史》緒論 *Xianggang wenxue* 香港文學 [Hong Kong Literature] 168, 1 December 1998, 11-19.

————.*Xianggang xiaoshuo shi* 香港小說史 [History of Hong Kong Novel]. Shenzhen: Haitian chubanshe, 1999.

Yuan, Yonglin 袁勇麟. "Jie du Xianggang de wenhua shenfen - *Xiaoshuo Xianggang de dute zhuishu shijiao* 解讀香港的文化身份——《小說香港》的獨特敘述視角. *Xianggang wenxue* 香港文學 [Hong Kong Literature] 228, 1st December 2003, 79-85.

Zhao, Xifang 趙稀方. *Xiaoshuo Xianggang* 小說香港 [Hong Kong Novels]. Beijing: Sanlian shudian, 2003.

Zhang, Xiaoxian 張小嫻 *Mianbaoshu shang de nuren* 麵包樹上的女人 [Woman on the Bread Tree]. Hong Kong: Tiandi tushu youxian gongsi, 1997.

————."Ai yu bishi" 愛與鄙視 [Love and Contempt]. *Huangguan zazhi* 皇冠雜誌 [Crown Magazine] 533, 1998, 32.

————.*Mai haitun de nuhai* 賣海豚的女孩 [The Girl Who Sells Dolphin]. Hong Kong: Tiandi tushu youxian gongsi, 1995.

————.*Zaijian ye youshu* 再見野融鼠 [Goodbye Rodent]. Hong Kong: Tiandi tushu youxian gongsi, 1996.

————.*Hebao li de danrenchuang* 荷包裏的單人床 [The Single Bed in the Wallet]. Hong Kong: Tiandi tushu youxian gongsi, 1997.

————.*San yue li de xingfubing* 三月裏的幸福餅 [Fortune Cookies in March]. Hong Kong: Tiandi tushu youxian gongsi, 1997.

————.*San ge A Cup de nuren* 三個A Cup 的女人 [Three Women of Cup Size A]. Hong Kong: Tiandi tushu youxian gongsi, 1997.

"Tongxiang minjian de lu - lun Jin Yong xiaoshuo chuangzhuo he Jin Yong yanjiu" 通向民間的路- 論金庸小說創作和金庸研究 [The way to the mass— Comments on Jin Yong novels and Jin Yong studies]. http://hwwx.stu.edu.cn/qikan/2003.6/20030614.htm (10 October 2005).

"Wu liu shi niandai de Xianggang wenxue" 五六十年代的香港文學 [Hong Kong Literature in the 1950s and 1960s]. http://www.ilf.cn/wxsl/xianggang/003.htm (10 October 2005).

Amy Lee

Amy Lee has a PhD in Comparative Literature from The University of Warwick, UK. Her research interests include the Chinese Diaspora, female self-writing, contemporary fiction and culture, and narratives of marginal experiences. She has published on women's diasporic writing, gender issues in contemporary fictions and detective fiction. Currently she is an Assistant Professor in the Humanities Programme and the Department of English Language and Literature of Hong Kong Baptist University.

CHAPTER TWELVE

CITY OF FANTASY: ROMANCE NOVELS IN LAS VEGAS

EVA STOWERS

I have been reading romance novels since I was a teenager. In the late 1960s and early 1970s, the majority of romance novels available to me were category, or series, romances, originally published by Mills and Boon in England, then reprinted by Harlequin in the United States and Canada. They were often set in exotic locations, such as Greece, Portugal, Spain, Turkey or Italy. They were much more exciting for a young girl than the novels written by Americans, such as Grace Livingston Hill, Faith Baldwin, and Emily Loring, although I will admit to devouring those as well. The American novels were rarely set in any location more exotic than the Wild West. Of course, Zane Grey made the West seem very exciting. I moved to Las Vegas when I was seventeen, more than thirty years ago. In the years since I have continued reading romance novels, and I have been struck by how many of them were set at least partially in Las Vegas.

This chapter presents a survey of my eventual research, which began with material I found serendipitously while browsing bookstore shelves and continued to include works in The Special Collections Department of the University of Nevada, Las Vegas Library, which has a collection of fiction set in Las Vegas. I have come to believe that Las Vegas is the exotic destination for American readers. It has the excitement of the unusual and thrilling without the perceived dangers of leaving American soil. Within a few blocks on the Strip you can visit sanitized versions of ancient Persia (The Aladdin), medieval England (the Excalibur), Egypt (the Luxor), Paris (the Paris), Rome (Caesar's Palace), and Venice (the Venetian). The city is an oasis in the desert, and the mystique of the desert has meant romance since at least Rudolph Valentino. It has, or had, the Mob—romanticized in its own way in popular fiction and movies. If romance is fantasy, well, so is Las Vegas. Furthermore, the concept of Las Vegas is so embedded in popular culture that the reader can draw upon her own mental image to set the scene. The author has little to do to set the mood and atmosphere of the place.

Romance fiction and Las Vegas have several other characteristics in common—they are both about risk, winning, and happy endings. Las Vegas, once associated with divorce, is now more commonly associated with marriage, which is still the end result of most romance novels. Modleski discusses romance as a way to "disappear" (36), which also resonates in Las Vegas. The city has a reputation for "otherness"—what happens in Las Vegas stays in Las Vegas. Watching local Las Vegas television news, it is amazing to see how often criminals get caught here, thinking they can disappear into the anonymity that is Las Vegas. Many readers of romance fiction acknowledge that they read it because of its escapist value. One of the readers who responded to a questionnaire put it plainly: "I guess I feel there is enough "reality" in the world and reading is a means of escape for me" (Radway 88).

As a long-time resident of Las Vegas, I have also been interested in how the perception of the city and its prime industry, gambling, or, as we like to say in Las Vegas, gaming, has evolved in these books over the years. The earliest book I found was published in 1963, *Las Vegas Nurse* (Sears). The author characterizes the desert as an inhabitable place where nothing grows. The love interest, a doctor (of course), complains that the sinful enterprise in the town has tainted the whole place. However, the doctor loses the nurse to the manager of a hotel—a tall, dark and handsome sort with a heart of gold. His chorus girls support elderly mothers and disabled brothers.

The next novel, published in 1975, coincidentally the year I moved to Las Vegas, is *Nurse in Las Vegas* (Converse). The medical romance was very popular in its time. In this story, a private duty nurse follows her hypochondriac patient, a comedian, to Las Vegas, where he is performing at the Tumbleweed Hotel. One of the amusing things I find in these novels is the names of the hotels the authors invent. A modern casino owner would never name a property the Tumbleweed Hotel because the concept of down and out is not a winning idea. A compulsive gambler, the comedian loses to some shady characters that run him out of town and eventually murder his son. The casino owners, although not in league with the cardsharps, are aware of them and have done nothing to stop them.

In the same year, Janet Dailey, a best-selling author of the time, published *Fire and Ice,* which begins in Las Vegas. For the first time we see the use of the setting as an excuse for irrational actions. The heroine, deciding to marry a stranger in order to gain custody of her sister, thinks to herself:

> Amid the fantasy world of Las Vegas with its myriad neon lights and dancing
> fountains, her actions had seemed quite reasonable and practical. The difference

between winning and losing before had depended on the throw of the dice or the turn of the card, but now it had been ironically decided by her signature on a marriage certificate. (Dailey 16)

Of course, Las Vegas has taken advantage of this reputation—witness the very well-known slogan, "what happens in Vegas stays in Vegas."

In his doctoral dissertation, "Las Vegas in Popular Culture," Edward Baldwin writes that in the 1980s "the romance novel, a genre generally dismissed by all but its own devoted readers, embraced Las Vegas as a key setting and symbol for many of its stories" (137). This is seen in at least nine romances published in the 1980s that are set in Las Vegas, and most of them offer a bleak look at the city. In *Midnight Memories,* the heroine is a blackjack dealer who decides to leave town because of how she feels the city wastes people's lives. In *Stardust and Sand,* a cocktail waitress, soon to be costume designer, has been abandoned in Las Vegas by her lover, a compulsive gambler who has lost all of their money. Angry at the gaming industry, she cries, "Your noble profession, catering to the obsessions of sick people like Marc. Damn you, you're as bad as a drug dealer!" (York 30). The owner of the bar she worked at runs a crooked poker game and winds up buried in the desert. In *Hearts Are Wild,* Andra is in Las Vegas to get a divorce from her husband, a professional poker player. For the first time we see gambling as a legitimate, albeit not particularly respected, profession. The heroine believes that "In Vegas, cheating was considered a more serious crime than murder" (Caimi 23). It probably does get a more immediate punishment because the penalties for cheating are often imposed by the casino operators and not the justice system.

In a novel published in 1989, *The Morning After,* a woman celebrating her thirtieth birthday gets drunk and wakes up in a hotel room in Las Vegas with a really bad headache and a wedding ring. The groom "strode to the window and stared out at the sprawl that was Las Vegas. In daylight, it lacked the glitter that made it seem almost magical at night. Now it was just a sprawling desert town with little to recommend it unless you wanted to gamble" (Schulze 45). The newlyweds can't annul the marriage because it has been consummated. Obviously this was before celebrity annulments such as pop star Britney Spears and Jason Alexander's 24-hour Las Vegas marriage, where we learned from media reports how easy it actually is to get an annulment.

Code Name Casanova (Carroll) features characters that live in Las Vegas. Many, if not most, of the other novels revolve around characters that are visiting and see the city as outsiders. In this book, the heroine owns a limousine company, and the hero operates a repair shop for high-end luxury vehicles.

When we reach the 1990s, Las Vegas is beginning to have a more positive image in the romance novels. In 1990 Carole Nelson Douglas published several short romances that feature a side character called Midnight Louie, who will go on to star in a series of mysteries set in Las Vegas. Midnight Louie is a talking cat—and they say romance fiction is unrealistic. In another of her stories, "The Show Girl and the Prof," the University of Nevada, Las Vegas is mentioned for the first time. The show girl in question is taking a creative writing class, and the professor is rather contemptuous of her writing. The professor displays a disdain for Las Vegas that was probably rather reflective of even local academics in the 1990s.

Although the image of Las Vegas in these novels is increasingly positive, the authors still emphasize its gaudiness. In *Valley of Fire*, a casino is described as

> decorated with purple carpet, pink marble columns, a life-size statue of Elvis, and as many chandeliers as there was space on the ceiling. Las Vegas's idea of elegance, Martha Ann thought. Still, the gaudy scene tugged at her. She had grown up near Vegas, had spent many hours in front of the felt-covered tables. Her future had once hinged on the roll of the dice. She felt a familiar surge of adrenaline, a clamoring of excitement, an itch to try her luck. (Webb 116)

We are starting to see the novelists describe the surrounding areas such as, in this case, Valley of Fire, a popular state park. The authors tend to underestimate the power of the desert, allowing their characters to walk miles through the summer desert with little or no water. Another romance, *Mackenzie's Mission* (Howard), is set primarily at Nellis Air Force Base and is centered around the testing of a secret aircraft. In a sequel, *Mackenzie's Pleasure*, the main characters go to Las Vegas to get married (Howard).

In another story that mentions Nellis, *If a Man Answers* (Lovelace), a test pilot is on disability leave. This story brings in some of the old clichés about Las Vegas, in that a woman overhears a murder after she has dialed a wrong number and suspects a mob hit because "Las Vegas has pretty well cleaned up its act in the past decade or so … but there is still a few of the old school around. Men with connections." I will admit, though, that for many years after moving to Las Vegas, I would hear old-timers talk about how the city was better when the Mob ran it. I suspect many of them still long for those good old days. It might explain the election of our current mayor, a lawyer who gained fame defending well known mobsters.

In 1998, Nora Roberts, a prolific and bestselling author, published *The Winning Hand*. In this story a woman down on her luck puts her last dollar in a slot machine and hits the jackpot. Her decision to buy a house in Las Vegas is revealing:

> She liked the hot winds, the sprawling desert, the pulse of life and promise that beat in the air. Las Vegas was the fastest growing city in the U.S., wasn't it, and reported to be one of the most livable? It said so in the glossy hotel guide on her coffee table." (Roberts 147)

In 1999, a short story titled "Jessie's Girl" (Baker) was published. You will be glad to learn that Elvis Presley did not die—he is a vampire working on the Las Vegas Strip as an Elvis impersonator. Interestingly, Elvis or his impersonators are often portrayed as minor characters in many romances set in Las Vegas. In *License to Thrill* (Wilde), an Elvis impersonator kidnaps an elderly couple. In *She Woke up Married* (MacPherson), the heroine awakes in bed with an Elvis impersonator. In *Light in Shadow* (Krentz), Zoe and Ethan fly to Las Vegas for their wedding and find that "The minister bore a striking resemblance to Elvis in one of his heavy phases. His assistant, who doubled as bridal attendant, witness, and secretary, was a retired showgirl" (Krentz 193). Krentz acknowledges the efforts made by resorts to draw tourists into gambling:

> Zoe knew that if she and Ethan allowed themselves to be lured into either the mall or the art gallery, they would eventually be fed straight into the resort's casino. That was how Las Vegas survived. The bellies of the great, glittering beasts were the gaming floors, and the creatures required around-the-clock feeding. (Krentz 196)

It is ironic that even when the author obviously disapproves of gambling, the characters still win.

One of the few novels that depicts the pre-gambling era Las Vegas is *Anywhere You Are* (O'Day-Flannery), published in 1999. A time-travel romance, a woman is caught up in a time-travel project being developed at Area 51 and is transported to the year 1877. Area 51 is a federal property where secret tests in the area of national security are conducted. Conspiracy theorists write that Area 51 is a secret area where the federal government keeps captured extra-terrestrials and their spacecraft. In this novel, the heroine becomes a guest at the Las Vegas Ranch, owned by O.D. Gass, who actually was one of Las Vegas's pioneers. When she and the hero return to the present, they bring back an herb given to them by a local medicine man. This herb holds the cure to AIDS. Granted, this miracle cure plot device may be rather silly, but one has to appreciate the attempt by the author to introduce an important social issue.

In the 2000s Las Vegas is for the most part depicted as a dynamic, exciting destination. The use of Las Vegas as a location has spread well beyond its use in category romances, where the city is often used as a device to get the couple married quickly in a tacky wedding chapel.

Las Vegas is used as a setting by some of the genre's most popular authors. Elizabeth Lowell wrote a novel titled *Running Scared*, in which a curator for a Las Vegas hotel/casino is setting up an exhibit of Celtic gold. How far has Las Vegas's image come that a hotel/casino would have a curator? Las Vegas can thank Steve Wynn for that since his hotel/casino, The Bellagio, was the first to have an arts gallery as a major attraction. My big question here is: why on earth would anybody name a casino the Golden Fleece? Yes, the Golden Fleece was a mythical artifact, but as a resident of Las Vegas, I automatically think of the word fleece as in "to plunder, rob heartlessly; to victimize." I have to believe that the author was attempting irony here. In this novel we do have a view of the seamier, poverty-stricken neighborhoods in Las Vegas, as well as an interesting depiction of rivalries among casino owners.

In *Catch Me If You Can*, Beau hates Las Vegas, sensing "a note of quiet frenzy, sadness even, as if the revelers were trying just a little too hard to have a good time" (Bruhns 25). In *The Nerd Who Loved Me* (Thompson), the heroine is a showgirl. In this and other novels, we see the example of the showgirls with hearts of gold. The heroine of *Skintight* (Andersen) is also a showgirl, one with dreams of opening a dance studio. *Double Down* points out that gambling is not restricted to Las Vegas. The heroine, a bookie's daughter and a compulsive gambler, falls in love with a football player who is faced with efforts to fix games. Dawn, in *Raising the Stakes*, is a card dealer who disapproves of gambling. She believes it is "wrong to be part of a process that separated people from their money" (Marton 67).

Martha, in *She's My Mom*, suffers from amnesia. The plotline covers construction fraud and offers a look at ordinary people in Las Vegas. The characters live in Green Valley, a development in the nearby town of Henderson. While suffering from amnesia Martha worked as a maid, but really was a CPA. It is nice to see Las Vegas viewed as a regular city with people that have non-gaming jobs. Another book with little mention of gambling is *Blue Skies* (Carr), where the plotline revolves around an attempt to start a new airline, and as such is indicative of the entrepreneurial spirit of the city.

In this decade gambling is mostly viewed without aversion, but there are some novels that depict the problem of compulsive gambling. *The Thrill of it All* (Ridgway) begins in Las Vegas at a convention, but the heroine leaves town in chapter one. There is an interesting secondary character who is a compulsive gambler. "Every win meant a few more minutes in this peaceful paradise where nothing—no worries, no grief, no confrontations—intruded" (Ridgway 161).

Romance novelists these days are experimenting with unusual elements of fantasy, such as fairies, goblins, vampires, and witches, and all of these have found a home in Las Vegas. In *Outsiders*, Sin City is obviously Las Vegas. The main characters are goblins and faeries. The author's note says:

> If there was ever a city where goblins would choose to dwell, it is there. Such a glittering jewel would cause unhealthy excitement in their greedy little hearts. They would covet the town above all others for its wealth and eye-catching brilliance. (Jackson "Introduction")

Interestingly, this novel contains a veiled reference to Yucca Mountain, which is about an hour's drive from Las Vegas. The federal government has targeted Yucca Mountain as a nuclear storage site. In reaction to this plan to store nuclear waste near a volcano, the hero says:

> The goblins arranged to have it brought there, of course. Plenty of rational people raised objections to storing nuclear waste in a region with energetic volcanic activity. But it isn't a heavily populated state—at least, not heavily populated by humans—and money talks, especially in Washington. (Jackson 60)

In another novel, *The Protector*, the heroine is a stage magician who can create true illusions. She describes the city as "magical, rising up in the distance like a fairyland, with castles, spires, and towers dotting the horizon" (Ruth 199). The description sounds similar to the hotel/casino, The Excalibur, to me. In *Absolutely Captivated* (Grayson), a private investigator is a 150-year-old "mage" who moved to Las Vegas in the 1950s. Oddly enough, this novel offers one of the most realistic depictions of Las Vegas, from the Star Trek Experience to the traffic jams on US 95. A sequel, *Totally Spellbound* (Grayson), is also set in Las Vegas.

For many years romance fiction has been looked down on as trivial fantasy. Las Vegas too has been denigrated as tacky, gaudy and soulless but has come into its own. In 2005 Las Vegas celebrated its centennial and rejoiced in its success as the embodiment of fantasyland. Because of this evolving image, Las Vegas is indeed a worthy subject for the romance novel.

Works Cited

Andersen, Susan. *Skintight*. Ontario: MIRA, 2005.

Baker, Madeline. "Jesse's Girl" In *Paradise*. New York: Leisure Books, 1999.

Baldwin, Edward. "Las Vegas in Popular Culture." Diss. U of Nevada, Las Vegas, 1997.

Bruhns, Nina. *Catch Me If You Can*. New York: Silhouette, 2000.

Caimi, Gina. *Hearts are Wild*. New York: Silhouette, 1985.

Carr, Robyn. *Blue Skies*. Ontario: MIRA, 2004.

Carroll, Dawn. *Code Name Casanova*. Toronto: Harlequin, 1989.

Converse, Jane. *Nurse in Las Vegas*. New York: New American Library, 1975.

Dailey, Janet. *Fire and Ice*. Toronto: Harlequin, 1975.

Elliot, Emily. *Midnight Memories*. New York: Dell, 1983.

Garbera, Katherine. *Sin City Wedding*. New York: Silhouette, 2004.

Grayson, Kristine. *Absolutely Captivated*. New York: Kensington, 2004.

———.*Totally Spellbound*. New York: Kensington, 2005.

Howard, Linda. *Mackenzie's Mission*. New York: Silhouette, 1992.

————.*Mackenzie's Pleasure.* New York: Silhouette, 1996.

Hudson, Tess. *Double Down.* Ontario: MIRA, 2005.

Jackson, Melanie. *Outsiders.* New York: Love Spell, 2003.

Krentz, Jayne Ann. *Light in Shadow.* New York: Jove Books, 2002.

Lovelace, Merline. *If a Man Answers.* New York: Silhouette, 1998.

Lowell, Elizabeth. *Running Scared.* New York: Avon, 2002.

Macpherson, Suzanne. *She Woke Up Married.* New York: Avon, 2005.

Marton, Sandra. *Raising the Stakes.* Toronto: Harlequin, 2002.

Modleski, Tania. *Loving with a Vengeance: Mass-produced Fantasies for Women.* New York: Routledge, 1982.

O'Day-Flannery, Constance. *Anywhere You Are.* New York: Avon, 1999.

Radway, Janice. *Reading the Romance: Women, Patriarchy, and Popular Literature.* Chapel Hill: U of North Carolina P, 1984.

Roberts, Nora. *The Winning Hand.* New York: Silhouette, 1998.

Ruth, Jenifer A. *The Protector.* Waterville, ME: Five Star, 2003.

Schulze, Dallas. *The Morning After.* Toronto: Harlequin, 1989.

Sears, Jane. *Las Vegas Nurse.* New York: Avon, 1963.

Thompson, Vicki Lewis. *The Nerd Who Loved Me.* New York: St. Martin's, 2004.

Webb, Peggy. *Valley of Fire.* New York: Bantam, 1990.

Wilde, Lori. *License to Thrill.* New York: Warner Books, 2003.

Winters, Rebecca. *She's My Mom.* Toronto: Harlequin, 2002.

York, Amanda. *Stardust and Sand.* New York: Silhouette, 1985.

Eva Stowers

Eva Stowers is the Medical Librarian at the University of Nevada, Las Vegas. She received a BA in Romance Languages from UNLV and an MA in Library Sciences from the University of Arizona.

CHAPTER THIRTEEN

UNDERSTANDING THE PLEASURE: AN UNDERGRADUATE ROMANCE READING COMMUNITY

SALLY GOADE

"Embarrassed by the passionate man and woman on the cover, I refused to read the book anywhere in public." Charley is an undergraduate student, writing her final exam essay for my course entitled, "Understanding the Pleasure: Women's Romance Fiction and Its Readers." Charley is explaining her feelings when she began to read the first text that she recognized as a popular romance novel. The novel was Kathleen Woodiwiss's 1972 *The Flame and the Flower*, which began as Avon Publishing Company's highly successful venture into publishing large, historical novels that did not follow the constraints of the long-established Harlequin and Silhouette series romances. Woodiwiss's novel became an absolute staple of the genre with its inclusion in Janice Radway's 1984 ethnographic study of the "Smithton" group of romance readers, in which *The Flame and the Flower* is identified as the readers' most "ideal" romance (Radway 67). Charley did not find the novel to be ideal, primarily because she reacted with strong aversion to the rape that occurs 29 pages into the book, a rape in which our eventual hero mistakenly identifies the heroine as a prostitute who is only pretending to be innocent and uninterested. The hero and heroine, Brandon and Heather, go on to fall in love and live happily ever after (a criterion for ideal romances), but Charley remained stuck on this question: "How could someone possibly fall in love with someone who raped her?"

Charley went on to read Laura Kinsale's 1992 *The Prince of Midnight* as one of several choices that she could make for her next romance novel, which she was reading along with Radway's book and several other theorists' essays. In her final essay, an account of her life as a romance reader, Charley states that she finds herself "irritated" that Kinsale brings several innovations into the romance narrative (among these, a physically impaired hero and an emotionally wounded and cold heroine). In response to her own irritation, this "new" romance reader then wonders, "How did I know so much about romance novels if I had only just read *The Flame and the Flower?*" noting that perhaps she had come into the class more familiar with romance narratives than she realized. Later, in response to her unequivocal enjoyment of Diana Gabaldon's 1991 *Outlander*, Charley asks, "Had I fallen into the trap? Was I to become a romance reader?" By the end of her final essay, Charley is not an absolute fan of the genre, but she does say that "many are laced with interesting innovations" and that "not all romances are 'trashy,' and the ones that are have probably failed miserably." She has even "begun to make recommendations" of romance novels to friends and has asked to be given the second book in Gabaldon's *Outlander* series as a holiday present.

Charley's journey from embarrassed, skeptical interest (she did register for a course in women's romance fiction) through aversion, recognition, attraction, and at last some resolution is not the only journey that students make as they learn more about popular romance novels (some enter the class as committed romance readers and are negotiating differently with an attraction they already recognize). However, Charley's reflection on her own reading is representative of the journey often made by students who begin as more resistant readers. In Understanding the Pleasure, students read, alongside the work of Radway and other theorists, a collection of essays written by popular romance novelists about the genre in which they write, entitled *Dangerous Men and Adventurous Women*. In her introduction to this collection, novelist Jayne Ann Krentz begins with the statement that "Few people realize how much courage it takes for a woman to open a romance novel on an airplane" (1). As Krentz describes the types of reactions her airline passenger is likely to experience, she is acknowledging cultural codes that both help to sell romance novels and help to keep the novels in the arena of "trash" literature. The novels' clinch covers, with various versions of Fabio embracing heroines with low-cut bodices, promise readers particular fantasies and pleasures unique to women's fiction. However, those same covers also serve to place unwelcome labels on readers, authors, critics, and teachers of literature who think that students can gain valuable insight from looking closely at both the covers and what is between them.

The focus for "Understanding the Pleasure" is women's fiction, chosen both because of my desire to understand the pleasure found in the texts and because fiction written by and overtly for women is often perceived as secondary to (or less academic than) corresponding "masculine" popular genres. Through reading and working in this course, students explore the line between literature and non-literature in their lives by connecting generic and audience reception theories to both canonical and popular women's fiction. By extending those connections into culture as a whole, they also begin to realize that they have been readers of the cultural codes of romance, in one form or another, all of their lives. By consciously entering a larger reading community, they are able to imagine themselves in the potential subject positions of author, critic, and even teacher, and they are able to see that for many romance readers, these roles cannot be kept distinct.

Throughout the course, students work to synthesize divergent voices within the romance reading community and add their own to the dialogue through their online reading journal/discussion board and in-class exchange. By the final exam, students are ready to write their own versions of Tania Modleski's short narrative, "My Life as a Romance Reader." Materials gathered from students for this chapter include their final essay exams (read in conjunction with initial surveys completed at the beginning of the semester) and students' online discussion board exchanges regarding their reading. All quoted material from students is used with their permission (and rather outspoken blessing) from a section of "Understanding the Pleasure" taught in the fall of 2003. This course was a "special topic," offered jointly within the English, Women's Studies, and Honors programs at our college. Thus, only about one third of the students were English majors, and all expressed an initial desire to fulfill their program requirements through an offering that seemed unusual and intriguing to them. However, only six out of sixteen students entered the course identifying themselves as romance readers.

A key outcome initially identified for "Understanding the Pleasure" was that by having students excavate their own position as critical readers, they would begin to recognize and question cultural ideology, thereby beginning the lifelong task of coming to terms with their own complicity in it. Students would then be able to enter a community of people who take pleasure in romance texts even as they wonder why those texts have such a strong hold on them. As an ultimate goal, students would learn that power over pleasure means understanding of the pleasure's source, not elimination of it.

Both terms, "pleasure" and "power," are inspired by Robert Scholes's assertion that a reader's power over any text begins with identification of the cultural codes that are her pleasure source in that particular text. According to Scholes, a student moves from the act of simple reading to the act of interpretation and finally to the act of criticism when she can identify these cultural codes and connect them to pleasure in the text (61). Early in Understanding the Pleasure, students are asked to walk over to a classroom window and explain what they see. Knowing that I must be up to something, a student will eventually note the smudges on the glass itself and the small squares of wood framing that break up the view. In *Mythologies*, Roland Barthes uses the metaphor of looking at a landscape through a glass to illustrate a point about semiotics, or the perception of signs. The myth or ideology, revealed by analysis, is the glass. Barthes maintains that, as a cultural critic, he must focus on the glass, the myth, and apply a systematic method in order to see or analyze it. He "must pass from the state of reader to that of mythologist" (110). One of the essential questions to be addressed in this course is whether students can recognize the construction of the window that holds their gaze, still have the ability to turn their attention from the glass to the scene beyond, and *enjoy* that scene. One of the reminders frequently offered after the window demonstration is for students to "knock on the glass." For students to analyze their own responses to the ideology presented by romance narratives, they must first develop the ability to recognize the ideology to which they are responding.

But Why Do We Read These Things?

Throughout popular romance criticism of the last three decades, the fundamental question critics have asked is stated bluntly in the title of Kay Mussell's 1983 essay, "But Why Do They Read Those Things?" By asking this type of question, directed to the text primarily as a means of understanding the audience, critics have focused on the role of romance novels in women's everyday lives and on the political power, located in a patriarchal system, that the novels may represent. The work done by Mussell, Radway, and Tania Modleski in the 1980's, which students read during the course, was part of a broad base of feminist criticism of women's popular fiction that sought to facilitate change in the patriarchal power structure by revealing how the ideology of the novels encouraged women to contribute to their own subjugation (an application of Antonio Gramsci's theory of hegemony).

The specific ideology in the case of feminist criticism of romance novels is what Leslie Rabine has called the "cultural myth of romantic love" (vii). This myth—that all problems can be overcome through true love—becomes an ideology so ingrained as to be nearly invisible as a conscious belief (hence Barthes's glass metaphor). The myth is considered oppressive to women because it teaches that a woman's ultimate success is always couched within her relationship to a lover/husband and her care of a domestic space where that relationship can flourish. In essence then, the romance heroine can evolve into increasingly spunky, intelligent, and accomplished forms, but she is never exempt from passing what Mussell calls the "domestic test," and without the ability to pass that test, she will not be successful (*Fantasy and Reconciliation* 110).

As an early critic of popular romance novels, Radway identifies potentially oppressive ideology in romance texts, but she also posits that readers can make multiple meanings from the texts, simultaneously engaging in both hegemonic reinforcement of patriarchal ideology and personal empowerment. Early in *Reading the Romance*, Radway introduces herself as a cultural scholar working from a base of semiotic theory (4). Radway's interpretation of semiotic theory adopts what Simon During calls the "culturalist" strand (During 5-7). This interpretation acknowledges that readers may make many meanings out of textual symbols, lending itself to the polysemic idea that readers negotiate meaning from texts in variable ways.

Partially because readers can make multiple meanings out of one signifier, the discipline of Cultural Studies allows for simultaneous empowerment and exploitation of the consumer within the act of consuming. According to Lawrence Grossberg in his introduction to *Bringing It All Back Home,* neither act is exclusive of the other (7). As consumers (readers) of popular texts, students who study the act of consumption (reading) struggle with characterizing their reading selves as both exploited and empowered by mass culture. Empowerment, as defined by Grossberg in *Dancing in Spite of Myself,* is not equivalent to resistance against exploitation. Instead, the "involvement and investment" of empowerment must be present in order for a consumer to take "any form of action or commitment, and hence any form of resistance or opposition" (14). The very act of taking pleasure then, if it is combined with recognition of the pleasure and reflection on its source, provides an opportunity for the consumer to take action.

The concept of semiotics and how consumers make multiple meanings from one signifier is implicit in Giroux and Simon's definition of the central question in an analysis of ideology as it intersects with pleasure.

> At stake here is the recognition that an overreliance on ideology critique limits our ability to understand how people actively participate in the dominant culture through processes of accommodation, negotiation, and even resistance. (17)

Giroux and Simon's accommodation, negotiation, and resistance correspond to Stuart Hall's description of three types of readings or "decodings" possible in reaction to texts: preferred, negotiated, and opposed ("Encoding, Decoding" 101-03). What Understanding the Pleasure has somewhat unexpectedly revealed is a mirroring among the students of these various responses to texts.

Even as students are learning that readers, theorists, and authors can be said to prefer, negotiate, or resist romance novels, they begin to see themselves as also preferring, negotiating, or resisting. Charley identifies her own negotiation fairly overtly when she notes that even as she felt "slightly guilty" for enjoying *Outlander* so much, when she "read something that [she] did not like" in the book, she "pretended that it didn't happen or forgot about it." This student, who strongly disliked her first romance novel, has discovered that if the narrative hails her own personal ideology enough, she is willing to overlook elements that she would otherwise consider distasteful (in the case of *Outlander*, a homosexual rape inflicted on the hero that he endures in order to save the heroine).

A preferred reading is that which follows the original intent of the text within a "dominant-hegemonic code." In a similar fashion, a reader making an accommodation to (or negotiation with) the preferred reading will alter her belief structure to accommodate that ideological model presented in the reading. In reaction to a fairly typical modern romance novel, a preferred reading would celebrate the love found by the hero and heroine, believing that both characters have found lasting fulfillment through the resolution of the story. Several of the students in Understanding the Pleasure were indeed able to set aside their aversion to the rape in *The Flame and the Flower*, accepting the novel's presentation of the act as a mistake, and finding themselves enthralled with the eventual union of the hero and heroine. In distinction to the assimilationist ethos of the preferred reading, a negotiated reading is one that allows the reader to accept parts of the dominant code while resisting others. In this case, a reader might enjoy the fantasy of lasting and fulfilling true love in a romance novel while simultaneously believing that real-life relationships will never be able to fully mirror the fantasy (to some degree, even the most preferred readers in the course viewed the narrative in Woodiwiss's novel as an unrealistic fantasy, but they admitted that while reading, they were buying it).

An opposed or resistant reading is one that completely refigures the text, reshaping it in another frame of reference. Modleski gives an example of an oppositional, resistant reading in her 1997 article when she quotes lesbian students who enjoy erotic heterosexual romance novel scenes by reading the masculine pronoun "he" in reference to the hero as "she" ("Romance Reader" 27). Even students who profess never to read mass literature, especially of the clinched cover variety, are still dealing with the texts (and the ideology represented within them) somehow. During points out that "though viewers need not accept the preferred code, they must respond to it in some way" (9). In Understanding the Pleasure, resistant readers find themselves required to continue reading if they are not willing to drop the course, so they may even oppose a text by maintaining a running argument with its ideology, but eventually, they realize that they are doing so. Through this course, students ideally learn not to separate their pleasure in or aversion to popular culture from their contemplative selves. For while the dual roles of consumption and critique may at times be uncomfortable, they are essential for individuals who would exercise true power over the texts in their lives.

Since many students have not been romance novel readers or may have relegated such reading to their past lives, it is essential that they recognize the ubiquitous nature of the cultural myth of romantic love in popular culture as a whole. The myth is easy enough to expose in an undergraduate classroom with three quick clips: (1) Sandra Bullock daydreaming in her lonely job as a subway token taker in *While You Were Sleeping*, (2) Julia Roberts alone in her bed with boyfriends spliced out of the pictures in *Pretty Woman*, and (3) Melanie Griffith hurrying to her secretarial desk in *Working Girl*. What are all of these women waiting for? What, as an audience member, do you already know is going to happen in these movies? Students answering those questions begin to get the idea that despite the strength and independence shown by each movie heroine, she is still portrayed as a woman waiting for the real adventure of her life to begin through advent of the hero. (For a helpful source on a range of popular films in which the myth of romantic love is easily exposed, see Crystal Kile's 1992 "Endless Love Will Keep Us Together.")

Exposure of the myth is often accompanied by an uncomfortable recognition for many students. These movies may be ones they have enjoyed in the past. If through classroom presentation and discussion, students agree that the movies work from a cultural myth of romantic love, they then face a schism between their pleasure and their beliefs if analytically, they also believe that a heroine should not be passively waiting for the advent of a hero. By acknowledging their own pleasure in any cultural ideology, students immediately become implicated as part of the culture that creates the ideology. At least in part, students' pleasure in the text exists in their identification of themselves and the ideals they hold dear in the text itself even if that identification has previously seemed too natural to recognize. However, if the self a student recognizes is reflected in ideals the student thought she had left behind, pleasure can be quickly followed by aversion. This aversion may be either to the text under study ("I'll never be able to enjoy *Pretty Woman* again") or to the act of analysis itself ("If I study that, I won't be able to enjoy it").

Recognizing that students are likely to experience this conflict, it becomes the instructor's job to intervene before aversion to the work and/or analysis prevents students from realizing their own power over the text. For this reason, the brief, preliminary classroom analysis of the cultural myth of romantic love is followed with a frank discussion of the conflicts students are likely to experience between pleasure and analysis. At this point, it becomes important to explicitly acknowledge a major theme of the course: romance readers in all subject positions, including fans, students, teachers, critics, and authors, are constantly negotiating their complicity in and resistance to dominant ideology.

Curricular Choices and Pedagogical Practice

The smallest innovations in any genre, and Scholes urges us to view the discipline of English as its own "genre," represent enormous struggle against established conventions (*Textual Power* 2). However, the innovations cannot be recognized without a corresponding recognition of the conventions against which they are made. For this reason, students in Understanding the Pleasure are encouraged from the course's outset to identify conventions of the popular romance narrative. The recognizable movie clips give them a start on this process, and with several romance novel readers in the room, it takes only a few moments to brainstorm a long list of conventions. By then putting the list that Radway gleaned from her ethnographic study of Smithton readers together with their reading of the Smithton group's favorite book (Charley's least favorite, *The Flame and the Flower*), students even become a little smug in their ability to describe a "typical" romance novel. Among the conventions they notice is recognition of a type that they later learn to identify as the Byronic hero. Through the Byronic hero, the hero of sensibility, child of nature, and Gothic villain are synthesized into one figure who retains many villainous elements but is a sympathetic character because of his capability for strong emotional attachment and passionate remorse. He holds both the reader's fascination and sympathy by becoming a combination hero-villain, or the classic hero/bad boy (Thorslev 134).

After students have begun to recognize their own knowledge of romance conventions—including character types, such as the Byronic hero, and plot outcomes, such as the happy ending—Understanding the Pleasure presents several viable and intriguing possibilities for organization. At the outset, it is important to admit to students that they are consumers not just of popular culture, but also of pedagogy. In fact, students' complicity in the ideology they analyze mirrors the complicity of any innovative pedagogical approach in the very pedagogical system that it proposes to change. Scholes urges a pedagogical approach that places "the teaching of literary consumption at the center of our apparatus and all our other activities positioned around it" (*Textual Power* 11). For students to start here, they must realize that the pedagogical canon, which has often marginalized feminine narratives and privileged realism over romance, also plays a significant role in which texts they have previously considered worthy of consumption and which texts are readily available for consumption.

There are three major pedagogical goals for the methodological approach to this course (for a detailed description of textual choices, see the sample syllabus, which is attached as an appendix). The first is to give students a rudimentary historical understanding of women's romance fiction. Students can then recognize the coherence of romance conventions between texts ranging from Classical to contemporary and from canonical to popular. In one sense, reaching this goal forces students to recognize that romance narratives must be dealt with somehow because they do not appear to be going away anytime soon. The second goal is to give students a unifying thread they can follow through the genre with real-life ideological consequences. My choice for this thread is the Byronic hero in his various, mutable forms, and students are asked to consider what consequences women readers' and writers' attraction to this hero might have in real-life relationship choices and behaviors. The third goal is to present romance texts themselves as the result of writers' ever-present role as readers also. In this way, consumption is placed at the center and writers are consumers who have managed to navigate their romance reading by utilizing generic and cultural codes to produce both accommodating models and innovative negotiations of earlier texts.

In order to accomplish this third goal, several of the primary works in the course are ones in which the authors have reacted significantly to the genre while still keeping their work within it. These choices include a set of two novels (half of the students read one, half the other, and they then share reading experiences), which is composed of Jane Austen's *Northanger Abbey* (along with excerpts from the popular eighteenth-century novel, Ann Radcliffe's *Mysteries of Udolpho*, that Austen's heroine is reading) and Margaret Atwood's *Lady Oracle* (in which the heroine is an author of costume gothics). Gabaldon's *Outlander*, which all students read, contains significant metatextual commentary on romance and employs enough innovations (among them a virginal hero and a married heroine who must abandon her first husband in another century) to give Gabaldon's facetious 2003 website comment that she "doesn't write romance novels" some credence. We also discuss Miguel de Cervantes's early parody of romance, using the legacy of *Don Quixote* and other parodies to show how those authors who negotiate with the genre can have a strong influence on it as well.

To some extent, students' likely familiarity with women's romances that have been established in the canon is employed as a bridge to less familiar texts. In doing so, it is then important to ask the question of why some texts are more familiar than others, why, for instance, a person might be considered more culturally literate because she recognizes the name "Heathcliff," while recognition of another romance hero might be considered trivial. The answer may be lodged in Heathcliff's function as a prototype, in the somehow surprising quality F. R. Leavis seems to recognize in Emily Brontë's *Wuthering Heights* (41), or simply in the fact that teachers of literature have traditionally consumed and critiqued Bronte's novel as literature students themselves. The answer probably lies at least in all three of these elements, but the important goal is for students to ask the question, refusing blind acceptance of my textual choices or anyone else's.

A Romance Reading Community

When students enter the dialogue surrounding women's romance, they can do so with written texts, each other, and me, but they can also enter that dialogue with several romance authors and readers outside the academic community. Mussell's introduction to a 1997 *Paradoxa* issue devoted to women's romance describes a dynamic dialogue between participants in the romance genre on an Internet listserv entitled "Romance Readers Anonymous" (RRA-L) (3). Since there is no charge for the listserv, students are required to subscribe to RRA-L during the time period of the course. They are often excited to find authors contributing to the listserv, and they find that those individuals who discuss modern women's fiction sometimes have college faculty logos by their names and often (whether or not they are college faculty) reach into the canonical romance tradition for references in their discussion. In an especially interesting survey in 2001, RRA-L members chose Emily Brontë's *Jane Eyre* as their second favorite romance novel of all time (Singh). Students in Understanding the Pleasure cheered when they learned that Gabaldon's *Outlander* had stolen first place from the canonical classic. No matter her favorite novel or occupation, each participant in the RRA-L is in fact a reader, and as such, is someone who has negotiated the sometimes treacherous territory of analyzing her (and very occasionally his) own pleasure in the text. The name of the listserv, like that of a confessional group for addicts, indicates a winking admission that at least some subscribers may not be entirely comfortable with admitting their membership in the group.

Part of revealing the pleasure of women's fiction to students is to include them in a reading community wherein they can discuss, recommend, and share texts. RRA-L provides a partial fulfillment of this objective, but it is also important for students to connect personally with an immediate peer group of readers. In an effort to keep, or in some cases discover, the pleasure of a reading community, students are required to keep an online journal in the form of a discussion board, in which they discuss their reactions to the primary texts, secondary criticism, and national listserv. Partially as a solution to the "so-many-texts, so-little-time" dilemma, the class is set up so that at three points in the semester, students are not all reading the same novel (see "sets" on syllabus in appendix). While logistics of ordering books and of being "on the same page" with students necessitate that the professor chooses the menu of texts, this approach shares similarities with a nonacademic reading community. Students are able and actually required to recommend texts to each other, and they vicariously learn about more novels than they can possibly read in fifteen weeks, often whetting their appetites to continue their membership in a larger reading community beyond the end of the semester (amazingly with the amount of reading for the course, some even sneak in a couple of "extra" readings during the semester by borrowing each other's books).

A sense of community among readers, a "fandom" in Grossberg's terminology, may be one method readers have of alleviating the "guilt" that often accompanies pleasure. Giroux and Simon identify this guilt as the result of a schism between ideology the consumer recognizes as desirable and actual ideology in products the consumer enjoys (17). At the least, a romance novel reader may feel tension between how she feels that others perceive her reading activity and how she represents the activity to herself. Additionally, students who feel guilt for enjoyment they have taken in the cultural myth of romantic love (through romance novels or other sources) may employ the image restoration strategy of mortification to distance their newly "educated" selves from their earlier selves. Mortification, identified by William Benoit, who builds on the work of Kenneth Burke, is a strategy used by a rhetor who wishes to acknowledge error or wrongdoing, accepting the blame but "placing it on one's 'bad' self" (87). In our case, the "bad" self would be the uneducated one who simply did not see the patriarchal ideology informing a romance fantasy. However, if students are allowed to stop at the point of mortification, the complexity of both the texts and the fantasy is denied. Instead, students can be encouraged to resist the urge to simply distance themselves from conflict, thus beginning the process of resolving the conflict.

Preferred, Negotiating, and Resistant Readers

While Charley was not conscious of having read romances before taking Understanding the Pleasure, she qualified as a negotiating reader because she came to find pleasure in romance narratives overall and found a way to acknowledge and work through her displeasure with some elements of the genre. In the 2003 section of Understanding the Pleasure, there were five total students who came to negotiate a positive relationship with texts that they had not considered worthy of reading before taking the course. One student, Erin, entitled her final essay: "My Life as a Romance Reader: The Journey from Skeptic to Addict," and in the essay, she takes a creative approach by setting herself up as a fictional, "negotiating" Harlequin editor who has come to hate the Harlequins she reads for a living but comes to enjoy historical romances that she stumbles upon through a book store clerk's recommendation. The reformed Harlequin editor even learns to find some pleasure in her work again as she notices conventions and innovations in those texts as well. Each of the five negotiating students ends the story of her reading on a positive note, saying that she has discovered pleasure in a source that she had always considered off limits and also found pleasure through the very act of analysis.

The seven "preferred" readers consisted of the six who entered the course as romance novel enthusiasts plus one who immediately recognized her own enjoyment of the romance narrative in popular film and unequivocally enjoyed the primary texts in the course from the outset. These students uniformly found justification for their personal reading choices in the knowledge that a long history of literary criticism surrounds romances, and they celebrated a sense of belonging to a larger reading community. One reason for this celebration was a sense that they no longer had to hide their romance reading or try to completely separate it from their academic work. One student, Cara, entitled her final essay: "My Life as a Romance Reader: My Intrinsic Dichotomy," expressing the division she had felt between her academic and personal reading. Another, Jessica, wrote a creative essay in which she joins several of her favorite romance characters in eighteenth-century Scotland (the setting for the *Outlander* series), eventually facing her "romantic half" (a side she says she had "buried" before taking the course), "having conversations and debates" with that half of herself, and embracing her "other" self. Interestingly, while the preferred readers expressed this type of struggle with earlier self-attempts to squelch their attraction to romance, none expressed resentment for the act of reflective analysis.

Rounding out the class romance-reading community were four "resistant" readers, students who in addition to never having read romance novels in the past, had experienced overtly negative reactions to the romance narrative when they had encountered it in film and other areas of popular culture. One of these students had to leave the course for medical reasons, but the other three attended regularly, read all the required texts, and participated actively in class and online discussions. Each wrote a thoughtful final exam essay, undoubtedly feeling that she must tread carefully in writing for a professor who could not quite hide her status as "academic fan" (another vexed subject position is that of teacher/fan). One student, Katelyn, resisted the heroines of romances throughout the course, taking spirited but good-natured issue with Woodiwiss's constant reference to Heather's incredible beauty in *The Flame and the Flower*, laughing uproariously at the fainting Pamela in Richardson's landmark eighteenth-century novel of the same name, seeing through what might be called the pseudo-independence of Johanna Lindsey's Tedra in *Warrior's Woman*, and finally suspending her resistance when she found herself admiring Gabaldon's Claire in *Outlander*. That novel, for all of the resistant students, was the one that came as a break, the one that had them letting their guards down, and the one that they saw as perhaps so innovative that it almost (but not quite) crosses the boundaries of the genre.

In Katelyn's essay, she experiences a turnaround in the end, saying that she had been "covering her feelings with humor" from the beginning because despite her protests, stories with happy endings (in her case identified as "mysteries and adventure stories") were always the ones that had appealed to her, but she didn't want to be seen as a romance reader and so had kept romances as distanced as she could from the reading she liked. Her final statement came as a bit of a shock to her teacher:

> This class has caused me to evolve into a more careful thinker. I realize now that romance novels are not the silly things that I supposed them to be, but a real facet of literature. This evolution as a reader kind of stunned me. I mean, I was a real critic before, and now I feel completely different about them.

While Katelyn may have experienced a turnaround, two resistant readers remained resistant throughout the class, but they coupled resistance with real self-reflection about why the texts elicited strong negative reactions for them. Andrea, acknowledging the idea that romance narratives are so ubiquitous as to be unavoidable, identifies herself at the beginning of her essay as someone who has had to "deal with" romances. She goes on to state: "I really did *want* to be able to understand the pleasure of these types of books. I still do." The deal breaker for Andrea and the final resistant reader, Courtney, was that rape within the first thirty pages of the first romance novel they read (*The Flame and the Flower*). Both students focused their final essays on the prevalence of rape in the popular genre, transformed from the 1970's (and they acknowledge even from the 1740's and Richardson's early novels) so that now the threat of rape tends to loom as something from which the hero saves the heroine, but is still too thinly disguised and unneeded to their minds.

Again, the goal of Understanding the Pleasure is for students to understand the attraction of popular romance through understanding the genre's history; following a cohesive thread, such as the Byronic hero, through the genre; and recognizing how authors have negotiated with the genre. In the case of resistant readers, the goal becomes helping students to understand what and perhaps why they are resisting, so that they too can feel power over the narratives, even if they never pick up romances for their own "pleasure." *The Flame and the Flower* was chosen as the first novel for all students to read because they would be simultaneously reading its description and critique in Radway's study and also because the novel represents a landmark change in the marketing of romance novels away from strictly series romance. In addition, the novel has uncanny similarities to Richardson's *Pamela*, which is arguably the first "romance novel" in English, and by reading *Pamela* and learning its history and legacy, students can place *The Flame and the Flower* in context within the genre. (Due to *Pamela's* imposing length, students are divided into groups, each of whom reads one-fifth of the abridged version, presenting their section to the rest of the class through a reader's theatre assignment and discussion.) Teaching *The Flame and the Flower* is valuable, but in addition to the advantages it presents, the book also unavoidably introduces the issue of rape in romance narratives directly into the class conversation. Because students deal quite differently with the presence of rape in Woodiwiss's novel, it is perhaps the ideal subject to follow in order to show the ways in which their reading community can function.

My discussion board prompt for the week students were reading *The Flame and the Flower* reveals that initial in-class discussion of a recognizable hero "type" (later introduced more fully as the Byronic hero) had affected students' interpretation of Brandon's character:

> In the first short class discussion of Katherine Woodiwiss's *The Flame and the Flower*, most students expressed attraction to the character of Brandon and at least forgiveness for (if not complete understanding of) his behavior in the first chapter. People also seemed to recognize Brandon as a "type" (mention was made of Johnny Depp). How would you describe this type in your words, and how does Brandon fit it and/or deviate from it?

Most of the students did manage to forgive Brandon, explaining the rape, as it is explained in the text, as a misunderstanding and seeing Brandon's eventual tender treatment of the heroine as his redemption. Interestingly, though, three of the students who later negotiated with the genre enough to find it quite agreeable reading could not reconcile with Woodiwiss's novel at this point in the course. In her online post, Erin points out that "[Rape] is an extremely painful trauma and no woman would forgive, much less fall deeply in love with, her rapist" (10 Sept 2003). Charley writes, "Although some may have forgiven Brandon for his behavior in the first chapter, I just can't seem to get past it" (15 Sept 2003). Those who defend Brandon online are careful not to contradict the above sentiments. Instead, they key into the qualities of the hero type that might help to explain his actions. Noelle, a preferred reader, writes of Brandon, "On the exterior he is all man—tough, rugged, and even violent. But there are moments when he forgets himself and shows his caring, gentle, even sensitive side." Noelle's description is common of students' early recognition of the Byronic hero, even before he had been formally introduced to them, but the opening of her post is also a typical acknowledgement of her classmates' concerns, as she states, "I do not totally forgive Brandon for what he did to [Heather], even though Heather seems to" (10 Sept 2003).

Reading *Pamela*, in which the heroine is threatened with rape and saved by her own virtue, and hearing also of Richardson's *Clarissa*, in which the heroine is drugged and molested, helps students to see that the threat of rape in literature is much older than *The Flame and the Flower* and its contemporaries (Rosemary Rogers's "Sweet-Savage" novels are perhaps the most notorious of the 1970's novels for this element). In his discussion of themes of ascent and descent in romance, Northrup Frye cites a transcendence that often occurs in the midst of a protagonist's descent into a hell-like sphere. The transcendence then becomes a spiritual ascent, raising the protagonist above the level of those who would have power over him/her (85; 91). A romance heroine's descent can be seen as her rape or near-rape when this element is introduced into a novel, a theory that is supported as women facing their worst fear by Radway's citation of Molly Haskell's 1976 article. Haskell posits:

> [The reader] makes projections about how she would react or whether she would survive. In effect, through her imagination she controls an occurrence that is widespread in her culture which she can neither predict nor prevent. (Radway 141)

Through their reading selections, students are also able to see how significantly the threat of rape has changed since the 1970's in novels, with heroines saved either by heroes or by their own ingenuity, but not becoming victims of their heroes, no matter what rationale might be offered.

Andrea, one of the resistant readers who continued to be perplexed by the threat of rape in romance, actually cites Haskell's theory in her final paper and shows that she understands its connection to Frye's theory as well. Andrea goes on to cite Susan Elizabeth Phillips (one of the authors whose novel, *It Had to Be You*, she had read for the course) from her essay in *Dangerous Men and Adventurous Women*. Phillips essentially describes the Byronic hero when she says that a "dangerous" protagonist "serves not only as the hero of the novel but also, more subtly, as its villain, a potent symbol of all the obstacles life presents to women" (57). Andrea draws from these sources the idea that "with the attraction to the bad boy comes a risk that, evidently, women need in order to fulfill the fears in their rape fantasies." While their introduction to these theories could not assuage Andrea's and Courtney's understandably resistant reactions to the threat of rape and that threat's connection to the Byronic hero's prevalence in romance novels, their study did give them a common theoretical ground on which to discuss these elements with other students, many of whom were preferred readers who accepted justification for the presence of rape in romance quite quickly.

A related theory that students—preferred, negotiating, and resistant alike—found especially intriguing was Laura Kinsale's "placeholder" theory. Kinsale's essay in *Dangerous Men and Adventurous Women* introduces an interpretation of the Byronic hero that builds on the idea of the romance narrative as triumph for the female reader. Kinsale's thesis is that the heroine is a "placeholder" for the reader. She distinguishes this function from reader identification by saying that "placeholding is an objective involvement" with an element of "analytical distance." The female reader "rides along with the character," but she is always measuring the heroine's actions against what she would do in the situation. According to Kinsale, actual reader identification, wherein "the reader *becomes* the character," happens with the hero rather than the heroine (32). In this way, the reader sees the placeholder character as the hero does, and she simultaneously experiences the hero's jolting emotional transformation as if it were her own.

As students sample popular romance texts published in more recent years, they find that the Byronic hero is often evoked rather than portrayed outright. As Mussell notes in "Where's Love Gone?" heroes have softened (4). In great part, this softening has taken place because authors like Kinsale are spending more time in the text on the hero's thoughts. The title of Kinsale's 1990 novel, *Prince of Midnight*, immediately promises a rendition of the Byronic hero, and the novel delivers with a former dashing nineteenth-century highwayman who, at the novel's opening, is an injured, jaded recluse. The reader continues to see the hero as a Byronic figure through the heroine's eyes, but very early in the novel, the hero's need for the heroine becomes clear as he mentally berates himself for dreaming about her (67).

To bring in one last common reading experience and a more subtle evocation of Byron's hero, the classroom community is brought together during the last week of the course to share excerpts from Catherine Anderson's 1994 *Shotgun Bride*, which is sadly out of print at this time but available through used book sellers. Anderson creates a hero who gives the heroine the immediate impression that he is "tall, dark and dangerous" (the title of the collection in which this short novel appears). Instead, he turns out to be a lonely cowboy who cooks biscuits and chocolate gravy with the heroine and eventually convinces her that the image she carries of herself as overweight and unattractive is entirely untrue. The Byronic hero is a familiar figure to romance readers; he need only be evoked by association for them to expect a different man on the inside than the one presented on the outside. *Shotgun Bride* depicts an anti-Byronic hero within a character that evokes the hero's tradition, showing a clear negotiation with this convention. The novel makes metatextual fun of itself, giving its heroine, Charlie, wild fantasies about men before she meets her hero, fantasies that she has gleaned from the pages of nineteenth-century "dime romances." As students note this negotiation with the genre, they also cannot help but notice that the heroine's struggle with body image is a decided innovation in a genre that has tended to showcase beautiful heroines who are somehow quite unaware of their beauty.

This 2003 reading community found great pleasure in their last shared reading experience of *Shotgun Bride*, but there was still room for resistance as well. Andrea notices in her final essay that Anderson's heroine "seems almost curious about the idea of a man taking advantage of her," and refers to sex as a "dangerous encounter." Erin, on the other hand, completing her "journey from skeptic to addict," finds herself thoroughly "enjoying [the book's] absurdity . . . Everything about it is wrong from the large, self-deprecating heroine to the all too appropriately named horse of the hero—Satan." Erin finds the hero to be quite right, however: "Yes, he is strong, good-looking, and carries a gun, but the only thing truly dangerous about him is his reputation." Through very different interpretations, both of these students are recognizing Anderson's metatextual negotiation with romance.

A final lesson from Understanding the Pleasure is that students are capable of learning from and appreciating not only differing theorists' views on romance but also differing views within their own classroom community. Fulfilling a requirement that each student quote another's online posting at least once in her final essay, students presented each other's reactions and arguments both in support of and in opposition to their own views. With each other's permission, Jessica (a preferred reader) brings Katelyn (a resistant reader) into her creative essay as a character and has Katelyn "duke it out" with Tedra, the warrior-heroine of Lindsey's *Warrior's Woman*. In turn, Katelyn brings Cara (a preferred reader) into her creative essay as the guide who shows why so many women take pleasure in romance narratives. Through a course that encourages understanding of and negotiation with popular culture and its effects on readers, students are able to move toward seizing their own power to recognize where pleasure lies in the text for them and for others, as well as where it does not.

Acknowledgement

I would like to extend heartfelt thanks and give well-deserved credit to the students who have allowed me to quote their work in this chapter. Thank you, Cara Baummer, Jessica Borchert, Noelle Cortese, Charley Dibble, Katelyn Galbraith, Andrea Laurencell, and Erin Mooney; you are women of influence, and you have taught me a great deal as you have allowed me a glimpse of your own negotiation with the pleasure of romance narratives.

Appendix – Understanding the Pleasure Sample Syllabus

Required Texts

Bittner, Rosanne. *Savage Destiny: Sweet Prairie Passion.* New York: Zebra, 1983.

Gabaldon, Diana. *Outlander.* New York: Dell, 1991.

Krentz, Jayne Ann, ed. *Dangerous Men and Adventurous Women: Romance Writers on the Appeal of the Romance.* Philadelphia: U of Pennsylvania P, 1992.

Radway, Janice A. *Reading the Romance: Women Patriarchy, and Popular Literature.* Chapel Hill: U of North Carolina P, 1984.

Richardson, Samuel. *Pamela.* 1740. New York: W.W. Norton, 1993.

Sappho. *Selected Poems.* c. 700 BC. Ed. Knox. New York: W. W. Norton, 1993.

Woodiwiss, Kathleen. *The Flame and the Flower.* New York: Avon, 1972.

Additional Texts (three are required)

Each student will choose two books from Set One and one from Set Two.

Set One:

Anderson, Catherine. *Coming Up Roses.* New York: HarperCollins, 1993.

Hill, Donna. *A Private Affair.* Washington, D.C.: BET Publications, 1998.

Kinsale, Laura. *The Prince of Midnight.* New York: Avon, 1990.

Krentz, Jayne Ann. *Absolutely, Positively.* New York: Pocket Books, 1996.

Lindsey, Johanna. *Warrior's Woman.* New York: Avon, 1990.

Phillips, Susan Elizabeth. *It Had to Be You.* New York: Avon, 1994.

Set Two:

Atwood, Margaret. *Lady Oracle.* New York: Simon and Schuster, 1976.

Austen, Jane. *Northanger Abbey.* (1818) New York: Penguin, 1972.

Course Description

"Few people realize how much courage it takes for a woman to open a romance novel on an airplane." With that sentence, novelist Jayne Ann Krentz begins her introduction to *Dangerous Men and Adventurous Women*, a collection of essays written by popular romance novelists about the genre in which they write. With that sentiment, we will begin our exploration of this offshoot of the larger Romance genre, examining the line traditionally drawn between "literature" and "non-literature," as well as claiming the power to critique and understand the texts that affect us on our own time. In addition, we will explore the critical debate that has surrounded the popular romance novel for thirty years now, asking whether these narratives contribute to women's oppression, empower women, or somehow do both simultaneously. Because literary criticism has so often focused on romance readers (or as Kay Mussell puts it, "But why do they read those things?"), the disciplines of cultural studies, psychology, and sociology will enter our conversation.

Course Outcomes

As demonstrated in a virtual reading journal, position papers, class presentations, and a comprehensive final exam essay, students successfully completing the course will be able to:

- explain the connection between canonical literature in the Romance genre and popular romance novels;
- explain a cursory history of the Romance genre from chivalric tales to modern popular literature;
- describe traditional romance novel conventions and recognize when authors are "bending" them;
- use principles from cultural and feminist literary criticism to analyze women's romance texts and the way those texts have traditionally been perceived;
- identify the ubiquitous nature of romance narratives in literature, film, other media, and the popular American consciousness;
- experience the romance novel reading community from both the outside and inside, confronting and articulating the often conflicted nature of ethnographic sociological and literary study;
- collaborate with peers to facilitate discussion and analyze their own written work;
- reflectively write on their experiences as romance readers, with particular attention to sources of both pleasure and discomfort.

Course Requirements

- Virtual Reading Journal: 20%
- Three Short Observation Papers on Specific Novel Characteristics (1½ -2 pages each): 15% (5% each)
- Two Position Papers, each using primary works and criticism from the "required list" to support a position regarding an aspect of a novel from one of the sets (4-5 pages each): 30% (15% each)

- Unannounced Reading Quizzes (one dropped): 10%
- *Pamela* Group Presentation: 5%
- Border's Field Trip Response & Scavenger Hunt: 5%
- Final exam essay - "My Life as a Romance Reader" (5-7 pages): 15%

Virtual Reading Journal: A Community of Readers

This is a course not only about the texts of women's fiction but also about the readers of those texts. One of the essential premises we will establish is that even if you are not regularly a reader of women's fiction ("romance novels" in the popular form), you have probably been exposed to the genre much more than you realize through other texts and types of entertainment in popular culture. As you proceed through the course, you will undoubtedly find pleasure in many of the romances you read. You may also find yourself shaking your head in amusement or dismay. Both reactions and the spectrum in-between are valid, and you should pay attention to them as you read and hear others' reactions to the same texts. As you form your reactions to readings, you will want to constantly keep other texts we have read and discussed in mind, making connections whenever you can.

A major portion of your grade will be your weekly virtual reading journal. Since our class is a small, seminar-style one, all members of the class will post their entries as part of an ongoing discussion group. I will initiate discussion with a prompt each week, but you are encouraged to take your responses beyond the prompt. Like any group of readers united by interest in a particular genre, you will have some texts in common (the "required" list) and some texts that only some of you have read (the two "sets"). Early in the semester, one of your tasks will be to help each of your fellow readers decide which book from set one she would like to choose as her second reading from the set. In addition to recommending and reacting, be sure that you are also making significant connections between texts and using what you learn through critical works and in-class discussion and lecture. The virtual journal will then become a wonderful source for paper ideas, giving you a place to test out your theories and be inspired by others.

In many ways, our model for this discussion group is a larger community of readers that you will also join, a listserv called Romance Readers Anonymous. The listserv is free, and you don't receive any marketing ploys or other annoying messages because you are a member. You will receive a digest each day with all of the messages posted. Several popular romance authors are members of the listserv, as well as librarians, academics, and everyday readers. Sometimes authors are definitely "selling" their books to other listserv members, but these entries are only a small percentage, so try skimming quickly by them to get to the real discussions. To encourage you to enter the dialogue on the listserv, you may earn up to 20 points extra credit on your journal grade by posting to the listserv (possible five points for each thoughtful post). However, you are only required to read your digests and comment on them in your e-mail journal. The digests can get a little long, so if you miss a day now and then, that's okay. Just be sure to comment at least once a week on the listserv discussion. You are encouraged to post entries on our "virtual journal" as often as you like. My suggestion would be to set aside some time every day to read for this course and to read/write e-mail at least every other day.

Minimum Messages Each Week:
- One significant entry (at least 200 words) in response to your current reading for class;
- One entry (at least 200 words) in response to the Romance Readers Anonymous Listserv;
- Two additional postings from you in response to your colleagues.

Observation Papers on Specific Novel Characteristics

For each of the popular novels that is required for everyone (*The Flame and the Flower, Sweet Prairie Passion,* and *Outlander*), you will write a short observation paper in which you will describe an element of the novel that seems either typical of the popular romance narrative or unusual in some way. If you have not been a regular romance novel reader, you may be worried that you won't recognize what seems "typical," but I think you will be amazed. The narrative is so common in Western culture that most people recognize typical characteristics (such as two potential lovers verbally sparring with each other, the heroine dressed as a man, and a happy ending) right away. An effective way to spot both typical and atypical characteristics is to notice spots where you feel irritated, unsettled, or delighted. Of course, in-class and online discussions will also help you with this process. As you describe the characteristic you choose, you will need to illustrate it with examples from the novel, citing page numbers for specific incidents and any quotes used.

Position Papers

For each position paper, you will use your choice of the texts, both primary and secondary, from the "required" list to support your position on an aspect of a novel from sets one or two. There are several approaches that can work well to develop and support your position. You might see the novel you are reading as an affirmation of or a contradiction of something a critic or enthusiast has said (Radway, Krentz, etc.). You might also notice a consistent trend in the genre that has its roots in earlier literature (Richardson, Austen, etc.), comparing the earlier and later works. You might also agree or take issue with the way readers are thought to use women's romance in their lives, working with your own response to the text and those of your classmates, as well what you will find written about readers in Radway, Krentz, Russ, etc. You are required to cite at least three works from the required list as support for your position, and you will need to work closely with your primary text (the "set" novel).

Final Exam Essay

For your final exam, you will write a polished, typewritten, 5-7-page essay in MLA format that you will bring to class at our scheduled final exam date and time. At the end of the semester, we will read an often-cited essay by Tania Modleski, entitled "My Life as a Romance Reader." Your final exam will be your version of this topic. More detailed information will follow later, but keep in mind that the final will require you to think reflectively about your own negotiation with romance texts, both before and during this class. You will be required to cite at least seven works (novels, essays, etc.) from the course in your paper. We will then use the exam time to share these "final" statements on what you have learned, and it will be required that you read a few sections of your paper out loud and come prepared to compare and discuss your conclusions with those of your classmates.

Sally Goade

Works Cited

Anderson, Catherine, Christina Dodd, and Susan Sizemore. *Tall, Dark and Dangerous*. New York: HarperCollins, 1994.

Atwood, Margaret. *Lady Oracle*. New York: Simon and Schuster, 1976.

Austen, Jane. *Northanger Abbey*. 1818. New York: Penguin, 1972.

Barthes, Roland. "Myth Today." 1973. *A Barthes Reader*. Ed. Susan Sontag. New York: Hill and Wang, 1982.

Benoit, William L. *Accounts, Excuses, and Apologies: A Theory of Image Restoration Strategies*. New York: State U of New York P, 1995.

Brontë, Emily. *Wuthering Heights*. 1847. Philadelphia: Courage Books, 1986.

Brontë, Charlotte. *Jane Eyre*. 1846. Philadelphia: Courage Books, 1988.

Cervantes, Miguel de. *The Ingenious Gentleman Don Quixote of La Mancha*. 1605. Ed. Joseph R. Jones and Kenneth Douglas. New York: W. W. Norton, 1981.

During, Simon, ed. *The Cultural Studies Reader*. New York: Routledge, 1993.

Eagleton, Terry. *Ideology: An Introduction*. New York: Verso, 1991.

Frye, Northrup. *The Secular Scripture: A Study of the Structure of Romance*. Cambridge, MA: Harvard UP, 1976.

Gabaldon, Diana. "Frequently Asked Questions." Home page. 26 Jan. 2003. 31 Jan. 2003. <http://www.cco.caltech.edu/~gatti/gabaldon/gabaldon.html>

———.*Outlander*. New York: Dell, 1991.

Giroux, Henry A., Roger I. Simon, and Paulo Freire, ed. *Popular Culture: Schooling and Everyday Life*. New York: Bergin and Garvey, 1989.

Grossberg, Lawrence. *Bringing It All Back Home: Essays on Cultural Studies*. Durham: Duke UP, 1997.

———.*Dancing in Spite of Myself: Essays on Cultural Studies*. Durham: Duke UP, 1997.

Hall, Stuart. "Encoding, Decoding." *The Cultural Studies Reader*. Ed. Simon During. New York: Routledge, 1993.

Kile, Crystal. "Endless Love Will Keep Us Together: The Myth of Romantic Love and Contemporary Popular Movie Themes." 1992. *Women and Romance: A Reader*. Ed. Susan Ostrov Weisser. New York: New York UP, 2001.

Kinsale, Laura. "The Androgynous Reader: Point of View in the Romance." *Dangerous Men and Adventurous Women: Romance Writers on the Appeal of Romance*. Philadelphia: U of Pennsylvania P, 1992.

Krentz, Jayne Ann, ed. *Dangerous Men and Adventurous Women: Romance Writers on the Appeal of the Romance*. Philadelphia: U of Pennsylvania P, 1992.

Leavis, F. R. *The Great Tradition: A Study of the English Novel.* Garden City, NY: Doubleday, 1954.

Lindsey, Johanna. *Warrior's Woman.* New York: Avon, 1990.

Modleski, Tania. "My Life as a Romance Reader." *Paradoxa* 3:1-2 (1997): 15-28.

————.*Loving with a Vengeance: Mass Produced Fantasies for Women.* Hamden, CT: Archon, 1982.

————."My Life as a Romance Writer." *Old Wives' Tales and Other Women's Stories.* New York: New York UP, 1998.

Mussell, Kay. "'But Why Do They Read Those Things?': The Female Audience and the Gothic Novel." *Female Gothic.* Ed. Juliann E. Fleenor. Montréal: Eden P, 1983.

————.*Fantasy and Reconciliation: Contemporary Formulas of Women's Romance Fiction.* Westport, CT: Greenwood P, 1984.

————."Where's Love Gone?   Transformations in Romance Fiction and Scholarship." *Paradoxa* 3:1-2 (1997): 3-14.

Nelson, Cary, Paula A. Treichler, and Lawrence Grossberg, ed. *Cultural Studies.* New York: Routledge, 1992.

Phillips, Susan Elizabeth. "The Romance and the Emowerment of Women." *Dangerous Men and Adventuous Women.*   Ed. Jayne Ann Krentz. Philadelphia: U of Pennsylvania P, 1992.

Pretty Woman. Dir. Garry Marshall. Rated version. Prod. Arnon Milchan and Steven Reuther. Videocassette. Touchstone Pictures, 1990.

Rabine, Leslie W. *Reading the Romantic Heroine.* Ann Arbor: U of Michigan P, 1985.

Radcliffe, Ann. *The Mysteries of Udolpho.* 1794. Ed. Bonamy Dobrée. New York: Oxford U P, 1998.

Radway, Janice. "Mail-Order Culture and Its Critics: The Book-of-the-Month Club, Commodification and Consumption, and the Problem of Cultural Authority." *Cultural Studies.* Ed. Lawrence Grossberg, Cary Nelson, and Paula Treichler. New York: Routledge, 1992.

————.*Reading the Romance: Women, Patriarchy, and Popular Literature.* 1984. Chapel Hill: U of North Carolina P, 1991.

Richardson, Samuel. *Clarissa or The History of a Young Lady.* 1748. Abr. and ed. George Sherburn. Boston: Houghton Mifflin, 1962.

————.*Pamela or Virtue Rewarded.* 1740. New York: W. W. Norton, 1993.

Russ, Joanna. "Somebody's Trying to Kill Me and I Think It's My Husband: The Modern Gothic." *Female Gothic.* Ed. Juliann E. Fleenor. Montréal: Eden P, 1983.

Scholes, Robert. *Textual Power: Literary Theory and the Teaching of English.* New Haven, CT: Yale UP, 1985.

Singh, Preeti. "2001 RRA-L Awards Winners." Online Posting. 1 Feb. 2002 to
    2 Feb. 2002. *Romance Readers Anonymous-Listserv Digest.* 9 Feb. 2002.
    <LISTSERV@LISTSERV.KENT.EDU>
Thorslev, Peter L., Jr. *The Byronic Hero: Types and Prototypes.* Minneapolis:
    U of Minnesota P, 1962.
While You Were Sleeping. Dir. Jon Turteltaub. Rated version. Prod. Joe Roth
    and Roger Birnbaum. Videocassette. Hollywood Pictures, 1995.
Woodiwiss, Kathleen E. *The Flame and the Flower.* New York: Avon, 1972.
Working Girl. Dir. Mike Nichols. Rated version. Prod. Douglas Wick.
    Videocassette. Twentieth Century Fox, 1988.

Sally Goade

Sally Goade holds a Doctor of Arts degree in English from Idaho State
University. She has been an Assistant Professor of English at The Sage
Colleges in Troy, New York, teaching American literature at Russell Sage
College for women and supervising graduate student teachers for Sage Graduate
School from 2000 to 2006. She was promoted to Associate Professor in the
spring of 2006 just before family needs necessitated a move to Tennessee. She
is currently under contract with Cambridge Scholars Publishing for a
monograph entitled *Negotiation with Romance: Authors Transforming the
Genre.* "Understanding the Pleasure" was taught for the third time in Fall 2006
as an online course for Russell Sage.

CHAPTER FOURTEEN

BECOMING BOTH POET AND POEM: FEMINISTS REPOSSESS THE ROMANCE

MARY BETH TEGAN

> She says Romance is a proper form for women.
> She says Romance is a land where women can be free to express their true natures. . . .
> She said in romance women's two natures can be reconciled. . . .
>
> My recent reading has caused me for some reason to remember myself as I was when a young girl,
> reading high Romances and seeing myself simultaneously as the object of all knights' devotion
> —an unspotted Guinevere—and as the author of the Tale. I wanted to be a Poet and a Poem. . . .
> It may be that this is the desire of all reading women. . . .
> —A. S. Byatt's *Possession*

Popular romance has vexed feminist thinkers for well over two hundred years, provoking ardent responses that range from delight to disquiet to disdain. Highly conscious of the power romance has—in its many discursive forms—over women's psychic and social existence, their desires and expectations, feminist critics in the late twentieth century have been anxious to understand its enduring appeal. The radical feminists of the 1960s and 1970s emphasized its covert ideological influence, and it is no coincidence that their "resistant reading" practices sought to liberate women readers from the unconscious identifications associated with popular genres. Later critics continued to mark the form's complicity with patriarchy, but they also took seriously the fantasies of women readers and examined why these texts proved so compelling. More recently, a new generation of romance scholars has taken issue with such critiques, asserting that readers maintain a sense of mastery over these texts and echoing Byatt's Victorian heroine's contention regarding the "proper form for women." But while romance may well be a proper form for women, the question remains as to whether it is a proper form for feminist readers.

This project engages the question imaginatively by offering feminist readers the opportunity to become both Poet and Poem, reader and read, participant and voyeur. I have asked critics of romance and women's narrative to re-imagine their institutionalized roles as the *subjects* of literary knowledge production and become, in effect, *objects* of study: to confront feminism's taboo text, to suspend their interpretive practices, and to assume a role more akin to that of the creative writer. Each critic selected a romance novel that provoked a strong affective response upon a first reading; participants then revised the original so it more closely approximated their own fantasies, focusing on a particular passage or scene, or, rewriting the entire plot in broad strokes. Musing about potential transformations, choosing which plots to manipulate and which to omit, and experimenting with a range of narrative techniques, the feminist reader engages with the textual object in a more intimate and implicated fashion.[24] In this sense, the act of revision compels the feminist reader beyond her politics and resistant interpretive practices to illuminate her unique reading processes and idiosyncratic desires. Within this more fluid critical scenario—a fantasy-centered scene where one might occupy the positions of romance reader or writer or critic—the feminist scholar is able to duplicate the practice of the "unconscious" romance reader who identifies multiply.[25] She might maintain

---

[24] With its evocative vocabulary and theoretical framework, Lynne Pearce's *Feminism and the Politics of Reading* (1997) proved enormously helpful in its discussion of the passionate struggle between reader and text. In constructing a model that accounts for the vicissitudes of a reader's "romance" with a text and the various "others" within that entice, Pearce relies on Roland Barthes's insights in *A Lover's Discourse* and manages to resist the hermeneutic focus of most theoretical discussions about reading. Examining the feminist reader's affective reading *process* in contradistinction to her considerably more conscious *practices,* she concludes that her emotional responses and her aesthetic/political analyses come from "different—and mutually incompatible—discursive sites" (23). The feminist reader's training in literary analysis has helped her to develop a number of strategies to avoid becoming "implicated" in the texts she encounters (27), including an appraisal of the work's aesthetic excellencies, its psychological realism, and its adherence to generic conventions. Equally useful in helping her to distance herself from the "textual others" that threaten to undermine her mastery are her politically conscious readings, which take gender and other identities into account—a task performed largely with the cache of re-visionary tools developed in the 1980s and 1990s.

[25] Feminist readers borrowing from Freud and Laplanche and Pontalis have amply theorized the possibilities of the structure of fantasy in their romance scholarship, but it is

the critical distance of the critic-voyeur (which, as Constance Penley has noted, is nonetheless an *implicated* position), wield the control of the writer and subject her heroine to desperate longings (or untold horrors), or even "become" the romance heroine—allowing "Scarlett (myself) to wind up with Ashley," as critic Judith Wilt imagined in an e-mail concerning this project. These uniquely negotiated "romance revisions" are then read alongside their creators' criticism and the rewritten romances of the other participants, a process that sheds light on the particularities of individual experience and desire as it reveals truths of a more collective nature.

The thirteen feminist readers who participated in this study were asked to explore their relationships to romance by rewriting a novel—popular or canonical—that compels their return. This "return to romance" occurs in at least one of two ways: the first, ubiquitous choice involves revising the romance so that new light is shed on familiar formal elements. The most significant changes to original texts are achieved through strategies of "resistance" like satire, inversion, or hyperbolic play—techniques employed more frequently by critics who rewrote a canonical text. In fact, with the exception of one writer whose revision ran roughshod over the form, the eight participants who rewrote a popular romance stayed remarkably close to generic expectations; in contrast, three of the five canonical rewrites included wildly anachronistic plot lines and characterization. The second type of return is an active revisiting of an early self-defining fantasy. In *Femininity Played Straight: The Significance of Being Lesbian* (1996), Biddy Martin suggests how a consciousness might be raised through revisiting those books that "generated a desire to read, the books in which we most thoroughly lost ourselves in that process through which the

---

interesting to note that romance writer Laura Kinsale also places an emphasis on "place" and "placeholding" in her essay, "The Androgynous Reader." Arguing that the reader makes a complex double identification, Kinsale claims that the female reader *becomes* the (more powerful!) hero but not the heroine; rather the heroine serves as a "placeholder" for the reader, who maintains a certain analytical distance, judging the heroine more because she "competes" with her (31). Watching the heroine "through her own and the hero's eyes" (35), the reader rarely loses her analytical edge, but when that distance collapses and she finds herself "spontaneously identifying" with hero *and* heroine, the "experience of the story is [so] utterly absorbing and vital" that she loses herself in the text (35). In accounting for the reader's judgment of the heroine, Kinsale's model obviously accords the female reader a *conscious* agency the structure of fantasy model doesn't, yet the emphasis on scene or place in both allow for a certain flexibility in readers' fantasies. Furthermore, the triangular relationship that emerges in both models—allowing for *both* identification and desire, and for (analytical) distance and merger—seems a crucial configuration for the reader's pleasures, and one, I would argue, appropriate to the feminist critic as well.

losing becomes the finding, or vice versa" (35), and seven out of thirteen participants chose this option. The self-reflexive commentary I received with each revision suggests that a more *textured* implicated reading is produced when one has to confront a younger, more ghostly reading self in the process. But despite these methodological differences, both approaches require the feminist critic to inhabit a strange position in reference to a familiar text—a destabilization that produces some rather surprising narrative effects.

Although the study's participants represent a range of positions within the academic hierarchy and vary in age (across approximately thirty years), they do not comprise as heterogeneous a group as I would have liked. The sample is predominantly American (including one Australian scholar) and white, though it is more diverse in respect to sexual identities. The sample includes feminists from the "first" generation to write seriously about romance in the late twentieth century—Jan Cohn, Nancy K. Miller, Kay Mussell and Tania Modleski—and those who have written more recently—Theresa Gregor, Sylvia Kelso, Pat Koski, and myself. When I began assembling the group in the summer of 2002, I contacted thirty-nine critics who had written on romance, the poetics and forms of women's narrative, and on feminist reading practices. I also acted upon referrals given by those contacts and strong-armed my colleagues in graduate school and my dissertation advisor. Of those I contacted, almost all responded generously—either with an enthusiastic "yes," or with encouragement and their regrets, or with lengthy e-mails that helped me to interrogate my assumptions and methods. Some of the regrets gave me insight into possible methodological problems: speaking of the 1.5-hour time limit I imposed for rewriting the romance, Carolyn Heilbrun could not "imagine how [she] could do what [I] want in two hours or even two weeks" (e-mail 9/08/02), a concern echoed by Helen Taylor; while other contacts—Nina Auerbach, Jennifer Cruise Smith, and Judith Wilt—didn't feel like they "fit" the sample, an indication to me that I had perhaps framed my goals, and perhaps, implicitly, my definitions of "romance" and "feminism" in too limiting a manner. Not surprisingly, the final sample group is considerably smaller than the one with which I maintained correspondence intermittently for a year; my colleagues' attrition was most often a consequence of other writing commitments.

The benefits of using "like subjects" have been many, not least of which was participants' assumption of authority within the study—questioning my terms and methodological premises, re-defining them to accommodate their own perceptions, and ignoring or modifying the guidelines given (often with great results). Indeed, I was bowled over by the amount of time and energy they were willing to put into this project, communicating with me over e-mail to clarify details, sharing their insights and materials, even suggesting (through their rigorous contextualization of their own readings) what additional information I needed from respondents and how to go about analyzing their revisions.[26] The collaboration began almost immediately. In my solicitation letters, I had framed the project as a consequence of my longing to learn how other feminist literary critics dealt with "suspect desires"—how they managed the tensions between their convictions as feminists and the pleasures or displeasures they discovered reading romance. While I had a pretty strong sense of the way the genre had evolved over time to accommodate a wider range of identities and desires (especially in the last thirty years), and I recognized that feminist readers managed all kinds of complex negotiations as "split subjects," I remained convinced that the generic parameters defined by romance writer Jayne Ann Krentz (and many other romance writers and scholars) would prove limiting for most feminist readers.[27]

Of all the assumptions I had made, this particular one generated the most ardent response. Early in the study, Kay Mussell asked if I believed that "no romance can be truly feminist" and therefore assumed that "all romances could use some feminist 'touching-up.'" It was a question that gave me pause (and the opportunity to work through my ideas a bit further), and, as a result, the "loose guidelines" I sent to participating subjects begin with some introductory comments about those very issues. I *had* assumed participants would want to make at least *some* changes in order to approximate their own ideal fantasy, but as I discovered, certain texts, like *Pride and Prejudice,* are apparently inviolable. Jan Cohn, when discussing her choice of a text to revise, wrote: "I did briefly consider a revision of *Pride and Prejudice,* but since I think that novel is perfect as it is, I could not imagine any purposeful revision or even any revision that would not impair its perfection" ("Gone With the Wind" 1).

---

[26] I am particularly indebted to Sylvia Kelso, whose "reading profile" helped me to construct the questionnaire I distributed to participants after receiving their revisions. She also helped me to identify one of the key analytical questions I've posed: what narrative event or convention has been revised, signaling the reader's "transformation from an assenting to a resisting reader?" ("Prolegemona" 2).

[27] Krentz writes: "A romance novel plot does not focus on women coping with contemporary social problems and issues. It does not focus on the importance of female bonding. It does not focus on adventure. [It] may incorporate any or all of these elements, but [. . .] the relationship between the hero and the heroine *is* the plot" (108). Her requirements are not necessarily incompatible with feminism, but this feminist reader would like to believe that other plots of ambition and relation might share equal time with the love plot in romance. And while I certainly don't view feminism and romance as two monolithic and opposed entities that create an easily defined conflict for feminist readers, I can imagine fantasies that might fall more easily under the label of "feminist" that *do* contrast markedly with many romance fantasies.

Other critics felt no real need to revise the romances they read. Cora Kaplan, for instance, explained:

> The specific task you ask me to perform for the project would be rather hard for me. You see I DON'T want to rewrite these romances particularly [. . .] I like the sad endings and the happy ones; I've no impulse to make *Gone With the Wind* more PC or revise *Katherine*. (e-mail 8/24/2002)

Furthermore, my assumption that feminist readers would have an uncomfortable experience reading romance was challenged by Judith Wilt's musing upon her own habits:

> The way I "deal with my suspect desires, and with the romance narrative in particular" while striving to be a feminist as well is . . . pretty much to keep both sets of desires unchanged, despite the internal incoherence. (e-mail 7/23/02)

Wilt's response, and comments made by Kaplan, Modleski, and others, potentially confirm Lynne Pearce's assertion in *Feminism and the Politics of Reading* (1997) about feminist readers and the way the political and the emotional pull apart: these readers seem able to "compartmentalize" their different reading experiences in ways that suggest the professional discursive site shuts down when the more personal is engaged.

The other contentious conversation to emerge circled around issues of textual choice, the most pressing of which was the novel's status. In fact, the distinction as to whether a text might be classified as canonical or popular romance became a persistent methodological question and one that will accompany me into the project's next incarnation. A number of critics, including my own readers and contacts, made the compelling argument that I was giving feminist critics too much latitude by letting participants define romance for themselves. That each of the published romance scholars in the study chose to rewrite a popular novel is telling, and the revisions of Jan Cohn, Sylvia Kelso, Pat Koski, Tania Modleski, and Kay Mussell demonstrate both an understanding of the genre's parameters and, more significantly, a respect for its limits, remaining in all cases but one *very* close to the formula. As Ann Rosalind Jones suggests in "Mills and Boon Meets Feminism," and Kelso observes here, the literary or canonical romance may well be less "restrictive," for it is somewhat sheltered from the pressures of the mass market and the hegemonic values holding sway there ("Stitching Time" 170). Romance writer and former academic Jennifer Crusie Smith raised the question of generic constraints more pointedly in a series of e-mails about the project three years ago. Recasting the project as a study of how "academic women try to redefine romance fiction to include fiction they're not ashamed to admit they've read," she argues: "the very elasticity of your definition of romance seems to be defeating your purpose [because] when you let your subjects define romance fiction in any way they want, you give them an out" (e-mail 9/13/02). I think Crusie makes two points worth considering: by collapsing the distinction between canonical and popular romance, I have potentially lessened the *risks* of reading romance, but perhaps this "redefinition" of romance fiction itself might be framed as a strategy of resistance—a uniquely feminist way of "dealing" with romance.

At the same time, I can't help but think that there are *some* risks attending the reading of the literary form as well: what of the critic who returns again and again to *Pride and Prejudice* or *Wuthering Heights?* Is it possible that canonical romance is more insidious, layering helpful fantasies over those that stoke our knottier desires, and offering all in a package that need embarrass no one? That its seductions may ultimately be even greater, aided by the beauty of the language itself? Julia Colyar observed in conversation that the teen romances she used to read, the similar films she still enjoys, are easier to manage *because* of their formulaic, "containable" quality: "I recognize it's romance, so it's harder to internalize it"; this is not, however, the case with more literary romances like those of Austen (Jan. 7). Because the literary text can prove perhaps even more unmanageable for feminists, in the following discussion I speculate about certain crossover conventions that prove troublesome for participants but maintain the fundamental distinction between the two types.

Choosing canonical romance over popular may, in fact, be the *most* effective means of resisting what Kay Mussell has called the "purest and simplest" romance type (*Fantasy* 30). All of the chosen texts have traits that appeal to the political reader, and three of the five novels were chosen specifically for that reason. Nancy Miller's avowedly "feminist text" is well known for its refusal of the erotic plot associated with romance, and Theresa Gregor's return to *Ramona* by Helen Hunt Jackson is similarly motivated. Acknowledging that the novel includes all of the elements of popular romance, she observes that the "best part for [her] is that it attempts to provide a racial critique of early California" ("Ramona Revisited" 1), that, in fact, the novel is itself a (romance) rewrite of Hunt's first book—*A Century of Dishonor,* which was a much more overtly political, critical work. My political impulse was considerably more unconscious, for when I reread Louisa May Alcott's *An Old-Fashioned Girl,* the "romance" that piqued my interest in the genre, I was stunned to find references to "women's rights" and "Boston marriages"; still, as my committee member, Hilary Schor, remarked at the time, "part of [me] must have known it was there all along," a deeply felt knowledge that may have prompted my return. These reflections and the reliance on "higher" or avant-garde forms in Lynn Pearce and Jackie Stacey's *Revising the Romance* (1995) and in Jean Radford's *The Progress of Romance* (1986) suggest that literary examples are more "accommodating" to feminism and so entail less risk for the feminist reader who wishes to avoid an "uncomfortable" experience. Equally suggestive is that the writers of the canonical revisions seem considerably less inhibited by the original; indeed, the comparatively open structure of these more literary texts seemed to encourage much wilder flights of fancy in three out of the five writers, while the other two were able to alter their endings substantially without affecting the narrative "logic" of the original text. It is not altogether surprising that most of the readers who chose to "return" to a well-thumbed text selected the more "capacious" literary examples, as a novel would have to consistently appeal to the reader as she herself changed through time. Of these, Beth Binggelli, Molly Engelhardt, and Theresa Gregor chose personal favorites; Nancy Miller made a rather different return—to a "romance" she'd critiqued in her highly influential essay, "Emphasis Added." What is intriguing is that *all* of these revisions focus almost exclusively on the heroine and her relationships with women; when the hero maintains a presence, it is a very muted one, as in Engelhardt's "Wuthering Heights Revisited." It is Cathy who haunts Engelhardt, who is also driven by a desire to establish a less masochistic relationship to the novel, and if Heathcliff figures in the beginning of the revision when his beloved rescues him on the moors, he all but disappears when they arrive at a gypsy camp. Engelhardt writes:

> Cathy and Heathcliff dismount, but just as their feet hit the ground, three dark-skinned, mean-looking men step up from behind them and encircle Cathy, and the largest of the three sweeps her up into his arms (she's very light and his brawny arms push against her large breasts) and carries her over to the tent where the party is going on. Heathcliff steps in front of the man, blocking his way, his fists clinched, but Cathy says, "No Heathcliff. I'll handle this." ("Wuthering" 2)

Reading more like popular romance than the classic we know so well, the forceful seduction scene that should, in all fairness, be Heathcliff's is here refigured as a potential gang rape. He is not even allowed the role of heroic savior, for Cathy insists she can protect herself. And indeed she can, presenting herself as the phallus personified in the next scene as the revision continues:

> Once inside the tent, the man puts Cathy on the ground and she immediately stands erect with her head held high staring defiantly into the eyes of the women sitting on the floor in front of her. These are some kind of women too. They are dark-skinned with black, wild hair and red lips, open in laughter at the sight of the young, angry Cathy; they wear big hooped earrings and colorful gowns that swoop all over the floor. They are everything that you could imagine beautiful,

gypsy women being. So what ends up happening is that the Queen of the gypsies takes a particular liking to Cathy and wants her to join the migrant tribe. [. . .] It takes no time at all for everyone to realize how smart Cathy is and how strong she is physically and after a year she becomes the queen's right-hand woman, known to everyone as the horse handler. ("Wuthering" 2)

What interests me here is that the gypsy women become objects of fascination for Cathy (and perhaps for Engelhardt as well), and the objectifying gaze that notes their skin and hair and lips and attire is her own. The bearer of the look is so often in romance still written as male, and yet here we meet a heroine who has both the power of the voyeur *and* the political clout of next in command. Managing to enjoy legislated sex once a year with another male in the gypsy camp for the sake of tribal order (while Heathcliff remains faithful), Cathy concludes her full life by taking up the pen to chronicle her time "with the gypsies" ("Wuthering" 3). She writes not of Heathcliff, turning her storytelling talents from romance to that of another genre—autobiography or, quite possibly, the political memoir.

Not surprisingly, Nancy Miller's heroine, Madame de Clèves, also pursues an authorial plot of ambition that is autobiographical, "writing a novel about a hopeless relationship between a man and a woman at the court" ("Princesse" 1). This is clearly an allusion to the focal love plot of *La Princesse de Cleves,* which Miller regards as feminist text, and it is striking that she gives Lafayette's heroine an opportunity to write her own story. The tale of a virtuous and beautiful young wife who finds herself pursued by the dashing Duke de Nemours, *Princesse* chronicles the longings of the hero and heroine but places almost equal emphasis on the despair of her husband and the moral corruption of the adulterous courtiers around them. When the husband dies of a broken heart, the Princesse is free to marry her beloved but chooses instead to sequester herself at home and in a convent for the rest of her days. Miller's discussion of *Princesse* in "Emphasis Added: Plots and Plausibilities in Women's Fiction" seeks to explain the "implausible" actions of the heroine who abandons the erotic plot expected of her, opting instead for a life of solitude and virtue that is more compatible with 1980s' feminist ideals. Reading the Princesse's choice as a "refusal of future suffering," Miller argues that her "self-mastery" may occasion "another kind of pleasure and power" (1). Nevertheless, the ending leaves Miller feeling somewhat unsatisfied, especially given its emphasis on "saintly occupations" (2), a closure she attempts to correct by imagining an

alternative resolution for her heroine.[28] Repeating verbatim the first sentence of
the novel's last paragraph, Miller writes:

> Madame de Clèves lived in a manner that gave no indication she would ever
> return. She invited a few of her friends, who were also young widows, to spend
> part of the year with her in her home and in her country estate in the south of
> France. Madame de Bauffremont, Madame de Longueville, and Madame de
> L'Espinasse were happy to join the Princess and escape from their own
> loneliness for a few months of every year. The young women, who were all
> beautiful as well as talented, enjoyed the time they spent together away from the
> demands and the gossip of the court. In both residences, the houses were large
> enough for each woman to have a separate apartment, with living quarters for her
> servants, as well as a study. The women decided to spend the mornings alone,
> reading and writing, but to come together in the afternoons for shared activities.
> Depending on the weather, they would ride horses or play music indoors. They
> would separate again for a few hours before dinner to pursue the arts. Each
> woman played a musical instrument and painted. At dinner, which in the warm
> summer months, was held out of doors, the women would discuss their works in
> progress—Madame de Clèves was writing a novel about a hopeless relationship
> between a man and a woman at the court—and reminisce. They loved to talk
> about marriage and how boring it was; Madame de Longueville and Madame de
> L'Espinasse said they hoped their daughters would never marry but they were
> resigned to the likelihood that they would. Often, friends living on nearby
> estates would join them after dinner for music or long walks along paths that led
> from the surrounding forest to the river. Invitations to the house were never
> turned down because everyone knew that to enter this world meant entering a
> world of exceptional pleasure.

Seeing to it that each of Madame de Clèves's friends has a "room of her own" in
which to create, Miller gives her heroine a utopic female community that recalls
the female cabal in Delariviére Manley's *The New Atalantis* (1709); the artists'
colony organized by Madame de Clèves is the perfect "support system" for her
labors, as she re-imagines her persistent longing for the Duke de Nemours as a
"scene [in] part of her novel" (2). Re-channeling her desire for the Duke into a

---

[28] For Miller, as for many feminist critics, the "ending" remains the crucial narrative
event, determining to a large extent how the rest of the work is to be understood. The
significance of "writing beyond the ending" was brought home with particular force
when I received a regret from Carolyn Heilbrun, who assumed that by "revision" I must
necessarily mean alternative closures. She cordially writes, "I'm grateful to you and
Nancy Miller for thinking of me in connection with different endings for romances" (e-
mail 9/8/03). Engelhardt's changes too were motivated by her dismay at the heroine's
end, so she returns to the novel's middle, reconstructing the trajectory so that it moves in
a much "happier" direction.

secondary love plot is a more effective strategy than marriage for holding him forever, and Miller seems to suggest through this "italicized" act that narrative is the only place where such intense feeling can endure. Banishing the Duke to relative obscurity in her heroine's anonymous novel, the critic redefines "pleasure" to describe a world of ambitious pursuits, conversation, and female companionship. Certainly the heroine's friends, who regret the inevitable marriages of their daughters, call into question the romance's promise of marital bliss, while the fact of the "disappearing man" arguably takes the "romance" right out of the tale.

While Miller's revision exposes the mechanical energies of plot by emphasizing the pleasures of deferral and the beloved's necessary absence, Beth Binggelli's "Jane X" highlights the function of its component parts through inversion and gleeful hyperbole. From the moment the reader meets the "pink pudding of a housekeeper," Mister Fairfax, she knows she's in a strange world, and with the introduction of Louisa May Alcott's March family, who function here as Jane X's "proto-punk girl band," the classic romance, *Jane Eyre*, becomes wishfully, wildly unfamiliar. The "other women" of the original novel—Blanche Ingram and Bertha Rochester—become Jane X's band-mates, joining "Jane Eyre" in an all-night jam session after Fairfax and Rochester prepare a meal for the women "under the guidance of Beth [March's] sword" ("Jane X" 2). Binggelli writes:

> Fairfax and Rochester sat in a dark corner of the room and observed the women from a distance. When he found the courage, Rochester approached Jane X during a break. She was drenched in sweat from her exertions, her hair hanging in loose snakes around her shoulders, her teeth smeared with lip rouge, her voice raspy from screaming lyrics. She smelled, he thought, like an earthy combination of Thornfield's dank, thrice-flooded root cellar, old Spanish port wine, and a bounding wooly dog. In her presence he had a sensation he never had before: he felt himself fall away, felt his substance evaporating to a fine mist, burning in a crucible to a smoke that coiled around the ceiling and bled through the windows to the ashen hills outside. Only this woman had made him feel so incomplete, so unfulfilled, so imperfect. Every fantasy of his own mastery in the steaming stew pot of her presence boiled away to nothingness. Jane smiled at Rochester's rapturous face and asked him to hold her chewed gum during sets. He cradled it like a relic. That night he finally set down a weight that had burdened and dragged him down his whole life, and in his lightness now appeared, in Jane's eyes, kinda cute. Just before finishing the last set, she slipped her room key in his hand. (2)

Trapped in the formulaic, passive, fretful role usually reserved for the romance heroine, Rochester observes Jane X from the sidelines, in much the same manner that the original Jane Eyre watched him. Possessed of a typical

242 Mary Beth Tegan

heroine's consciousness, he is consumed with the mystery of the more powerful lover's motives. The scene also turns the post-Freudian preoccupation with "the female enigma" on its end by exposing what is really at stake: man's terror in the face of his own vacuity. Consider Rochester's sense of himself as a "fine mist, burning in a crucible to a smoke that coiled around the ceiling and bled through the windows to the ashen hills outside." Rochester's "incomplete" characterization is emblematic of the "disappearing" or "shadow" men in the revisions by Miller and Engelhardt, and by keeping the uneven power dynamic intact but inverting the players, these examples perform to a tee the kind of feminist revision one might expect. The other technique remarked in feminist narratology is intertextual revision, which raises the question of whether narrative pleasure might be enhanced through a layering of fantasies: such incorporations give the reader access not only to the familiar (and widely divergent) delights associated with *Jane Eyre* and *Little Women* but also to the somewhat perverse pleasures of seeing her own desires thwarted and then redirected through textual disruptions like hyperbole or inversion.[29] I can relish the transformations inherent in the *bildungsroman*, the uncommon displays of female anger and jealousy, and the discovery of true and unforeseen loves, while simultaneously reveling in the idea of Jane X walking out on Rochester. The intertextual revision therefore appeals to a wider array of what might be termed "progressive" and "regressive" pleasures as well as to our many reading selves within.

My own encounter with the repressed reader of Alcott's *An Old Fashioned Girl* was illuminating; I found she "imbibed" a good deal more than macaroons and *pelisses* when I reread the book after many years. The two-volume novel tells the story of "country mouse" Polly Milton, who changes the lives of Fanny Shaw and her Bostonian family over the course of ten years. Polly is "old-fashioned" and comes from an Alcott-like family that is rich in education but lacking in capital. Drawn in sharp contrast, the Shaw family is recently moneyed, and their conspicuous display of their wealth is emphasized repeatedly. The heroine doesn't exert much influence over her friend Fanny until the family is ruined, and the latter must reform her fashionable ways to win her beloved, Mr. Sidney. The scene I chose to rewrite calls Fanny's fashionable pursuits into question, for it takes place in the home of two young women—a sculptor and an engraver who "take care of one another in true Damon and Pythias style." As if the allusion to the two Greek friends weren't enough, Fanny's comment, "Let a lover come between them and their friendship won't

---

[29] See, for instance, Susan S. Lanser's "Toward a Feminist Narratology," a feminist revision of Genette's *Discours du récit* that constructs a theory concerning the different levels of narrative and the strategies employed by women writers.

last long," is answered by Polly's refutation: "I think it will. Take a look at
them, and you'll change your mind." Fanny becomes enthralled by the art of
Rebecca—the sculpture of a beautiful woman, and she impresses the artist and
her friends with her 'reading' of the piece. She marks especially the figure's
"imposing" air. What follows is a discussion of how that woman might be
rendered even more imposing, and options like "giving her a child" are
dismissed, while "giving her a ballot-box" is embraced along with other objects
that speak to her talents: "a needle, pen, palette, and broom." (I'd like to think
this last is a witchery reference.) It is a prime pedagogical opportunity, and
Fanny is subtly changed by her time with the women. Alcott writes:

> Fanny had been to many elegant lunches, but never enjoyed one more than that
> droll picnic in the studio; for there was a freedom about it that was charming,
> and artistic flavor to everything, and such a spirit of good-will and gayety, that
> she felt at home at once. As they ate, the others talked and she listened, finding
> it as interesting *as any romance* to hear these young women discuss their plans,
> ambitions, successes and defeats. It was a new world to her, and they seemed a
> different race of creatures from the girls whose lives were spent in dress, gossip,
> pleasure or *enuui.* They were girls still, full of spirits, fun, and youth; but below
> the lightheartedness each cherished a purpose, which seemed to ennoble her
> womanhood, to give her a certain power, a sustaining satisfaction, a daily
> stimulus, that led her on to daily effort, and in time to some success in
> circumstance or character, which was worth all the patience, hope, and labor of
> her life. (177, emphasis added)

On the brink of self-discovery and finding a new purpose for living, Fanny
seems poised for a new plot. But this potential trajectory is brought to an abrupt
halt and subsumed back into the more conventional "reform" narrative that will
end with her winning her love object through her transformation into a more
Polly-like woman. Watching the girls and reflecting upon the beauty of their
lives, Fanny muses that girls like these would easily earn the respect and love of
men, "for in spite of their independence, they are womanly." She wishes she
had a talent to live for, imagining that it would make her more interesting to the
much-desired Sydney ("dear to everyone" in fact) and acknowledging that she
would like these things for herself—things "money can't buy."

I want another plot for Fanny; in fact, I want Book 2 to be about her self-
transformation, and I want it to begin here. Why focus on Polly who is already
perfection? Fanny is conflicted, she's struggling for something more, and I
think she draws the wrong lesson from this exchange. I want Fanny to see
beyond the conventional love plot (she can have that too, down the line, and
with someone more interesting than Mr. Sydney, who is constantly assessing her
through comparisons with her friend). In Alcott's plot, she encounters much
hardship when her father loses their fortune, and it is her ability to cope fairly

well (with Polly's guidance) and provide her parents with comfort that convinces Sydney she is worth loving. I want Fanny to help differently—to make her family's fortune and send money home, using the talent and knowledge she has gained as an avid consumer of women's clothing. In an earlier doll dressmaking scene, Fanny shows a great deal of interest in the design of a "red merino frock": I want her to tap into this interest and to develop her vision and skills with the help of the artistic community Polly has provided. Fanny will, therefore, return to see these women, who will help her shape her aesthetic sensibility and encourage her to go to Paris on her own—not to buy gowns but to design them. With fashions cut for the new woman Rebecca envisions in her sculpture, Fanny will become a sort of Coco Chanel, a girl from the "provinces" who takes Paris by storm. Some of "A Re-Fashioned Girl" might highlight her struggles as an American who must become acquainted with the subtle codes for conduct and discourse in Parisian society, but I think most of her difficulty will come through the conflict generated by her corset-less designs, which allow for more freedom of movement and expression. She will eventually return to America, setting up a house that rivals those of Paris and making it possible for women to buy at home. Clearly there is more than "one" reader at work here—the youthful original who thrilled to the details of dress and design, her shadowy elder who longs for the road not taken, and their feminist counterparts; what delights me most about revision is that the process can accommodate us all.

Like mine, Theresa Gregor's revision, "Ramona Revisited," recasts a moment that interests her politically. Helen Hunt Jackson's novel is about a young Native American woman who leaves the Mexican family with whom she has grown up in order to follow her lover Alessandro—a ranch hand who dies before the novel's end and leaves the heroine widowed with a child. Gregor chooses to rewrite the ending, and what is perhaps most intriguing about her revision is that she does not bring Ramona's husband back to life but focuses instead on Felipe's assessment of Ramona's motives at the novel's close.

> Felipe Ortegna has asked the widowed, single-Indian-mother Ramona to return to Mexico with him because California is increasingly hostile to Mexican rights. When she agrees to go, he surmises "that she would spare her daughter the burden she had gladly, heroically borne herself, in the bond of race."

> However, we catch a glimpse into Ramona's thoughts and her reason for going to Mexico is not so much to spare her daughter any racial turmoil, but to chart a new destiny for her daughter. "[Ramona's] imagination was kindled. An untried future beckoned—a future which she would embrace and conquer for her daughter." This passage intrigues me because both representatives of the two largest racial groups in California at this time (the Indians and the Mexicans) are

removed, literally written out of the novel's landscape, in the end. An end that many American settlers actually wished for since it would resolve the nagging "Indian question" (what to do with them when their land was wanted) as well as address the problem of dealing with the previous colonizers, the Mexicans. For this reason, and for all of Jackson's claims to advocate for Indian reform, it seems that in the end, she was incapable of imagining any other kind of world except for a white one. I imagine, on the other hand, another ending for Ramona. She remains and teaches her daughter to survive in California.

Gregor's imagined ending is much more satisfying politically, delivering an implicit critique of race relations and American imperialism as it valorizes the mother-daughter bond. This is, significantly, the *only* revision to deal directly with the question of race, suggesting that despite feminist romance scholars' growing sensitivity to this set of issues, the "assumed whiteness" of romance persists (Perry 172). Arguably, Engelhardt's revision engages with race implicitly, for Cathy's fascination with the gypsy women is attributed to their "dark-skin, black, wild hair and red lips, open in laughter" ("Wuthering" 2). Whether the white English heroine's speculative pleasure comes at the *expense* of the racialized, eroticized "other" is questionable, though Cathy's deep attachment to the Queen suggests otherwise. Broadly outlining her heroine's new life trajectory, Gregor's revision commences with the act of *choosing*:

> Ramona refuses to move to Mexico with Felipe. Instead she tells him that she wishes to return to San Jacinto and live at her and Alessandro's home on the mountain. Felipe adamantly rejects Ramona's proposal at first. He confesses his love to her and tells her that he would do anything for her except allow her to live out a barely subsistent life with her child.

> Ramona's resolve is steadfast. Her calm, quiet, nearly ethereal demeanor finally convinces Felipe that Ramona is living in another realm and that she has never accepted Alessandro's death. Felipe finally begins to understand that Ramona would feel closer to Alessandro if she were at their home.

> Before Felipe sails for Mexico he shows Ramona the Senorita Ortegna's letter describing Ramona's birth origins and the jewels that Ramona inherited from her father Angus Phail. Felipe explains to Ramona that she is entitled to take the treasure. She reluctantly accepts the jewels, and then is heartened at the prospect of becoming completely independent of Felipe. She now has the resources to provide a comfortable life for her small family. Felipe offers Ramona several other gifts—tokens of his love really—but she quietly refuses all, except for Baba and Benito—her loyal steeds.

Gregor's Ramona is considerably less pliable than the original, refusing the protection of the wealthy, faithful Felipe and insisting upon making her own way. Her decision to accept her inheritance is predicated on her desire for autonomy, but it also mirrors her commitment to her own daughter's destiny. I believe Gregor's choice to highlight the significant role played by property in women's attempts to secure independence is suggestive, and it is a factor addressed by Miller and Engelhardt's revisions as well. It is, however, largely maternal love that motivates these choices: Ramona wants to provide Little Majella with a community and history that reinforces her racial affiliation, and she puts these even before her own quasi-filial ties to Felipe.

That mother-daughter relations are closely linked to the narrative desires of romance is a theory given much play by romance scholars past and present, so it is not terribly surprising to recognize its centrality in revisions like Gregor's and this rewrite of *The Thornbirds*. The novel by Colleen McCullough is a highly unconventional romance itself, focusing on the love that develops between an ambitious priest and the young woman who has known him all her life. Written by a critic who wishes to remain anonymous, this revision pursues a "taboo" relationship of a different sort, recovering the buried plot of Anne, Meggie's landlady at Himmelhoch and recasting the women's relationship as lesbian romance. Highly critical of marriage, and of emotionally draining husbands and lovers, "Anne" is by far the most subversive of the romance revisions, in part because the heroine's trajectory is the most developed and her consciousness the most examined, but also because the lesbian affair between Meggie and Anne is both central and contextualized. The concluding scene in this overflowing text (six pages) brings many of the strands together—the secret love of Anne and Meggie, the vanquishing of Ralph, her weak and fickle lover, and the unspoken understandings between mother and daughter:

> One by one everyone excused themselves to their bedrooms leaving just the three of them: Fee, Meggie, and Anne. They sat in near silence, each attending to whatever trivial task she had chosen to distract her. Once when Anne looked up from her book to catch Meggie looking at her she could swear she saw Fee, out of the corner of her eye, observe the exchange. But by the time Anne noticed, Fee's eyes were once again fixed on what she was doing. Anne closed her book, gathered up her crutches, "Good night Meggie, Fee," she said as she struggled to get to her feet and balance herself leaning on the crutches. Meggie looked up and smiled warmly, as she said her good nights. Fee just nodded. Anne did not look back as she exited the room and made her way to her cottage, but she had a good idea of what was happening in the main house. Meggie would wait a respectable length of time, then put down the sewing she was pretending to work on. She would rub her eyes, tired from so much attention to the detailed stitching, and bid Fee goodnight. Then she would come to Anne, like she had whenever possible since Anne had arrived. They had come together without thinking, as if it was something that they had both always known. They had always shared in each other's secrets; now their love for one another had

become their most passionate secret. Meggie never stayed. That was the one thing that they both regretted, but neither was certain of what the others in the house, the family, would say. Anne suspected that they would, in fact, say nothing at all, but could never quite bring herself to press Meggie on this. The Catholic in Meggie was not quite extinguished. "But," thought Anne, "I have the one I have always loved, the one I have wanted, the one I gave to that priest, the one who returned from his bed to mine. If Ralph only knew." In fact, if Mary Carson knew, she would be so envious. She had used all of her vast power and wealth to take down the arrogant priest, but this cripple had all but done the same thing with much fewer resources, and was still alive to enjoy it.

Inside the main house things had proceeded much as Anne predicted. After thirty minutes Meggie rubbed her tired eyes and put aside the sewing that she actually had been working on. She walked over to Fee's desk and said a somewhat stiffly formal goodnight. Fee responded in kind, and Meggie walked quickly from the room.

Moments later the light went out in the main room and Fee, unseen by anyone, stood by the window looking out. She didn't have to wait long until she saw her daughter hurry along the path leading to Anne's cottage. Standing silently in the dark watching her daughter enter the cottage, a ghost of a smile briefly crossed her face. And she turned and went to her own bed. (5-6)

The desire for the mother's acceptance is as much an undercurrent here as the love between the two women, a parallel that recalls Lizzie Thynne's reading of the film, *Anne Trister,* in which the bond between mother and daughter stands as the psychoanalytic origin of the heroine's affection for her female lover. There is a kind of "warrant" established in this revision, with the mother quietly licensing the unacknowledged desires of the daughter. Matriarchal power is suggested through the figure of Mary Carson—however problematic her power may be, by the fatal business of Anne's own midwife mother, and by the small female community's preeminence at the end: all suggest that Fee's ghostly smile does "mean" significantly. This revision supports Suzanne Juhasz's contention that the lesbian romance is most often simultaneously a "coming out" story, with the "closet" serving as the primary obstacle to love and the mechanism by which the development of plot and character are brought together. As the sole example of lesbian romance among the collected revisions, "Anne" also offers the only sustained glimpse into the heroine's mind and provides a much more striking example than one would find in heterosexual romance of the process by which one claims a new identity through love.

While the previous revisions arguably took the "man" out of "romance," those remaining conform more to generic expectations by keeping men at the center of the heroine's plot and consciousness. I have therefore organized the pieces by Pat Koski, Sylvia Kelso, Tania Modleski, Jan Cohn, and Kay Mussell in a rather rough schema that moves from those revisions with a lesser male presence to those in which the hero figures more prominently. Exhibiting considerably less resistance to the romance form, these writers not only chose texts that were more emblematic of popular formulas, they also show a greater willingness to engage more immediately with the text—an "intimacy" achieved by rewriting actual scenes and grappling with the language of the text. Their willingness to "get their hands dirty" in this fashion may reflect a greater degree of intellectual or emotional investment: these writers are published romance scholars.

Pat Koski's revision of Mary Stewart's *Nine Coaches Waiting* turns on Linda Martin's interior monologue in a moment of crisis, as she attempts to give the heroine greater confidence in her own judgment. A romantic suspense novel, this particular example is often mentioned by feminists who admit to liking romance—a choice that is not difficult to understand if one considers the equal importance of the mystery plot. Linda Martin is an English governess who returns to her French origins in order to care for the young heir of the de Valmy family, Philippe. Ensconced in their isolated chateau, she must hide from her employers the flawless French she speaks and manage the vague menace she detects in almost every corner and figure in the house. She falls in love with the second son and guardian of young Philippe, but for much of the novel he too is suspect. In one of five revisions that engage with the language of the novel directly, Koski observes:

> . . . if I could rewrite parts of *Nine Coaches Waiting*, I would change Linda Martin to recognize her own strength, and to compare herself more favorably both in terms of gender and wealth. This would be made clear when she finds that there is a plot to kill the child under her care and she is told that the man she loves is involved in that plot. I'm willing to understand why she doesn't immediately discount this news—after all, she cannot really take the chance that she is wrong, as it involves a child's life. My rewriting of this scene [will allow her to] trust her motives. The specific passage from the book will make clear what I mean.

> "...I had seen even while shock reacting on weariness had driven me stupidly and headlong from him up the stairs. And now I saw the look that came down over his face, bleak bitter pride shutting down over anger, and I knew that I had turned my world back to cinders, sunk my lovely ship with my own stupid, wicked hands. I couldn't speak, but I began to cry..." (234)

Well, I mean really "stupid, wicked hands"? My rewriting:

"...I had seen even while shock reacting on weariness had driven me headlong from him up the stairs. And now I saw the look that came down over his face, bleak bitter pride shutting down over anger, and I knew that he could have been trusted. Nonetheless, my reasons for protecting Philippe were sound and I would have to make Raoul understand."

What the juxtaposition of the original and rewritten texts makes clear is that the heroine's capacity for meaningful action—signaled by her focus on her "hands"—is being called into question as much as her judgment and understanding. Eradicating not only the heroine's negative characterization of her hands (and metonymically her actions) but the allusion to the "Cinder"-ella ending she has potentially lost, Koski presents a considerably more realistic and favorable self-assessment, but she loses a degree of the heroine's *imaginative* insight and the richness of her fantasy-life. She also brings the two male figures out of the shadows by naming them, and Linda's more embodied awareness of the hero, Raoul, reinforces his status as more than an idealization and hers as a woman firmly grounded in the "real" world.

Sylvia Kelso chose to revise Jennifer Crusie's *Fast Women,* a novel that follows the professional and sexual adventures of a recent divorcee. Through family connections, Nell gets a job as secretary to a private investigator, Gabe McKenzie. While attracted to one another, they disagree on just about everything when it comes to running the office. They begin a relationship, but their conflicts prove to be too great and Nell quits. Although she would rather go into business with her former sister-in-law, Suze, she is forced to take another job among family, giving her access to information Gabe needs to solve a case in which he is personally implicated. When she is caught, Gabe must rescue her from death by refrigeration. They reconcile, and she goes back to work with him as a partner. Kelso focuses primarily on the novel's ending—the "limitingly heterosexual vision [that] remains one of [her] main political and imaginative problems with romance" ("Prolegemona" 3). While her changes also guarantee the requisite happy ending, it is not the conventional closure one expects from popular romance. Reflecting on the other "sticking point" that motivated her rewrites, Kelso identifies the moment when

Nell and her close mate Suze veered toward lesbian sex, got as far as trying a kiss, and found it "vanilla" (Crusie, *Women*, 281). "I'm ... into penetration," says Nell (274). As a heterosexual reader, I had no trouble figuring why Nell would want to jump Gabe and go on doing it. As a fantasy reader and a long-term feminist, I had a good many second thoughts about that other lost opportunity. In both cases, I felt, as I once felt about the love-ties in A. S. Byatt's *Possession,* that the text had suffered from a lack of imagination. Or, in this case, perhaps, from an unconscious acceptance of the limits of its genre.

She herself chooses to push at those limits, first allowing Suze to rescue Nell from the freezer where Gabe originally finds her, then bringing Suze's love interest, Riley, in at the crucial moment to witness their attraction. Kelso writes:

> Riley is devastated. Gabe is furious and devastated. Suze's husband is furious and devastated and wants to make the scandal of all time, but is gagged by the revelation of the Dysart-Ogilvie crimes. Margie, busily selling off her china on E-Bay after brushing off her accountant lover, says mildly, "We could always go to New York and find Janice." Battered by conflicting desires, family disbelief, and the uproar of a major scandal, Nell and Suze find themselves saying, "s Why not?"

> Nell's son Jason lets the word slip to Gabe's daughter Lu, who tells Gabe. Gabe and Riley descend on the women as they are packing. After a long and desperate confrontation, Suze and Nell reach a compromise. "We're leaving," Suze tells the men, "but perhaps not permanently. We need time to sort this out. To sort ourselves out. And to let you sort yourselves out. We're flying to New York with Margie, tonight. [. . .] We're planning to stay a while. All three of us. But it needn't be forever. If you decide you want us back—all three of us—you can let us know. ("Fast Women" 3)

This emphasis on "three" at the revision's conclusion suggests one way in which Kelso makes good on the epigraph with which she begins: "One is not enough, and two is only one possibility" (Donna Haraway). The other, of course, is through the choice she gives *this* reader by offering two different closures—and, indeed, "choice" seems to be the paramount concern in the two revisions—alone and together. Both resolutions offered by Kelso function as compelling critiques of the institution of marriage: the first because it points to the need for women to establish a life (and identity) separate from (but in addition) to the marriage, and not just because that "other" life makes the wife more interesting to her husband; and the second because it suggests that women might be happier if they recognize that they will never find happiness if they put all their energy into one limiting role. Beth Binggelli's "Jane X" and Nancy Miller's "Princesse" display a similar savvy when it comes to experiential knowledge and romantic expectations: Nell learns from her previous marriage that owning a business with a husband can result in self-effacement and so resists that choice the second time around; the Princess is convinced from her period at court that love cannot endure within the bonds of marriage, and she and her friends delight in discussions about its boredoms; Jane X refuses Rochester based on her knowledge that she'd make a "crappy wife" and Bertha's report. Even if a woman chooses not to limit herself in the fashion of these re-imagined heroines, the weight of that cultural imperative, and the expectations that arise from it, continue to shape the perceptions of most women concerning their single or married status. The more stories circulating that question the "happy-heterosexual-couple-ending," as Kelso calls it, the more choices women may perceive. Certainly, the "both/and" demand made by the women at the end is a welcome alternative for the woman who "wants it all," but the ending also makes clear that the women are confused and conflicted, that the costs of "both/and" are not negligible.

In marked contrast, Tania Modleski's revision of *Nerd in Shining Armor* attempts to reinscribe the formulaic gender roles of romance by reversing the original author's "nerdification of the hero" in order to resuscitate the alpha male figure and by recuperating the oppositional erotics of the 1970s bodice ripper. Using the feminist technique of "inversion" to re-establish the generic status quo, she resists the accommodations of *Nerd,* which is itself a rewrite of the rapaciously "sensual romance" that Carol Thurston celebrates in *The Romance Revolution.* The original novel thwarts readerly expectation by presenting an office romance that goes awry when the alpha male "hero" turns out to be a truly dangerous man. Gen, the heroine, has fallen for her boss Nick, who takes her and a "computer nerd" by the name of Jackson on his private plane, but then stages a plane crash so that he can escape with embezzled money and parachute to safety while leaving them to die. Gen and Jackson manage to crash land the plane, and much of the plot depends on their struggle to survive on a deserted island. Their difficulties allow them to recognize in each other equal partners, and the novel ends with their union and Nick's capture.

In Modleski's version Jen is a filing clerk who works in one of Nick's many corporate offices, and the two have a history together—an early sexual encounter that stops just short of consummation. She has taken "a couple of courses in feminism" at college, which helps her to recognize that Nick is still a "male chauvinist pig" (2), but she nevertheless finds herself "melting" whenever she encounters him in the filing room. Emphasizing that Jen's "principles are at odds with the attraction she feels" (2), Modleski uses the character's feminist politics to establish the first significant obstacle to her inevitable union with the hero. (The second is the budding romance between Gen and Jackson.) By choosing to use the very tools that occasioned her own awakening in service to the heroine's love plot, Modleski subordinates her progressive politics to her reading pleasures, thereby suggesting that her emotional responses do come from "different—and mutually incompatible—discursive sites than her aesthetic or political analyses of texts" (Pearce 23). Her facility for compartmentalizing is further suggested by her adherence to formula, and she makes her recuperation of romance explicit in her protagonists' first exchange:

"Let's face it, you need taking care of," he murmurs . . .

"Oooo, you are insufferable, a cave man, a throwback to the dark ages of the 70s; I can take care of myself, I . . . ." He cuts her off with a swift brutal kiss, then pinning her against the wall with his hard muscled body, says "Yeah? Who would you rather be stranded with on a desert island? Him or me?"

"See? That's my point, Nick. Nobody ever does get stranded on a desert island anymore. You're obsolete."

He reminds her of his vast real estate and corporate holdings. "Then how did I get to the top of the ladder if I'm obsolete? I got there because I'm the original Robinson Crusoe. (3)

When Jen declares she'd "rather take her chances with Jackson on a desert island" (3), Nick arranges a little experiment, flying the two to a desert island and leaving them stranded. While Gen "proves herself to be highly resourceful" (4), Jackson disappoints considerably, and Gen soon realizes that Nick has orchestrated the whole adventure. She retaliates by staging a hot romance with Jackson, which brings Nick to the island. Hoping to disrupt what is only a phony affair, Nick

arrives just in time to save Gen and the wimpy Jackson from a very real danger by slashing in two a huge snake that's about to attack them or something of the sort. Never has anyone appeared so magnificent; Gen realizes at once that for good or for ill, she is really in love with Nick. (Modleski 4)

While his misperception of her feelings for Jackson keeps Nick from declaring his love, the two are shortly reconciled. After inviting him over for champagne, which he presumes they will share with Jackson, she sends him into the bathroom to change his attire: "they each emerge simultaneously (of course!) from their rooms, he wearing a loincloth, she wearing the tatters of a skimpy dress, with a bodice that looks eminently rippable" (Modleski 4). This conclusion to her romance—which highlights once again the fantasy of eroticized gender inequalities and the 1970s form that immortalized it, suggests that Modleski is concerned here far less about shaping the romance *for* feminism than saving the romance *from* it.

Jan Cohn—another of the three romance scholars who wrote first about the form in the 1980s—takes on the classic *Gone with the Wind,* a work inviting particularly compulsive repetitions "because in the reader/viewer's secret heart, she hopes the story will turn out differently this time" ("Wind" 1). Like Modleski, Cohn rewrites the novel, and, most significantly, the ending, so it conforms to the parameters of the popular romance. She writes:

Considered in the terms of romance, the problem is that the hero and heroine, though married, have not achieved a happy ending, have not admitted their

mutual love. What I want here is a 'real' happy ending, Rhett and Scarlett
contentedly—and passionately—in each other's arms. [. . .] I want to rearrange
things so that Scarlett can outgrow her feelings for Ashley before it is too late—
in time for a happy ending to take place. As the novel stands Melanie's death
bed scene serves to bring Scarlett to her senses; she realizes that she loves Rhett
and not Ashley. That's fine, of course, but it's too late. The scene that should
bring Scarlett to her senses takes place when Rhett carries her to her bed and—
here come all the asterisks that indicate wild, passionate sex. That sex should, of
course, cement their love or, if one thinks that Scarlett does love Rhett and is
simply too besotted with her memories to recognize this, it should make her
understand that Rhett is indeed her true love. (That is, I imagine, the
point. Romance heroines cannot have wild, passionate sex with men they don't
love.) Of course, everything goes wrong: Rhett is abashed and Scarlett, now
ready to fall permanently into his arms, is dismayed and hurt by his
brusqueness. (This scene, by the way, makes me crazy! Here is where I do want
that happy ending.) Another problem with this scene is that it comes too early in
the novel, before Melanie's death and thus before it is time for the resolution.

[. . .] as in the original, [Scarlett] rushes home. But instead of finding Rhett
angry, fed up, and prepared to leave her, she finds no one there. Scarlett broods
and paces, waiting for Rhett. But no drinking, no nipping brandy! She should,
though, become somewhat distraught, as revealed in her hair and clothing. In
other words, her defenses are down. Rhett returns and Scarlett's disarray, and
dishabille, awakens both his sympathy and his lust. At this point, he carries her
up the stairs for that asterisked scene, and then everyone lives happily ever after.
("Wind" 3)

Her Scarlett is considerably reformed—no tippling, no hiccoughing, and, more
in keeping with popular formulas, incapable of enjoying rapacious sex with her
husband while still in love with another man (as she is in Mitchell's version).
She is also less avaricious and hard-bitten. Cohn's revision centers much more
upon the heroine's character in part because she believes Rhett has earned his
heroic status by rescuing the women from the Atlanta siege and embracing the
South's lost cause in the final hour. Explaining that she feels more sympathy
for the pre-war heroine, Cohn offers an alternative revision, which ends the
book midway through. Recognizing that Scarlett's romance with the Old South
is for many as seductive a story as her love plot with Rhett, Cohn considers
leaving Tara much more intact after Sherman's march. After the trek from
Atlanta, Scarlett will return to find her mother alive and her father "striving
courageously" at home, where she will await Rhett's return from war sheltered
in the bosom of her family. While Cohn presumes that all will end happily, the
resolution is nonetheless "open," and she de-emphasizes it in relation to the
version excerpted above. As she herself implies, most at issue for Cohn is the
requisite "happy ending" of romance, and what is intriguing about her choice is

that the original's "refusal" of the conventional closure is what has secured its reputation with feminist readers as "antiromance."

While Kay Mussell attempts to balance the gender inequalities desired by Modleski and Cohn, she nevertheless manages to keep the romance formula intact. Her revision is much more implicit than implicated, for she remains at arm's length, taking the more conventional revisionary approach by commenting on what dissatisfies. What doesn't work for Mussell is the "declaration scene" between hero and heroine in Georgette Heyer's *Frederica,* a novel that features a Marquis who is also a determined bachelor, much to the chagrin of the London *ton.* He becomes the guardian of a longtime friend's orphaned children and finds himself greatly charmed by the two young women and three young boys in his care. Frederica is the eldest girl, a young woman determined to capitalize on her younger sister's beauty in the marriage market that masks as "the Season." She herself ends up winning the love of the Marquis, Alverstoke, and making a much better match. Mussell argues that the scene in which the hero declares his love to Frederica "undermines the heroine's competence and understanding and ends by reinforcing unequal gender relationships" ("Commentary" 1). She writes of the bothersome resolution:

> The only issue to be resolved is Frederica's lack of awareness of Alverstoke's feelings for her as well as hers for him. The impediment to their betrothal is slim indeed and easily fixed. Although Alverstoke has been of great help to her throughout the book as she attempts to deal with raising three siblings on her own, Frederica is capable, sensible, and intelligent and has won his admiration through her independence and competence. Until this scene, the relationship between them has never seemed unequal. The overt power disparity in the declaration scene, then, comes as a surprise and reinforces the disparity in their social stations and gender. Alverstoke never really bends or changes. He says he wants to marry her because she has never bored him, because he is interested in her brothers, because he can't live without her. But there appears to be no emotional intensity in these statements, which seem distant and ironic rather than sincere. Frederica, in turn, takes on the role of child/student when he teaches her that what she feels for him is really love. ("Commentary" 1)

Frederica—who has shown herself to be a skillful problem-solver throughout the novel is uncharacteristically overwhelmed in this scene, and her teeming emotions are contrasted sharply with Alverstoke's seeming detachment and self-control. She "trembles," her "brain in a whirl" (Heyer 382), and her lengthy, confused response to his claim that "he cannot live without her" is all but silenced when "his lordship [takes] her ruthlessly into his arms" (384).

With Frederica emerging from "an embrace which threatened to suffocate her" (Heyer 384), the erotics of dominance identified by Mussell become difficult to refute. And yet the control exerted by the critic herself is also worth noting: reinterpreting the revision guidelines to accommodate a critical approach that is more familiar, Mussell manages a considerably more distanced engagement with *Frederica* by avoiding an actual rewrite. She reproduces, in fact, a critical reading she made almost twenty years ago, but while the scene obviously haunts her, the discomfort she feels is not sufficient to prompt "real" changes to text. While discussing the relative power of Heyer's hero and heroine in *Fantasy and Reconciliation* (1984), Mussell focuses on the hero's agency and the didactic role he assumes:

> Alverstoke seems less authoritarian than some other romance heroes because he does not know how Frederica feels, but he has enough authority to define love for her and to give her the information she requires to respond properly to his proposal. Male knowledge and authority in matters of love are constants in romance fiction; but, paradoxically, expertise in human relationships belongs to woman's sphere. Conventionally, in the act of being chosen—when the hero makes his declaration—a woman knows she has earned the right to take on the responsibilities inherent in her intuitive expertise. He bears the responsibility of making the choice before she can perform her womanly duties. (137)

I can't help wondering—given the test of time—if there isn't something appealing about the hero's unwavering self-control after all. Ostensibly most pressing for the critic is the restoration of Frederica's "competence," but perhaps her interest in competence is *really* associated more with Alverstoke; he is, after all, one of Mussell's exemplary "competent" heroes—a taxonomical term used in her earlier work to describe heroes like Mr. Darcy in contrast to the more passionate, mysterious men of the Brontë novels. The critic's own display of self-control when challenged to implicate herself more fully is suggestive, a sign that she may be identifying as much with the hero in her rewrite as the heroine.[30] More significantly perhaps, it also serves to remind us that revision is a task undertaken most frequently with an eye toward protecting one's self and one's interests.

At the other end of the "implicated reader" spectrum is the anonymous writer who wrote "Anne." In that revision the romance is all but obliterated by the heroine's successive trauma—a displacement that echoes the narrative dynamic in Wollstonecraft's *Maria,* where Jemima's tale of misery brings the budding romance to a halt. As the author makes clear in her response to the

---

[30] Jessica Benjamin's comments in *Like Subjects, Love Objects* (1995) are illuminating in this context: "The point Freud got right here was that women engage in 'narcissistic'— that is identificatory—love when they love in a man the ideal self they would have wished to be" (58).

post-revision questionnaire, her highly unconventional fantasy scenario owes much to her immediate psychic situation:

> [At the time of writing] I was forced to deal with some pretty unpleasant real-life stuff that involved spending lots of time in a shock-trauma unit of a hospital (this, I think, is probably evident in the resulting text). When I sat down to start writing I found it much easier than I thought I would—though I had to cut out some of the detail that I had envisioned because it was getting pretty long. To be honest, I sort of felt that it wrote itself, like I didn't really have control over the process. (e-mail 5/6/04)

Suggested in these reflections (as well as in the revision they comment upon) are the *limits* of the romance formula's binding power: while it may accommodate certain feminist ideals and principles, what it cannot do so easily is contain the energies of its readers' real-life sorrows and struggles. This writer's revision experience is clearly cathartic, facilitating a rush of emotion that doesn't so much "control" or "act upon" the text as exceed it; the writer has made the text almost completely her own, displacing the primary plot and redirecting the flow of desire.

What is highlighted by the anonymous author and Mussell's rather polarized textual engagements is the way revision—when imagined differently—can enable a productively unfamiliar relationship to a familiar text. It can bring affect to the fore, unleashing the unconscious within for one "reader," yet allow another to keep the "threatening" romance at "arm's length." This is apparently a much more comfortable distance for Beth Binggelli, whose comments in a series of e-mail and actual conversations illuminate the complicated performance such implicated readings entail. Having approached this task by "writing herself into" *Jane Eyre*—the most "engaged" revisionist position I had imagined—she reports, "I'm in there, but I'm wearing a disguise. I'm definitely in it, but no one would recognize me" (Jan. 7 2004). Yet despite her immersion in both text and task, she felt that her self-conscious satire left her feeling more in control. And perhaps most intriguing (and surprising to me) was that she felt *more* empowered in the act of rewriting romance than she had writing about the form in the more conventional mode of feminist criticism. Binggelli writes:

> Writing about the genre made me feel vulnerable; rewriting the romance made me feel powerful. I [wrote] an essay [. . .] on my relationship with the romance called "Intolerable Texts"—something very autobiographical. [. . .] Strangely, the revision also feels very personal, but in an incredibly controlled way. The essay on the genre felt like confession; the revision felt like vengeance. Of course, vengeance feels much better! (e-mail 5/3/04)

Testifying to her highly personal encounter *and* the control she felt, this feminist reader suggests that agency need not be sacrificed to affect nor the reverse, an experience that challenges the idea that feminist reading and emotional responsiveness come from "mutually incompatible" discursive sites. When juxtaposed with the other readers' experiences, Bingelli's reveals the idiosyncratic nature of this form of revision, which brings the feminist reader beyond a sanctioned set of *practices* to illuminate each participant's very unique process and her own peculiar desires.

Not surprisingly, then, the motivations for revision among participants varied greatly: Cohn and Modleski expressed a desire to "write to formula"; Kelso wished to "fix" something that left her feeling dissatisfied; Engelhardt, Miller, and I wanted "livelier" trajectories for our heroines. But Binggelli's comments about her own impulses toward revision helped me to frame our varying purposes in a more harmonious light. Writing of an earlier instance when she found herself "compelled" to rewrite a Katherine Mansfield short story called "The Little Governess," she reports making the same general changes she did for "Jane X":

> . . . reverse gender roles, empower women, make men do the cowering for a change. And what is even weirder about this is that I LOVE Mansfield (definitely an author with feminist sensibilities), so my impulse was not to fix something that was evil and broken but to save it for me, to force a space where it could be saved for me. (e-mail 7/17/2003)

The two occurrences of "save" in this statement of purpose are provocative, pointing as they do to two possible meanings (which may, ultimately, be two sides of the same narcissistic coin). The first possibility recalls the chivalric imperative that underlies much feminist criticism—a persistent desire to "save" imperiled texts, as well as their authors, their characters, and their readers. Modleski, Mussell, and Robinson once sought to redeem the readers of romance by explaining the texts' appeal, Miller to explain the Princesse de Clève's preferences to a critical community that found her choice "implausible," and Kelso to demonstrate the feminist ideals of Gothic novelist Barbara Michaels. And the heroic motivations of chivalric romance—paterfamilias to the popular form—emerge in the revisions as well: Binggelli imports the entire March family so Jane is not without protection and companionship; Engelhardt saves Cathy's life; there is even the case of text saving reader, as in "Anne," where solace is provided vis-à-vis the romance. Indeed, all of the revisions feature some element of rescue or recuperation, and one could easily view *most* of what is written by feminist critics as motivated by this generous impulse toward the "other." But "saving," as Binggelli's comments suggest, is a rather complicated response for the feminist reader because saving others is simultaneously "saving a space for me"—a way of asserting the self, a way of becoming a heroine. The merger desired here might be viewed as an act of intellectual penetration, recalling Wolfgang Iser's notion that "filling in the gaps" is a way of taking control of the text. Alternatively, it might signal a desire for greater textual intimacy or for a prolonged connection with the authorial subject or a beloved character like Jane Eyre.[31] Most probably, of course, the heroic desire to "save/save a space for me" is about achieving all three—omnipotence, intersubjective connection, and the recuperation of what has been lost, in effect, the fantasy of omnipotence and merger associated with primary narcissism. And as many other feminist critics have suggested, the projection of one's self, one's fantasies, into a textual encounter is clearly unavoidable. In an e-mail exchange I had with Judith Wilt, I suggested that if she were short on time, she might authorize my use of her essay on Richardson's *Clarissa*—"He Could Go No Farther"—as a revisionary text. In this essay Wilt speculates about the possibility that the *women* actually rape Clarissa and that Lovelace is impotent, and because it raises the possibility that he has not truly obtained the object of his desire, it leaves at least *this* reader with a keen sense of pleasure (as well as the horror that she may be victimized by other women). Because Lovelace's dream is central to Wilt's analysis, I became quite taken with the idea that feminist criticism might function *itself* as a form of fantasy. She wrote that she was "fascinated by [my] notion that [her essay] might be a feminist-fantastic revision of *Clarissa,* that it made her "start thinking about ALL her critical work in that way" (e-mail 7/23/02). Are feminist readers simply another group of fantasizing women readers, recasting their pleasures as their politics? When we critics read, are we always "romancing" the text—that is, creating our own fantasy of meaning? Are feminist readers simply another group of fantasizing women readers, recasting their pleasures as their politics? And if so, how are readers' wishes and ambitions fueled and supported by the fantasies of feminist criticism?

When I returned to the ethnographic portion of my project in 2002 after a period of academic *ennui*, I discovered that revisiting the romance in the company of women not only vividly illustrated the identificatory possibilities of

---

[31] Because Lynne Pearce's discussion of intersubjective connection and the feminist reader's longing for the "textual other" is particularly elegant, I will not take time to elaborate upon this idea here but rather refer the reader to *Feminism and the Politics of Reading.* She too recognizes the feminist reader's desire to save a space for herself and observes that readers move about in texts voyeuristically, exploring our textual others from all angles and "looking for ways in which we may make them respond to us and include us in their script" (18).

this fantasy structure, it actually manufactured desire.   The energy of participating critics—the enthusiasm with which they responded to my requests for help and discussed their own revisions—reawakened my curiosity in, and commitment to, this project.   I was, in effect, "turned on" by the narrative and critical desires that animated their writing—the (no longer guilty) pleasures to be discovered in their romance revisions as well as the lengthy e-mails that interrogated the project's design.   My sense of purpose and confidence as a feminist critic was rekindled, and my own writing greatly enlivened, by their contributions; indeed, the pre-oedipal pleasure and support suggested by one respondent's reference to "our project" has helped me to realize the power and potential of women speaking together in an Irigarayan fashion.   I believe this sense of power and pleasure can be enhanced even further by inviting the romance reader into our conversation, collapsing further the distinction between critic and reader, subject and object, and raising our collective consciousness about the desires we share in common.   For if we take Byatt's romance reader at her word—accept that the "desire of all reading women" is to be both "Poet and Poem"—we can explore more effectively the tension between women's desire to craft their own stories and explanatory narratives, and their longing for mediation—to have their tales told by someone they can trust, someone who sees them clearly and can help them become their most perfect selves. Romance may, in fact, be the perfect vehicle through which feminist readers (and their doubles) explore what it means to be both Poet and Poem: the subjects and objects of our speculative endeavors, the ambitious authors of our collective story, the beloved creation of our best collaborative efforts, the deserving recipients of our chivalry and devotion.

Works Cited or Consulted

Anonymous. "Anne, a Revision of *The Thornbirds*."

Benjamin, Jessica.   *Like Subjects, Love Objects: Essays on Recognition and Sexual Difference.* New Haven: Yale UP, 1995.

Binggelli, Beth. "Jane X."

Brooks, Peter.   *Reading for the Plot: Design and Intention in Narrative.* Cambridge: Harvard UP, 1984.

Brownstein, Rachel.   *Becoming a Heroine: Reading About Women in Novels.* 2nd ed. New York: Columbia UP, 1994.

Byatt, A. S.   *Possession: A Romance.* New York: Random House, 1990.

Cawelti, John G.   *Adventure, Mystery, and Romance: Formula Stories as Art and Popular Culture.* Chicago: U of Chicago P, 1976.

Chappel, Deborah K.   "LaVyrle Spencer and the Anti-Essentialist Argument." *Paradoxa* 3.1-2 (1997): 107-120.

Christian-Smith, Linda K. *Becoming a Woman Through Romance.* New York: Routledge, 1990.

Coddington, Lynn. "Wavering Between Worlds: Feminist Influences in the Romance Genre." *Paradoxa* 3.1-2 (1997): 58-77.

Cohn, Jan. *Romance and the Erotics of Property: Mass-Market Fiction for Women.* Durham, N.C.: Duke UP, 1988.

———."Gone With the Wind."

Cranny-Francis, Anne. *Feminist Fiction: Feminist Uses of Generic Fiction.* New York: St. Martin's, 1990.

Crusie Smith, Jennifer. "Romancing Reality: The Power of Romance to Reinforce and Re-vision the Real." *Paradoxa* 3.1-2 (1997): 81-93.

Engelhardt, Molly. "Wuthering Heights Revisited."

Freud, Sigmund. *Beyond the Pleasure Principle.* Trans. James Strachey. New York: Norton, 1961.

———."Creative Writers and Daydreaming." *Critical Theory Since Plato.* 2nd ed. Ed. Hazard Adams. New York: Harcourt Brace Jovanovich, 1992. 712-716.

———."On Narcissism." *The Freud Reader.* Ed. Peter Gay. New York: Norton. 1995. 545-561.

Fuss, Diana. *Identification Papers.* New York: Routledge, 1995.

Gamman, L. and M. Marshment, eds. *The Female Gaze: Women as Viewers of Popular Culture.* London: Women's Press, 1989.

Gregor, Theresa. "Ramona Revisited."

Hutton, Elaine. "Good Lesbians, Bad Men and Happy Endings." Beyond Sex and Romance?: The Politics of Contemporary Lesbian Fiction. Ed. Elaine Hutton. London: Women's P, 1998. 175-201.

Jones, Ann Rosalind. "Mills and Boon Meets Feminism." *The Progress of Romance.* Ed. Jean Radford. London: Routledge & Kegan Paul, 1986.

Juhasz, Suzanne. "Lesbian Romance Fiction and the Plotting of Desire: Narrative Theory, Lesbian Identity, and Reading Practice." (1998). *Women and Romance: A Reader.* Ed. Susan Ostrov Weisser. New York: New York UP, 2001. 276-291.

Kelso, Sylvia. "Stitching Time: Feminism(s) and 30 Years of Gothic Romances." *Paradoxa* 3.1-2 (1997): 164-179.

———."Prolegemona."

———."Revision of Fast Women."

Kinsale, Laura. "The Androgynous Reader: Point of View in the Romance." *Dangerous Men & Adventurous Women.* Ed. Jayne Ann Krentz. Philadelphia: U of Pennsylvania P, 1992. 31-44.

Kofman, Sarah. *The Enigma of Woman: Woman in Freud's Writings.* Trans. Catherine Porter. Ithaca: Cornell UP, 1985.

Koski, Patricia, Lori Holyfield, and Marcella Thompson. "Romance Fiction as
    Women's Myth." *Paradoxa* 3.1-2 (1997): 3-14.
————."Mary Stewart Rewritten."
Krentz, Jayne Ann. *Dangerous Men & Adventurous Women: Romance Writers
    on the Appeal of the Romance.* Philadelphia: U of Pennsylvania P, 1992.
Lanser, Susan S. "Toward a Feminist Narratology." *Feminisms: An Anthology
    of Literary Theory and Criticism.* Eds. Robyn R. Warhol and Diane Price
    Herndl. New Brunswick: Rutgers UP, 1991. 610-629.
LaPlanche, Jean, and Jean-Bertrand Pontalis. "Fantasy and the Origins of
    Sexuality." *Formations of Fantasy.* Eds. Victor Burgin *et al.* London:
    Methuen, 1986.
Light, Alison. "'Returning to Manderley'—Romance Fiction, Female Sexuality
    and Class." *Feminist Review* 16 (April 1984): 7-25.
Lyon, Beverly Clark, Karen Gennari Bernier, Michelle Henneberry-Nassau,
    Lauren Beth Jenks, Angie J. Moorman, and Marah Bianca Rhoades.
    "Reading Romances, Reading Ourselves." *Women and Romance: A Reader.*
    Ed. Susan Ostrov Weisser. New York: New York UP, 2001. 355-374.
Manley, Delariviére. *New Atalantis.* 1709. Ed. Rosalind Ballaster. New York:
    New York UP, 1992.
Martin, Biddy. *Femininity Played Straight: The Significance of Being Lesbian.*
    New York: Routledge, 1996.
Massé, Michelle A. *In the Name of Love: Women, Masochism, and the Gothic.*
    Ithaca: Cornell UP, 1992.
Meizei, Kathy. *Ambiguous Discourse: Feminist Narratology and the British
    Women Writers.* Chapel Hill: U. of North Carolina P, 1996.
Miller, Nancy K., ed. "Arachnologies: The Woman, The Text, and the Critic."
    The Poetics of Gender. New York: Columbia UP, 1986.
————."Decades." *Changing Subjects: The Making of Feminist Literary
    Criticism.* London: Routledge, 1993. 31-47.
————."Emphasis Added: Plots and Plausibilities in Women's Fiction." *PMLA*
    96 (1981): 36-48.
————."Princesse."
Modleski, Tania. *Loving with a Vengeance: Mass-Produced Fantasies for
    Women.* New York: Routledge, 1982.
————."Nerd in Shining Armor."
————.*Old Wives Tales and Other Women's Stories.* New York: New York UP,
    1998.
————."Some Functions of Feminist Criticism: Or, the Scandal of the Mute
    Body." *Feminism Without Women: Culture and Criticism in a
    "Postfeminist" Age.* New York: Routledge, 1991.

Mussell, Kay. *Fantasy and Reconciliation: Contemporary Formulas of Women's Romance Fiction.* Westport, Conn.: Greenwood Press, 1984.

———."Frederica."

———."Where's Love Gone?" *Paradoxa* 3.1-2 (1997): 3-14.

Pearce, Lynn. *Feminism and the Politics of Reading.* London: Arnold, 1997.

Pearce, Lynn and Jackie Stacey. *Romance Revisited.* New York: New York UP, 1995.

Penley, Constance. "Feminism, Psychoanalysis, and the Study of Popular Culture." *Cultural Studies.* Eds. Lawrence Grossberg, Cary Nelson, and Paula Treichler. New York: Routledge, 1992. 494-500.

Perry, Kathryn. "The Heart of Whiteness: White Subjectivity and Interracial Relationships." *Romance Revisited.* Eds. Lynn Pearce and Jackie Stacey. New York: New York UP, 1995. 171-184.

Rabine, Leslie. *Reading the Romantic Heroine: Text, History, Ideology.* Ann Arbor, MI: U of Michigan P, 1985.

———."Romance in the Age of Electronics: Harlequin Enterprises. *Feminist Criticism and Social Change.* Eds. Judith Newton and Deborah Rosenfelt. New York: Methuen, 1985. 249-265.

Radford, Jean, ed. *The Progress of Romance.* London: Routledge & Kegan Paul, 1986.

Radway, Janice. *Reading the Romance: Women, Patriarchy, and Popular Literature.* Chapel Hill, NC: U of North Carolina P, 1991.

Regis, Pamela. "Barrier and Point of Ritual Death in Nora Roberts' Category Fiction." *Paradoxa* 3.1-2 (1997): 145-154.

Regis, Pamela. *A Natural History of the Romance Novel.* Philadelphia: U of Pennsylvania P, 2003.

Robinson, Lillian S. "On Reading Trash." *Sex, Class, and Culture.* Bloomington: Indiana UP, 1977. 200-222.

Rose, Jacqueline. *States of Fantasy.* Cambridge: UP, 1996.

Seidel, Kathleen Gilles. "Judge Me By the Joy I Bring." *Dangerous Men & Adventurous Women: Romance Writers on the Appeal of the Romance.* Philadelphia: U of Pennsylvania P, 1992. 161-179.

———.*Till the Stars Fall.* New York: Onyx/Penguin, 1994.

Snitow, Ann Barr. "Mass Market Romance: Pornography for Women is Different." *Radical History Review* 20 (Spring/Summer 1979): 141-161.

Snitow, Ann Barr, Christine Stansell, and Sharon Thompson. *Powers of Desire: The Politics of Sexuality.* New York: Monthly Review, 1983.

Stacey, Jackie. *Star Gazing: Hollywood Cinema and Female Spectatorship.* London: Routledge, 1994.

Taylor, Helen. "Gone With the Wind: The Mammy of Them All." *The Progress of Romance.* Ed. Jean Radford. London: Routledge & Kegan Paul, 1986. 113-136.

Tegan, Mary Beth. "A Re-Fashioned Girl."

Thurston, Carol. *The Romance Revolution: Erotic Novels for Women and the Quest for a New Sexual Identity.* Urbana, IL: U of Illinois P, 1987.

Thynne, Lizzie. "The Space Between: Daughters and Lovers in Anne Trister." *Romance Revisited.* Eds. Lynn Pearce and Jackie Stacey. New York: New York UP, 1995. 103-116.

Weisser, Susan Ostrov, ed. *Women and Romance: A Reader.* New York: New York UP, 2001.

Wilt, Judith. *Ghosts of the Gothic.* Princeton: Princeton UP, 1980.

Winnett, Susan. "Coming Unstrung: Women, Men, Narrative, and Principles of Pleasure." *PMLA* 105 (1990): 505-518.

Mary Beth Tegan

Mary Beth Tegan now holds an assistant professorship in Nineteenth-Century British Literature at Saint Xavier University in Chicago, where she is working on two book projects emerging from her dissertation. The first, "Vanity's Heirs: Women Writers' Reproductions Within the Mirror of Romance," is a comparative study of the fragmented reception theories of late eighteenth- and nineteenth-century female critics; the light romances they dismiss as reflexive productions of vanity; and the reviewers' own novels—works that reflect the deeper ambitions of their authors but are nonetheless inheritors of the mimetic impulse that characterizes lesser fictions. The second project is an extension of the study discussed in the featured essay and one for which she hopes to engage many more participants. Please contact the author at tegan@sxu.edu if interested.

INDEX